THE CLASS

1000

VIDEOS

TO RENT OR BUY

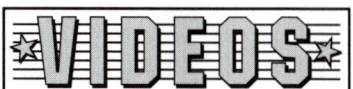

TO RENT OR BUY

SANDY ROBERTSON

foulsham
LONDON • NEW YORK • TORONTO • SYDNEY

foulsham
The Publishing House, Bennetts Close,
Cippenham, Berkshire, SL1 5AP, England

ISBN 0-572-02389-8

Copyright © 1999 Strathearn Publishing

All Rights Reserved

The Copyright Act prohibits (subject to certain very limited exceptions) the making of copies of any copyright work or of a substantial part of such a work including the making of copies by photocopying or similar process. Written permission to make a copy or copies must therefore normally be obtained from the publisher in advance. It is advisable also to consult the publisher if in any doubt as to the legality of any copyright which is to be undertaken.

Printed in Great Britain by St Edmundsbury Press, Bury St Edmunds, Suffolk

To Janine, Californian girl

Thank you to:

Harvey Fenton at *Flesh & Blood* magazine; More Munchies, Acton Vale, London for the *soup du jour*; Tony at Psychotronic Video; Hollywood Flicks, Askew Road, London; Cathal Tohill; John at Zwemmers; Cinema Store; Cinema Bookshop; the British Film Institute; Columbia TriStar; Nicholas Rochford at Compendium Bookshops; HMV, Oxford Street; Edwin Pouncey; Wendy Hobson, Jane Hotson and Barry Belasco at Foulsham; and my editor, Gill Crossley.

Contents

Introduction	9
How to Use This Book	11
Action and Adventure	15
Adult	39
Animation	53
Comedy	61
Drama	87
Epics	123
Family Entertainment	139
Gangsters	149
Hong Kong	167
Horror	175
Musicals	205
Romance	221
Science Fiction	237
Thrillers	257
War	277
Westerns	293
World Greats	313
Further Reading	319
Index of Titles	321
Index of Stars	335
Index of Directors	361

Introduction

This is not meant to be an encyclopaedia of movies on tape – rather, it's a snapshot of what I believe to be the very best films currently available to rent or buy on video, guaranteeing you a good night's entertainment across a broad range of mainstream categories. So when you are looking for a video for an evening's viewing – or even if you arrive at the shop too late to grab a copy of the latest release – you know how to select the best. It's not a list of my personal favourites (although I could hardly avoid trusting my own taste and letting a few of those slip in!), nor is it one of those dubious roll-calls of 'The Greatest Films of all Time' as defined by the critics. But it should ensure that every time you rent a video, you know you're getting one which you will enjoy rather than a disappointing piece of trash which doesn't live up to the blurb on its cover.

Take note that the selection does include Horror and Adult films. Our views on what is acceptable have modified considerably over the years, but you must, of course, use your own judgement when choosing tapes for you and your family. I have included the certificate rating to help you in making appropriate choices.

Buying and renting videos is big business these days as the presence of now-familiar big-name stores in our high streets testifies. Paradoxically, they actually present a real threat to viewer choice as we lose our friendly local video shops. You know the sort: the ones who will find that old Western you just *have* to see even though it's been out of print for years or who will turn a blind eye when a regular customer brings back a tape a day late. Please support your local corner shop – we need them!

May I also suggest you complain if you're not happy with a tape? I see no reason why a tape costing £12.99 or more to buy should be vastly inferior in quality to a film taped off TV, yet that can be the case.

We hope to produce future editions of this book to keep up to date with the constantly changing selection of movies available on tape – so if you spot any errors of fact you can write to me care of the publisher. Similarly, write to me if there are any changes or improvements you wish to suggest – or any superb videos you feel should be considered for inclusion.

Now press 'PLAY!'

Sandy Robertson.

How to Use This Book

The reviews in this book are of films which, as far as we're aware, are currently available to rent and/or buy on UK video labels. They are presented in categories broadly consistent with the shelf titles in most British stores (Westerns, Horror, Comedy etc.). If a film fits into more than a single genre, however, stores will often shelve copies of the same film in more than one location (*Annie Hall*, for example, might be found in both Romance and Comedy in some shops – if in doubt, ask the assistants).

Titles are listed alphabetically within each section, though definite/indefinite articles like 'The' and 'A' are ignored unless they are in a foreign language (hence a film beginning with the German 'Das' for 'The' would be listed under 'D'). Titles starting with numerals are placed in ascending numerical order, if they occur, before the As in each segment.

Reviews give the title, director, main stars, year of original production, the country of origin, video label, running time, BBFC certificate and a rating (see overleaf) based on the artistic/entertainment merit of the film. This is followed by a review, giving an outline of the plot, a short comment on performances, and so on. Where I thought it appropriate, I inserted details of USA Academy Awards (Oscars) gained, source material such as books or plays (unless stated otherwise, the book source has the same title as the film), movies related to the one under scrutiny, subtitles and so on. I've tried to include details of any related controversies, cuts, alternative versions and other anecdotal material.

The BBFC certificates below give you a guide on the suitability of the video for the family but you must use your own judgement.

Uc   Universal: suitable for all, but especially for kids.
U   Universal: suitable for all.
PG   Parental Guidance: some scenes may be unsuitable for children.
12   For persons of 12 or over.
15   For persons of 15 or over.
18   For persons of 18 or over.
R18 Only sold from licensed sex shops to persons 18 or over.

There is no obligation to indicate on the box whether a video is a cut version, though this may change in the future.

Each film is given a 'rating', although this is intended as a guide only as one person may not enjoy a '5' film even though ten others would rate it as the best they have seen in years.

1   Will have some cult appeal or historic merit, but not a 'great' film.
2   Not entirely successful, but worthwhile sequences or performances. Worth a look!
3   Solid entertainment, and certainly worth renting or buying.
4   A really good film, with great acting and visuals.
5   Top-notch stuff. Direction, performances and cinematography of the very highest order. A classic.

Films are assumed to be in colour. If they are in black and white, the indication 'B&W' is given. If a film is a mix of colour and monochrome, this will be shown as 'Col/B&W'.

Running times should be treated as a rough guide only, as they are not always precisely accurate on the video. They will not vary by more than a few minutes. The running times of films on UK VHS-PAL video and TV are about four per cent shorter as they are shown at a faster speed. Tapes from France using the SECAM system will only play in black and white, and NTSC tapes from the US will not play at all unless you have a multi-standard VCR. Fortunately, these are now widely available.

The indication 'two-for-one' is used when a film is available on the same tape as (or on a separate tape, packaged with) another film; the two films should be sold at a lower price than one would normally expect to pay if they were bought separately.

The terms 'letterboxed' and 'widescreen' are interchangeable, and mean that since the film is being presented in an approximation of the original cinematic aspect ratio, there will therefore be black areas above and below the picture on normal TV screens (the first term is based on the fact that a widescreen image resembles a letterbox). Most TVs are one-third wider than they are tall, but widescreen films can be well over twice as wide as they are high! Sadly, I use the word 'approximation' because many firms seem to treat widescreen as a gimmick which allows them to charge more than for standard fullscreen 'pan-scan' or 'cropped' tapes which fill the TV screen but lose the extreme ends of the cinema picture. Sometimes the image is not letterboxed fully in order to minimise the black areas on the TV screen; or the film is blown up to make actors' faces closer, then re-cropped to make it look like the proper ratio. All these tricks ignore the fact that punters buy widescreen tapes precisely because they want the full cinema picture – and even firms which show the ratio on the back of the box don't always play the game.

Films change label frequently and it's sometimes hard to tell just who owns a movie, so you may find a video has a different labelling on the box, in a catalogue, on the video itself, or on a cut-price version. It makes no difference to the viewing!

I've not noted catalogue numbers: you'll rarely need them to buy or rent a tape, though HMV and Virgin regularly produce catalogues of currently obtainable tapes, with numbers, for about £1.50 each. Neither have I noted when a film is in stereo, nor when it is close-captioned for the deaf. Check the boxes for this information. The HMV/Virgin booklets also give a good listing of tapes captioned for the deaf. (The captions are only revealed when accessed via a special unit.)

ACTION AND ADVENTURE

The big-selling cliché of the cinema of the moment is the movie as a 'rollercoaster ride'– as in *Twister* or *Speed* – with huge effects sequences. These are really an update of the terrible disaster-movie genre of the 1970s, albeit a lot more fun. Action and adventure come in many guises, from the James Bond pix to Indiana Jones, Batman and even the old classic Errol Flynn romps, but however you look at them, they are all pure entertainment, ideal for that evening in: sit back, relax, enjoy ...

48 HOURS

EDDIE MURPHY, NICK NOLTE, JAMES REMAR, ANNETTE O'TOOLE

WALTER HILL

USA (CIC) 1982

92m (18)

A cop gets a villain out of prison to help him on a case in this energetic action thriller, made before Nolte was a big star and when Murphy still made an effort to be amusing. There was a cut '15' certificate version around at one time, so check out the box for details. A sequel, *Another 48 Hours*, was a turgid re-run of the same situation.

THE ADVENTURES OF ROBIN HOOD

ERROL FLYNN, OLIVIA DE HAVILLAND, BASIL RATHBONE, CLAUDE RAINS

WILLIAM KEIGHLEY, MICHAEL CURTIZ

USA (WARNER) 1938

102m (U)

The definitive Technicolor version of the myths of the philanthropic bandit of Sherwood Forest and his battles with Prince John and his henchmen. Flynn still cuts a dash and makes the recent Kevin Costner attempt at the part look threadbare, while Rains and Rathbone are deliciously sneering villains. Only whey-faced Olivia de Havilland fails to stir the blood. Three Oscars, including one for Erich Wolfgang Korngold's magnificent score. Also on a two-for-one tape with Flynn's *Captain Blood* (see page 19).

CLASSIC 1000 VIDEOS

THE AFRICAN QUEEN

 HUMPHREY BOGART, KATHARINE HEPBURN, ROBERT MORLEY, PETER BULL

 JOHN HUSTON

USA (FOX) 1951

 105m (U)

Based on CS Forester's novel, this unusual film sees an oddball romance emerge when the slovenly captain of a small African steamboat is forced to rescue a prim spinster after her missionary brother dies. Laughs, thrills and heroism abound as they confront the might of the German navy in the days of World War One. Some find Hepburn's performance grating – you may be interested to know she's no less feisty in real life: I once asked her permission to write a poetry cycle based on her career and got a brisk note of refusal for my pains! Bogie won an Oscar for his role as the drunken skipper. Special box available.

AIR FORCE ONE

 HARRISON FORD, GARY OLDMAN, DEAN STOCKWELL

 WOLFGANG PETERSEN

USA (TOUCHSTONE) 1997

 120m (15)

When America and her president are seen to be corrupt and ineffectual, the tried and true answer is to turn to the movies for new hope. As in *Independence Day* (see page 247), here we have a pres who can physically kick butt with the best of 'em when under attack.

This time we have a nutball (Oldman) taking over the top man's plane in order to force the release of the leader of a small Soviet breakaway state – utter hooey, of course, but Ford (as the feisty pres) and Oldman (nasty in the extreme) do their stuff well and Petersen handles the tense action like a master.

BACK TO THE FUTURE

 MICHAEL J FOX, CHRISTOPHER LLOYD, LEA THOMPSON

 ROBERT ZEMECKIS

USA (CIC) 1985

 111m (PG)

Wacky time-travel adventure about teenager Marty McFly and his interference in the lives of his parents via a mad professor who turns one of the ill-fated De Lorean sports cars into a temporal racer. Back in the past, the kid invents distorted heavy guitar rock ten years too early. Eat your heart out Jimi Hendrix! Oscar for SFX. Available in widescreen boxed edition with both sequels and a documentary.

BACK TO THE FUTURE PART 2

 MICHAEL J FOX, CHRISTOPHER LLOYD, LEA THOMPSON

 ROBERT ZEMECKIS

USA (CIC) 1989

 103m (PG)

Lacklustre sequel to the first film, shot back-to-back with Part 3 to save cash – not usually a notion one associates with Hollywood blockbusters. It shows.

ACTION AND ADVENTURE

BACK TO THE FUTURE PART 3

★ MICHAEL J FOX, CHRISTOPHER LLOYD, MARY STEENBURGEN, LEA THOMPSON

🎬 ROBERT ZEMECKIS

USA (CIC) 1989

⏱ 113m (PG)

Against all expectations, this third part of the saga (shot at the same time as Part 2 for reasons of economy) represented a partial return to form for our heroes: McFly finds himself in the old West, with all the cowpoke-spoofing nonsense one might expect that to entail. A good send-off for the series, but let us hope director Zemeckis doesn't push his luck with another come-back-to-the-future any time soon.

BATMAN

★ MICHAEL KEATON, JACK NICHOLSON, KIM BASINGER, JACK PALANCE, MICHAEL GOUGH

🎬 TIM BURTON

USA/UK (WARNER) 1989

⏱ 121m (15)

Noting recent adult-oriented comics which returned Batman to his dark roots, Hollywood let young director Burton loose with this disturbing, perverse version of the antics of the cowled detective. A million miles from the primary colours of the camp 1960s TV show, with Oscar-winning sets and a hilarious scene-stealing Jack Nicholson as The Joker, this is not a movie for young viewers. Widescreen available. Also boxed with *Batman Returns*.

BATMAN FOREVER

★ VAL KILMER, JIM CARREY, TOMMY LEE JONES, NICOLE KIDMAN

🎬 JOEL SCHUMACHER

USA (WARNER) 1995

⏱ 115m (PG)

Third (and worst) of the current series of big-screen adventures for the Caped Crusader, with Val Kilmer taking over from Michael Keaton in the lead. Carrey does a typically manic Riddler, but the makers need to learn that stories (rather than stars) are what's needed. Widescreen available.

BATMAN RETURNS

★ MICHAEL KEATON, DANNY DeVITO, MICHELLE PFEIFFER, CHRISTOPHER WALKEN

🎬 TIM BURTON

USA (WARNER) 1992

⏱ 126m (15)

If anything, this sequel to the first film is even darker: The Penguin, known to comics fans as a tuxedoed twit, is here shown as a bitter creature with flippers for hands. Sick enough to alienate the studio, their sponsor Burger King and the film's intended audience, but cleverly made. The series continued without Burton and with Val Kilmer instead of Keaton in the cape for *Batman Forever*, followed by *Batman And Robin*, starring George Clooney in the title role. As noted above, *Batman* and *Batman Returns* are available in a boxed set.

BATMAN AND ROBIN

GEORGE CLOONEY, ALICIA SILVERSTONE, CHRIS O'DONNELL, UMA THURMAN, ARNOLD SCHWARZENEGGER

JOEL SCHUMACHER

USA (WARNER) 1997

120m (PG)

Fourth Batman flick, and it's another turkey despite heart-throb Clooney in the lead and the gallery of big-name villains. Available in a widescreen special boxed edition.

BLUE THUNDER

ROY SCHEIDER, WARREN OATES, MALCOLM McDOWELL, CANDY CLARK

JOHN BADHAM

USA (SPEARHEAD) 1983

105m (15)

Excitingly staged drama about a super helicopter and shenanigans surrounding same. Scheider and smug McDowell are great as the pilot and his old forces adversary (now the big bad boss) respectively. Lots of impressive swooping and crashing. Inspired a TV series of poor quality, but this original is Hollywood craftsmanship at its best.

BOILING POINT

WESLEY SNIPES, DENNIS HOPPER, LOLITA DAVIDOVICH, VIGGO MORTENSEN

JAMES B HARRIS

USA (4-FRONT) 1992

89m (15)

Snipes is developing into one of the few reliable black action stars possessed of genuine acting ability and an appeal which crosses racial divides. This revenge thriller was one of his earlier hits and also boasts a fine support turn from movie madman Dennis Hopper.

BROKEN ARROW

JOHN TRAVOLTA, CHRISTIAN SLATER, SAMANTHA MATHIS, DELROY LINDO

JOHN WOO

USA (FOX) 1996

86m (15)

Hong Kong action director Woo has had some trouble translating his hyperkinetic style into the more regimented Hollywood way of working, but this is a pretty agreeable compromise. Travolta is a turncoat intent on killing his pal (Slater) and hijacking their plane full of atomic missile warheads. Plenty of nail-biting moments and furious action, even if it doesn't quite match the insane delirium of Woo's best Hong Kong pix such as *The Killer* (see page 171). 'Broken Arrow', incidentally, is allegedly the military term for an aircraft lost while carrying nuclear bombs. Widescreen available.

ACTION AND ADVENTURE

CAPTAIN BLOOD

 ERROL FLYNN, OLIVIA DE HAVILLAND, BASIL RATHBONE, LIONEL ATWILL

 MICHAEL CURTIZ

USA (WARNER) 1935 B&W

 94m (PG)

Spirited version of Raphael Sabatini pirate story, with the same three stars who went on to great success in *The Adventures Of Robin Hood* (see page 15). Duels, ruffled shirts, and many swashes are buckled (or should that be 'buckles are swashed'?). This is apparently a cut print – the original cinema release is listed at 119m. Also on a two-for-one tape with *The Adventures Of Robin Hood*.

CLEAR AND PRESENT DANGER

 HARRISON FORD, WILLEM DAFOE, ANNE ARCHER, JAMES EARL JONES

 PHILIP NOYCE

USA (CIC) 1994

 136m (12)

Ford returns as Jack Ryan, the CIA character he played in *Patriot Games* (see page 32) – also essayed by Alec Baldwin in *The Hunt For Red October* (see page 26) in another flick based on Tom Clancy's series of novels. Competent rather than masterful, but a reliable cast just about carry it off.

CLIFFHANGER

 SYLVESTER STALLONE, JOHN LITHGOW, MICHAEL ROOKER

 RENNY HARLIN

USA (GUILD) 1993

 106m (15)

A breathtaking opening signals what to expect in this action adventure about mountain-rescue daredevil Stallone on the trail of bank heisters. There are some superb stunts and Lithgow is a great slimy villain. An efficient piece of enjoyable nonsense.

CON AIR

 NICOLAS CAGE, JOHN MALKOVICH, JOHN CUSACK, STEVE BUSCEMI, COLM MEANEY, VING RHAMES, RACHEL TICOTIN

 SIMON WEST

USA (TOUCHSTONE) 1997

 111m (18)

Spectacular action movie, with Cage as an ex-military hero about to be released from jail after serving time for killing a thug who menaced his wife. Unfortunately he hitches a ride home on a plane carrying psychos like Cyrus the Virus (Malkovich) and serial killer Garland Green (Buscemi), and a hijack ensues. The only dubious element is the ending, hinting that vile but witty Green deserves escape and a chance at freedom because he spares a small girl.

CONAN THE BARBARIAN

 ARNOLD SCHWARZENEGGER, SANDAHL BERGMAN, JAMES EARL JONES, MAX VON SYDOW

 JOHN MILIUS

USA (FOX) 1982

 121m (15)

Fascist individualism as filtered through the old pulp-mag tales of Robert E Howard's sword 'n' sorcery hero, here incarnate in musclebound Arnie. Spectacularly mounted, but Milius just doesn't have the magical touch needed – compared to the 1960s Italian 'Hercules' films of the likes of Mario Bava and Vittorio Cottafavi starring Arnie's hero Reg Park: (see *Hercules Conquers Atlantis*, page 131), there's something lacking. Available in widescreen.

CONAN THE DESTROYER

 ARNOLD SCHWARZENEGGER, GRACE JONES, MAKO, WILT CHAMBERLAIN

 RICHARD FLEISCHER

USA (ENTERTAINMENT) 1984

 96m (15)

Fleischer is more adept at this kind of cod-historical effort than Milius but it's a pity he wasn't hired to do the first pic – this is tired stuff, yet still beautiful-looking for all that.

DANTE'S PEAK

 PIERCE BROSNAN, LINDA HAMILTON, CHARLES HALLAHAN

 ROGER DONALDSON

USA (CIC) 1997

 104m

Volcano films seem to be a minor Hollywood fetish just now, and this average disaster movie is nothing more than a competent piece of work. It remains to be seen whether or not Pierce Brosnan can parlay his James Bond success into a wider career of megastar dimensions. Issued with some behind-the-scenes footage as a bonus.

DAYLIGHT

 SYLVESTER STALLONE, DAN HEDAYA, VIGGO MORTENSEN, CLAIRE BLOOM

 ROB COHEN

USA (CIC) 1997

 110m

Above-average Stallone action film, with the star as a disgraced fellow proving his heroic stature by leading folks trapped in a New York river tunnel to safety. Akin to the formula of the disaster movies of yore, but superior in SFX and execution. The end is ridiculous, but so what?

ACTION AND ADVENTURE

DELIVERANCE

★ JON VOIGHT, BURT REYNOLDS, NED BEATTY, RONNY COX

🎬 JOHN BOORMAN

USA (WARNER) 1972

⏱ 109m　(18)

Four city guys take a canoeing trip into backwoods wilderness only to be stalked by degenerate hillbillies. The message (if there is one) appears to be that men who act macho and 'in control' are not always the ones with the will to survive when things get serious. The male rape sequence still packs a punch though very little is actually shown. Now in a new, pristine widescreen version.

DEMOLITION MAN

★ SYLVESTER STALLONE, WESLEY SNIPES, SANDRA BULLOCK, NIGEL HAWTHORNE

🎬 MARCO BRAMBILLA

USA (WARNER) 1994

⏱ 111m　(15)

Daft but sporadically dazzling action flick set in the future, a peaceful have-a-nice-day world where the only means of coping with a crook freed from suspended animation (Snipes) is to unleash his also-frozen police nemesis (Stallone). Really, this comes into the so-bad-it's-good category, with costumes and story like an old TV *Blake's 7* episode. Enjoy!

DICK TRACY

★ WARREN BEATTY, AL PACINO, MADONNA, DUSTIN HOFFMAN, PAUL SORVINO

🎬 WARREN BEATTY

USA (TOUCHSTONE) 1990

⏱ 103m　(PG)

Oscars for sets, make-up and the Sondheim tune 'Sooner or Later' cannot disguise the thinness of Beatty's recreation of the pulp comic 'tec hero of yore. He acts like a plank of wood, Madonna wishes she was Marilyn Monroe, the story is zero. Only Pacino mugging away madly under a ton of weird latex make-up and the primary-coloured cityscapes and costumes make it all watchable.

DIE HARD

 BRUCE WILLIS, BONNIE BEDELIA, WILLIAM ATHERTON, ALAN RICKMAN

JOHN McTIERNAN

USA (FOX) 1988

126 m   (18)

This was the movie that made TV actor Willis a big-screen star. He's an off-duty cop, visiting his estranged wife's LA offices for Christmas, who stumbles into a robbery-and-hostage situation. Willis is charismatic as the outnumbered, outgunned guy, while Alan Rickman nearly runs away with the film as the wily, callous terrorist robber. A key '80s film which never loses the human element amongst the gunfire and explosions. There have been two sequels: the first, *Die Hard 2* (aka *Die Harder*) came about by accident when the studio noted a story it had bought was too similar to a Die Hard-type plot. Solution? Just change the character to that of Willis in the first pic and film it as a sequel! Much better was *Die Hard With A Vengeance*, but the first movie remains the only really classic action picture of the three. Widescreen.

DIRTY HARRY

 CLINT EASTWOOD, HARRY GUARDINO, JOHN VERNON, RENI SANTONI, ANDY ROBINSON

DON SIEGEL

USA (WARNER) 1971

98m   (18)

Originally a vehicle for Frank Sinatra, this super-duper action film has Clint as likeable rogue cop 'Dirty' Harry Callahan, taking on a psycho terrorising San Francisco and its supposedly lame bosses, the police chief and mayor. Condemned as right-wing by some, mainly due to the fact that the psychopath (ably played by Robinson) had a peace symbol on his belt. I think we can assume that was meant as an ironic touch – at least I hope so! I've heard this was much cut by the studio, but there's no mention of this in Don Siegel's autobiography, *A Siegel Film* (Faber). Many sequels, none as entertaining as this tough classic.

DOCTOR NO

 SEAN CONNERY, URSULA ANDRESS, BERNARD LEE, JOSEPH WISEMAN

TERENCE YOUNG

UK (MGM/UA) 1962

105m   (PG)

The first of the never-ending series based on Ian Fleming's spy hero James Bond was quite a low-budget affair – but with the way the stories later became swamped in gadgetry this may have been a blessing in disguise. Connery is still the only 007 for me, and this tale of a criminal genius in Jamaica remains one of his best. See also *Goldfinger* (page 26), *Thunderball* (page 37) and *You Only Live Twice* (page 256). All the 'Bonds' have been made available recently in digitally remastered versions, and widescreen. In the case of this film, such letterboxing is somewhat superfluous as it wasn't lensed in a true widescreen ratio.

ACTION AND ADVENTURE

THE DOGS OF WAR

CHRISTOPHER WALKEN, TOM BERENGER, COLIN BLAKELY, JO BETH WILLIAMS

JOHN IRVIN

UK (WARNER) 1980

114m (15)

Frederick Forsyth's novel is the basis for this story of double-dealings and mercenaries in contemporary Africa, with Walken a bit too young and clean as the killer-with-a-conscience. He's always an arresting actor, however, and workman-like direction from Irvin and a good support cast make for a flick that hardly deserves its bad reputation.

DROP ZONE

WESLEY SNIPES, GARY BUSEY, YANCY BUTLER, MICHAEL JETER

JOHN BADHAM

USA (CIC) 1994

97m (15)

Reliable action director Badham does a competent job on this sky-diving effort, released around the same time as *Terminal Velocity* (see page 36), a broadly similar movie. This is marginally the better film, mainly due to Snipes as the good guy and Busey as the twitchy leader of an airborne team of dangerous crooks.

THE EIGER SANCTION

CLINT EASTWOOD, GEORGE KENNEDY, JACK CASSIDY, VONETTA McGEE

CLINT EASTWOOD

USA (CIC/4-FRONT) 1975

113m (15)

Improbably set-up spy-actioner has Clint as the agent brought out of retirement to spot a traitor on a climbing jaunt. Lots of odd touches, such as Eastwood being paid in artworks, Cassidy as a gay with a poodle that's as camp as he is, and so on. Based on a John Trevanian novel. Seems to be cut, as original running time is noted at 125m.

EMPEROR OF THE NORTH

LEE MARVIN, ERNEST BORGNINE, KEITH CARRADINE, ELISHA COOK Jnr

ROBERT ALDRICH

USA (FOX) 1973

119m (15)

Also known as *Emperor Of The North Pole*, this exciting movie by cult director Aldrich concerns the attempt by hobo Marvin to ride vicious rail-guard Borgnine's train in revenge for his brutality against other tramps. Plenty of heart-in-mouth-moments.

CLASSIC 1000 VIDEOS

ESCAPE FROM LA

KURT RUSSELL, STACY KEACH, STEVE BUSCEMI, PETER FONDA

JOHN CARPENTER

USA (CIC) 1996

96m (15)

Virtually a blow-by-blow remake of the earlier (and superior) *Escape From New York* (see below): Russell is despatched into the city/prison on an important mission. Cynical and lacking in imagination, though it has better stars than it deserves and always looks good.

ESCAPE FROM NEW YORK

KURT RUSSELL, LEE VAN CLEEF, ISAAC HAYES, ERNEST BORGNINE, DONALD PLEASENCE

JOHN CARPENTER

USA (POLYGRAM) 1981

106m (15)

I suppose when this was made, 1997 seemed far off – it predicted that New York would by then be a dumping ground for incorrigibles, given the choice of painless death or fending for themselves in a rancid Big Apple. Russell is promised a third option: freedom if he goes in and rescues the stranded USA President, with the added incentive of a timed explosive planted in his neck to make him return as planned. Sprawling, cynical and fun. The recent *Escape From LA* (see above) is virtually a remake.

FACE/OFF

NICOLAS CAGE, JOHN TRAVOLTA, GINA GERSHON, JOAN ALLEN

JOHN WOO

USA (TOUCHSTONE) 1997

133m (18)

After *Broken Arrow* (see page 18) expat Hong Kong action stylist Woo really gets into his stride with this absurd-but-wonderful tale of Cage swapping faces and mannerisms with Travolta in a cat-and-mouse game of secret agents v terrorists. It's a hoot to see the two actors trying to ape each other's tics in this meld of *Eyes Without A Face* and James Bond – insanely inventive entertainment with Woo managing to translate the 'anything goes' Hong Kong feel to the USA.

FIREFOX

CLINT EASTWOOD, FREDDIE JONES, WARREN CLARKE, NIGEL HAWTHORNE

CLINT EASTWOOD

USA (WARNER) 1982

121m (15)

Thrill-a-minute tale which starts out as a complicated espionage story until Clint reaches his destination in the heart of Russia, when it becomes a fine adventure flick as he has to steal a new computer-controlled MIG jet. Great special effects in this adaptation of the Craig Thomas novel. Sadly only available in a pan-scan and cut version, the original running time being 137m.

ACTION AND ADVENTURE

FIRST BLOOD

 SYLVESTER STALLONE, RICHARD CRENNA, DAVID CARUSO, BRIAN DENNEHY

 TED KOTCHEFF

USA (POLYGRAM) 1982

89m (15)

The initial Rambo movie, based on David Morrell's novel, is a solid action thriller with a downbeat feel quite different from its fantasy-type sequels. Sly is a war hero who objects to being thrown out of a town just for looking a bit dodgy, and minor conflict with the law soon escalates. Has a point to make.

FLESH AND BLOOD

 RUTGER HAUER, JENNIFER JASON LEIGH, RONALD LACEY, JACK THOMPSON

 PAUL VERHOEVEN

HOLLAND/SPAIN/USA (4-FRONT) 1985

 122m (18)

Down-and-dirty epic of sex and violence in medieval times. Realistically nasty stuff with lots of action from the director who went on to major Hollywood success with *RoboCop* (see page 251) and *Total Recall* (see page 255). Hauer is devilish fun and Lacy has a ripe cameo as a grimy priest.

GOLDENEYE

 PIERCE BROSNAN, SEAN BEAN, ISABELLA SCORUPCO, JOE DON BAKER

 MARTIN CAMPBELL

UK/USA (MGM/UA) 1995

124m (12)

This first Bond movie with Brosnan in the role marks a return to form for the series – it is certainly better than any of the risible Roger Moore vehicles, which treated the series like a 'Carry On' comedy romp. The stunts are genuinely clever rather than simply relying on bigger and bigger explosions, the story is acceptably convoluted, the support more than mere cannon fodder and Brosnan has a hint of Connery's wry glint. Great!

GOLDFINGER

	SEAN CONNERY, HONOR BLACKMAN, GERT FROBE, SHIRLEY EATON, HAROLD SAKATA
	GUY HAMILTON
	UK (MGM/UA) 1964
	105m

Possibly the best 'Bond' film, where spectacle was on the up but the technology hadn't yet dwarfed the plot. Great scenes: Ms Eaton murdered by being painted in suffocating gold; Bond having a laser aimed at his groin and asking the villain of the piece (who plans to rob Fort Knox) if he expects him to talk: 'No, Mr Bond, I expect you to *die!*'; the fight between Bond and Oddjob (Sakata) with his razor-rimmed bowler; and the crooked golf match. The only thing that might offend modern audiences, even when making allowances for the pic's era, is the idea that the naughtily-named Pussy Galore (Blackman) is 'cured' of her implied lesbianism by big, hunky Bond! Letterboxed and digitally remastered. See also *Thunderball* (page 37), *Doctor No* (page 22) and *You Only Live Twice*, (page 256). Latest incarnation of James is Pierce Brosnan in *GoldenEye* (see page 25) and *Tomorrow Never Dies* (see page 37).

HIGHLANDER

	CHRISTOPHER LAMBERT, SEAN CONNERY, CLANCY BROWN, HUGH QUARSHIE
	RUSSELL MULCAHY
	UK/USA (WARNER) 1986
	111m

This silly but moderately entertaining story about duelling immortal warriors has become something of a cult. The UK and USA versions are different, and the director recently combined elements of both for a special laserdisc cut. It inspired sequels and a TV series, which seems strange as it wasn't a mega-blockbuster. Connery and Lambert carry it off, though. Widescreen available.

THE HUNT FOR RED OCTOBER

	SEAN CONNERY, ALEC BALDWIN, TIM CURRY, SCOTT GLEN
	JOHN McTIERNAN
	USA (CIC) 1990
	129m

Tom Clancy's novel inspired this tale of a Russian captain who defects and has to convince the West that he wants to hand over his state-of-the-art stealth submarine to them – to some extent it's like an underwater *Firefox* (see page 24). Connery is no Russki ('We shail into hishtory') but he has authority and star magnetism. Baldwin's CIA man character has also been played by Harrison Ford in *Patriot Games* (see page 32) as part of an ongoing plan to adapt other Clancy tales. Widescreen available.

ACTION AND ADVENTURE

ICE STATION ZEBRA

ROCK HUDSON, ERNEST BORGNINE, PATRICK McGOOHAN, JIM BROWN

JOHN STURGES

USA (WARNER) 1969

139m (U)

Based on an Alistair MacLean novel about treachery aboard a submarine. Plenty of tension and drama amid the icy wastes, but McGoohan all but abducts the pic from under Rock's wooden nose.

THE ITALIAN JOB

MICHAEL CAINE, NOEL COWARD, BENNY HILL, RAF VALLONE

PETER COLLINSON

UK (CIC/4-FRONT) 1969

96m (PG)

Cult adventure about Brit villains pulling off a robbery in Italy with a fleet of Mini Minors. The stunts are delightful and amazing, while Coward camps up his cameo as a jailed crime lord. Dated.

THE JACKAL

BRUCE WILLIS, RICHARD GERE, SIDNEY POITIER, DIANE VENORA

MICHAEL CATON-JONES

USA (CIC) 1998

119m (18)

Loose updating of *The Day Of The Jackal* (see page 264), now turned into an action romp full of loud bangs and sensationalism (Willis's first screen kiss *with a man*.) Mercilessly panned by the critics on its release, this is actually quite solid, mindless, entertaining fun.

JAWS

ROY SCHEIDER, ROBERT SHAW, RICHARD DREYFUSS, MURRAY HAMILTON

STEVEN SPIELBERG

USA (CIC) 1975

118m (PG)

Peter Benchley's novel about small-town politics and relationships affected by a killer shark is here presented as a thrill-machine, with a fake-looking rubber beast belying the book's subtleties. Many sequels, but even the best was inferior to Italian rip-off *The Last Jaws* – an upstart gore-fest which the American studio took legal action to suppress. Spielberg is allegedly planning a *Jaws* remake or special edition. Oscars include one for the haunting John Williams score. Widescreen.

THE JEWEL OF THE NILE

MICHAEL DOUGLAS, KATHLEEN TURNER, DANNY DeVITO, SPIROS FOCAS

LEWIS TEAGUE

USA (FOX) 1985

101m (PG)

Sequel to *Romancing The Stone* (see page 34), same cast, but not a patch on the original. Typical Hollywood logic: a film is a hit, so they make it all over again and hope that no one'll notice the con. Very light, but nonetheless enjoyable – in a stupid kind of way.

27

JOURNEY TO THE CENTRE OF THE EARTH

 JAMES MASON, PAT BOONE, ARLENE DAHL, DIANE BAKER

 HENRY LEVIN

USA (FOX) 1959

 126m (U)

Energetic rendering of the Jules Verne classic about an expedition to the earth's core, which is depicted as a world of marvels. The art direction, Bernard Herrmann's score and Mason's acting make it perfect for kids of all ages from nine to 90, but using real lizards instead of animation for the dinosaur sequences was a mistake. It's a travesty that this is released as an 'All-time Great', but not in its original CinemaScope framing.

JURASSIC PARK

 SAM NEILL, LAURA DERN, JEFF GOLDBLUM, RICHARD ATTENBOROUGH

 STEVEN SPIELBERG

USA (CIC) 1993

 126m (PG)

A Michael Crichton story of a theme park on an island off Costa Rica, run by geneticists and featuring live dinosaurs created from ancient DNA (extracted from prehistoric blood samples obtained via the guts of mosquitoes trapped in amber). Mad idea, but you'll believe it when you see the mix of animatronics and computer images used to create the dinos – which run wild just as the park is being road-tested. There are holes in the plot: at least one strand about a sick saurian is simply dropped and never returned to, but with all the excitement you'll hardly care. Sequel, *The Lost World* (Sir Arthur Conan Doyle will turn in his grave), is out now. Widescreen available – though I believe the image has possibly been blown up within the frame to make the image more readable on small TVs. This was certainly the case with the USA tape and disc release. Though the film has a PG cert, there's an added note that some scenes may be too intense for some young viewers.

THE KILLER ELITE

 JAMES CAAN, ROBERT DUVALL, BURT YOUNG, BO HOPKINS, GIG YOUNG

 SAM PECKINPAH

USA (MGM/UK) 1975

 122m (18)

Peckinpah's bizarre version of Robert Rostand's novel about conflict between renegade spies and their ex-employers is a mad, violent piece of fluff – even shorn of the director's preferred ending, which had a dead character coming back to life as if to indicate that the whole movie was a joke! In my book, even minor Sam Peckinpah is great Sam Peckinpah.

ACTION AND ADVENTURE

LEGEND

☆ TOM CRUISE, TIM CURRY, MIA SARA, DAVID BENNENT

🎬 RIDLEY SCOTT

UK (WARNER) 1985

⏱ 90m (PG)

Scott's attempt to film an original myth rather than an extant fable fell flat with critics, though it's enchanting to look at, not least due to devilish Curry in his outsize red horns as he stalks the last unicorn in order to bring on an age of darkness. There are two versions with two entirely different music scores. BBC TV often shows the USA version.

LETHAL WEAPON

☆ MEL GIBSON, DANNY GLOVER, GARY BUSEY, TOM ATKINS

🎬 RICHARD DONNER

USA (WARNER) 1987

⏱ 105m (18)

Action-packed story of unhinged policeman and the effects of his demented, near-suicidal ways on his partner. Lots of mayhem, bangs and whizzes made for a smash hit, propelled by Gibson's star power and his interaction with Glover. Two sequels (see right). Available in widescreen.

LETHAL WEAPON 2

☆ MEL GIBSON, DANNY GLOVER, JOE PESCI, PATSY KENSIT

🎬 RICHARD DONNER

USA (WARNER) 1989

⏱ 109m (18)

Formulaic sequel to the first film. Our dynamic duo are up against drug-dealing diplomats, while Gibson finds time for romance with Kensit. Humour is added to the mix by Pesci. Widescreen available.

LETHAL WEAPON 3

☆ MEL GIBSON, DANNY GLOVER, JOE PESCI, RENE RUSSO

🎬 RICHARD DONNER

USA (WARNER) 1992

⏱ 118m (15)

Tired sequel to the earlier pix. Rene Russo appears as a martial-arts expert copper in this escapist fodder, which finds our boys chasing cop-killers. Widescreen available. A fourth in the series, with hit USA comic Chris Rock joining the team, is now on release.

CLASSIC 1000 VIDEOS

THE LOST WORLD: JURASSIC PARK

 JEFF GOLDBLUM, RICHARD ATTEN-BOROUGH, PETER POSTLETHWAITE, JULIANNE MOORE, ARLISS HOWARD

 STEVEN SPIELBERG

USA (CIC) 1997

 123m (PG)

By-the-numbers sequel to *Jurassic Park* (see page 28): turns out there are even more saurians to be dealt with, stashed on a secret island near the one in the original flick. Edgy maths genius Goldblum is along for the ride, this time with a big-game hunter (Postlethwaite) intent on bagging a male Tyrannosaurus Rex, and another couple of pesky kids (just like the first film) for the young audience to identify with. Great FX, but the jaw-dropping factor is diminished the second time out.

THE LONG KISS GOODNIGHT

 GEENA DAVIS, SAMUEL L JACKSON

 RENNY HARLIN

USA (NEW LINE) 1996

 115m (18)

There's a touch of self-parody about this deliberately over-the-top actioner with its crazy stunts, big bangs and flamboyant heavy-weapon wielding. Directed by Davis's then-husband Harlin, with a nicely judged performance from Samuel L Jackson of *Pulp Fiction* (see page 163) fame. A good evening's entertainment.

MAD MAX

 MEL GIBSON, TIM BURNS, STEVE BISLEY, JOANNE SAMUEL

GEORGE MILLER

AUSTRALIA (WARNER) 1979

 100m (18)

The film which made Gibson a star. The USA actor, who'd lived in Australia since boyhood, stars in this story about a near future world where petrol is short and cops spend their time chasing bikers on the highways. The original picture opened on the bottom of a double bill in London's Leicester Square, where it soon emerged that punters were paying to see the little Aussie flick and not the big picture. *Mad Max* became a world-wide hit. Widescreen.

MAD MAX 2: THE ROAD WARRIOR

 MEL GIBSON, BRUCE SPENCE, VERNON WELLS, EMIL MINTY

 GEORGE MILLER

AUSTRALIA (WARNER) 1981

 91m (18)

The best of the 'Mad Max' pix. Director Miller had a bigger budget and put it to good use in a display of stunts and pyrotechnics to shame the largest Hollywood studio. Our hero, devastated by the loss of his wife in the first film, roams the wastelands until he encounters a settlement threatened by a crew of punk bikers. Released as *The Road Warrior* in the USA, as the original film was not so well known there.

ACTION AND ADVENTURE

MAD MAX: BEYOND THE THUNDERDOME

 MEL GIBSON, TINA TURNER, FRANK THRING, ANGELO ROSSITTO

 GEORGE MILLER, GEORGE OGILVIE

USA (WARNER) 1985

 102m (15)

The third 'Mad Max' movie sees another increase in budget and a dip in story quality. It seems like two plots glued together: first Max stumbles into a community run by Aunty Entity (Turner) and has to fight for his life in a bizarre gladiator arena. Then, thrown into the desert to die, he comes upon a tribe of lithe, lost kids who see him as a messiah. Pretentious, mythic overtones of religiosity finally drag the action down.

THE MARK OF ZORRO

 TYRONE POWER, LINDA DARNELL, BASIL RATHBONE, GALE SONDERGAARD

 ROUBEN MAMOULIAN

USA (FOX) 1940 B&W

 93m (U)

Swashbuckling classic from one of the great American directors. Power poses as a fop in old Mexico, while in reality he's the righter-of-wrongs, the masked hero Zorro. Rathbone is at his slimy best. Magnificent swordfight at the climax.

MISSION: IMPOSSIBLE

 TOM CRUISE, JON VOIGHT, EMMANUELLE BEART, HENRY CZERNY

 BRIAN DE PALMA

USA (CIC) 1996

 106m

One of De Palma's less personal films, this is an adaptation of an old TV series (like his earlier film *The Untouchables*, see page 165). Little remains of the original, except the basic format of agents doing improbable things to a background of that noodling theme tune. The plot is ridiculous, with people continually pulling off rubber masks to reveal that we've been misled, but the action is pure celluloid-packaged adrenalin: look out for the scene where Cruise dangles above a burglar-proof room in a harness. A great night's entertainment.

NEVER SAY NEVER AGAIN

 SEAN CONNERY, EDWARD FOX, MAX VON SYDOW, KLAUS MARIA BRANDAUER

 IRWIN KERSHNER

UK (WARNER) 1983

 128m

Connery outraged his ex-employers by starring in this unofficial remake of *Thunderball* (see page 37), the rights being owned by Irish entrepreneur Kevin McClory. It's inferior to the original, yet there are apparently plans to remake the story for a third time! Please, no!

OUTBREAK

	DUSTIN HOFFMAN, RENE RUSSO, MORGAN FREEMAN, DONALD SUTHERLAND
	WOLFGANG PETERSEN
	USA (WARNER) 1995
	113m (15)

All-too-plausible tale of a killer virus plague carried to the USA by an escaped monkey. The aura of controlled panic is well maintained throughout, and, while it may not be in the league of *The Graduate* or *Midnight Cowboy* (see page 111), the part of the army doctor on the trail of the disease makes a welcome return to form for Hoffman after an arid spell of many years.

PATRIOT GAMES

	HARRISON FORD, ANNE ARCHER, PATRICK BERGIN, SEAN BEAN
	PHILIP NOYCE
	USA (CIC) 1992
	117m (15)

Ford's first outing as Tom Clancy's novel-series hero, CIA man Jack Ryan – see also *Clear And Present Danger* (page 19) and *The Hunt For Red October* (page 26) for more on this character. On holiday in the UK he thwarts an IRA attack, is knighted (!) and then becomes a target. Plenty of action and excitement, but a bit overlong.

THE PEACEMAKER

	GEORGE CLOONEY, NICOLE KIDMAN, ARMIN MUELLER-STAHL
	MIMI LEDER
	USA (DREAMWORKS) 1997
	120 m (15)

TV hunk Clooney teams up with Kidman to thwart mad, bad folk threatening the UN building with stolen Russian nuclear hardware. Predictable explosive melodrama which has seemingly (inexplicably, to me) proved a big hit in the video rental market in the UK. It's good to look at, at least.

THE POSEIDON ADVENTURE

	GENE HACKMAN, ERNEST BORGNINE, SHELLEY WINTERS, RODDY McDOWALL
	RONALD NEAME
	USA (FOX) 1972
	112m (PG)

This adaptation of a Paul Gallico novel makes for perhaps the best of the 1970s disaster movies – but that's not saying much! The usual formula: a group of people in a bad situation (this time an upturned ocean liner) reveal their personal problems as they battle to get free. And of course they're all played by stars. Oscars for SFX and for song ('The Morning After').

ACTION AND ADVENTURE

PREDATOR

ARNOLD SCHWARZENEGGER, CARL WEATHERS, BILL DUKE, JESSE VENTURA

JOHN McTIERNAN

USA (FOX) 1987

102m (18)

Top troops on a rescue up the jungle find themselves battling a shape-shifting alien in this effective, gory, shoot-'em-up. Not a classic, but it has its moments.

THE PRISONER OF ZENDA

STEWART GRANGER, DEBORAH KERR, JAMES MASON, ROBERT COOTE

RICHARD THORPE

USA (WARNER) 1952

97m (U)

This remake of the 1937 Ronald Colman version of Anthony Hope's novel is often derided, but it's actually a nifty fairytale picture. Granger plays two parts: the lazy royal of a small country and the distantly-related Englishman who has to take his place to prevent political disaster. Rich colour and a typically vile villain (Mason) make for unimpeachable and jolly nonsense.

RAIDERS OF THE LOST ARK

HARRISON FORD, KAREN ALLEN, PAUL FREEMAN, JOHN RHYS-DAVIES

STEVEN SPIELBERG

USA (CIC) 1981

112m (PG)

First and undoubtedly the best of the three 'Indiana Jones' pix, with Ford as the raffish archaeologist on the track of the lost Ark of the Covenant – also sought by the Nazis for its mysterious powers. Closely modelled on serials of the World War Two era, but with a much improved budget, this is full of whip-cracking, snake-pits and rotting skeletons. The edge-of-your-seat pre-credits sequence sets the tone brilliantly. The two sequels just don't have the same magic, though they were hugely successful. Oscars include one for SFX.

RAMBO: FIRST BLOOD PART 2

SYLVESTER STALLONE, STEVEN BERKOFF, RICHARD CRENNA, CHARLES NAPIER

GEORGE P COSMATOS

USA (POLYGRAM) 1985

92m (15)

Sequel to the superior *First Blood* (see page 25). Army boss Crenna is aiming to harness alienated veteran Rambo's deadly talents, offering him a mission to rescue long-forgotten USA POW's from the Vietnam conflict who're being held in Cambodia. Lots of explosions and lingering shots of Sly's oiled chest.

RAMBO 3

SYLVESTER STALLONE, RICHARD CRENNA, MARC DE JONGE

PETER McDONALD

USA (POLYGRAM) 1988

94m (18)

Rambo goes to Afghanistan to fight the Reds and rescue bossman Crenna. The most expensive (and least effective) of the three Rambo pix, and cut heavily by the UK censor for violence. Next came a kiddy cartoon and the inevitable sex parodies.

ROB ROY

LIAM NEESON, TIM ROTH, JESSICA LANGE, JOHN HURT, BRIAN COX

MICHAEL CATON-JONES

USA/UK (MGM/UA) 1995

113m (15)

Issued at the same time as *Braveheart* (see page 124), this is another tale of a Scots hero battling against both the English and enemies closer to home. Neeson makes a dashing lead, but the picture is nearly stolen by Roth as a foppish, evil cad who violates our hero's woman. Great action and top scenery.

THE ROCK

SEAN CONNERY, NICOLAS CAGE, ED HARRIS, MICHAEL BIEHN

MICHAEL BAY

USA (HOLLYWOOD) 1996

131m (15)

Blockbuster thriller about a political prisoner (Connery) let out of clink by nasty USA authorities to help agent Cage battle an aggrieved military man (Harris) who has taken over the prison on the island of Alcatraz. The pace never lets up, and it has become increasingly apparent that any pic like this which takes Connery on board is doing itself a big, big favour. Totally ludicrous but a decided hoot.

ROMANCING THE STONE

MICHAEL DOUGLAS, KATHLEEN TURNER, DANNY DeVITO, ZACK NORMAN

ROBERT ZEMECKIS

USA (FOX) 1984

101m (PG)

Soldier-of-fortune and woman-in-peril form uneasy alliance in this comic upstart partially inspired by the success of *Raiders Of The Lost Ark* (see page 33). Lame sequel: *The Jewel Of The Nile* (see page 27).

ACTION AND ADVENTURE

THE RUNNING MAN

 ARNOLD SCHWARZENEGGER, MARIA CONCHITA ALONSO, YAPHET KOTTO, JIM BROWN

PAUL MICHAEL GLASER

USA (ENTERTAINMENT) 1987

97m (18)

Based on a novel by Stephen King (penned under the pseudonym Richard Bachman) and helmed by TV's *Starsky and Hutch* star Glaser, this is one of many thrillers with the theme of modern sports taken to a logically deadly extreme. Has a reputation among Arnie's fans, but looks a tad cheap.

THE SEA HAWK

 ERROL FLYNN, FLORA ROBSON, CLAUDE RAINS, DONALD CRISP

 MICHAEL CURTIZ

USA (WARNER) 1940 B&W

 122m (U)

A Rafael Sabatini novel again provides the basis for a Flynn swashbuckler, as in *Captain Blood* (see page 19). Sir Francis Drake hassles the piratical Spaniards – or is that the other way around? Flynn at his handsome, strutting best. Show it to your kids to let them know there was life before Tom Cruise.

SPEED

 KEANU REEVES, SANDRA BULLOCK, DENNIS HOPPER

JAN DE BONT

USA (FOX) 1994

 111m

A movie for which the term 'rollercoaster' was made. Our heroes are aboard a bus with a bomb planted by madman Hopper, the catch being that it will go off if the vehicle drops below a certain speed. A massive hit and rightly so. It ain't art, but ... Widescreen available.

SPEED 2 – CRUISE CONTROL

 JASON PATRIC, SANDRA BULLOCK, WILLEM DAFOE

 JAN DE BONT

USA (FOX) 1997

 120m

By-the-numbers retread of the previous 'Speed' movie by director De Bont. With only the overrated Bullock and lacking his hero (Keanu Reeves) and villain (Dennis Hopper) from the debut flick (see above), the director is left treading water and no number of explosions can save the picture.

CLASSIC 1000 VIDEOS

SUPERMAN – THE MOVIE

 CHRISTOPHER REEVE, MARLON BRANDO, MARGOT KIDDER, GENE HACKMAN

 RICHARD DONNER

USA/UK (WARNER) 1978

 137m (PG)

Epic, star-stuffed version, recounting comic hero's origins, suffers slightly from the difficulty of gluing the backstory to a final resolution. Numerous sequels, offshoots, TV shows, etc. The part seems jinxed: early Superman George Reeves killed himself, while Christopher Reeve has since been paralysed in a tragic riding accident. Oscars for SFX. (Note: apparently, there's a cheapo, unauthorised Indian rip-off of this film that makes for weird viewing!) Widescreen available.

TERMINAL VELOCITY

 CHARLIE SHEEN, NASTASSJA KINSKI, JAMES GANOLFINI, CHRISTOPHER McDONALD

 DERAN SARAFIAN

USA (HOLLYWOOD) 1994

 98m (15)

Convoluted spy film revolving around sky-diving and hijacked Russian gold. There are some breathtaking stunt sequences, but the cast and plot are strictly routine by comparison. Still, a sure-fire lager-and-curry midnight movie.

THE TERMINATOR

 ARNOLD SCHWARZENEGGER, LINDA HAMILTON, MICHAEL BIEHN, LANCE HENRIKSEN

 JAMES CAMERON

USA (VISION) 1984

 102m (18)

Inventive, low-budget story about an android (Arnie) who comes back in time to kill the woman who will give birth to a revolutionary hero of the future. Rekindled Arnie's career and put director Cameron into the major league. See sequel below.

TERMINATOR 2: JUDGEMENT DAY

 ARNOLD SCHWARZENEGGER, LINDA HAMILTON, ROBERT PATRICK, EDWARD FURLONG

 JAMES CAMERON

USA (GUILD) 1991

 130m (15)

This sequel to the first pic has a mega-budget and was one of the first films to use computer 'morphing' in a big way. Arnie returns, this time as a 'good' android bent on protecting the kid who is the future saviour of the world, at the same time getting the boy's mum out of the asylum where she's been placed because of her ravings about time-jumping machine-men. Unfortunately for them all, a far superior android is on their trail. Astounding effects that can hardly be put into words – a perfect wedding of tricks and plot. Don't miss it. Longer version for TV.

36

ACTION AND ADVENTURE

THUNDERBALL

SEAN CONNERY, ADOLFO CELI, CLAUDINE AUGER, LUCIANA PALUZZI

TERENCE YOUNG

UK (MGM/UA) 1965

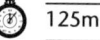

125m (PG)

Great 'Bond' film about hijacked bomb-carrying plane, rather similar to the recent *Broken Arrow* (see page 18). Soaring John Barry score and thrilling undersea fights. Remade as *Never Say Never Again* (see page 31). Now available in widescreen, digitally remastered version. See also *Doctor No* (page 22), *Goldfinger* (page 26) and *You Only Live Twice* (page 256). Celi, the baddie here, made a rip-off Italian flick called *Operation Kid Brother* – with Connery's sibling Neil!

TOMORROW NEVER DIES

PIERCE BROSNAN, JOE DON BAKER, TERI HATCHER, JONATHAN PRYCE, MICHELLE YEOH

ROGER SPOTTISWOODE

UK/USA (WARNER) 1997

114 m (12)

Brosnan's second stab at the 007 mantle is something of a let-down after the refreshing heights of *GoldenEye* (see page 25), despite the presence of Pryce, TV *Superman*-babe Hatcher and Hong Kong starlet Yeoh. Spottiswoode directs in reliable ho-hum manner but it's a tired mix of cocktails and bangs. Neither shakes nor stirs, but will please die-hard fans of the series. Available in widescreen.

TOP GUN

TOM CRUISE, KELLY McGILLIS, VAL KILMER, TOM SKERRITT

TONY SCOTT

USA (CIC) 1986

110m (15)

Flash-bang-wallop action/ romance about USA Navy fliers competing to be 'top gun' in their F-14 squadron. I rate it three for the undeniably fine action sequences. The song 'Take My Breath Away' won an Oscar. Widescreen available. Note: director Scott is the less-talented sibling of Ridley Scott, who directed classics like *Alien* (see page 240) and *Blade Runner* (see page 242). The film got a memorable come-uppance in a recent movie called *Sleep With Me*, in which motormouth film director Quentin Tarantino does a cameo as a party guest with a theory that *Top Gun* has a homosexual subtext which involves the other fliers urging Tom Cruise to ditch Kelly McGillis and 'go the gay way'; in defence of this notion he draws dark inferences from alleged dialogue about fliers 'riding each other's tails'.

TRUE LIES

ARNOLD SCHWARZENEGGER, JAMIE LEE CURTIS, ART MALIK, TIA CARRERE

JAMES CAMERON

USA (CIC) 1994

135m (15)

The director of *Aliens* (see page 240) and *The Abyss* (see page 239) helms above-par spy action for big Arnie, with some great stunts – especially the helicopter-dangling one re-enacted by Ms Curtis at the Oscars. Art Malik makes a nicely evil villain, too. Available in widescreen, though some sources state that the image has been blown up/cropped.

TWISTER

BILL PAXTON, JAMI GERTZ, HELEN HUNT, CARY ELWES

JAN DE BONT

USA (CIC) 1996

108m (PG)

Another spectacle from De Bont, maker of *Speed* (see page 35). A hit, but the tornado SFX lose their impact on the small screen and the package isn't aided by the fact that the actors and script simply don't manage to make us give two figs about the characters, estranged boy and girl weather scientists, would you believe?

ADULT

Video provides an ideal medium for 'adult' entertainment. After all, most of us, I think it would be fair to say, would rather indulge in such pursuits in the privacy of our own home. However, if you are hoping that your local video store will provide you with an ever-changing supply of porn, you will be sadly disappointed.

In the USA and most of Europe, adults are allowed free access to hard-core movies – by which term I mean films where the stars indulge in real sexual acts on-screen under the unflinching gaze of the camera. In the UK the situation is very different: only soft-core (simulated) sex is normally permitted, and the few hard-core movies which do get a release are censored. I'm not being pedantic here or saying that a movie is worthless if the BBFC removes a few seconds, but the fact is that nobody watches sex films for the plot – and even some of the more artistically ambitious flicks (like those of cult figure Michael Ninn) lost their flavour when shorn of minutes of sex content before being deemed fit to be viewed by British adults.

Things may be changing, however. In recent years the censor has passed hard sex scenes in so-called 'educational' videos, and some hard core was controversially passed in an attempt to 'test the waters' with the public. Also significant was the *Evening Standard* story about a Soho video dealer charged with selling uncertificated pornography. As his lawyer had anticipated, the case against him collapsed when the judge advised the police to reconsider the charge, on the basis that the average 1997 jury just wouldn't find heterosexual sex obscene.

My own favourite sex film is *Baby Face*, an old classic by USA director Alex De Renzy, although the film was issued here only in bowdlerised form, and it may be years yet before your average high-street dealer (or even licensed sex stores where R18 material is sold) will freely offer such pix. In the meantime, what follows is a trawl through what you can currently rent or buy on tape in the Adult section.

9½ WEEKS

☆ MICKEY ROURKE, KIM BASINGER, DAVID MARGULIES, MARGARET WHITTON

🎬 ADRIAN LYNE

USA (FOX) 1986

⏱ 112m (18)

Unjustly over-valued, pseudo-sadomasochistic bonkfest. The title derives from the duration of the lust-fuelled collision of the two leads, and inspired many similarly-titled movies. Rather a patina of glitzy, arty pretension to my mind, although to be fair, you get to see Basinger before she began to fade – though she's made a comeback of sorts with the recent *LA Confidential* (see page 109) – ditto Mickey Rourke, a fine actor who is criminally under-used these days. Based on Elizabeth McNeill's novel of the same name. Available in widescreen.

AI NO BOREI

☆ TATSUYA FUJI, KAZUKO YOSHIYUKI, TAKAHIRO TAMURA

🎬 NAGISA OSHIMA

JAPAN/FRANCE (CONNOISSEUR) 1978

⏱ 100m (18)

Companion film to the infamous *Ai No Corrida* (1976) – still banned on tape, due, no doubt, to the gruelling penis-severing scene – this is another tale of doomed love, with a man and woman embarking on an affair and bumping off the girl's inconvenient husband, only to find themselves plagued by his ghost. Luminescent photography and impassioned playing make this a classic of its kind. Widescreen. Subtitled.

THE ALCOVE

☆ LILLI CARATI, ANNIE BELLE, AL CLIVER, LAURA GEMSER

🎬 JOE D'AMATO

ITALY (JEZEBEL) 1985

⏱ 88m (18)

Cut (one assumes) version of decadent sex 'n' drugs miasma from cult horror/porn director D'Amato, the man whose name and predilection for gorefests spawned many 'D'Amato Ketchup' headlines. His real name is Aristede Massaccesi, but when you sit through material like this you can see why a pseudonym (this is one of many) must seem like a neat idea.

THE ART OF LOVE

☆ MARINA PIERRO, MICHELLE PLACIDO, MASSIMO GIROTTI

🎬 WALERIAN BOROWCZYK

ITALY/FRANCE (JEZEBEL) 1984

⏱ 93m (18)

Arthouse director who edged his way into classy eroticism, Borowczyk may have now been abandoned by the serious critics, but that doesn't mean he has ditched genuine commitment to his work. He fetishises objects and images, and this visualisation of a series of sex lectures for lechers given by Ovid to an audience of ancient Romans gives ample rein to his propensity for ripe and passionate action. Subtitled and widescreen.

ADULT

THE BELT

JAMES RUSSON, ELEONORA BRIGLIADORI, KAREN MOORE

GUILIANA GAMBA

ITALY (ART HOUSE/ANGEL) 1989

90m (18)

Tired story about a married couple who enliven their sex life by whacking each other with the implement of the title, though this doesn't seem to stop the husband ending up in court accused of abusing his wife. Doesn't really get going either as drama or as porn.

BEYOND THE VALLEY OF THE DOLLS

DOLLY READ, CYNTHIA MYERS, EDY WILLIAMS, JOHN LAZAR

RUSS MEYER

USA (FOX) 1970

102m (18)

Rare big-studio outing for breast-fetishist Meyer is a witty lampoon of the Hollyweird milieu of the original *Valley Of The Dolls* (1967), though not an actual sequel. Busty all-girl rock group move to California and become involved in many ups 'n' downs (and in 'n' outs) when they join the entourage of crazed manager Z-Man, who throws pervy parties that drive him to exclaim things like, 'This is my happening and it freaks me out!' (a line recently reprised in comedy hit *Austin Powers – International Man Of Mystery*). Energetically photographed in psychedelic Hieronymous Bosch tones by Fred J Koenekamp with a climactic massacre inspired by the Manson murders – but you wouldn't know it from this faded, cut, non-widescreen tape. Available as a letterboxed import laserdisc, and has been shown semi-widescreen (and uncut) by Channel 4 TV.

BLACK CANDLES

MARTHA BELTON, BETTY WEBSTER, JEFFREY HEALEY

JOSE LARRAZ

SPAIN (REDEMPTION) 1981

81m (18)

Cut and with the cast lurking under pseudonyms, this is cult horror director Larraz's infamous *Los Ritos Sexuales Del Diablo*, a pic some thought lost and which fans were dying to see because of the lurid posters. Methinks it should have stayed lost: the censor used to get terribly upset by any juxta-position of sex and the occult, but this tale of a naughty diabolical sect would be unlikely to enrage even the staunchest Christian reactionary.

BLANCHE

MICHEL SIMON, GEORGES WILSON, LIGIA BRANICE

WALERIAN BOROWCZYK

FRANCE (CONNOISSEUR) 1971

90m (PG)

Early Borowczyk film about the young bride of a nasty aristocrat who finds herself at the mercy of powerful men who lust after her beauty. Typically opulent costumes and authentic historical feel, though lacking the explicit sex that became the director's trademark in later pix.

COMMON-LAW CABIN

ALAINA CAPRI, BABETTE BARDOT, ADELE REIN

RUSS MEYER

USA (TROMA/RM) 1967

69m (18)

Meyer has been called the 'rural Fellini' on account of an early run of pix like this, cod morality tales full of earthy sex in backwoods surroundings. Take a man and a couple of girls running a dump of a tourist lodge miles from anywhere, then more guys 'n' babes turn up and the fireworks begin. Crisply transferred from the original negative, but was it worth the effort? Strangely, there is virtually no bare flesh on show despite the 18 certificate. Save your cash for Meyer's later works.

CRIMES OF PASSION

KATHLEEN TURNER, ANTHONY PERKINS, BRUCE DAVIDSON, ANNIE POTTS

KEN RUSSELL

USA (VISION) 1984

102m (18)

Classy professional girl has an alternative identity as China Blue, call-girl catering to the lubricious fantasies of all and sundry while freeing her own wild side. Bizarre performance from Perkins as a pseudo-priest wielding a killer dildo. Heavily censored before being issued.

CRASH

JAMES SPADER, DEBORAH UNGER, ROSANNA ARQUETTE, ELIAS KOTEAS, HOLLY HUNTER

DAVID CRONENBERG

CANADA (COLUMBIA TRISTAR) 1996

96m (18)

Controversial screen version of JG Ballard's futuristic novel which gave the BBFC and the tabloids apoplexy is here released (finally) on tape in its uncut cinema form. Set among a group of pervos who get their kicks re-enacting celebrity car accidents and sexualising the resultant wounds and scar tissue, it shows how a rather numb young couple (Spader and Unger) are drawn into the weird circle in an attempt to revive their feelings. Filmed with the cold glamour of sleek car ads, it's sick, stylish and brilliant. There is no explicit sex, in case you're interested, at least not in the traditional sense of the phrase.

ADULT

DARK HABITS [3]

CARMEN MAURA, LAURA CEPEDA, CRISTINA S PASCUAL

PEDRO ALMODOVAR

SPAIN (TARTAN) 1983

111m (18)

*S*panish cult sleazemaster Almodovar spins a sick story about a singer on the run who enters a convent. But this is no jaunt in the manner of Whoopi Goldberg's 'Sister Act' films – these nuns are lesbians, junkies, sex novelists, acid casualties and all-round weirdos. Sure to offend, especially in a Catholic land such as Spain. Subtitled and widescreen.

THE DARK SIDE OF LOVE [3]

MONICA GUERRITORE, LORENZO LENA, GILLA NOVAK

SALVATORE SAMPERI

ITALY (JEZEBEL) 1985

88m (18)

Disabled teenage boy living with his aunt gets involved in her naughty sex life, amid bouts of oddball attempts at philosophising. Plenty of atmosphere. Widescreen.

DIRTY WEEKEND [5]

LIA WILLIAMS, DAVID McCALLUM, RUFUS SEWELL, SYLVIA SYMS, IAN RICHARDSON

MICHAEL WINNER

UK (POLYGRAM) 1993

96m (18)

As *Flesh & Blood* magazine recently noted, the bad press Michael Winner gets is just journalistic laziness as he has actually done some fine work – and this, I'd say, is one of his best. Like Abel Ferrara's *Angel Of Vengeance*, aka *Ms 45* (1980), it's about a woman who tires of constant male abuse – from rape to stalking and straightforward everyday yobbery – and decides to take violent punitive action. The grimy, drab Britain shown is not shabby film-making (as some critics said) but is in fact entirely apt for the mood the picture tries to convey. Anyone who has seen Winner's USA pix with Charles Bronson will know that he can turn out slickly glossy work with the best of them. Even as they panned *Dirty Weekend*, the hacks had to give credit to Lia Williams' gutsy-yet-fragile lead performance, which makes this a must-see lost classic.

EDUCATION ANGLAISE [1]

JEAN ANTOLINOS, VERONIQUE CANTAZARO, CAROLINE LAURENCE

JEAN-CLAUDE ROY

FRANCE (JEZEBEL) 1982

89m (18)

Naughty boarding school frolics involving ageing teens and a pervy sadomasochist villain on the run. Porn star Brigitte Lahaie makes an all-too-brief appearance. Widescreen.

EGON SCHIELE EXCESSES

MATHIEU CARRIERE, JANE BIRKIN, CHRISTINE KAUFMAN

HERBERT VESELY

W GERMANY (REDEMPTION) 1980

83m (18)

*Story of the end of the Austrian artist's life and the trouble he got himself into by painting a teenage girl – she accused him of making advances and his nude drawings of her were used as evidence that he was a child pornographer. A serious and adult work about the effect of moral hysteria on art. How apt.

EMILIENNE

BETTY MARS, PIERRE OUDRY, NATHALIE GUERIN

GUY CASARIL

FRANCE (ART HOUSE/ANGEL) 1975

90m (18)

*Soft-core drama about husband and wife both having it off with the same girl. Interesting because it is well made but, if it's sex you're after, give it a miss. Widescreen.

THE EROTIC DREAMS OF CLEOPATRA

MARCELLA PETRELLI, RITA SILVA, ANDREA COPPOLA

CESAR TODD

ITALY/FRANCE (JEZEBEL) 1983

85m (18)

More stylishly set up than most of these porn efforts in the style of *Caligula* (see page 125), *The Erotic Dreams Of Cleopatra* may not, in terms of spectacle, be a patch on Liz Taylor's *Cleopatra* (see page 126), but it presents the sexual frolics in imaginative and lush settings. Surprisingly, considering the scene of horse-masturbation (similar to that in *Caligula II – The Untold Story*, which is banned in the UK) the censor has apparently resisted the urge to snip away at the action. This may be because the animal sex in this case is shown in shadow only – how artistic! Letterboxed at near fullscreen ratio.

EROTIKA

SAMANTHA STRONG, PORSCHE LYNN, NIKKI SINN

ROBERT McCALLUM

USA (PURGATORY) 1995

83m (18)

Glossy, stylised hard core shot under a pseudonym by indie director Gary Graver. Small-town American gal moves to Los Angeles and shags lots of people, with some fake feel-good feminist philosophising thrown in. Way better that the average USA porno, but (of course) the hard-core footage has been brutally excised. Many scenes of the star being orally pleasured by both sexes, for those who are looking for that sort of thing.

ADULT

ESCAPE FROM BROTHEL [3]

PAULINE CHEN, ALEN FONG, RENA MURAKAMI

WONG LUNG WEI

HONG KONG (EASTERN HEROES) 1991

97m (18)

This is one of the films from Hong Kong classified as 'Category III' – their censor rating for movies with lots of sex and violence, usually featuring permutations of both. This sort of thing doesn't sit well with the BBFC and this print has been totally butchered by them, which is a shame as a lot of effort seems to have been put in by the video company – the tape is in widescreen, subtitles are in the black area under the picture, and there's an original trailer. The opening line ('Suzie, I can't wait much longer, my aphrodisiac has already worn off!') will give you some idea of what to expect.

ESKIMO NELL [3]

KATY MANNING, ROY KINNEAR, ANNA QUAYLE, CHRISTOPHER BIGGINS

MARTIN CAMPBELL

UK (MEDUSA) 1974

81m (18)

Better-than-usual cheesy Brit sex farce directed by the man who went on to helm the hit James Bond pic *GoldenEye* (see page 25). Real-life movie-maker Michael Armstrong (see *Mark Of The Devil*, page 193) stars as a director asked to film the erotic ditty of the title. According to exploitation veteran David McGillivray in the excellent *Sexadelic* magazine, this is what actually happened in real life! Bored by the idea, he made up the film as we have it here: director has to make the pic in four different versions for various backers (family film/hard core/gay Western/martial arts musical) and mayhem results. Pals were cast and the characters are allegedly spoofs of certain film-industry folk, with Armstrong's psychedelic clothes supposedly based on the garb of Michael Winner. Lots of odd cameos – note the appearance of one-time British TV's *Dr Who* girl Katy Manning.

EVIL SENSES [2]

MONICA GUERRITORE, GABRIELLE LAVIA, MIMSY FARMER

GABRIELE LAVIA

ITALY (ART HOUSE/ANGEL) 1986

90m (18)

Gorgeously filmed erotic thriller from husband-and-wife team Lavia and Guerritore, with the former as a killer-for-hire, hiding out in a whorehouse. Soft sex and some nasty violence, though the censor has inflicted cuts (on the latter especially).

FASTER PUSSYCAT, KILL ... KILL!

TURA SATANA, HAJI, LORI WILLIAMS, SUSAN BERNARD, STUART LANCASTER

RUSS MEYER

USA (TROMA/RM) 1966 B&W

83m (18)

Kitsch domination fantasy from breast-lover Meyer, with rough, tough girls dishing out butch violence in the American desert. A cult pic with no real nudity or overt sex, just fast cars and faster women.

FLESH GORDON

JASON WILLIAMS, SUZANNE FIELDS, JOHN HOYT

HOWARD ZIEHM, MICHAEL BENVENISTE

USA (ENTERTAINMENT) 1974

84m (18)

*S*pot-on parody of the original *Flash Gordon* serial. Planet Mongo becomes Planet Porno, Dr Zarkov is now Dr Jerkoff, etc. Apparently began life as a hard-core effort but, when the makers saw how good the film was looking, they decided to go for a more mainstream approach. SFX are wonderful, including a stop-motion animated 'Penisaurus'! Very, very funny. A poor sequel, *Flesh Gordon 2* aka, *Flesh Gordon Meets The Cosmic Cheerleaders*, was made some years later and is also available on tape.

IMMORAL TALES

LISE DANVERS, FABRICE LUCHINI, PALOMA PICASSO

WALERIAN BOROWCZYK

FRANCE (CONNOISSEUR) 1974

99m (18)

Four-tale compendium of Borowczyk's typically luscious, overheated fetishisation of the female sex in historical mode. One story is about legendary vampire Countess Bathory, another about Lucrezia Borgia and so on. Widescreen and subtitled print of a movie that was obviously a labour of lust.

MIRANDA

SERENA GRANDI, ANDREA OCCHIPINTI, MALISA LONGO

TINTO BRASS

ITALY (ART HOUSE/ANGEL) 1985

95m (18)

Village barmaid just can't help driving the lads wild. Weak story, but Tinto Brass, director of *Caligula* (see page 125), brings a down-to-earth horniness to the proceedings – indeed, sex movie expert David Flint has described the film (in *Flesh & Blood* magazine) as 'a knicker-lover's delight'! Need I say more. Widescreen.

ADULT

MONDO TOPLESS [2]

BABETTE BARDOT, DIANE YOUNG, PAT BARRINGER

RUSS MEYER

USA (TROMA/RM) 1966

60m (18)

Cheap mockumentary about the alleged topless craze of the 60s, lensed by tit-crazed Meyer in the wake of *Faster Pussycat, Kill ... Kill!* (see page 46). Lots of outsize jiggling mammaries.

NAKED – AS NATURE INTENDED [2]

PAMELA GREEN, BRIDGET LEONARD, ANGELA JONES

GEORGE HARRISON MARKS

UK (JEZEBEL) 1961

58m (15)

Legendary tits 'n' ass pic from photographer Harrison Marks, starring his muse Pamela Green (who also appears in *Peeping Tom* (see page 197). No real sex – the BBFC made sure of that even before the production began – but it's an amusing relic of what was once thought risqué.

ORGY OF THE DEAD [2]

CRISWELL, FAWN SILVER, PAT BARRINGER

STEPHEN C APOSTOLOFF

USA (WARNER) 1965

91m (18)

Produced by famed 'bad' moviemaker Ed Wood and starring his pal, gleefully mad Hollywood 'psychic' Criswell, this is a fitfully fun piece of trash about a couple who get stranded in a graveyard only to have our ghoulish hero totally torture them by having the naked dead folk dance for his delectation. Has to be seen to be believed, but the bizarre camp novelty value soon wears off due to the lack of plot and the over-extended running time.

SCANDALOUS GILDA [3]

MONICA GUERRITORE, GABRIELLE LAVIA, PINA CEI

GABRIELE LAVIA

ITALY (JEZEBEL) 1985

88m (18)

More from the Lavia/Guerritore team. Demented philosophical crap, with nasty rapes, cartoon penises and casual shagging. So off-handedly odd that it does succeed in holding the interest for much of the running time.

SCHOOL FOR SEX [2]

🌟 DEREK AYLWARD, ROSE ALBA, FRANCOISE PASCAL

🎬 PETE WALKER

UK (JEZEBEL) 1968

⏱ 80m (18)

Allegedly a mega-hit all over the world but this, sadly, is the less naughty UK print. Cult trash thriller/horror director Walker made this unremarkable film about an academy that trains girls to get dosh out of rich guys. The original would be more worth watching.

THE SEXUAL LIFE OF THE BELGIANS [3]

🌟 JEAN-HENRI COMPERE, NOE FRANCQ, SOPHIE SCHNEIDER

🎬 JEAN BUCQUOY

BELGIUM (TARTAN) 1994

⏱ 81m (18)

Autobiographical story of the director's sex life as a young man: scenes of him getting seduced by a randy schoolgirl when he saves her from fellow pupils, nipping his dick on some dentures, penning porn and sleeping with an inflatable bedmate. And this apparently is only the first part of a trilogy! Slightly letterboxed. Subtitled.

SHATTER DEAD [3]

🌟 STARK RAVEN, FLORA FAUNA, MARINA DEL REY

🎬 SCOOTER McCRAE

USA (SCREEN EDGE) 1994

⏱ 84m (18)

Screen Edge specialise in releasing cutting-edge low-budget (this was shot on tape) indie films, and this is probably their best release so far. Set in a future world where death is defunct and people must choose whether to 'die' young and keep their looks forever or to sink into an eternity of decrepitude, this is more imaginative than most big studio sex/violence fare. Scene of a girl being sexually penetrated with a gun has been cut by the BBFC.

SHOWGIRLS [3]

🌟 ELIZABETH BERKELY, GINA GERSHON, KYLE MACLACHLAN, ROBERT DAVI

🎬 PAUL VERHOEVEN

USA (FOX) 1995

⏱ 126m (18)

Derided on cinema release, Verhoeven's exposé of tacky sex-opera goings-on among Las Vegas strip dancers ought to achieve cult status on tape: lotsa tits and unintentional hilarity. Available in widescreen.

ADULT

SPANKING THE MONKEY 🎬3

JEREMY DAVIES, ALBERTA WATSON, CARLA GALLO

DAVID O RUSSELL

USA (TARTAN) 1996

⏱ 98m (18)

Unwholesome sexual frustrations beset the hero of this witty look at small-town USA life as he endlessly attempts to find solace in the act of the title (masturbation) while locked in the loo. Occasionally hilarious and subversive in the extreme.

STRANGE DAYS 🎬3

RALPH FIENNES, JULIETTE LEWIS, ANGELA BASSETT

KATHRYN BIGELOW

USA (CIC) 1995

⏱ 141m (18)

Future *noir* about a hustler who sells illicit video clips that the buyer can play back mentally in order to experience directly the originator's own thrills. When a 'snuff' tape of a real killing falls into his hands trouble isn't far behind ... It's a very long movie but a great performance from Fiennes as the video dealer will keep you glued to the screen. Though the film release was untouched, the BBFC have cut 13 seconds of sexual violence from the video. Ironic, given the plot.

SUPERVIXENS 🎬4

SHARI EUBANK, CHARLES NAPIER, USCHI DIGARD, HAJI

RUSS MEYER

USA (TROMA/RM) 1975

⏱ 104m (18)

One of Meyer's best films, *Supervixens* is like a live-action, sexed-up 'Road Runner' cartoon. A man goes on the run after being falsely accused of killing his wife and gets involved in several sexy encounters of the bra-busting kind. One violent scene has apparently been cut by the BBFC, losing 47 seconds of footage; this is odd, as Meyer recently stated that he would not allow any of the films he owns (of which this is one) to come out in a cut form. The cut doesn't spoil the pic however.

TANDEM 🎬3

KINO MAHITO, ISHIWARA YURI, HAZUKI HOTARU

TOSHIKI SATO

JAPAN (PINK JAPAN) 1994

⏱ 57m (18)

Pink films are Japan's porn, and, though hard sex acts and even pubic hair are usually digitally masked, the makers substitute lots of S&M, masturbating, piddling – you name it, they do it. In this short entry, a biker and an office worker make friends and fall out and in between the two events we see their sexual dreams. Part art, part porno, very Japanese. Subtitled and widescreen.

49

CLASSIC 1000 VIDEOS

UP!

RAVEN DE LA CROIX, KITTEN NATIVIDAD, CANDY SAMPLES

RUSS MEYER

USA (TROMA/RM) 1976

80m (18)

'Who-killed-the-Nazi?' plot (Meyer is always including Martin Bormann references in his pix) is intermingled with the usual japes and cantilevered bosoms in what is undoubtedly one of Meyer's best nudie efforts. Typically over the top.

VAMPYROS LESBOS

SOLEDAD MIRANDA, DENNIS PRICE, EWA STROEMBURG

JESS FRANCO

W GERMANY/SPAIN (REDEMPTION) 1970

86m (18)

The prolific Franco helms a dreamy 70s sex-vampire saga starring his then favourite muse, the late Soledad Miranda. A mix of the director's speciality nightclub strip stuff and arty sex where kites stand in for bats, sunlight for darkness and the camera lingers on scorpions, mannequins and blood. There are two versions available: one packaged to resemble the recent hit soundtrack CD (which includes the promo music video clip), the other in normal Redemption packaging (which includes a trailer). Subtitled and widescreen.

VENUS IN FURS

ANNE VAN DER VEN, RAYMOND THIRY, MEREDITH CHAN-A-HUNG

MAARTJE SEYFERTH, VICTOR E NIEUWENHUIJS

NETHERLANDS (VISIONARY) 1994 B&W

70m (18)

One of several stabs at the Sacher-Masoch story (there is also one by Jess Franco), this was put together on a minuscule budget by two documentary-makers and follows the novel faithfully. The author gave his name to masochism, so you won't be surprised to learn this is a tale of a man who is a slave to his whip-swishing mistress. Dazzling, considering the budget; this is worthy of investigation.

VIXEN

ERICA GAVIN, HARRISON PAGE, VINCENTE WALLACE

RUSS MEYER

USA (TROMA/RM) 1968

70m (18)

One of Meyer's better 'domestics': yet another tale of a rural babe tired of husband and on the lookout for randy tourists. The success of *Vixen* gave Mayer his shot at the major leagues with *Beyond The Valley Of The Dolls* (see page 41) for Fox.

ADULT

WHORE [4]

THERESA RUSSELL, ANTONIO FARGAS, SANJAY

KEN RUSSELL

USA (POLYGRAM) 1991

81m (18)

Russell transposes cabbie David Hines' play *Bondage* (about Kings Cross prostitutes) from London to the USA with some success. Ms Russell (no relation) talks to the camera as she goes through the highs and lows of her day as a not-so-happy hooker. Eventful, sad, funny and superbly acted by the small cast. The only flaw I can see is that Theresa Russell is just *too* damn good-looking for a cheap streetwalker!

WR MYSTERIES OF THE ORGANISM [3]

MILENA DRAVIC, IVICA VIDOVIC, JACKIE CURTIS

DUSAN MAKAVEJEV

YUGOSLAVIA/WEST GERMANY (CONNOISSEUR) 1971

80m (18)

Legendary movie based on the works of sex-guru Wilhelm Reich. This is the version the director prepared for British TV's Channel 4 in which the scene of Jim Buckley having his penis plaster-casted is optically obscured, but it really makes little difference. Impenetrable (!) but never boring.

ZETA ONE [2]

YUTTE STENSGAARD, VALERIE LEON, DAWN ADDAMS, JAMES ROBERTSON JUSTICE

MICHAEL CORT

UK (JEZEBEL) 1969

84m (18)

Looks like a science-fiction secret-agent romp, but it's really just another weak Brit sex comedy. Notable for starring the sexy Ms Stensgaard, one-time Hammer horror starlet.

51

ANIMATION

There's no doubt about it: you can't beat a good cartoon video for keeping the kids quiet. But there's far more animation on video nowadays than just good ol' *Tom And Jerry*.

With the advent of increasingly sophisticated computer technology, animation now turns up alongside other special effects tools in all kinds of movies: it not only conjured up many of the dinosaurs for *Jurassic Park*, but furnished some of the wilder lion footage for the recent *The Ghost And The Darkness*. It's funny to think that when Disney first used computer animation 'shortcuts', they were heavily criticised by purists – although techniques such as 'rotoscoping' (where scenes are drawn using live footage as a basis) had been in use for years. Of course, the first computer animations were relatively simple: a sequence for the 1982 Disney live-action film *Something Wicked This Way Comes,* of a train magically turning into a carnival site, was scrapped because it simply didn't look real.

There are many types of animation and if you're into this, your video store should have plenty to offer you. The new computerised genre culminated in *Toy Story*, where the imagery looks three-dimensional rather than having the 'flat' appearance of cartoons – but for years experts like Ray Harryhausen have been lensing models a frame at a time to make monsters that can even be made to interact with live footage. The UK's own Nick Parks has won Oscars with his *Wallace and Gromit* shorts (which are available to buy on video), using similar techniques. For some, though, the classic cartoons like *Tom And Jerry* and the numerous Warners shorts by Chuck Jones (*Bugs Bunny, Road Runner, et al*) are the ones to see. Again, there are many collections of these shorts available to buy on tape. Recently there have been releases of Japanese adult cartoons *(anime)* with an emphasis on sex and gore. Some extend over several tapes but they are often cut by the BBFC.

For the purpose of this book, I've decided simply to present a short selection of feature-length movies, classics where animation is the main (in most cases, the sole) film technique used. A note on the Disney films I've featured: the studio continues to make feature-length cartoons, with *The Hunchback Of Notre Dame* and *Hercules* recently on release in cinemas.

While they do release their cartoons to video, they have a policy of making only a few titles available to buy for a limited period. This is very frustrating, I know, but you should be able to rent classic titles from your local tape library.

THE 7TH VOYAGE OF SINBAD [5]

☆ KERWIN MATTHEWS, TORIN THATCHER, KATHRYN GRANT, RICHARD EYER

🎬 NATHAN JURAN

USA (CINEMA CLUB V) 1958

⏱ 89m (U)

Everyone has a film which made an impact on them when they were very young – this is mine. I'll never forget the moment when Ray Harryhausen's animated giant Cyclops emerges roaring from his lair – mind-boggling stuff. And this 'Arabian Nights' fantasy has more wonders to dwarf the sketchy human characters: a sword-fighting skeleton, a snake-woman, a fire-breathing dragon, two-headed birds. There's also an imposing score by Bernard Herrmann. Harryhausen made two further 'Sinbad' movies many years later, but they lack the naive passion of this first classic.

101 DALMATIANS [4]

☆ Voices of: ROD TAYLOR, BETTY LOU GERSON, J PAT O'MALLEY and others

🎬 WOLFGANG REITHERMAN, HAMILTON S LUSKE, CLYDE GERONIMI

USA (DISNEY) 1961

⏱ 79m (U)

A better bet than the recent live-action version, this telling of Dodie Smith's classic tale is one of the best Disney cartoon features. Nasty Cruella de Vil is hoarding dalmatian puppies to make herself a spotted fur coat, but when she steals the brood of feisty Pongo and Perdita she's messed with the wrong pooches! Atmospheric recreation of the 'twilight barking', where dogs across the land howl messages in relay, and stylish artwork make it great for adults as well as kids.

54

ANIMATION

ALADDIN [4]

Voices of:
ROBIN WILLIAMS and others

RON CLEMENTE, JOHN MUSKER

USA (DISNEY) 1992

91m (U)

The highlight of this magic carpet ride is Robin Williams as the voice of the genie – his improvisational skills seem to have driven the animators to new heights of inspiration as the character transforms himself and the world around him to match his array of voices – dazzling. Which makes the insipid nature of the two pretty-pretty lead characters all the more wet by comparison. Oscars for best score and song ('A Whole New World').

AN AMERICAN TAIL [3]

Voices of:
DOM DeLUISE, NEHEMIAH PERSOFF, CHRISTOPHER PLUMMER and others

DON BLUTH

USA (CIC) 1986

78m (U)

Delightful and moving cartoon about a family of poor mice who flee the pogroms of mother Russia and leave their *shtotl* for a new life in America. Bluth is an escapee himself – from the Disney studios. His picture is as well animated as any Disney effort, but one doubts whether *they* would have made this story. A smashing little cartoon.

BASIL, THE GREAT MOUSE DETECTIVE [5]

Voices of:
VINCENT PRICE, BARRIE INGHAM, MELISSA MANCHESTER and others

JOHN MUSKER, RON CLEMENTE, DAVE MICHENER, BURNY MATTISON

USA (DISNEY) 1986

80m (U)

Fab confection about a mouse version of Sherlock Holmes dubbed Basil as a tribute to the screen's great player of the part, Basil Rathbone. Our little hero fights not Moriarty but the evil Professor Rattigan, voiced to fruity perfection by the late Vincent Price. This was the first Disney cartoon to use computer animation, thus enraging the purists. Shame on 'em: it's a smashing film.

BEAUTY AND THE BEAST [4]

Voices of:
PAIGE O'HARA, ROBBY BENSON, ANGELA LANSBURY and others

GARY TROUSDALE, KIRK WISE

USA (DISNEY) 1992

85m (U)

Sumptuous version from Disney of the classic fairy tale. Embellishments include the amusing walking/talking household objects. Oscars for the Menken/Ashman score. Definitely the best of the studio's more recent pix.

55

FANTASIA 🎬5

☆ DEEMS TAYLOR (Narrator),
LEOPOLD STOKOWSKI AND THE PHILADEPHIA ORCHESTRA, MICKEY MOUSE

🎬 BEN SHARPSTEEN

USA (DISNEY) 1940

⏱ 120m (U)

Ambitious undertaking for Disney in which pieces of classical music are wedded to cartoon imagery with varying degrees of success. High points include Mickey Mouse as the Sorcerer's Apprentice (where you could almost believe the music was written for the film rather than the reverse) and the demonic 'Night on Bare Mountain' sequence. The film has lost a few snippets, including a 'racist' clip of a black centaur polishing its hooves like a shoeshine boy. I'm not sure I approve – one can't condone racism but how will we ever know where it existed if we keep going back and rewriting history by erasing 'offensive' images? The film won a special Oscar for Stokowski and the orchestra.

JAMES AND THE GIANT PEACH 🎬4

☆ Voices of:
SIMON CALLOW, RICHARD DREYFUSS, JANE LEEVES, SUSAN SARANDON, DAVID THEWLIS, MIRIAM MARGOLYES

🎬 HENRY SELICK

USA (GUILD) 1996

⏱ 76m (U)

Weird screen retelling of Roald Dahl's popular children's fantasy from the director of *Tim Burton's The Nightmare Before Christmas* (see page 59) using computer animation to crazed effect. Demented fun for all ages, which works just as well on the small screen as it did in cinemas.

JASON AND THE ARGONAUTS 🎬4

☆ TODD ARMSTRONG, NIALL MacGINNIS, HONOR BLACKMAN, NIGEL GREEN

🎬 DON CHAFFEY

UK (CINEMA CLUB V) 1963

⏱ 104m (U)

Only marginally less satisfying than *The 7th Voyage Of Sinbad* (see page 54) – though some prefer it – this is animator Ray Harryhausen tackling Greek mythology via a horde of stop-motion animation creatures, including bat-winged harpies and the seven-headed hydra. Todd Armstrong makes a handsome Jason in search of the golden fleece (though his voice was dubbed by another actor) and Bernard Herrmann comes up with another imaginative score. A nice touch is the notion of the gods looking down and toying with the lives of mortals. Harryhausen tried to repeat the formula many years later with *Clash Of The Titans*, but it was a pale imitation of this glorious epic.

ANIMATION

KING KONG [5]

FAY WRAY, ROBERT ARMSTRONG, BRUCE CABOT, FRANK REICHER

MERIAN C COOPER, ERNEST SCHOEDSACK

USA (4-FRONT) 1933 B&W

100m (PG)

Based on an idea by Edgar Wallace, this is the classic (for once the word is completely justified) story of a huge ape brought back to civilisation from a prehistoric island. In New York he escapes and climbs the Empire State Building with Fay Wray in his hairy hand – one of the most instantly recognisable images in movie history. Animator Willis O'Brien (the man who inspired Ray Harryhausen) had already created the monsters for the silent version of Conan Doyle's *The Lost World*, and his Kong looked so real that at least one reviewer at the time of release thought it was a man in a suit. The fingerprints of the animator positioning the model between frames made the fur appear to move on film – a fault he passed off as intentional, saying it was the ape bristling with anger! For years only prints shorn of some of the more violent footage were in circulation, but happily this video is from an uncut archive copy.

LADY AND THE TRAMP [3]

Voices of: PEGGY LEE, STAN FREBERG, BARBARA LUDDY and others

HAMILTON S LUSKE, CLYDE GERONIMI, WILFRED JACKSON

USA (DISNEY) 1955

77m (U)

Lesser fare from Disney, about a romance between two dogs, though many have a soft spot for it. Highlight is Peggy Lee's voicing of the sexy Peggy in the dogs' home. This was Disney's first CinemaScope cartoon feature, but it's pan-scan on tape, I'm afraid.

THE LION KING [4]

Voices of: JEREMY IRONS, JAMES EARL JONES and others

ROGER ALLERS, ROB MINKOFF

USA (DISNEY) 1994

84m (U)

Founded on the notion that there's a lotta mileage in the old good-v-evil family sagas, this predictable but fun cartoon tells of a cute young lion due to inherit the throne from his King of Beasts pop. But nasty uncle Scar (a wonderfully slimy voicing by Jeremy Irons) has other plans. Grrreat pack of gangsterish hyenas. Oscar-winning musical score from Tim Rice and Elton John may or may not be to your taste.

THE LITTLE MERMAID 3

Voices of:
BUDDY HACKETT, KENNETH MARS, JODI BENSON and others

JOHN MUSKER, RON CLEMENTE

USA (DISNEY) 1989

82m (U)

Slight confection from Disney about cute li'l undersea gal. Apparently she was originally topless, but the moralists got cold feet and gave her a seashell bra! Oscars for best score and song ('Under the Sea').

MYSTERIOUS ISLAND 3

HERBERT LOM, MICHAEL CRAIG, JOAN GREENWOOD, NIGEL GREEN

CY ENDFIELD

UK (CINEMA CLUB V) 1961

101m (U)

Jules Verne story about escapees in a prison break via balloon during the American Civil War who end up on a weird isle populated by Captain Nemo (Lom) and oodles of outsize Ray Harryhausen creatures. Rather than construct a crab model, he improvised with a dead one bought from MacFisheries! Another fine Bernard Herrmann score.

ONE MILLION YEARS BC 4

JOHN RICHARDSON, RAQUEL WELCH, MARTINE BESWICK

DON CHAFFEY

UK (WARNER) 1966

100m (PG)

Hammer's foray into (relatively) big-budget films, a remake of an old Victor Mature caveman romp, bolstered by Ray Harryhausen's animated saurians and starlet Raquel Welch in that itsy-bitsy, teeny-weeny, furry little rabbit bikini. What a combination! The monsters may not be as smoothly rendered as the beasts in *Jurassic Park* (see page 28), but they have character which comes from having one man at the helm. Thunderous, percussive score from Mario Nascimbene.

PINOCCHIO 4

Voices of:
DICKIE JONES, DON BRODIE, CLIFF EDWARDS and others

BEN SHARPSTEEN, HAMILTON S LUSKE

USA (DISNEY) 1940

88m (U)

Oft-filmed story of a puppet boy who comes to life. The scenes of him being abducted on his way to school and spirited to an evil place full of bad lads may scare some younger children. Oscars for best score and song ('When You Wish Upon a Star').

ANIMATION

POCAHONTAS 3

Voices of:
MEL GIBSON, BILLY CONNOLLY, LINDA HUNT and others

MIKE GABRIEL, ERIC GOLDBERG

USA (DISNEY) 1995

81m (U)

Bears very little relation to the true story of Native American girl Pocahontas, and it's all rather sickly in spite of the rumbustious presence of Billy Connolly as the voice of one amiable rascal.

SLEEPING BEAUTY 4

Voices of:
MARY COSTA, BILL SHIRLEY, BARBARA LUDDY and others

CLYDE GERONIMI

USA (DISNEY) 1958

75m (U)

Lovingly drawn fairy story from Disney, with a splendidly evil witch casting her spell over the innocent heroine. The 70mm widescreen grandeur will be lost here, though: Disney really ought to consider issuing their widescreen material in letterbox format.

THE SWORD IN THE STONE 3

Voices of:
RICKY SORENSON, ALAN NAPIER, GINNY TAYLOR and others

WOLFGANG REITHERMAN

USA (DISNEY) 1963

80m (U)

Arthurian legend gets the Disney treatment in this adaptation of TH White's *The Once and Future King*. Not considered one of the studio's high points, but I've always had a soft spot for it: the battle of magic between Merlin and the witch is a belter of a sequence, at least.

TIM BURTON'S THE NIGHT- 4 MARE BEFORE CHRISTMAS

Voices of:
DANNY ELFMAN, CHRIS SARANDON and others

HENRY SELICK

USA (DISNEY) 1993

76m (PG)

Many assume that this was directed by Burton: in fact, it is based on an idea he had for a story while he was an animator at Disney. When people leave Disney (like Don Bluth, of the 'American Tail' films), they are often seen as rivals and rarely have any further dealings with the studio – but the old firm have definitely done themselves a favour by agreeing to make this project. Using computer animation, it conjures up a world eerily similar to that of Burton's *Beetlejuice* (see page 66). Bad boy Jack Skellington, who 'runs' Hallowe'en, decides to do the dirty on Santa and usurp the Christmas hols for his own evil ends. The dark imagery may frighten some youngsters, but it is a beautifully made film. Very Charles Addams-like, which is a compliment.

TOY STORY

Voices of:
TOM HANKS, TIM ALLEN and others
JOHN LASSETER
USA (DISNEY) 1995
77m (PG)

The first full-length computer animation film is a hilarious bit of fluff about toy cowboy Woody (voiced by Tom Hanks) being jettisoned by his owner in favour of dumb spaceman Buzz Lightyear (voiced by Tim Allen), and has proved a hit with adults and kids alike. Although created by computer, the images have none of the 'flatness' of cartoons: they look like real toys walking and talking. This is surely only the beginning ...

WHO FRAMED ROGER RABBIT?

BOB HOSKINS, CHRISTOPHER LLOYD, STUBBY KAYE, JOANNA CASSIDY
ROBERT ZEMECKIS
USA (TOUCHSTONE) 1988
99m (PG)

Bravura mix of real actors and cartoon characters, based on Gary K Wolf's novel *Who Censored Roger Rabbit?* about a private eye who enters 'Toontown' – a film studio where animated characters supposedly exist for real. If you enter into the silly spirit of the thing you'll enjoy yourself no end, as the makers overcame initial reluctance by different franchise-holders and managed to include famous 'toon characters from various studios. Opens with a clever example of star Roger's own work to get us in the mood. His sensual wife, Jessica Rabbit, even became a *Playboy* centrefold in real life! Amazingly, there has never been a sequel to this massive hit. Oscars for editing and audio/visual effects work.

COMEDY

If it's home entertainment for all the family you're after, then where better to start than in the comedy section? However, making a selection of good comedy videos is no easy task: what is funny to one person may be excruciatingly dull to another; so all I can do here is play safe by including the massively popular giants of the genre (Woody Allen, The Marx Brothers, Mel Brooks, Robin Williams, etc.), the latest finds (Jim Carrey, for example), and a few personal favourites. Due to the vast output of some screen comics and the restriction that choices must be currently on tape, I've only been able to include the smallest sampling of the work of Peter Sellers and Bob Hope. 'Carry On' movies are also virtually a genre in themselves, so rather than review one or two, I've reviewed the series as an entity in a separate note.

At the moment, Hollywood appears to be treating comedy like all other movies: a hit must be copied or spawn sequels. Hence *Driving Miss Daisy* (about a driver and his tetchy old charge) was virtually reincarnated as *Guarding Tess* (about a bodyguard and his tetchy old charge) – and can anyone tell the difference between headbanging comic duos Bill and Ted, Wayne and Garth *(Wayne's World)* and Beavis and Butthead? Party on, dudes!

10

DUDLEY MOORE, JULIE ANDREWS, BO DEREK, ROBERT WEBBER

BLAKE EDWARDS

USA (WARNER) 1979

118m (18)

Married songsmith pursues a young woman he sees and rates as a perfect '10' on the hit parade of beauty in this sporadically funny sex romp. The message that beauty has more to do with what's inside a person than superficial looks will be lost on most male members of the audience, who will be content to drool over Ms Derek's justly famed body.

1941

JOHN BELUSHI, TIM MATHESON, NANCY ALLEN, DAN AYKROYD, CHRISTOPHER LEE

STEVEN SPIELBERG

USA (CIC) 1979

112m (PG)

A major flop for Spielberg, but now something of a hip cult, this is a big spectacle based on the supposed invasion of California by the Japanese in World War Two. It's his attempt to do an epic laff-riot like *It's A Mad, Mad, Mad, Mad World* (see page 78) and it fails. It really needs a huge screen to pull it off.

ACE VENTURA: PET DETECTIVE

JIM CARREY, COURTENEY COX, SEAN YOUNG, TONE LOC

TOM SHADYAC

USA (WARNER) 1994

87m (PG)

Carrey is not my favourite type of actor – to me he seems to be a rubber-faced, rubber-stamp of Jerry Lewis circa the early 60s – but he does have a popular following so he is certainly doing something right. This is the best of his works, and is agreeably silly enough.

THE ADDAMS FAMILY

ANJELICA HUSTON, RAUL JULIA, CHRISTOPHER LLOYD, DAN HEDAYA

BARRY SONNENFELD

USA (CINEMA CLUB V) 1991

96m (PG)

Lovingly crafted update of the old TV show adapted from Charles Addams' drawings of a ghoulish cartoon family. Some of the acid commentary on American society may be gone, but the sets and acting are a delight throughout. See sequel on page 63.

COMEDY

ADDAMS FAMILY VALUES 🎬 4

⭐ ANJELICA HUSTON, RAUL JULIA, CHRISTOPHER LLOYD, JOAN CUSACK

🎬 BARRY SONNENFELD

USA (CIC) 1993

⏱ 94m   (PG)

A sequel that's every bit as much fun as the first film, with a particularly mischievous showing from little Christina Ricci as the coolly calculating daughter of the family. Sadly, with star Raul Julia deceased, the series seems to be stalled for good.

AIRPLANE 🎬 5

⭐ ROBERT HAYS, JULIE HAGERTY, ROBERT STACK, LLOYD BRIDGES

🎬 JIM ABRAHAMS, DAVID ZUCKER, JERRY ZUCKER

USA (CIC) 1980

⏱ 84m   (PG)

Madcap, risqué spoof of the stupid 'Airport' series of disaster flicks, with several reliable players sending themselves up something rotten. Ideally suited to video: the jokes come so rapidly that the ability to rewind for a second glance is essential. A hoot.

AMERICAN GRAFFITI 🎬 4

⭐ RICHARD DREYFUSS, HARRISON FORD, RON HOWARD, CHARLES MARTIN SMITH

🎬 GEORGE LUCAS

USA (CIC) 1973

⏱ 108m   (PG)

Wacky, slapstick comedy about the coming-of-age of small-town American buddies as they leave school and prepare for the wide world. Lucas became a top film-maker with the 'Star Wars' movies, Howard switched to directing, and Ford is now a megastar legend. This pic was much copied but never improved upon.

AND NOW FOR SOMETHING COMPLETELY DIFFERENT 🎬 4

⭐ JOHN CLEESE, ERIC IDLE, GRAHAM CHAPMAN, MICHAEL PALIN, TERRY JONES

🎬 IAN McNAUGHTON

UK (CINEMA CLUB V) 1972

⏱ 85m   (PG)

Many of the *Monty Python's Flying Circus* TV sketches are here, re-shot on film stock, making a nice time-capsule for those who weren't around for the original BBC broadcasts. Personally, though I loved the Python style in my schoolboy days, I now find that the increased sophistication of today's comedy (which has taken on board the anarchic social criticism of the team and expanded upon it) makes some of the material look very dated indeed. The same could be said of the Goons, of course: the price of innovation? Note: all the Python TV shows are now available in a huge box-set, released as we went to press.

63

ANIMAL CRACKERS [3]

★ THE MARX BROTHERS, MARGARET DUMONT, LILLIAN ROTH

▸ VICTOR HEERMAN

USA (CIC) 1930 B&W

⏱ 98m   (U)

"**T**his morning I shot an elephant in my pyjamas – how he got in my pyjamas I'll never know!' So says Groucho Marx in this adaptation of the comic team's hit Broadway show. Groucho, Harpo, Chico and Zeppo are all here in a classic piece of wisecracking, slapstick mayhem.

ANIMAL HOUSE [4]

★ JOHN BELUSHI, TIM MATHESON, TOM HULCE, JOHN VERNON

▸ JOHN LANDIS

USA (CIC) 1978

⏱ 104m   (15)

First and funniest of the 'National Lampoon' gagfests, brimming with rude slapstick, set in and around college fraternities and featuring the late Belushi at his gross best. Hulce went on to star in hit drama *Amadeus*. Also known as *National Lampoon's Animal House*.

ANNIE HALL [5]

★ DIANE KEATON, WOODY ALLEN, TONY ROBERTS, CAROL KANE, PAUL SIMON

▸ WOODY ALLEN

USA (WARNER) 1977

⏱ 89m   (15)

One of Allen's best, a touching, funny romantic comedy about a wacky girl and a nerdish comedian, with typically Allen-ish observations on life: 'a relationship is like a shark – if it doesn't keep moving forward it dies. I think what we've got here is a dead shark'. Keaton's mismatched, Oxfam-style clothes became a fashion trend. Oscars: best film, actress (Keaton), direction, screenplay (Allen and Marshall Brickman).

ARSENIC AND OLD LACE [3]

★ CARY GRANT, PRISCILLA LANE, PETER LORRE, RAYMOND MASSEY

▸ FRANK CAPRA

USA (WARNER) 1941 B&W

⏱ 113m   (PG)

Near-screwball film of the old chestnut about crazed murdering grannies, with sharp direction from Capra and a wonderful cast of top players. Sick and sardonic – perhaps that's why release was held back until 1944 though the pic was filmed three years earlier. A camp classic.

COMEDY

ARTHUR 🎬 4

DUDLEY MOORE, LIZA MINELLI, JOHN GIELGUD, TED ROSS

STEVE GORDON

USA (WARNER) 1981

93m (15)

This easy-going comedy about a layabout millionaire who spends his days in an agreeable haze of booze and casual sex until true love strikes was a surprise hit. Both Moore as the loveable lush and Minelli as his gal acquit themselves well, but Gielgud steals the show (and won an Oscar) in the support part of the droll, filthy-mouthed butler who has to clear up the empties and dismiss last night's hookers after his master's excesses. The theme tune also won an Oscar. There was a sequel, *Arthur 2: On The Rocks*, but it failed to match the louche charm of its predecessor.

AUSTIN POWERS – INTERNATIONAL MAN OF MYSTERY 🎬 4

MIKE MYERS, ELIZABETH HURLEY, MIMI ROGERS

JAY ROACH

USA (FOX) 1997

91m (15)

Deliciously camp homage to 60s spy spoofs like *Our Man Flint* and *Dr Goldfoot And The Girl Bombs*. How do you spoof a spoof? I dunno, but *Wayne's World* honcho Myers manages it in this pic, lensed in authentically garish psychedelic colour, in the twin roles of shag-mad Powers and his nemesis Dr Evil, a groovy secret agent and a Blofeld-like baddy both released from the suspended animation they've been frozen in since those fabulous 60s. On hand to update Powers on the advances in civilisation is modern babe Vanessa Kensington (a surprisingly able Hurley). Great fun.

BAD TASTE 🎬 4

PETER O'HERNE, PETER JACKSON, MIKE MINETT, TERRY POTTER

PETER JACKSON

NEW ZEALAND (POLYGRAM) 1988

90m (18)

First film from highly-rated director Jackson is a ghastly, gory, sick, hilarious horror piece about idiotic secret agents fighting cannibal aliens. Minuscule-budget 'shock' flicks like this are apt to get a hammering from the censor, but the BBFC realised what the director was trying to do, saw the joke and let the film through unscathed. Don't see it on a full stomach!

BEDAZZLED 🎬 3

PETER COOK, DUDLEY MOORE, ELEANOR BRON, RAQUEL WELCH

STANLEY DONEN

UK (FOX) 1967

101m (PG)

Update of *Faust*, with Devil Cook tempting his then-partner Moore with the seven deadly sins: naturally, in the swinging 60s Raquel Welch was trotted out as Lust. Not as nimble as it wants to be, but it's great to see the late Cook in his prime. A faded relic.

65

BEETHOVEN 🎬3

CHARLES GRODIN, BONNIE HUNT, DEAN JONES, STANLEY TUCCI

BRIAN LEVANT

USA (CIC) 1992

87m (U)

Knockabout funny concerning the havoc wrought by a rescued St Bernard on the family who saved it from a nasty geezer. A sure bet for children, with a nice appearance by Tucci (who played Richard Cross in TV hit *Murder One*). Has already spawned one sequel so far: *Beethoven's 2nd* (1993).

BEETLEJUICE 🎬4

MICHAEL KEATON, GEENA DAVIS, ALEC BALDWIN, WINONA RYDER

TIM BURTON

USA (WARNER) 1988

88m (15)

Showcase for director Burton's insane ideas and the pic which first matched him with Keaton, with whom he worked on *Batman* (see page 17) and its first sequel, *Batman Returns* (see page 17). Mad story involves a couple who come to realise they're dead after a car smash, and who hire freelance ghoul Keaton to rid their beloved home of new tenants. In the process, they form a bond with the new family's morbid daughter because she's the only human who seems able to tune in to what's going on! The imagery is unique, skewed and unsettling: like a Charles Addams aiming for the 90s and beyond. Amazing. (Also on a two-for-one tape with *The Witches Of Eastwick* (see page 85), the devilish Jack Nicholson comedy.)

BEVERLY HILLS COP 🎬3

EDDIE MURPHY, JUDGE REINHOLD, STEVEN BERKOFF, RONNY COX

MARTIN BREST

USA (CIC) 1984

101m (15)

Motormouth Murphy in first of the action/comedy films about a black street cop, Axel Foley, and his adventures in the refined purlieus of California. His wisecracks are undeniably amusing first time around, but while this is the best of his pix it already looks tired and passé by current standards. Catch it on TV instead, unless you're a diehard Eddie fan.

COMEDY

BILL AND TED'S BOGUS JOURNEY

KEANU REEVES, ALEX WINTER, GEORGE CARLIN, JOSS ACKLAND

PETER HEWITT

USA (ENTERTAINMENT) 1991

98m (PG)

Originally to be called *Bill And Ted Go To Hell*, this second story of the dumb-but-cool rock dudes sees them murdered by robot doubles before they meet the grim reaper and ... you don't really want to hear this, do you? Sort of live-action *Beavis And Butthead* and immense fun, the only worrying thing being the apparent message that it is okay to be stupid as long as you are pure in spirit and love rock 'n' roll, because then you can beat the baddies who want to control the world. Sadly, that's just what the real bad guys would love you to believe! Wake up, the reaper's coming! Two-for-one tape with *Bill And Ted's Excellent Adventure* (see below) available.

BILL AND TED'S EXCELLENT ADVENTURE

KEANU REEVES, ALEX WINTER, GEORGE CARLIN, BERNIE CASEY

STEPHEN HEREK

USA (ENTERTAINMENT) 1989

90m (PG)

Low-budget time-travel comedy about two rock-loving California nerds who discover that they're the future of mankind – but only if they pass their exams! Stupid-yet-funny: became a 'sleeper' hit through word-of-mouth and propelled Reeves towards stardom. Spawned sequel and TV cartoons. I'll leave it to you to decide whether it is better/worse than similar *Wayne's World* and *Beavis And Butthead*. Two-for-one tape with sequel (see above) also available.

BILLY LIAR

TOM COURTENAY, JULIE CHRISTIE, MONA WASHBOURNE, WILFRED PICKLES

JOHN SCHLESINGER

UK (WARNER) 1963 B&W

98m (PG)

Overpraised, sad, dour story about a dreamer who finally is unable to take the steps to freedom urged on him by his girlfriend. You come away angry at him for being such a loser, despite the many hilarious touches. I mean, what guy wouldn't scoot away to London with a young Julie Christie along for the run?

BLAZING SADDLES [3]

☆ CLEAVON LITTLE, GENE WILDER, MADELINE KAHN, DOM DE LUISE

▶ MEL BROOKS

USA (WARNER) 1970

⏱ 94m   (15)

A mega-hit at the time of first release, this cowboy spoof is still full of healthy vulgarity but to me feels slightly smug and dated. Unfortunately, it led Mel Brooks to embark on a series of progressively less amusing parodies of other genres, of which the best was 1974's *Young Frankenstein* (see page 86). He is an immensely astute and talented producer, but he still continues with these 'spoofs' to the present day, even though they all seem to play for only a week or so in cinemas and get a critical drubbing. One can only suppose they make money somehow, somewhere. This remains his best work, along with cult film *The Producers* (see page 82).

THE BLUES BROTHERS [3]

☆ JOHN BELUSHI, DAN AYKROYD, CAB CALLOWAY, CARRIE FISHER

▶ JOHN LANDIS

USA (CIC) 1980

⏱ 127m   (15)

This wildly successful cult flick about two cool dudes trying to save an orphanage is really just an excuse for the late Belushi to goof off amid superb action stunts and guest spots for many music legends. At the time of release, the duo recorded a live album of old soul songs which was a Number One hit in the USA record charts, and there has recently been a successful *Tribute To The Blues Brothers* stage show in the UK. A new 'Blues Brothers' film has recently emerged, to bad reviews.

BOB ROBERTS [4]

☆ TIM ROBBINS, ALAN RICKMAN, GORE VIDAL, GIANCARLO ESPOSITO

▶ TIM ROBBINS

USA (CINEMA CLUB V) 1992

⏱ 104m   (15)

Shrewd pseudo-documentary about the rise of a right-wing USA political candidate who cleverly uses the weapons of the counterculture in a 'straight' context: he sings folk songs deriding alleged welfare scroungers and his album covers ape the designs of old Dylan hits. Sinister and possibly prophetic despite the humour. Unbelievably, one major UK film critic opined that the joke was on the director because the ideas put forward by the conniving politician in the movie were jolly good and made perfect sense to him! Now that's even more disturbing than the film. As Oscar Wilde said, life imitates art ...

COMEDY

THE BREAKFAST CLUB 🎬4

EMILIO ESTEVEZ, JUDD NELSON,
MOLLY RINGWALD, ALLY SHEEDY

JOHN HUGHES

USA (CIC) 1984

93m (15)

Touching, funny, believable story about a group of misfits stuck in a detention class for high-school troublemakers. As we listen to them talk, they gradually reveal, not without barbed wit, their personal problems. Judd Nelson appears to have got lost in the wake of his 'Brat Pack' fame, but this movie shows just what a fine actor he really is. And whatever happened to Ringwald and Sheedy, so affecting and effective here? A little lost classic ensemble job.

BRITANNIA HOSPITAL 🎬3

LEONARD ROSSITER, JILL BENNETT,
FULTON MACKAY, GRAHAM CROWDEN

LINDSAY ANDERSON

UK (WARNER/LUMIERE) 1982

111m (15)

Typically grim humour from Anderson, with a chaotic, demented NHS hospital standing for the collapse of the Britain of Thatcher and big business. You'll laugh until you're sick to your stomach, that is if you manage to raise a chuckle at all. Not much fun, but I hardly suppose it was intended to be.

BROADCAST NEWS 🎬5

WILLIAM HURT, HOLLY HUNTER,
ALBERT BROOKS, JACK NICHOLSON

JAMES L BROOKS

USA (FOX) 1987

127m (15)

Romantic comedy about a TV producer torn between her smitten, clever best friend and the handsome-but-dumb newscaster who gets all the breaks simply because of his looks. A witty, incisive examination of the way news on the box is sold as mere entertainment for the brain-dead, with a great cast. Do see it!

THE BURBS 🎬3

TOM HANKS, COREY FELDMAN,
CARRIE FISHER, BRUCE DERN

JOE DANTE

USA (CIC) 1989

97m (PG)

Dante's oddball fantasy about the corruption lurking beneath suburbia for those who pry too much into their neighbours' affairs. Not a hit, but now has a following. The BBFC made slight cuts because film clips seen on TV during the pic are from films not legally available in the UK(!).

THE CABLE GUY 🎬3

☆ JIM CARREY, MATTHEW BRODERICK

🎬 BEN STILLER

USA (COLUMBIA TRISTAR) 1996

⏱ 92m (12)

Bizarre hybrid comedy-thriller about a depressed young man (Broderick) whose life is invaded by the deranged cable TV installer (Carrey) whom he bribes to provide him with free access to movie channels. Carrey is his usual crazed self, but the fact that we are never sure if we're watching comedy or tragedy finally undermines what might have been a great story.

'CARRY ON ...' A SPECIAL NOTE!

Instead of reviewing individual entries in the 'Carry On' series, I think it is best simply to insert this note looking at the films as a whole. The series is virtually a genre in itself, vulgar Brit humour of the panto and seaside postcard transferred to film. Cast members came and went, but a core group of Kenneth Connor, Charles Hawtrey, Sid James and the marvellous Kenneth Williams were around for most of the pix – though the posthumous release of Williams' diaries reveal that he felt (rightly) that not enough effort went into the writing or acting by many of those involved. From *Carry On Sergeant* (1959) to *Carry On Columbus* (1992), there were 30 films plus compilations and offshoots. The movie known as *Carry On Don't Lose Your Head* (1966) was initially issued as simply *Don't Lose Your Head*, because the makers wrongly thought the series had had its day. *Carry On Columbus* was a belated attempt to revive the series for the 90s with new stars to cash in on the serious (eh?) 'Columbus' movies being made at the time – an old trick they'd pulled off at the time of Liz Taylor's *Cleopatra* (see page 126) with *Carry On Cleo* (1965). Gerald Thomas directed most of the films and many are still around on video, but I think most pundits agree that it's definitely now time to call a halt to all this carry on! (Most of the available films are on Warner, Cinema Club Video and 4-Front.)

CASANOVA'S BIG NIGHT 🎬3

☆ BOB HOPE, JOAN FONTAINE, BASIL RATHBONE, VINCENT PRICE

🎬 NORMAN Z McLEOD

USA (CIC) 1954

⏱ 82m (U)

Hope takes a break from the never-ending 'Road' pictures with Bing Crosby to appear in this handsomely mounted piece of tosh about the great lover and his troubles. Throwaway nonsense, but Hope is as amusing as ever and Rathbone and Price beef up the cast no end. Only the most churlish will fail to smile.

COMEDY

CITY SLICKERS

BILLY CRYSTAL, HELEN SLATER, JACK PALANCE, BRUNO KIRBY

RON UNDERWOOD

USA (CINEMA CLUB V) 1990

109m (15)

Chucklesome adventure of city boys learning to be cowboys under the unforgiving tutelage of leathery old hand Palance, who won an Oscar for his efforts. The film was successful enough to spawn a sequel and to be parodied in a jeans advert. Harmless and very funny in places: definitely worth renting, if not owning.

CRIMES AND MISDEMEANORS

MARTIN LANDAU, WOODY ALLEN, ALAN ALDA, CLAIRE BLOOM, MIA FARROW

WOODY ALLEN

USA (VISION) 1989

100m (15)

One of Woody's better serious/comic hybrids, a musing on murder and infidelity with a sterling turn from Landau, an actor who has only recently been recognised as the fine performer he is. Allen plays his usual glum worry-wart, providing comic relief just when things look to be getting too dramatic for comfort. A lovely bit of film-making.

CROCODILE DUNDEE

PAUL HOGAN LINDA KOZLOWSKI, DAVID GULPILIL, MARK BLUM

PETER FAIMAN

AUSTRALIA (POLYGRAM) 1986

93m (15)

Screen debut for comic Hogan, in which he plays a rough bushman lured from the Aussie outback to the concrete jungle of New York – which he takes on with a mixture of charm and a Very Big Knife Indeed. An amusing romantic comedy which certainly changed Hogan's life – he ditched his wife for his co-star, blonde bombshell Kozlowski. He has never quite equalled its success, even with the 1988 sequel *Crocodile Dundee 2*.

A DAY AT THE RACES

THE MARX BROTHERS, MAUREEN O'SULLIVAN

SAM WOOD

USA (WARNER) 1937 B&W

109m (U)

Another Marx Brothers classic slice of tomfoolery. Also on a two-for-one tape with *A Night At The Opera* (1935), yet another Marx Brothers effort and also helmed by Sam Wood.

DEAD MEN DON'T WEAR PLAID

STEVE MARTIN, RACHEL WARD, CARL REINER, RENI SANTONI

CARL REINER

USA (CIC/4-FRONT) 1982 B&W

88m (PG)

One-note spoof of the classic monochrome private eye movies of yore. Clips from many favourites are skilfully woven into the story, with Martin on form as he responds to the dialogue with amusing quips. If it was being put together nowadays, of course, new technology would enable the comic to be placed in the old footage for a much funnier and smoother effect. Still offers a fair share of laughs, but you may tire of it before the finale.

DEATH BECOMES HER

MERYL STREEP, BRUCE WILLIS, GOLDIE HAWN, ISABELLA ROSSELLINI

ROBERT ZEMECKIS

USA (CIC) 1992

104m (PG)

Fast-and-furious comic roller-coaster from Zemeckis (who made the 'Back to the Future' films (see pages 16–7). Oscar-winning computer effects – which show the stars twisting and rubbernecking all over the shop – are astonishing the first time around.

DIRTY ROTTEN SCOUNDRELS

STEVE MARTIN, MICHAEL CAINE, BARBARA HARRIS, DANA IVEY, GLENNE HEADLY

FRANK OZ

USA (4-FRONT) 1988

110m (PG)

Remake of the 1964 Brando film *Bedtime Story*. Two rival con-artists on the French Riviera take a bet to see who can swindle a glamorous TV star first. Quite well written, but really it's the silly japes of Martin and Caine which make it a reasonably engaging (if overlong) story.

COMEDY

DR STRANGELOVE, OR HOW I LEARNED TO STOP WORRYING AND LOVE THE BOMB [4]

PETER SELLERS, STERLING HAYDEN, SLIM PICKENS, GEORGE C SCOTT

STANLEY KUBRICK

UK (ENCORE) 1963 B&W

91m (PG)

Based on Peter George's novel *Red Alert* (aka *Two Hours To Dream*), this classic cold war comedy has Sellers in three parts: the USA President attempting to recall bombers sent (by a mad militarist) to nuke Russia, a demented ex-Nazi adviser and a stiff-upper-lip Brit. Like its non-comedy equivalent *Fail Safe* (see page 103), the movie is very much of its time but remains a sour commentary on atomic stalemate. A typically icy Kubrick picture, with Sellers, Hayden and Scott acting manically. Characters with names such as Buck Turgidson immediately clue you in that this is to be played as high farce. Unique.

DRIVING MISS DAISY [4]

JESSICA TANDY, MORGAN FREEMAN, DAN AYKROYD, PATTI LUPONE

BRUCE BERESFORD

USA (WARNER) 1989

94m (U)

Slushy yet genuinely warm and amusing story of the quarter-century relationship between a tetchy white woman and her black chauffeur in America's deep south. Based on Alfred Uhry's play, it won Oscars for best film, actress (Tandy), adapted screenplay and make-up. The recent movie *Guarding Tess* was an obvious attempt at replicating the formula.

DUMB AND DUMBER [3]

JIM CARREY, JEFF DANIELS, LAUREN HOLLY

PETER FARRELLY

USA (FIRST INDEPENDENT) 1994

102m (12)

Carrey and Daniels are two slapstick fools in this amusing but thoroughly inconsequential piece of nonsense. A hit at the box-office but hardly classic comedy, let alone a great movie.

EDUCATING RITA [4]

MICHAEL CAINE, JULIE WALTERS, MAUREEN LIPMAN, MICHAEL WILLIAMS

LEWIS GILBERT

UK (RANK) 1983

110m (15)

Willy Russell's mega-hit play transfers smoothly to the screen, with Walters as a working-class girl anxious to better herself by studying for a university degree, and Caine as the alcoholic lecturer who urges her to go for it. Bittersweet romance which garnered Oscar nominations for Caine and Walters.

73

ENTERTAINING MR SLOANE [3]

BERYL REID, HARRY ANDREWS, PETER McENERY, ALAN WEBB

DOUGLAS HICKOX

UK (WARNER/LUMIERE) 1969

90m (15)

Half-arsed (ooh-er!) attempt to film the late Joe Orton's bisexual comedy of manners, with Reid and Andrews as the old duffers lusting after McEnery's leather-clad houseboy. Orton's work is notoriously hard to bring off (double ooh-er!) in that the farcical elements have to be played dead straight (*triple* ooh-er!) for the humour to bite, and while it's nice to have a filmed record of the play the cast can't quite pull it off (anyone for a quadruple ooh-er?).

FIRST WIVES CLUB [3]

BETTE MIDLER, GOLDIE HAWN, DIANE KEATON

HUGH WILSON

USA (CIC) 1996

98m (PG)

Revenge fantasy for the Hormone Replacement Therapy generation, with trio of glamorous and successful women uniting to take a swipe at the hubbies who ditched them. Fairly witty script and glossy smirking from the three stars. Some great one-liners from Bette Midler but suffers slightly from trying to get a message across instead of concentrating on the comedy.

A FISH CALLED WANDA [4]

JOHN CLEESE, KEVIN KLINE, JAMIE LEE CURTIS, MICHAEL PALIN

CHARLES CRICHTON

UK (WARNER) 1988

103m (15)

Veteran director Crichton came out of retirement to direct this hit farce about missing loot being chased by a misfit gang of jewel robbers. Curtis is sexy and Kline won the Oscar for best supporting actor, but the result doesn't quite live up to its inflated reputation as the craziest comedy of the 80s.

THE FULL MONTY [4]

ROBERT CARLYLE, PAUL BARBER, MARK ADDY, TOM WILKINSON

PETER CATTANEO

UK (FOX) 1997

88m (15)

Surprise Brit hit about unemployed men escaping the horrors of the dole by forming a male strip troupe, with great performances all round (in the film, *not* the troupe!). The story isn't *that* original (a similar tale had appeared as a TV play) but the exuberant execution made it a success in America, a market normally resistant to parochial Brit stories. A real measure of the film's impact is that when the title phrase is used these days people immediately think of the movie, rather than the subject under discussion. Funny, and quite touching in places.

COMEDY

GEORGE OF THE JUNGLE

LESLIE MANN, JOHN CLEESE, RICHARD ROUNDTREE, HOLLAND TAYLOR

SAM WESMAN

USA (BUENA VISTA) 1997

88m (U)

Puzzling (as in, why bother?) but sporadically chucklesome live-action revamp of a 60s TV cartoon about a terminally-thick Tarzan-esque hero who can't swing on a jungle vine without crashing into the nearest tree trunk. Stupid, but it has an imbecilic energy that keeps you watching in spite of better judgement. Or maybe it's just nostalgia. Wonder if they'll do 'Super Chicken' next?

GHOSTBUSTERS

DAN AYKROYD, BILL MURRAY, SIGOURNEY WEAVER, RICK MORANIS

IVAN REITMAN

USA (CINEMA CLUB V) 1984

101m (PG)

Like a comedy version of TV's *X-Files*, with a bunch of loony parapsychologists using hi-tech to combat the supernatural infestations of the modern world. Startling SFX and some good jokes. Sequel: *Ghostbusters 2* (1988).

GOOD MORNING, VIETNAM

ROBIN WILLIAMS, FOREST WHITAKER, ROBERT WUHL, TUNG TUANH TRAN

BARRY LEVINSON

USA (TOUCHSTONE) 1988

116m (15)

Based on real-life American forces disc jockey Adrian Cronauer, this showcases Williams' ad-libbing style to perfection. He plays a DJ broadcasting to US troops in Vietnam who comes into conflict with his superiors when he refuses to toe the line with staid music and chat – but, predictably, the ordinary soldiers love his anarchic style. Hilarious moments, but precious little story beyond some spurious romance – the problem lies in the fact that there is no way you can make the Vietnam conflagration seem like fun.

GREMLINS

ZACH GALLIGAN, PHOEBE CATES, HOYT AXTON, JUDGE REINHOLD

JOE DANTE

USA (WARNER) 1984

102m (15)

Demented and cartoonish riot about some odd little creatures which multiply and get nasty if you don't follow the pet care rules, with typically dark subtext from director Dante. Fab scenes of the evil little devils running amok and creating havoc in a Spielbergian small American town. Available in widescreen. Sequel: *Gremlins 2: The New Batch* (1990).

GROUNDHOG DAY [3]

BILL MURRAY, ANDIE MacDOWELL, CHRIS ELLIOTT, MARITA GERAGHTY

HAROLD RAMIS

USA (COLUMBIA TRISTAR) 1993

101m (PG)

Daft premise about a TV man sent to a small town to cover the witless annual festival, only to find that he must constantly relive the same day over and over again. Some romance, some laughs and a romantic ending. Don't look too deeply for meaning, just enjoy at a light-hearted level. Widescreen available.

HANNAH AND HER SISTERS [4]

WOODY ALLEN, MICHAEL CAINE, MIA FARROW, BARBARA HERSHEY, DIANNE WIEST, CARRIE FISHER, MAX VON SYDOW

WOODY ALLEN

USA (VISION) 1986

102m (15)

Typically classy romantic comedy from Allen centred around the complex love lives of a group of sisters and their suitors, husbands and friends. Won deserved supporting performance Oscars for Caine and Wiest.

HARVEY [5]

JAMES STEWART, JOSEPHINE HULL, VICTORIA HORNE, PEGGY DOW

HENRY KOSTER

USA (CIC) 1950 B&W

107m (U)

Splendid version of the Mary Chase play about attempts to lock a dipsomaniac in an asylum because he holds conversations with the giant white rabbit of the title, which is invisible to all but himself. Non-stop screwball confusion and a nice message about the sanctity of the individual, driven by a wonderful performance from Stewart. He revived the play in the 1970s on the London stage to deserved acclaim. The play won a Pulitzer Prize and the movie won Hull a best supporting actress Oscar.

HEAR MY SONG [4]

NED BEATTY, ADRIAN DUNBAR, SHIRLEY ANN FIELD, DAVID McCALLUM

PETER CHELSOM

UK (CIC) 1991

104m (15)

Entertaining tale about a plan to stage a concert starring legendary Irish tenor Josef Locke. Ned Beatty, usually confined to secondary character parts, gives an outstanding performance in this great little film.

HEATHERS 🎬 4

WINONA RYDER, CHRISTIAN SLATER, SHANNEN DOHERTY, KIM WALKER

MICHAEL LEHMANN

USA (CINEMA CLUB V) 1989

98m (18)

Slyly nasty tale of a girl who tires of her membership of a snobby group of high school girls all named Heather, only to be prompted by her new weirdo beau into bumping them off (along with other sundry twerps). Goes a bit cock-eyed towards the end, but still an original debut for the director with nifty work from the two lead stars. Humour at its blackest.

HOT SHOTS 🎬 3

CHARLIE SHEEN, LLOYD BRIDGES, CARY ELWES, EFREM ZIMBALIST Jnr

JIM ABRAHAMS

USA (FOX) 1991

81m (PG)

From the makers of *Airplane* (see page 63) and *Naked Gun* (see page 80) comes this madcap send-up of *Top Gun*, with lots of visual puns and foolishness. Tries a tad too hard, but not bad. Sequel: *Hot Shots Part Deux*.

THE HUDSUCKER PROXY 🎬 4

TIM ROBBINS, PAUL NEWMAN, JENNIFER JASON LEIGH, CHARLES DURNING

JOEL COEN

USA (COLUMBIA TRISTAR) 1994

107m (PG)

Homage of sorts to the screwball comedies of Frank Capra from the brothers Coen. Robbins is the eager-to-please nerd, plucked from obscurity to the top of the tree by scheming boss Paul Newman in an attempt to grab big bucks. Hilarious, and the 30s-style sets amaze.

THE IMPORTANCE OF BEING EARNEST 🎬 4

MICHAEL REDGRAVE, MICHAEL DENNISON, EDITH EVANS, JOAN GREENWOOD

ANTHONY ASQUITH

UK (RANK) 1952

91m (U)

Classic screen version of Oscar Wilde's sparkling comedy of manners, with Evans making the perfect Lady Bracknell. She's supported by a glittering cast of top British thespians, including Margaret Rutherford and Miles Malleson as well as the big stars. Witty, wonderful, marvellous. May seem dated to younger audiences, but that's their loss.

IT'S A MAD, MAD, MAD, MAD WORLD

SPENCER TRACY, PHIL SILVERS, JERRY LEWIS, TERRY-THOMAS, JACK BENNY

STANLEY KRAMER

USA (WARNER) 1963

148m (U)

The idea of making an epic, widescreen, spectacular comedy is an odd one, but that's what Kramer attempted in this multi-star pic about a bunch of disparate folk in search of buried loot. It doesn't quite come off, but the star cameos and Oscar-winning SFX carry the thing along. Not available in widescreen. The original running time was 192m, but the last copy I saw had the above-listed 148m timing. Worth checking before you buy or rent to ascertain if you're getting the full movie.

JERRY MAGUIRE

TOM CRUISE, KELLY PRESTON, CUBA GOODING Jnr, RENEE ZELLWEGER

CAMERON CROWE

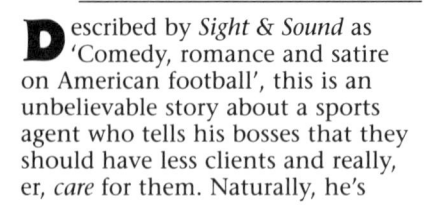

USA (COLUMBIA TRISTAR) 1996

133m (15)

Described by *Sight & Sound* as 'Comedy, romance and satire on American football', this is an unbelievable story about a sports agent who tells his bosses that they should have less clients and really, er, *care* for them. Naturally, he's fired. How he fights back takes up the rest of the story. If only life was like that. Well reviewed but overrated.

KIND HEARTS AND CORONETS

DENNIS PRICE, ALEC GUINNESS, JOAN GREENWOOD, MILES MALLESON

ROBERT HAMER

UK (WARNER/LUMIERE) 1949 B&W

101m (U)

Roy Horniman's novel *Noblesse Oblige* ably transferred to screen, with Price as murderer bumping off eight aristocrats (all played by Guinness) on his way to a title. Smooth as a perfect sherry and a British comedy classic.

KING OF COMEDY

ROBERT DE NIRO, JERRY LEWIS, SANDRA BERNHARD, TONY RANDALL

MARTIN SCORSESE

USA (WARNER) 1981

105m (U)

Scorsese's comment on obsessive fans has De Niro and shark-mouthed Bernhard as devotees of star Lewis who kidnap the man, with a ransom demand that results in De Niro getting a comedy spot on TV. A twisted look at the blurring of notoriety and fame, it proved one of Scorsese's few flops and was quickly shown on TV. Interesting rather than funny.

COMEDY

THE LAVENDER HILL MOB [4]

ALEC GUINNESS, STANLEY HOLLOWAY, SIDNEY JAMES, ALFIE BASS

CHARLES CRICHTON

UK (WARNER/LUMIERE) 1951 B&W

77m (U)

Oscar-winning screenplay about bank employee (Guinness) and his pals robbing a gold shipment. Delightful Ealing classic which still packs a load of laughs. Unforgettable cast of old hands and famous faces. See it at least once.

LOST IN AMERICA [4]

JULIE HAGERTY, ALBERT BROOKS, MICHAEL GREEN, GARY MARSHALL

ALBERT BROOKS

USA (WARNER) 1985

88m (15)

An executive drops out after missing a promotion and takes to the road with his wife in a camper van, only to lose all their savings at Las Vegas when the lady gets gambling fever. Hilarious, but the ending in which our hero goes back and grovels for a job at his old firm is misjudged and depressing, albeit true to life. Not a hit, but a cult film.

LOVE AT FIRST BITE [3]

GEORGE HAMILTON, SUSAN ST JAMES, RiCHARD BENJAMIN, DICK SHAWN

STAN DRAGOTI

USA (MIA) 1979

96m (15)

Dracula spoof with old smoothie Hamilton romancing the girl he meets when he emigrates to the USA. Horror comedies are notoriously difficult to pull off, but this has a deserved reputation as a daft slice of lightweight foolishness.

THE MEANING OF LIFE [3]

JOHN CLEESE, GRAHAM CHAPMAN, ERIC IDLE, TERRY GILLIAM; MICHAEL PALIN

TERRY JONES

UK (CIC) 1983

107m (15)

The third Python movie, with the usual *mélange* of bizarre and sick sketches – including a musical number about sperm and the exploding gut of greedy Mr Creosote! Aka *Monty Python's The Meaning Of Life*. Note: the running time given is for the original, but some references claim that video editions exist which run for as little as 86m. As always, check the box!

MONTY PYTHON AND THE HOLY GRAIL

JOHN CLEESE, MICHAEL PALIN, TERRY JONES, GRAHAM CHAPMAN

TERRY GILLIAM, TERRY JONES

UK (FOX) 1975

90m (15)

Medieval madness from the Python team, with severed limbs and silly jokes. Classed as their best effort by some fans, but I find it wears thin after one screening.

MONTY PYTHON'S LIFE OF BRIAN

JOHN CLEESE, GRAHAM CHAPMAN, MICHAEL PALIN, TERRY JONES

TERRY JONES

UK (CIC) 1979

93m (15)

Very controversial in its time, Python's spoof of a false biblical messiah lampoons the life of Jesus with such delights as the famed sequence of crucified men singing *Always Look on the Bright Side of Life*. Guaranteed to offend someone, somewhere, even today.

MY COUSIN VINNY

JOE PESCI, RALPH MACCHIO, MARISA TOMEI, FRED GWYNNE

JONATHAN LYNN

USA (FOX) 1992

119m (15)

The normally scary Pesci brings his comedic talents to the fore here as an inept lawyer called down south to help his young relative and his friend, who've been wrongly accused of violent crime. The culture clash is dryly presented, and the sultry Tomei rightly won a Best Supporting Actress Oscar as Vinny's smart but long-suffering babe.

NAKED GUN

LESLIE NIELSEN, PRISCILLA PRESLEY, OJ SIMPSON, GEORGE KENNEDY

DAVID ZUCKER

USA (CIC) 1988

81m (15)

Subtitled *From The Files Of Police Squad*, this movie was inspired by the cult TV gagfest of that name. From the same team as *Airplane* (see page 63), with much the same quickfire style of idiotic humour. It's amazing to see how Nielsen has changed course in late career from being a straight actor to become a droll funnyman. Other noticeable cast members include Priscilla Presley and the now-notorious OJ Simpson. Two sequels so far.

NATIONAL LAMPOON'S VACATION

CHEVY CHASE, RANDY QUAID, BEVERLY D'ANGELO, JOHN CANDY

HAROLD RAMIS

USA (WARNER) 1983

98m (15)

National Lampoon began as a college humour mag, went to news-stands, branched into records parodying the foibles of the rock world, and finally moved on to the silver screen. This is one of many 'National Lampoon' flicks, featuring typically earthy, stupid jokes as a middle-American family undergo a nightmare journey when they decide to visit a naff theme park for their holidays. It was popular enough to spawn a series of vacation-themed 'Lampoon' pix.

THE NUTTY PROFESSOR

EDDIE MURPHY, JAMES COBURN, JADA PINKOTT

TOM SHADYAC

USA (CIC) 1996

91m (12)

This remake of a Jerry Lewis comedy from the 60s is basically the Jekyll and Hyde story played for laughs. Murphy goes from nerdy fatty to smooth lothario via the (superbly executed) SFX and, as in his patchy *Coming To America*, much fun comes via the star being rendered unrecognisable under a series of clever make-ups.

THE ODD COUPLE

JACK LEMMON, WALTER MATTHAU, JON FIEDLER, HERB ELEMAN

GENE SAKS

USA (CIC) 1968

106m (PG)

Neil Simon's stage hit about two mismatched flatmates (one obsessively neat, the other a slob) makes for one of Lemmon and Matthau's spirited, superb pairings. Not to be missed. Spawned a hit TV series with Tony Randall and Jack Klugman taking over the parts. Delightful stuff.

PRIVATE BENJAMIN

GOLDIE HAWN, ARMAND ASSANTE, ROBERT WEBBER, EILEEN BRENNAN

HOWARD ZIEFF

USA (WARNER) 1980

110m (15)

Wry, sprightly comedy with Hawn as a spoiled rich girl who joins the army thinking she's going to a special version where the recruits bed down in luxury condominiums and get breakfast in bed. Soon waking up to the fact that she's been duped, she buckles down and makes a real career for herself. Fun, but the tale gets bogged down in turgid romance. Inspired a lame TV series.

PRIVATE PARTS [3]

★ HOWARD STERN, ROBIN QUIVERS, JENNA JAMESON, MARY McCORMACK

🎬 BETTY THOMAS

USA (ENTERTAINMENT) 1997

⏱ 105m (18)

Ribald biopic of outspoken USA radio host Howard Stern, directed in breezy style by Betty Thomas (who starred as Lucy Bates on TV's *Hill Street Blues*) and with long-haired foulmouth Stern playing himself. He was the first of the shock-jocks and was never equalled, spewing forth obscenities while battling with phone-in listeners, sponsors and bosses alike. Very funny if you're broad-minded.

THE PRODUCERS [5]

★ ZERO MOSTEL, GENE WILDER, DICK SHAWN, KENNETH MARS

🎬 MEL BROOKS

USA (4-FRONT) 1967

⏱ 84 m (PG)

The first and best Mel Brooks comedy romp is a characteristically oddball tale about two conmen who plan to make a killing by finding a play that is bound to fail and then selling the shares in the production several times over, thus ensuring that no one will expect to see a payday. They choose a musical about Hitler penned by a mad Nazi – but their plans go awry. A gallery of weirdos and some hilarious set pieces make this a comedy that stands up to repeated viewings. Oscar: screenplay (Brooks).

A SHOT IN THE DARK [4]

★ PETER SELLERS, ELKE SOMMER, GEORGE SANDERS, HERBERT LOM

🎬 BLAKE EDWARDS

USA (WARNER) 1964

⏱ 101m (PG)

First sequel to *The Pink Panther*, charting the further adventures of bumbling Inspector Clouseau (Sellers). The series went downhill from here, ending in dire efforts issued after Sellers's death, but this still cuts the mustard. The Henry Mancini music was used in a series of cartoons starring the Pink Panther character familiar from the credit sequences of many of the films.

SIR HENRY AT RAWLINSON'S END [4]

★ TREVOR HOWARD, PATRICK MAGEE, VIVIAN STANSHALL, HARRY FOWLER

🎬 STEVE ROBERTS

UK (TARTAN) 1980

⏱ 75m (15)

Poetic and surreal Brit whimsy about a crusty aristo in his crumbling pile. Based on records and radio readings by the late Vivian Stanshall of anarchic UK rock/trad jazz abusers The Bonzo Dog Band. Stanshall was a man who trod a fine line between madness and genius, not always carefully, and it's great to have this filmic record of one of his finest conceits.

COMEDY

THIS IS SPINAL TAP ★4

MICHAEL McKEAN, ROB REINER, CHRISTOPHER GUEST, HARRY SHEARER

ROB REINER

USA (POLYGRAM) 1984

82m (15)

On-the-money spoof rockumentary charting the supposed excesses of an imaginary band, all the way from teen psychedelia to heavy metaldom and exploding drummers. Anyone who has served time in the pop biz will find it even more amusing than the ordinary viewer, what with complaints about backstage sandwiches and albums with titles like 'Smell the Glove'. A much-needed jab in the beergut for an over-inflated business.

TIN CUP ★4

KEVIN COSTNER, RENE RUSSO

RON SHELTON

USA (WARNER) 1996

130m (15)

Sort of a *Rocky* for golf fans; an amusing, well-acted and scripted piece about the struggles of a golf professional and his girlfriend. Much fun is to be had from this nicely observed movie.

TO DIE FOR ★5

NICOLE KIDMAN, JOAQUIN PHOENIX, MATT DILLON, DAVID CRONENBERG

GUS VAN SANT

USA (POLYGRAM) 1995

102m (15)

The normally freckle-faced Kidman is transformed here as a steely-thighed, ambitious blonde determined to make it big as a TV reporter at any cost. Using sex and seduction, she stops at nothing to get her way, but her amorality recoils on her in this hilarious, murderous black comedy. A sweetly sardonic indictment of the cult of the cathode personality. Movie director Cronenberg cameos as a hitman.

TOOTSIE ★4

DUSTIN HOFFMAN, TERI GARR, JESSICA LANGE, BILL MURRAY, GEENA DAVIS, ELLEN FOLEY, CHARLES DURNING

SYDNEY POLLACK

USA (CINEMA CLUB V) 1982

112m (15)

Engagingly silly farce about a desperate actor who dresses as a woman to get a role in a popular soap opera, only to find himself with a dilemma when he falls in love with a girl star of the show. Immensely successful, and Lange won an Oscar for best supporting actress. Also available in a widescreen edition from Columbia Tristar.

CLASSIC 1000 VIDEOS

TRADING PLACES [4]
★ EDDIE MURPHY, DAN AYKROYD, JAMIE LEE CURTIS, DON AMECHE, RALPH BELLAMY

🎬 JOHN LANDIS

USA (CIC) 1983

⏱ 111m (15)

A couple of jaded old millionaires bet on whether a homeless bum can do as well as a rich man if they are simply forced to swap lives. Very funny picture with a hint of the style of the old Frank Capra screwball comedies from Hollywood of yore. Curtis is *très* sexy and Murphy was still a new star who felt compelled to make an effort when he made this, but the film is nearly stolen by Ameche and Bellamy as the old rogues.

TWINS [3]
★ DANNY DeVITO, ARNOLD SCHWARZENEGGER, CHLOE WEBB, KELLY PRESTON

🎬 IVAN REITMAN

USA (CIC) 1988

⏱ 102m (PG)

Two men meet and realise that, in spite of appearances, they are twins. Unbelievable, but the stars hurry it along and there are enough laughs along the way to make it worth renting. Schwarzenegger shows a previously unsuspected flair for comedic playing.

UNCLE BUCK [3]
★ JOHN CANDY, MACAULAY CULKIN, AMY MADIGAN, LAURIE METCALF

🎬 JOHN HUGHES

USA (CIC) 1989

⏱ 96m (15)

A kind, but slovenly, uncle babysits some recently bereaved kids with unexpectedly hilarious results. A good performance by the late John Candy in this competent, well-executed, if sentimental, domestic comedy.

THE WAR OF THE ROSES [3]
★ MICHAEL DOUGLAS, KATHLEEN TURNER, DANNY DE VITO, SEAN ASTIN

🎬 DANNY DeVITO

USA (FOX) 1989

⏱ 111m (15)

Bitter, black farce about a battling married couple who engage in a war of attrition that destroys all around them. The fun gradually wears out, but the stars do their best. Based on a novel by Warren Adler.

COMEDY

WAYNE'S WORLD [4]

MIKE MYERS, DANA CARVEY, ROB LOWE, TIA CARRERE

PENELOPE SPHEERIS

USA (CIC) 1992

95m (PG)

Expanded from characters first seen in TV snippets, this is about two heavy-metal nerds who run a public access TV show from home. Comparisons with *Bill And Ted/Beavis And Butthead* notwithstanding, it laughs at itself while staying hip enough to get the youth vote – though the plot is predictable. Rob Lowe sends up his sex-god image and Carrere makes a believable rock babe, but Myers and Carvey carry the show. Sequel: *Wayne's World 2* (1993).

WHAT'S NEW PUSSYCAT? [3]

PETER O'TOOLE, PETER SELLERS, WOODY ALLEN, URSULA ANDRESS

CLIVE DONNER

USA/FRANCE (MGM/UA) 1965

108m (15)

Dated Woody Allen script, delivered in very flashy swinging 60s style by Donner. Now a cultish curio, with the neurotic sex-therapy theme a hint of the concerns Allen would return to in a more sophisticated mode. Tom Jones had a smash hit with the Hal David/Burt Bacharach theme song.

WHITE MEN CAN'T JUMP [3]

WESLEY SNIPES, WOODY HARRELSON, ROSIE PEREZ

RON SHELTON

USA (FOX) 1992

111m (15)

Amiable comedy about two basketball hustlers – one black, one white – who form a partnership rooking the gullible punters they meet on street corner courts. Harrelson and Snipes make a likeable double act.

THE WITCHES OF EASTWICK [2]

JACK NICHOLSON, CHER, MICHELLE PFEIFFER, SUSAN SARANDON

GEORGE MILLER

USA (WARNER) 1987

114m (18)

Based on the John Updike novel, this tells the story of three randy ladies who conjure the Devil (a typecast Nicholson) to satisfy their needs but find him a little more trouble than they bargained for. Quite funny, but never seems sure whether it means to be a comedy or a scare ride. Also on a two-for-one tape with horror/comedy *Beetlejuice* (see page 66).

WITHNAIL AND I [5]

RICHARD E GRANT, PAUL McGANN, RICHARD GRIFFITHS, MICHAEL ELPHICK

BRUCE ROBINSON

UK (CIC) 1986

103m (15)

Hilarious and irreverent 60s story of a couple of failing actors who plan a holiday in the country cottage of a flamboyantly homosexual relative. Recently reissued on the tenth anniversary of first release, this has a cult reputation due, mainly, to the fruity, eye-rolling performance of Grant. Brilliant. Widescreen available.

WORKING GIRL [4]

SIGOURNEY WEAVER, MELANIE GRIFFITH, HARRISON FORD, ALEC BALDWIN

MIKE NICHOLS

USA (FOX) 1988

109m (15)

Dumped-on secretary Griffith uses her boss Weaver's absence to take over her job, designer wardrobe *and* boyfriend – but what'll happen when the bitch queen gets back? A morality tale with a bite and plenty of laughs, not to mention Carly Simon's Oscar-winning song 'Let the River Run'. A deserved smash hit.

YOUNG FRANKENSTEIN [3]

GENE WILDER, MARTY FELDMAN, TERI GARR, PETER BOYLE, GENE HACKMAN, MADELINE KAHN

MEL BROOKS

USA (FOX) 1974 B&W

106m (15)

One of Brooks's best gagfests is an uncannily accurate and loving spoof/tribute to the early Universal horror films, notably Rowland V Lee's *Son Of Frankenstein*. Shot in authentic monochrome and utilising Kenneth Strickfaden's spectacular lab FX from the originals, this is a treat for kids of all ages.

DRAMA

While there are movies in this section which could arguably have made interesting and acceptable appearances in other categories (*Se7en*, say, on page 119), the main purpose here is to ensure the inclusion of films that are worthy of note but which don't easily lend themselves to pigeon-holing: *Quiz Show*, for instance, which is not a romance, a comedy, a thriller or an adventure, yet remains a deftly made, brilliantly acted, thought-provoking piece of cinema. Skip this section at your peril, for if you do, you'll miss some of the best pictures in the book – and some of the best additions to your tape collection.

7 YEARS IN TIBET

BRAD PITT, DAVID THEWLIS, MAKO

JEAN-JACQUES ANNAUD

USA (ENTERTAINMENT) 1997

129m (18)

Moody Pitt vehicle, extolling the life-changing qualities of Tibet. Dull, dull, dull, but fans of Brad will hardly care. Tibet is a big thing with Hollywood liberals outraged by China's human rights abuses and fascinated by Buddhism and the exiled Dalai Lama, the subject of Scorsese's recent *Kundun*.

ABSENCE OF MALICE

PAUL NEWMAN, SALLY FIELD, BOB BALABAN, WILFORD BRIMLEY

SYDNEY POLLACK

USA (VIDEO COLLECTION) 1980

111m (PG)

This tale of a news reporter who runs a story which has dire consequences for a blameless man is eternally topical with the on-going debate about balance between press rights and the need for a privacy law. Solid acting from the two stars.

THE ACCUSED

JODIE FOSTER, KELLY McGILLIS, BERNIE COULSON, LEO ROSSI

JONATHAN KAPLAN

USA (CIC/4-FRONT) 1988

116m (18)

Harrowing drama about a girl who gets gang-raped in a bar after drunkenly flirting with the customers. Her lawyer (McGillis) infuriates her by letting the perpetrators off with lesser charges, but makes amends by bringing to book the men who cheered as the rape took place. Grim rumination on the question of whether doing a bit of reckless carousing should ever be allowed to render a woman open to the accusation of 'asking for it' – and whether doing nothing to stop a crime is a crime in itself. Foster won an Oscar for her performance as the victim.

ALL THE PRESIDENT'S MEN

ROBERT REDFORD, DUSTIN HOFFMAN, MARTIN BALSAM, HAL HOLBROOK, JASON ROBARDS, JACK WARDEN

ALAN J PAKULA

USA (WARNER) 1976

132m (15)

Talky but well-acted story of Woodward and Bernstein, the two *Washington Post* reporters who exposed the political espionage and financial corruption behind the Watergate burglary and ultimately brought about the downfall of Presdent Nixon. Oscars: supporting actor (Robards), screenplay (William Goldman, from book by Woodward and Bernstein), sets and sound.

AMERICAN BUFFALO

DENNIS FRANZ, DUSTIN HOFFMAN, SEAN NELSON

MICHAEL CORRENTE

USA (FILMFOUR) 1997

83m (15)

David Mamet's play provides the basis for this character study of three crooks involved in a plot to steal a rare coin. Set in a crummy pawn shop, the downbeat essay in duplicitousness is carried along by fine acting from Dennis Franz (of TV's *NYPD Blue*) and a nasty Hoffman. The less-than-cinematic setting betrays its stage origins, but this is another compelling story from a master yarn-spinner.

AMERICAN GIGOLO [3]

RICHARD GERE, LAUREN HUTTON, NINA VAN PALLANDT, HECTOR ELIZONDO

PAUL SCHRADER

USA (CIC) 1980

112m (18)

Sexual athlete for hire is accused of murder and only one of his women clients can get him off – but he doesn't want to use her name. Calvinist rebel Schrader concocts a typically jaundiced look at LA sleaze, with a nice performance from Gere as the male tart with a noble heart.

APOLLO 13 [4]

TOM HANKS, KEVIN BACON, BILL PAXTON, GARY SINISE, ED HARRIS

RON HOWARD

USA (CIC) 1995

134m (PG)

Even though the historically-minded will know the outcome, this is a thoroughly engrossing real-life adventure set aboard the malfunctioning USA space-capsule of the title. Tom Hanks gives a believable, measured performance as astronaut Jim Lovell, battling against all the odds to get his crew back to earth alive.

AWAKENINGS [3]

ROBIN WILLIAMS, ROBERT DE NIRO, JOHN HEARD, PENELOPE ANN MILLER

PENNY MARSHALL

USA (CINEMA CLUB V) 1990

115m (15)

Based on the career of Dr Oliver Sacks, this moving film tells of an unorthodox medic (Williams) who discovers that a group of patients thought to be mindless vegetables have, in fact, been aware of their condition despite being immobile for decades. If the realisation is horrifying, the scenes of the 'awakenings' under experimental drug treatment are both moving and funny. Contains the simple message that every moment of life is precious and not to be wasted. Much good acting, including a touching performance by De Niro as one of the patients.

BACKDRAFT [3]

ROBERT DE NIRO, KURT RUSSELL, WILLIAM BALDWIN, DONALD SUTHERLAND

RON HOWARD

USA (CIC) 1991

131m (15)

Tale of sibling rivalry between two Chicago firemen. Too long, but great SFX and the film is saved by De Niro as a shrewd arson detective on the track of pyromaniac Sutherland.

THE BAD AND THE BEAUTIFUL [4]

☆ KIRK DOUGLAS, LANA TURNER, WALTER PIDGEON, DICK POWELL, BARRY SULLIVAN, GLORIA GRAHAME, GILBERT ROLAND

▦ VINCENTE MINELLI

USA (WARNER) 1952 B&W

⏱ 118m (PG)

To its credit, Hollywood is always pretty vicious when it turns its critical gaze on itself: this prime piece of navel-contemplation is a flamboyant tale of the ups-and-downs of a megalomaniac producer and the effect he has on those around him, with a confident central performance from Douglas and nice work from those in his orbit. Several Oscars, including best supporting actress for Grahame as a southern belle.

BAD DAY AT BLACK ROCK [3]

☆ SPENCER TRACY, ROBERT RYAN, LEE MARVIN, ANNE FRANCIS

▦ JOHN STURGES

USA (WARNER) 1954

⏱ 81m (PG)

Sadly available only in pan-scan, this tense tale involves a one-armed man arriving in an unfriendly desert town to investigate what happened to a Japanese-American pal. Suspenseful, but rather worthy and over-regarded by critics, and diminished on the small screen. Top cast, though.

BARTON FINK [3]

☆ JOHN GOODMAN, JOHN TURTURRO, JUDY DAVIS, STEVE BUSCEMI

▦ JOEL COEN

USA (COLUMBIA TRISTAR) 1991

⏱ 112m (15)

Murder and mystery assail a young writer new to Hollywood in this slab of weirdness from the acclaimed Coen brothers writer/director team. Despite its cult reputation, this is a tad over ambitious and isn't quite up to the dazzling standard of heir best pix, such as *Fargo* (see page 104) and *Blood Simple* (see page 259).

BASQUIAT [4]

☆ JEFFREY WRIGHT, DAVID BOWIE, DENNIS HOPPER, CHRISTOPHER WALKEN

▦ JULIAN SCHNABEL

USA (GUILD) 1996

⏱ 102m (15)

Biopic of street artist who was taken up by the New York cognoscenti, worked with Warhol and died of drug abuse, leaving behind paintings that are now worth a bundle. Rock star Bowie plays Warhol quite effectively here and the film is a fascinating glimpse into the hip art world of the time.

DRAMA

BEACHES 🎬3

⭐ BETTE MIDLER, BARBARA HERSHEY, SPALDING GRAY, JOHN HEARD

🎬 GARY MARSHALL

USA (TOUCHSTONE) 1988

⏱ 118m (15)

Based on Iris Rainer Dart's novel, this is a mildly engaging story of the enduring friendship of two women from disparate backgrounds – a rich girl and a would-be singer. Maudlin ending, but the occasional laughs and the two stars will keep you watching.

THE BEDFORD INCIDENT 🎬3

⭐ RICHARD WIDMARK, SIDNEY POITIER, JAMES MacARTHUR, MARTIN BALSAM

🎬 JAMES B HARRIS

USA (ENCORE) 1965 B&W

⏱ 98m (PG)

One of the better cold war 'brink of nuclear insanity' pix of the 60s with USA warship captain Widmark playing cat and mouse with a Russian sub in icy waters. Real sweaty-palms stuff, with some fine acting.

THE BIG BLUE 🎬4

⭐ JEAN RENO, ROSANNA ARQUETTE, JEAN-MARC BARR, PAUL SHENAR

🎬 LUC BESSON

FRANCE (FOX) 1988

⏱ 114m (15)

Unusual movie of friendship, love and competition set against the strange sport of 'free diving' – the divers have no breathing gear, but test their endurance by holding on to a rope at incredible depths for amazing lengths of time. Beautiful photography and an astonishing dream sequence make up for the lukewarm acting. The film was cut for international release, but the full 174m version is available in a special boxed set.

BIG WEDNESDAY 🎬3

⭐ JAN-MICHAEL VINCENT, WILLIAM KATT, GARY BUSEY, ROBERT ENGLUND

🎬 JOHN MILIUS

USA (BLACK DIAMOND) 1978

⏱ 119m (PG)

Hymn to the glories of male bonding in the Californian surfing culture of the 60s. The young pals gradually see their idyllic existence eroded by age, responsibilities and the Vietnam War. The most personal of Milius' pix. Available in widescreen.

BILLIONAIRE BOYS CLUB [4]

JUDD NELSON, RON SILVER, FREDRIC LEHNE, BRIAN McNAMARA

MARVIN J CHOMSKY

USA (VIDEO COLLECTION) 1987

175m (15)

The most underrated of the 'Brat Pack' actors of the 80s, Nelson excels in this made-for-TV story based on the true tale of a charismatic young wheeler-dealer whose schemes led to murder. This appears to be a slightly edited version.

THE BIRDMAN OF ALCATRAZ [5]

BURT LANCASTER, KARL MALDEN, THELMA RITTER, NEVILLE BRAND

JOHN FRANKENHEIMER

USA (WARNER) 1961 B&W

148m (PG)

Classic account of Robert Stroud, a 'lifer' who became an expert on avian diseases while imprisoned. Lancaster gives a towering performance, and there's no attempt to whitewash Stroud's murderous nature. Able support from Ritter as his supportive but jealous mother, and from Malden and Brand as his jailers. A genuine masterpiece.

THE BLACKBOARD JUNGLE [3]

GLENN FORD, ANNE FRANCIS, SIDNEY POITIER, VIC MORROW

RICHARD BROOKS

USA (MGM/UA) 1955 B&W

101m (12)

Dated but well-made version of Evan Hunter's novel of classroom violence. The 'kids' look to be in their thirties, and the rock 'n' roll of Bill Haley hardly seems likely to inspire mayhem – but the story still carries us along.

BODY HEAT [4]

WILLIAM HURT, KATHLEEN TURNER, TED DANSON, MICKEY ROURKE, RICHARD CRENNA

LAWRENCE KASDAN

USA (WARNER) 1981

108m (18)

Rich bitch uses sex to draw her lawyer beau into a plot to slay her husband. Considered wildly naughty at time of release, but with passage of time its virtues as a worthwhile steamy thriller are more likely to impress.

DRAMA

THE BOUNTY

ANTHONY HOPKINS, MEL GIBSON, LIAM NEESON, LAURENCE OLIVIER, EDWARD FOX, DANIEL DAY-LEWIS

ROGER DONALDSON

UK (FOX) 1984

128m (15)

Based on Roger Hough's book *Captain Bligh and Mr Christian*, this Robert Bolt script was intended as a vehicle for the late, great David Lean – but director Donaldson does an excellent job of attempting to convey a more rounded portrait of the main protagonists involved in the 'Mutiny on the Bounty' tragedy than seen in previous films on the tale. Hopkins is a brilliant but irascible and aloof Bligh, with Gibson as a brattish Christian seduced by sun and sex. Well worth seeing.

BOYZ 'N' THE HOOD

ICE CUBE, CUBA GOODING Jnr, LARRY FISHBURNE, ANGELA BASSETT

JOHN SINGLETON

USA (COLUMBIA TRISTAR) 1991

107m (15)

Interesting first film from director Singleton about efforts of a lone black father to keep his kids out of gang trouble in their poor Los Angeles ghetto home. Sprawls and drifts a bit but is highly rated by many critics.

BREAKING THE WAVES

EMILY WATSON, UDO KIER, JEAN-MARC BARR

LARS VON TRIER

DENMARK/SWEDEN/NORWAY/ FRANCE/NETHERLANDS (GUILD) 1996

152m (18)

Cult hit about the tortured mind of a girl married to a European oil-rig worker and her dire life in a dreary coastal dump in Scotland. Rave reviews all round, apparently, but I'm mystified. Looks good, I'll say that! Widescreen.

THE CAINE MUTINY

HUMPHREY BOGART, FRED MacMURRAY, VAN JOHNSON, LEE MARVIN

EDWARD DMYTRYK

USA (CINEMA CLUB V) 1954 B&W

119m (U)

A crew rebel against their disturbed captain and then have to justify their actions in a court-martial. Bogart excels as Captain Queeg in this taut version of Herman Wouk's Pulitzer Prize-winning novel. Charlton Heston took the part in the London stage version, *The Caine Mutiny Court Martial*, many years later – though the play was more concerned than the movie with exploring the dubious motives of some of the crew (and the heroic actions which led to Queeg's mental problems). The play was later remade as a TV movie with a different cast.

CAT ON A HOT TIN ROOF [3]

ELIZABETH TAYLOR, PAUL NEWMAN, BURL IVES, JACK CARSON

RICHARD BROOKS

USA (WARNER) 1958

103m (15)

Steamy Tennessee Williams play provides the basis for this epic about a southern family dripping with neurotic sexuality, avarice and mendacity. Lusty tosh with much gloriously bad acting, especially from Ives as the bulky Big Daddy, patriarch of the clan. Remade for TV in 1984.

THE CHAMBER [3]

GENE HACKMAN, FAYE DUNAWAY, CHRIS O'DONNELL

JAMES FOLEY

USA (CIC) 1996

108m (15)

Young lawyer meets his estranged grandad to defend him on a last-ditch death-row attempt to escape execution for a racist bombing murder. In the process he tries to discover why the old man took the rap for others, but John Grisham's story doesn't translate well to the screen. O'Donnell is a blank space and the grizzled, nasty Hackman acts him into a corner.

CHARIOTS OF FIRE [4]

BEN CROSS, IAN CHARLESON, NIGEL HAVERS, IAN HOLM, JOHN GIELGUD

HUGH HUDSON

UK (FOX) 1981

118m (U)

Rather plodding and overrated, yet still a quality piece of entertainment, this fact-based story tells of two students (one Christian, one a Jew) who compete in races at the 1924 Olympics. Skilful depiction of the prejudices and mores of the era in Colin Welland's Oscar-winning script, and a nicely judged performance by the late Ian Charleson. Other Oscars: best picture/score (Vangelis)/costumes.

CHINATOWN [4]

JACK NICHOLSON, FAYE DUNAWAY, JOHN HUSTON, BURT YOUNG

ROMAN POLANSKI

USA (CIC) 1974

131m (15)

Classic private eye adventure of corruption and incest set in Los Angeles of the 30s with Nicholson as Jake Gittes, the bewildered 'tec at the heart of the case. Great period feel, and Robert Towne's literate screenplay won an Oscar. Director Polanski turns up in a cameo as the thug who slits Jake's nose open. An underrated sequel, *The Two Jakes*, appeared in 1990. Widescreen available.

DRAMA

THE CINCINNATI KID

STEVE McQUEEN, EDGAR G ROBINSON, KARL MALDEN, ANN-MARGRET, TUESDAY WELD, RIP TORN

NORMAN JEWISON

USA (WARNER) 1965

101m (15)

Card-sharp tale that is a rather poor attempt to ape the hot-youngster-against-old-pro story of the Paul Newman film *The Hustler*. Would have worked better in black-and-white, and the proceedings cannot have been helped by director Sam Peckinpah being replaced by Norman Jewison shortly after shooting began on the spurious charge that Peckinpah wanted to make a 'dirty' movie. Worth seeing however for old hands like Robinson and the wonderfully-named Rip Torn.

CITIZEN KANE

ORSON WELLES, JOSEPH COTTEN, EVERETT SLOANE, AGNES MOORHEAD, DOROTHY COMINGORE, GEORGE COLOURIS

ORSON WELLES

USA (4-FRONT) 1941 B&W

120m (U)

Oft-cited as the best film of all time, this drama of a ruthless press baron was highly controversial in its day. Young Welles, fresh-faced and already famed for scaring the USA with his radio broadcast of HG Wells' *War of the Worlds* (presented as a news bulletin spoofing a real Martian attack), was given an unprecedented total-control deal and used every cinematic trick in the book (and some that weren't) to dazzle his audience. News boss WR Hearst assumed the pic was based on him and tried to have the negative bought and destroyed, but it was released and won an Oscar for best screenplay for Welles and Herman J Mankiewicz. Gregg Toland's cinematography and the acting by Welles' Mercury Players make this a film largely deserving of its inflated reputation. Welles was never again granted this kind of control or budget, and spent the rest of his life making movies with flashes of brilliance and taking cameo parts to scare up cash for his projects. It is indeed sad to think what films he could have created with the budget of just one of today's trashy blockbusters.

THE COLOR OF MONEY

PAUL NEWMAN, TOM CRUISE, MARY ELIZABETH MASTRANTONIO, JOHN TURTURRO

MARTIN SCORSESE

USA (TOUCHSTONE) 1986

115m (15)

One of Scorsese's least successful movies and a follow-up to Newman's 60's classic *The Hustler*. This time his pool-shark character is older and wiser and takes on young Cruise as an apprentice, but it drifts toward the end and has none of the impact of the earlier film. Newman won the Best Actor Oscar. Based on the novel by Walter Tevis.

THE COLOR PURPLE

WHOOPI GOLDBERG, DANNY GLOVER, RAE DAWN CHONG, OPRAH WINFREY

STEVEN SPIELBERG

USA (WARNER) 1985

148m (15)

Epic attempt at a serious, sentimental story by Spielberg, based on the novel by Alice Walker about the ups and downs of a black woman in America's Deep South. Over-long and rather maudlin but nicely shot and directed. Available in a widescreen version.

COOL HAND LUKE

PAUL NEWMAN, GEORGE KENNEDY, DENNIS HOPPER, STROTHER MARTIN

STUART ROSENBERG

USA (WARNER) 1967

121m (15)

Based on Donn Pearce's novel, this is the effective story of a young rebel without a cause who, jailed for drunkenly lopping the heads off parking meters, inspires fellow inmates in a brutal southern chain-gang. It boasts an outstanding showing from Newman in the lead and an Oscar-winning performance from Kennedy as his buddy. The tragic ending and an unusually (for him) understated score from Lalo Schifrin make this a picture well worth seeking out.

COURAGE UNDER FIRE

MEG RYAN, DENZEL WASHINGTON, LOU DIAMOND PHILLIPS, SCOTT GLENN

EDWARD ZWICK

USA (FOX) 1996

111m (15)

Investigation into the death of a female military hero fuels a great and gruelling drama dealing with battlefield ethics, machismo and truth. The question is: does Ryan deserve her posthumous decoration and glory, or condemnation as a bad leader? Duplicity abounds, but will the facts come out? Plenty nervous tension, guilt and fine acting here.

A CRY IN THE DARK

MERYL STREEP, SAM NEILL, CHARLES TINGWELL, BRUCE MYLES

FRED SCHEPISI

USA/AUSTRALIA (MGM/UA) 1988

116m (15)

True story of Lindy Chamberlain, who claimed her baby was carried off by a wild dingo during a camping trip in the Australian outback. She was jailed for murder but subsequently exonerated and released. Streep is convincing, but her usual facility with accents deserts her here and led to people coming out of cinemas squawking 'A ding-go's gawt mawyee *bay-bee*'.

DRAMA

CRY FREEDOM

KEVIN KLINE, DENZEL WASHINGTON, PENELOPE WILTON, ALEC McCOWEN, JOHN THAW

RICHARD ATTENBOROUGH

UK (CIC) 1987

158m (PG)

Worthy true-life story of how writer Donald Woods escaped with his family from South Africa in order to tell the world how the authorities had murdered his friend, black activist Steve Biko. Like many films of its type, it was criticised for concentrating on the white characters, but it does get an important message across while holding the attention. Washington was nominated for an Oscar. The American TV version is somewhat longer.

THE CRYING GAME

STEPHEN REA, FOREST WHITAKER, JAYE DAVIDSON, MIRANDA RICHARDSON

NEIL JORDAN

UK (POLYGRAM) 1992

108m (18)

Cult hit involving the IRA and matters of sexual identity. Even if the final revelation is known to most people these days, whether they've seen the movie or not, the acting and direction carry it along. Still Jordan's best effort – in the eyes of most punters at least.

DANGEROUS GAME

HARVEY KEITEL, JAMES RUSSO, MADONNA

ABEL FERRARA

USA (POLYGRAM) 1995

108m (18)

Originally released in the USA as *Snake Eyes*, this typically weird (and autobiographical?) film from the director of *Bad Lieutenant* (see page 150) is about a manipulative moviemaker and his effect on the lives of his actors, both on and off the set. Madonna is dire.

DANGEROUS LIAISONS

GLENN CLOSE, JOHN MALKOVICH, MICHELLE PFEIFFER, KEANU REEVES, UMA THURMAN, PETER CAPALDI

STEPHEN FREARS

USA (WARNER) 1988

115m (15)

Classic French novel by Choderlos de Laclos (and the play based on it by Christopher Hampton) inspired this wickedly amusing story of an eighteenth-century lady who passes her time in scheming with the love lives of friends and enemies. Close and Malkovich are excellent, and it's nice to see Peter Capaldi in a big movie – I first interviewed him when he was an unknown rock singer working the bars near my home town back in Scotland, but he went on to win an Oscar for a short he made; a marvellous actor. Oscars: art, costumes, script.

DEAD MAN WALKING 🎬 5

⭐ SUSAN SARANDON, SEAN PENN, SCOTT WILSON, ROBERT PROSKY

🎬 TIM ROBBINS

USA (POLYGRAM) 1995

⏱ 122m (15)

Oscar-winning story based on the life of Sister Helen Prejean, an American nun who gives spiritual comfort to both death row prisoners and the victims of their crimes, urging the former to realise their offences and the latter to attempt forgiveness. The film never flinches from showing the righteous anger of bereaved families, and also makes the obscenity of capital punishment the subject of a more honest protest by contrasting the execution of one man (Sean Penn, outstanding in a part based on a composite of real-life cases handled by Prejean) with flashbacks to his hideous crime. Penn moves from arrogance to self-realisation, gradually making the audience sympathise with his initially repulsive character, and Sarandon is never sanctimonious. A must-see, whatever your thoughts on the death penalty.

DEAD POETS SOCIETY 🎬 4

⭐ ROBIN WILLIAMS, ROBERT SEAN LEONARD, ETHAN HAWKE, JOSH CHARLES

🎬 PETER WEIR

USA (TOUCHSTONE) 1989

⏱ 123m (PG)

Best of the 'inspirational teacher' genre which flourished in the 80s (and far superior to the later, racially patronising *Dangerous Minds*), this pic gives Robin Williams one of his best non-comic roles as a young master at an expensive boys' school whose pupils admire him so much that they resurrect the secret club he once belonged to – with tragic consequences. Oscar: screenplay.

THE DEFIANT ONES 🎬 4

⭐ TONY CURTIS, SIDNEY POITIER, THEODORE BIKEL, LON CHANEY Jnr

🎬 STANLEY KRAMER

USA (WARNER) 1958 B&W

⏱ 96m (U)

Chase story of two prisoners – one black, one white – who escape while chained together and have to learn to understand each other. Fine work from the two leads. Inferior TV remake appeared circa 1985.

DRAMA

DETOUR

TOM NEAL, ANN SAVAGE, CLAUDIA DRAKE, EDMUND MacDONALD

EDGAR G ULMER

USA (VISIONARY) 1945 B&W

65m (15)

Classic from a 'poverty row' studio by cult director Ulmer involves a hitch-hiker who accidentally becomes enmeshed in murder. A legendary *film noir* and a textbook example of no-resource genius. Based on the Martin Goldsmith novel.

THE DEVILS

OLIVER REED, VANESSA REDGRAVE, DUDLEY SUTTON, GEMMA JONES, GEORGINA HALE, MAX ADRIAN, MURRAY MELVIN, MICHAEL GOTHARD

KEN RUSSELL

UK (WARNER) 1971

103m (18)

Russell's film, still controversial today, explores how one woman's sexual obsession became the vehicle for political and ecclesiastical corruption in seventeenth-century France. Based on John Whiting's play and on Aldous Huxley's book *The Devils of Loudun*, Russell's movie embellishes the facts with all manner of gore and naked nuns. Reed gives his best-ever performance as the worldly priest who, accused of satanism by Redgrave, finds faith in martyrdom. There are great sets by Derek Jarman and a weird score from Peter Maxwell Davies. The picture was slightly cut by the BBFC. BBC TV showed the UK print in semi-widescreen some time ago, though an NFT attempt to find the BBFC-cut footage was unsuccessful. Warner have now issued that master to replace the previously available pan-scan of the cut US version. The letterboxing remains cropped as on television.

DEVIL'S ADVOCATE

AL PACINO, CRAIG T NELSON, CHARLIZE THERION, KEANU REEVES

TAYLOR HACKFORD

USA (WARNER) 1997

135m (18)

After a young defence lawyer gets a child molester off, the suggestively-named John Milton (Pacino) hires him to look after his chums, who include a homicidal politico (Nelson). Pacino is, of course, the Devil, there to tempt folks down the left-hand path. Pulls the viewer in and Pacino is neat, but the film reminds me of an old *film noir* (*Alias Nick Beal*, with Ray Milland) to which it can't come close.

DISCLOSURE

MICHAEL DOUGLAS, DEMI MOORE, DONALD SUTHERLAND, DENNIS MILLER

BARRY LEVINSON

USA (WARNER) 1994

123m (18)

Typical blend of intrigue and hi-tech from the pen of Michael Crichton, with Douglas wrongly accused of sex abuse by an ambitious colleague, high-flier Demi Moore. A tight script, clever use of computer FX and superb acting make this a film which grips right up until the final frames. Highly topical, in both the aspects of sexual politics in the workplace and of the explosion of electronic storage of secrets.

DO THE RIGHT THING

DANNY AIELLO, OSSIE DAVIS, JOHN TURTURRO, SPIKE LEE

SPIKE LEE

USA (CIC) 1989

114m (18)

Not entirely successful blending of laughs and sociology, with black customers rioting after the boss of the local pizza joint refuses to put pictures of black stars on the wall alongside snaps of Italian-Americans such as Sinatra and Co. Starts off amusing but finally leaves a sour taste in the mouth as one contemplates the follies and pettiness of humanity.

DOG DAY AFTERNOON

AL PACINO, JOHN CAZALE, CHARLES DURNING, LANCE HENRIKSEN

SIDNEY LUMET

USA (WARNER) 1975

119m (15)

Pacino scored an early hit in this story, based on true facts, of an inept bank robber who gets involved in a siege with a vault full of hostages while attempting to steal cash for his gay lover's sex-change operation! Oscar for screenplay. Widescreen.

DRAMA

THE DOORS 〔4〕

VAL KILMER, MEG RYAN, KYLE MACLACHLAN, KEVIN DILLON, FRANK WHALEY, MICHAEL MADSEN, MIMI ROGERS

OLIVER STONE

USA (GUILD) 1991

134m (18)

Not a musical, though the soundtrack is greatly enhanced by the music of the group of the title, but a warts 'n' all biopic of Doors singer Jim Morrison, played with uncanny verisimilitude by Kilmer, as he progresses from rising young sex god of 60s LA to dying alcoholic blues poet in 70s Paris. The pop milieu of the period is dazzlingly recreated by Stone. The film needs a widescreen showing, but as far as I'm aware the only time it has been made available on video in this format was via a short-lived special edition sold only by WH Smith.

DRUGSTORE COWBOY 〔4〕

MATT DILLON, KELLY LYNCH, JAMES REMAR, JAMES LE GROS, WILLIAM S BURROUGHS

GUS VAN SANT

USA (VISION) 1989

97m (18)

Based on an unpublished novel by James Fogle, this was a bizarrely compelling and successful film about a gang of junkies who rob chemists to sustain their habits, detailing their hit-and-miss escapades and run-ins with the law. Leader Dillon decides to come off drugs after one of his gang dies of an overdose, but his past catches up with him. Strange visual effects and convincing acting made this an oddly moving salute to lost youth. Lovely cameo appearance by one of your humble scribe's acquaintances, famed addict and author, the late William S Burroughs (playing a junkie priest, of all things).

EAST OF EDEN 〔3〕

JAMES DEAN, RAYMOND MASSEY, JO VAN FLEET, JULIE HARRIS

ELIA KAZAN

USA (WARNER) 1955

115m (PG)

Dean died with only three pix under his belt and became a legend, the first American teenager of real note. This version of the John Steinbeck novel about two sons battling for the love of a stiff-necked father shows him at his tortured best. Van Fleet got an Oscar for best supporting actress. Available in a widescreen edition. Remade as a TV mini-series many years later. For the economy minded, there's a two-for-one package with Dean's *Rebel Without A Cause*.

EASY RIDER

PETER FONDA, DENNIS HOPPER, JACK NICHOLSON, PHIL SPECTOR

DENNIS HOPPER

USA (COLUMBIA TRISTAR) 1969

94m (18)

Quintessential low-budget road movie, which made Hollywood realise that the youth market wanted their own stories, their own music, and that it did not take multi-million-dollar profligacy to provide them. Hopper and Fonda play two hippy bikers on a drug-dealing trip across America which ends in death. Nicholson's cameo as a soused southern wastrel began his inexorable rise to stardom. Soundtrack by then-hot groups such as Steppenwolf, the Jimi Hendrix Experience, the Byrds and others more obscure. Available in widescreen.

ED WOOD

JOHNNY DEPP, MARTIN LANDAU, SARAH JESSICA PARKER, BILL MURRAY

TIM BURTON

USA (TOUCHSTONE) 1994 B&W

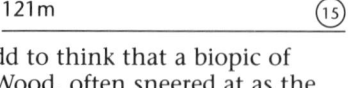

121m (15)

Odd to think that a biopic of Wood, often sneered at as the most inept Hollywood director ever (though his films have a bizarre mood all their own), should garner two Oscars: one for make-up, the other for Martin Landau's wonderful performance as faded, morphine-addicted star Bela Lugosi. Director Burton obviously empathises with Wood's weird vision, but even in monochrome the film looks too glossy to be authentic, and Depp too young for a transvestite war hero (!) See it anyhow.

THE ELEPHANT MAN

JOHN HURT, ANTHONY HOPKINS, JOHN GIELGUD, FREDDIE JONES, ANNE BANCROFT

DAVID LYNCH

USA/UK (WARNER) 1980 B&W

118m (PG)

Hurt is unrecognisable as Victorian sideshow freak John (in real life Joseph) Merrick, whose face and body were hideously distorted by tumours – possibly resulting from the disease neurofibromatosis or perhaps Proteus syndrome – and who was rescued by surgeon Sir Frederick Treves (played here by Hopkins in the days before he too became a 'Sir'). The direction is rather tear-jerking for the normally unflinching Lynch, but the pic is lensed in luminous monochrome by Freddie Francis. It's based on the memoirs of Treves, though the film hints at the parallels between the surgeon's use of the Elephant Man and those who showed him as a freak. Widescreen available. Nominated for seven Oscars and won best film and actor (Hurt) at the BAFTAs.

DRAMA

ELMER GANTRY [4]

BURT LANCASTER, JEAN SIMMONS, DEAN JAGGER, SHIRLEY JONES

RICHARD BROOKS

USA (WARNER) 1960

142m (PG)

Lancaster exploits his acrobatic athleticism in this story of a phoney evangelist in 20s America, running, jumping and ranting about God and the Devil to rake in the donations. Well-written by the director from the Sinclair Lewis novel. Oscars: best actor (Lancaster), best supporting actress (Jones), screenplay.

EMPIRE OF THE SUN [3]

CHRISTIAN BALE, JOHN MALKOVICH, NIGEL HAVERS, MIRANDA RICHARDSON

STEVEN SPIELBERG

USA (WARNER) 1987

146m (PG)

Based on JG Ballard's autobiographical novel, this tells the story of a boy in a Japanese prison camp after he's separated from his parents in World War Two China. Has its moments but is a largely overblown mix of Brit stiff-upper-lips and large explosions.

THE ENGLISH PATIENT [3]

RALPH FIENNES, KRISTIN SCOTT THOMAS, JULIETTE BINOCHE, WILLEM DAFOE

ANTHONY MINGHELLA

USA (BUENA VISTA) 1996

155m (15)

Sorry, but this version of Michael Ondaatje's post-colonial novel seems an over-praised bore to me. A badly burned pilot in 1943 North Africa tells his story of love, espionage and betrayal to his nurse amid desert scenery and his Italian hospital bed. A staggering nine Oscars, including best pic! Available in widescreen.

FAIL SAFE [3]

HENRY FONDA, DAN O'HERLIHY, WALTER MATTHAU, LARRY HAGMAN

SIDNEY LUMET

USA (ENCORE) 1963 B&W

108m (PG)

Nuclear disaster movie. When an American weapons system goes wrong and bombs the USSR, the President's only hope of averting a world war is to offer to destroy one of his own cities in order to prove to the enemy that he's told the truth. Suspenseful stuff, based on the novel by Harvey Wheeler and Eugene Burdick.

FALLING DOWN 🎬4

MICHAEL DOUGLAS, ROBERT DUVALL, FREDERIC FORREST, BARBARA HERSHEY

JOEL SCHUMACHER

USA (WARNER) 1992

108m (18)

Anyone who has ever lost their temper under stress will sympathise with this story of a redundant man, estranged from his family, who simply walks away from his car in an LA traffic jam and gets involved in a series of violent confrontations. After he defeats muggers and then uses their gun to deal with a snotty shop assistant, a weary cop, Duvall, is sent on his trail. Both Duvall and Douglas (as the protagonist) give thoroughly realistic performances – though I fear many will find it hard to identify with the cop's admonition that Douglas has no right to act on the anger he feels towards those in power who made false promises of job security for those who obey society's rules. Still, our anti-hero's fate may make you lie down and count to ten next time you feel yourself about to explode. Looks eerily prescient in the light of 1996's tragic events in Scotland and New Zealand.

FARGO 🎬5

FRANCES McDORMAND, STEVE BUSCEMI, HARVE PRESNELL, PETER STORMARE

JOEL COEN

USA (POLYGRAM) 1995

98m (18)

Off-beat tale of heavily pregnant police chief (McDormand, who deservedly bagged an Oscar for her work here) investigating a car dealer who has arranged for two inept kidnappers to fake the abduction of his wife. Whimsical, funny, bloody and engrossing, with the Scandinavian accents of the small USA town of the title adding to the air of other-worldliness. Also won an Oscar for best screenplay for director Coen (husband of McDormand) and his brother Ethan. Please do see it.

FATAL ATTRACTION 🎬4

MICHAEL DOUGLAS, GLENN CLOSE, ANNE ARCHER, ELLEN FOLEY

ADRIAN LYNE

USA (CIC) 1987

114m (18)

The dangers of illicit romantic entanglements are pointed up in this story of a married man who has a fling only to find that the object of his lust has become psychotically fixated on him. Based on the short *Diversion*, to which the makers bought the rights in order to make sure it will never be seen again – so much for studio dedication to film history and preservation! Available in a widescreen version, with a bonus of the original ending which was dumped after previews. Pity they didn't include *Diversion* as well.

DRAMA

A FEW GOOD MEN 4

TOM CRUISE, JACK NICHOLSON, DEMI MOORE, KIEFER SUTHERLAND

ROB REINER

USA (COLUMBIA TRISTAR) 1992

138m (15)

Military courtroom drama about an investigation into the circumstances surrounding the death of a young US Marine at the hands of his buddies. Agreeable work from Cruise and Moore as the lawyers on the case, but the star is undoubtedly Nicholson. Though he only has a handful of scenes, his performance as a mad-eyed commander who demands complete loyalty from his boys, dominates the movie. The final confrontation between Nicholson and Cruise is an absolute corker. Widescreen available.

THE FIELD 3

RICHARD HARRIS, JOHN HURT, SEAN BEAN, BRENDA FRICKER, FRANCES TOMELTY, TOM BERENGER

JIM SHERIDAN

UK (CINEMA CLUB V) 1990

109m (15)

Harris is outstanding as the tenant of an Irish peat field who has long coveted ownership of the land and is outraged when a visiting American dares to bid against him for it. Fine acting from the supporting cast, especially Hurt as a wily yokel, but this tragic little tale sags towards its sad end and looks too much like something shot for TV. Based on the play by John B Keane.

FIELD OF DREAMS 4

KEVIN COSTNER, RAY LIOTTA, JAMES EARL JONES, BURT LANCASTER, AMY MADIGAN

PHIL ALDEN ROBINSON

USA (ENTERTAINMENT) 1988

101m (PG)

Delightful fantasy about a farmer who, having felt compelled to raze his crops to build a baseball field, then sees it filled with members of a (real-life) disgraced team who threw the World Series years before – except that they're ghosts. He ends by bringing a famous writer out of retirement and manages a reconciliation with his own late father. If it all sounds mad and twee on paper, on screen it works as a message about never giving up on your most personal dreams. If only life were really like this! Based on the novel *Shoeless Joe*, by WP Kinsella, in which the writer character was named as real author JD Salinger, reclusive creator of *The Catcher in the Rye*.

FRIED GREEN TOMATOES AT THE WHISTLE STOP CAFE ③

JESSICA TANDY, MARY STUART MASTERSON, MARY LOUISE PARKER, KATHY BATES

JON AVNET

USA (CINEMA CLUB V) 1991

130m (PG)

Old woman tells young feminist about restaurant run by her two pals in 30s USA. A funny, touching fable of female empowerment in the face of male boorishness. Too long, but worth the effort. Based on Fannie Flagg's novel.

FROM HERE TO ETERNITY ④

BURT LANCASTER, DEBORAH KERR, MONTGOMERY CLIFT, FRANK SINATRA, DONNA REED

FRED ZINNEMANN

USA (COLUMBIA TRISTAR) 1953 B&W

114m (PG)

Classic film version of the James Jones novel of the lives and loves of those in and around a rough US army camp in Hawaii just before the attack on Pearl Harbor. Magnificent acting by Clift as the man who irritates his superiors by refusing to box due to the death of a previous opponent, and there's that famous love scene between Burt and Deborah in the foaming surf. Eight Oscars, including best picture, director, supporting actor and actress (Sinatra and Reed), cinematography and screenplay.

GI JANE ③

DEMI MOORE, VIGGO MORTENSEN, ANNE BANCROFT

RIDLEY SCOTT

USA (FIRST INDEPENDENT) 1996

125m (15)

A 'serious' version of *Private Benjamin* (see page 81): a woman's battle to get respect in the army. Panned mercilessly, but the antics of shaven-headed Demi hit it big with the girl-power constituency and the pic has apparently been a rental video hit in the UK.

GORILLAS IN THE MIST ③

SIGOURNEY WEAVER, BRYAN BROWN, JULIE HARRIS, IAIN CUTHBERTSON

MICHAEL APTED

USA (WARNER) 1988

124m (15)

Romanticised biopic of Dian Fossey, who was murdered by poachers in 1965 while studying and attempting to save the endangered mountain gorillas of Rwanda. The story hardly needed the slushy love interest the makers added, as her life and work were clearly interesting enough without it. Weaver seems to realise this and acts throughout as if to make her character as unfanciable as possible. Not to be sniffed at – and that's not a gorilla joke!

DRAMA

THE GRAPES OF WRATH

HENRY FONDA, JOHN CARRADINE, CHARLEY GRAPEWIN, JANE DARWELL

JOHN FORD

USA (FOX) 1940 B&W

129m (PG)

Ford's version of John Steinbeck's novel of the dustbowl depression embodies much the same pioneer spirit as his Westerns, albeit in a less mythical context. Over-reverent, perhaps, but well-made. Oscar: best supporting actress (Darwell).

HENRY – PORTRAIT OF A SERIAL KILLER

MICHAEL ROOKER, TOM TOWLES, TRACY ARNOLD

JOHN McNAUGHTON

USA (ELECTRIC) 1990

83m (18)

One of the most important independent pix of recent years. Based on the (alleged) confessions of real serial killer Henry Lee Lucas, this is a gruesome near-documentary presentation of Henry and his buddy planning and executing various sex murders. The UK censor was upset by the director's refusal to insert implicit criticism of the actions of the protagonists, so there are cuts and at least one sequence has been re-edited in the version on sale here. McNaughton has not lived up to the promise of this film with his later mainstream movies, though Rooker (see *JFK*, page 108) and Towles have become regular Hollywood support players of some ability.

HOW GREEN WAS MY VALLEY

WALTER PIDGEON, MAUREEN O'HARA, RODDY McDOWALL, DONALD CRISP, ANNA LEE

JOHN FORD

USA (FOX) 1941 B&W

118m (U)

Sentimental but enjoyable film version of Richard Llewellyn's novel about life in a Welsh village. Coal mining was never this cosy in real life, but fine actors and sharp script carry it along. Oscars: best picture, director, cinematography, art direction and supporting actor (Crisp).

IN THE NAME OF THE FATHER

DANIEL DAY-LEWIS, PETER POSTLETHWAITE, EMMA THOMPSON

JIM SHERIDAN

UK (CIC) 1993

127m (15)

Critics moaned over some factual errors, but this true story of the people wrongly imprisoned for many years for the IRA bombs in Guilford remains a shocking, sobering experience that will shatter your faith in British justice. Police are shown as both brutal and cynical. Day-Lewis is fine as Gerry Conlon, but Postlethwaite steals the film as his bewildered father.

107

JFK

KEVIN COSTNER, TOMMY LEE JONES, GARY OLDMAN, SISSY SPACEK, JOE PESCI, WALTER MATTHAU, JACK LEMMON, DONALD SUTHERLAND, JOHN CANDY, MICHAEL ROOKER

OLIVER STONE

USA (WARNER) 1991

189m (15)

Over-long, star-laden account of lawman Jim Garrison's attempt to unveil the conspiracy that led to the 1963 assassination of President Kennedy. Deftly uses flashbacks and monochrome inserts to explore the various possibilities, but unless you pay rigid attention you are liable to get lost trying to work out what is established fact and what is mere supposition. Costner tries hard as an upright Henry Fonda-type, but looks too boyish for the role. The real Garrison appears as Judge Warren, whose commission whitewashed the murder as the act of lone nut Lee Harvey Oswald. A terrible crime against democracy was committed, but the benefit of hindsight has changed our hither-to rose-tinted view of the victim. Available in pan-scan, in widescreen and even in a widescreen director's cut, packaged with a documentary tape on the case. Take your choice – at least it's better than Stone's execrable *Nixon*, his companion biopic of Kennedy's nemesis.

THE KILLING FIELDS

SAM WATERSTON, HAING S NGOR, JOHN MALKOVICH, JULIAN SANDS

ROLAND JOFFE

UK (WARNER) 1984

136m (15)

True story of a USA reporter's attempt to regain contact with his Cambodian guide, left behind when the Khmer Rouge took over the country. Superbly authentic work from Ngor as the guide – hardly surprising as he was a victim of the terror himself. Dr Ngor, who was, sadly, murdered recently, won a richly deserved best supporting actor Oscar. Other Oscars: editing and cinematography.

KISS OF THE SPIDER WOMAN

WILLIAM HURT, RAUL JULIA, SONIA BRAGA, MILTON GONCALVES

HECTOR BABENCO

BRAZIL/USA (ELECTRIC) 1985 COL/B&W

120m (15)

Unusual story of a political prisoner whose spirits are kept up by the recounting of a tacky film plot by his drag-queen cellmate. The late Julia is good as the politico, but the star is Hurt as the homosexual who initially infuriates his friend but who finally inspires him by the resilience he finds through fantasy. The inserts from the imaginary movie, which is loosely based on a character in a couple of real Hollywood movies, are shown in black and white. Oscar: best actor (Hurt).

DRAMA

LA CONFIDENTIAL [4]

KEVIN SPACEY, KIM BASINGER, DANNY DeVITO, RUSSEL CROWE

CURTIS HANSON

USA (WARNER) 1997

132m (18)

Streamlined version of one of James Ellroy's complex Los Angeles novels, telling the story of cops, junkies, police brutality, etc., etc., in early 50s Hollywood. Despite the simplification and the ditching of some characters, the story is still somewhat hard to follow but is redeemed by nicely-judged performances all round. Justifiably lauded at the Oscars (Basinger won best-supporting actress) and well worth seeing.

LAST EXIT TO BROOKLYN [4]

JENNIFER JASON LEIGH, STEPHEN LANG, BURT YOUNG, STEPHEN BALDWIN

ULI EDEL

WEST GERMANY (POLYGRAM) 1989

98m (18)

Darkly compelling movie of Hubert Selby Jnr's controversial novel about 50s hookers, dopers and sundry other sleazy folk. Jason Leigh gives the outstanding performance here, but not a film to watch if you're looking for a pick-me-up!

LEGENDS OF THE FALL [3]

BRAD PITT, ANTHONY HOPKINS, AIDAN QUINN, JULIA ORMOND

EDWARD ZWICK

USA (COLUMBIA TRISTAR) 1994

129m (15)

Ins-and-outs of brothers in love and war as they move between their wilderness home and civilisation, between romance and hate-fuelled rage. The full plot is too complex to detail here, but director Zwick (of *Glory* fame) keeps the action ticking over as the picture moves in an ever more tragic direction. Savagely superior soap-opera. Widescreen and boxed set available.

LENNY [4]

DUSTIN HOFFMAN, VALERIE PERRINE, GARY MORTON, JAN MINER

BOB FOSSE

USA (WARNER) 1974 B&W

111m (18)

Biography of Lenny Bruce, the first alternative standup comic and a man whose numerous brushes with the law over drugs and obscenity led to his downfall. Hoffman's performance was criticised at the time, but it's hard to see how it could have been bettered. It may be a truism that funny men don't have funny lives, but this movie illustrates the fact all too harrowingly.

LONE STAR

KRIS KRISTOFFERSON, FRANCES McDORMAND, MATTHEW McCONAUGHEY, RON CANADA

JOHN SAYLES

USA (COLUMBIA TRISTAR) 1996

130m (15)

Deep mystery as modern-day sheriff Kristofferson investigates events in the past. Support from the marvellous McDormand and the up-and-coming McConaughey make this an intriguing drama that's worth a look. Available in widescreen.

LOOKING FOR RICHARD

AL PACINO, KEVIN SPACEY, ALEC BALDWIN, WINONA RYDER

AL PACINO

USA (GUILD) 1996

112m (12)

Thought-provoking piece by Pacino, as he records his efforts to stage Shakespeare's *Richard III* and tries to fathom the fascination of the play with the help of actors, friends and passers-by. A brave and entertaining piece of documentary genius. Widescreen.

THE MADNESS OF KING GEORGE

NIGEL HAWTHORNE, HELEN MIRREN, IAN HOLM, RUPERT EVERETT, AMANDA DONOHOE

NICHOLAS HYTNER

UK (COLUMBIA TRISTAR) 1995

106m (PG)

Based on Alan Bennett's play *The Madness of George III* (allegedly renamed in case Americans wondered if they'd missed the first two films!), this has wonderfully affecting performances all round, especially from Hawthorne as a man who realises his sanity is in danger yet is unable, for once in his life, to control events. Bennett slyly draws parallels with the current British Royal Family: 'To be the Prince of Wales is not a position, it is a predicament.' Available in a letterboxed de luxe package, this is a film which rightly garnered many awards. Intelligence and entertainment need not be incompatible.

THE MAN WITH THE GOLDEN ARM

FRANK SINATRA, KIM NOVAK, DARREN McGAVIN, ELEANOR PARKER

OTTO PREMINGER

USA (VISIONARY) 1955 B&W

120m (PG)

Controversial in its day, this film of Nelson Algren's book stars Sinatra as Frankie Machine, whose 'golden arm' refers to both his card-dealing skills and his heroin addiction. This was probably the first movie to play out the highs and lows of junkiedom with any truth. Sinatra scores (ahem) brilliantly in the lead. Worth catching.

MICHAEL COLLINS 🎬4

LIAM NEESON, ALAN RICKMAN, JULIA ROBERTS, STEPHEN REA

NEIL JORDAN

UK (WARNER) 1996

⏱ 127m ⓡ15

A massive fuss was expected by the distributors of this biopic of the original IRA godfather, but there were few protests, except from those who questioned the accuracy of some scenes. Collins, who negotiated the ill-fated treaty that led to the division of Ireland and is the cause of the 'troubles' today, ended up wearing an army uniform and was killed by his own ex-comrades. He seems to have been aware of his own fall-guy status, compounding the air of tragedy in this well-made picture. Neeson gives a fine performance in the lead and is shaping up to be one of the major stars of the future.

MIDNIGHT COWBOY 🎬3

JON VOIGHT, DUSTIN HOFFMAN, BRENDA VACCARO, SYLVIA MILES, VIVA

JOHN SCHLESINGER

USA (WARNER) 1969

⏱ 108m ⓡ18

Dated version of James Leo Herlihy novel about a non-sexual love affair between two hustlers in 60s New York, Voight as a naive cowboy stud and Hoffman as the tramp 'Ratso' Rizzo. Influenced by Warhol flicks of the time and featuring members of his 'Factory' entourage, it's a clever subverting of underground image into overground substance, a tragi-comic paean to not-so-beautiful losers. Singer Harry Nilsson is often erroneously credited with the score; in fact he merely sang Fred Neil's song *Everybody's Talkin'*: the score is by John Barry. Oscars: picture, director, screenplay.

MIDNIGHT EXPRESS 🎬4

BRAD DAVIS, JOHN HURT, RANDY QUAID, BO HOPKINS

ALAN PARKER

UK (COLUMBIA TRISTAR) 1978

⏱ 121m ⓡ18

Oscar-winning script by Oliver Stone is an exaggerated version of the true story of a young American's imprisonment in a Turkish jail for attempting to smuggle cannabis out of the country – interesting in the light of the accusations of untruths levelled at later Stone projects such as *JFK* (see page 108). Good performances from Hurt and Quaid as the jailed misfits who adopt the scared kid in the corrupt prison, but the ending seems a bit too pat. Some grim violence, including a man having his tongue bitten off. Widescreen available.

MRS BROWN

JUDI DENCH, BILLY CONNOLLY, ANTONY SHER, GEOFFREY PALMER

JOHN MADDEN

USA/UK/IRELAND (BUENA VISTA) 1997

99m (15)

Well-made story of the irreverent relationship between Queen Victoria (Dench) and her highland ghillie John Brown (Connolly), as he attempts to assuage her prolonged mourning over the death of her husband Prince Albert. The subtext of continuing Scottish servility to the English has been criticised, but nothing can detract from the accomplished acting and production values. Although the title of the film is *Mrs Brown*, the video box has the legend *Her Majesty Mrs Brown*, just in case audiences are in any doubt of what the film is about.

MY BEAUTIFUL LAUNDERETTE

DANIEL DAY-LEWIS, SAEED JAFFREY, ROSHAN SETH, SHIRLEY ANNE FIELD

STEPHEN FREARS

UK (PVG) 1985

97m (15)

Cult movie about a young British Asian and the luxury washeteria he runs with his gay lover. Occasionally touching, with moments of violence, but the average viewer may find it a bit dull.

MY LEFT FOOT

DANIEL DAY-LEWIS, RAY McANALLY, BRENDA FRICKER, FIONA SHAW

JIM SHERIDAN

UK (ELECTRIC) 1989

103m (15)

The story of Christy Brown, the Irish writer, who fought against cerebral palsy to become an author by using the one part of his body he could control – the eponymous foot – to tap out words on a keyboard. Oscars for Day-Lewis and Brenda Fricker, who plays his mother. An inspiring movie about the power of the human will to overcome seemingly insurmountable odds.

DRAMA

NAKED LUNCH ▢4

⭐ PETER WELLER, JUDY DAVIS, IAN HOLM, ROY SCHEIDER, JULIAN SANDS

🎬 DAVID CRONENBERG

UK/CANADA (FIRST INDEPENDENT) 1980

⏱ 111m (18)

A synthesis of the 'unfilmable' literary sex/dope fantasy by the late William S Burroughs and his experiences in trying to write the book, including his accidental shooting of his wife. Hallucinatory imagery and talking insect typewriters, not to mention bug killers hooked on their own exterminating powder. The mad alien world of lifelong gay junkie Burroughs fits in with director Cronenberg's body-loathing world view just fine, but the result only proves the impossibility of translating the book's scattergun ideas into narrative cinema. A marvellous try, though! Available in widescreen.

THE NAME OF THE ROSE ▢4

⭐ SEAN CONNERY, F MURRAY ABRAHAM, CHRISTIAN SLATER, RON PERLMAN

🎬 JEAN-JACQUES ANNAUD

FRANCE/ITALY/WEST GERMANY (POLYGRAM) 1986

⏱ 124m (18)

Billed as a 'palimpsest' (look it up) of Umberto Eco's fat intellectual novel, this tells of a Sherlock Holmes-style monk investigating murder and mystery in an ancient monastery with the help of his Watsonish young assistant. The grubby fourteenth-century atmosphere is well handled, and Connery is at his best.

NELL ▢2

⭐ JODIE FOSTER, LIAM NEESON, NATASHA RICHARDSON

🎬 MICHAEL APTED

USA (POLYGRAM) 1994

⏱ 108m (12)

Dull tale of wild-child of the backwoods (Foster), who is rescued and romanced by well-meaning Neeson. The sort of 'worthy' pic that Hollywood loves, but on this occasion the ball has been well and truly fumbled.

OF MICE AND MEN ▢3

⭐ JOHN MALKOVICH, GARY SINISE, SHERILYN FENN, CASEY SIEMASZKO

🎬 GARY SINISE

USA (MGM/UA) 1992

⏱ 111m (PG)

Decent, if a little too subdued, version of John Steinbeck's story of two poor men in depression America: the childlike Lennie (John Malkovich) and his minder George (Sinise). Doesn't stand comparison with the 1939 version which featured Lon Chaney Jnr's classic turn as Lennie, but still worth renting if you're a fan of the story.

ON GOLDEN POND [3]

HENRY FONDA, KATHARINE HEPBURN, JANE FONDA, DABNEY COLEMAN

MARK RYDELL

USA (4-FRONT) 1981

109m (PG)

Henry Fonda's final movie sees him paired with daughter Jane in a story about a grump coming to terms with the onset of old age and the need to settle up emotional accounts with his wife and child. Oscars for Henry Fonda and Katharine Hepburn, and for Ernest Thompson for the screenplay based on his own play. Slush, but quality slush.

ON THE WATERFRONT [4]

MARLON BRANDO, LEE J COBB, ROD STEIGER, EVA MARIE SAINT, KARL MALDEN

ELIA KAZAN

USA (COLUMBIA TRISTAR) 1954 B&W

103m (PG)

Classic version of Budd Schulberg's novel of corruption among dockers and union officials. Brando is fabulous as the ex-fighter who finally decides to take a stand in the face of opposition from his brother (Steiger) and the boss (Cobb), both of whom give larger-than-life performances. Oscars: best picture, director, actor (Brando), supporting actress (Saint) and cinematography.

ONE FLEW OVER THE CUCKOO'S NEST [5]

JACK NICHOLSON, LOUISE FLETCHER, DANNY DeVITO, WILL SAMPSON, CHRISTOPHER LLOYD, BRAD DOURIF

MILOS FORMAN

USA (POLYGRAM) 1975

134m (18)

Marvellous film adaptation of Ken Kesey's novel about a rebel who elects to go to a mental hospital thinking it'll be a softer option than jail, with tragic consequences when his free-spirit nature squares up to a sadistic nurse. Nicholson and Fletcher are stunning as the rebel and the nurse, and the cast includes several actors who would go on to bigger things. Oscars: best actor (Nicholson), best actress (Fletcher), best picture, director and screenplay. Available on a two-for-one tape with the Nicholson vehicle *Carnal Knowledge*.

PACIFIC HEIGHTS 🎬3

⭐ MICHAEL KEATON, MELANIE GRIFFITH, MATTHEW MODINE, MAKO

🎬 JOHN SCHLESINGER

USA (FOX) 1990

⏱ 98m (15)

Another of the early splurge of thrillers where ordinary life choices prove deadly, (like *The Hand That Rocks The Cradle* (see page 267) or *Single White Female* (see page 275). Respected Brit Schlesinger tries to make something of this one, which is about a couple who take a tenant to make ends meet and (just about) live to regret it. Soon he's stopping the rent, gutting the place and (amazingly) getting the law on his side. It's all too plausible (at least until the main climax), with Keaton as the charming, loony scam artist, and liable to put you off being a landlord for life.

A PASSAGE TO INDIA 🎬3

⭐ ALEC GUINNESS, JUDY DAVIS, VICTOR BANERJEE, PEGGY ASHCROFT, NIGEL HAVERS

🎬 DAVID LEAN

UK (WARNER) 1984

⏱ 163m (PG)

Ashcroft is superb as the adventurous old lady who goes on a trip with her son's future wife to India, where she befriends a local doctor, only to end up accusing him of a sex attack. Oscars for best actress (Ashcroft) and best score (Maurice Jarre) can't hide the fact that this lovingly-shot version of the EM Forster novel is too slow and not one of Lean's best films. Compare it to *Lawrence Of Arabia* (see page 133) and you'll agree.

THE PEOPLE vs LARRY FLYNT 🎬4

⭐ WOODY HARRELSON, COURTNEY LOVE

🎬 MILOS FORMAN

USA (COLUMBIA TRISTAR) 1996

⏱ 124m (18)

Biopic of the publisher of politically-incorrect US porn mag *Hustler*, showing his battles with the courts, drugs and the aftermath of an assassination attempt that left him confined to a wheelchair and flirting with Christianity. If it wasn't true, the story would be deemed too far-fetched to film! Harrelson makes a likeable monster who says all he's guilty of is bad taste. The message is that free speech is for everybody, not just those we think are worthwhile.

CLASSIC 1000 VIDEOS

PERFORMANCE

JAMES FOX, MICK JAGGER, ANITA PALLENBERG, MICHELE BRETON, ANTHONY VALENTINE

NICOLAS ROEG, DONALD CAMMELL

UK (WARNER) 1970

102m (18)

Classic hallucinatory comment on 60s decadence, with Fox as gangster on the run seeking refuge with fading rock star Jagger in his weird, *ménage-à-trois* household. Directed by two cult moviemakers and full of great music and jarring editorial flourishes, this is a much-pondered and acclaimed piece. Pristine print, plus trailer. Widescreen.

PHILADELPHIA

TOM HANKS, DENZEL WASHINGTON, JASON ROBARDS, MARY STEENBURGEN, ANTONIO BANDERAS

JONATHAN DEMME

USA (COLUMBIA TRISTAR) 1994

125m (12)

Demme made this movie as a sop to gay activists who had been outraged by his portrayal of a queer killer in *The Silence Of The Lambs* (see page 275). The story is maudlin yet curiously effective and moving (largely due to Hanks), revolving around a gay lawyer who enlists homophobe Washington to sue the firm that fired him because he had AIDS. While his staunchly supportive parents don't ring true, Hanks carries the picture and won an Oscar for his performance.

POSTCARDS FROM THE EDGE

MERYL STREEP, SHIRLEY MACLAINE, DENNIS QUAID, GENE HACKMAN, RICHARD DREYFUSS

MIKE NICHOLS

USA (COLUMBIA TRISTAR) 1990

97m (15)

Funny drama about fraught relations beetween a movie star and her daughter, well acted by Oscar-nominated Streep with a fine support cast. Based on Carrie Fisher's autobiographical novel, inspired by her relationship with her own Hollywood parents, Debbie Reynolds and Eddie Fisher.

PRESUMED INNOCENT

HARRISON FORD, GRETA SCACCHI, RAUL JULIA, BRIAN DENNEHY

ALAN J PAKULA

USA (WARNER) 1990

121m (18)

Based on Scott Turow's hit novel, this is a competent and fairly engrossing drama about a respected lawyer (Ford) suspected of murdering an attractive female colleague. There are enough twists to sustain interest to the surprise ending. Quality formula.

DRAMA

PRICK UP YOUR EARS 🎬4

⭐ GARY OLDMAN, ALFRED MOLINA, VANESSA REDGRAVE, JULIE WALTERS, WALLACE SHAWN

🎬 STEPHEN FREARS

UK (VISION) 1987

⏱ 111m (18)

John Lahr's biography of gay playwright Joe Orton – murdered by his lover who then took his own life – is brought hilariously and lovingly to the screen via a scintillating script by Alan Bennett and stellar acting from Oldman and Molina as the doomed literary jesters. Great stuff.

QUIZ SHOW 🎬5

⭐ RALPH FIENNES, PAUL SCHOFIELD, JOHN TURTURRO

🎬 ROBERT REDFORD

USA (HOLLYWOOD) 1994

⏱ 128m (15)

True story of an academic who fell from grace when it was discovered he was being 'fed' the answers on a TV quiz of the 50s in order to keep the public tuning in to root for a popular winner. Fiennes is a revelation as the tempted innocent and Scofield nearly steals the pic as his deeply disappointed intellectual dad. May not sound much on paper but you'll be doing yourself a grievous wrong if you pass this one by. One of the best films of the 90s.

RAGING BULL 🎬4

⭐ ROBERT DE NIRO, CATHY MORIARTY, JOE PESCI, THERESA SALDANA

🎬 MARTIN SCORSESE

USA (WARNER) 1980 B&W

⏱ 124m (18)

Scorsese's tribute to the great boxing pix of yesteryear is based on the life of Jake La Motta, who crashed from ring hitter to nightclub owner. De Niro gained weight for the later stages of the film to show the angry man's decline, and rightly won an Oscar for his effort. Slow-motion vision and sound (plus colour effects) are employed in the gruelling fight scenes. The film also won an Oscar for editing.

RAIN MAN 🎬4

⭐ DUSTIN HOFFMAN, TOM CRUISE, VALERIA GOLINO, JACK MURDOCK

🎬 BARRY LEVINSON

USA (WARNER) 1988

⏱ 128m (15)

Attending his dad's funeral, Cruise finds he has an autistic sibling who has been left everything in his father's will. He hopes to get the estate made over to him but soon finds that his irritating brother is in many ways a brilliant man. Oscars: best film, director and screenplay and best actor (Hoffman). Note: according to some sources, the original print was 140m (136m on video), so check the box if this matters to you.

REMAINS OF THE DAY

EMMA THOMPSON, ANTHONY HOPKINS, JAMES FOX, CHRISTOPHER REEVE

JAMES IVORY

UK/USA (COLUMBIA TRISTAR) 1993

130m (U)

This elegant film of Kazuo Ishiguro's novel tells the story of a repressed English servant and his love. It was nominated for several Oscars – Emma Thompson won for best actress. Widescreen available.

REVERSAL OF FORTUNE

JEREMY IRONS, GLENN CLOSE, RON SILVER, ANNABELLA SCIORRA

BARBET SCHROEDER

USA (CINEMA CLUB V) 1990

106m (15)

Oscar-winning role for Irons as Claus von Bulow, the real-life aristocrat accused of attempting to kill his wife (and consigning her to a coma) with an injection of insulin. Von Bulow was freed by master lawyer Alan Dershowitz, on whose book the film is based (he also worked on the OJ Simpson case), but the movie manages to avoid libel while still leaving doubt in the viewer's mind about his guilt or innocence. Extremely entertaining even when you know the outcome.

ROCKY

SYLVESTER STALLONE, TALIA SHIRE, BURT YOUNG, BURGESS MEREDITH

JOHN G AVILDSEN

USA (WARNER) 1976

114m (PG)

Those who snigger at Stallone as if he was some incurably thick hunk are having to eat their words due to his impressive part in the recent *Copland* – but more mature observers never forgot that his leap to the big time began with his writing and starring in this moving little pic about a broken-down fighter's last chance at romance and fame. All the dreadful sequels notwithstanding, *Rocky* still stands up as a model of what Stallone can do on a good day. Oscars: best pic/ director/editing.

SCHINDLER'S LIST

LIAM NEESON, RALPH FIENNES, BEN KINGSLEY, CAROLINE GOODALL

STEPHEN SPIELBERG

USA (CIC) 1994 COL/B&W

197m (15)

Spielberg was finally accepted as a serious film director with this true story of Oskar Schindler, a Nazi speculator in Poland during World War Two who felt the tug of conscience and ended up using his money to save the Jewish slave

DRAMA

workers in his employ. Neeson is smooth as Schindler and Fiennes is unnerving as a concentration camp boss who likes nothing better than shooting a few inmates during pre-breakfast target practice. Though in monochrome, the film has some colour effects and a final colour coda which shows the actors who played the Jews accompanying their real-life models to Schindler's grave. Nominated for ten Oscars, it won only one, for best picture. Available in widescreen.

SE7EN

BRAD PITT, MORGAN FREEMAN, KEVIN SPACEY, GWYNETH PALTROW

DAVID FINCHER

USA (ENTERTAIMENT) 1994

126m   (18)

Icy tale of a serial killer working his way through murders based on the seven deadly sins. Super acting, but many found it too dark and disgusting. Some prints, including the one used for video mastering, were struck using a special recovered-silver process called CCE which makes even the dimmest scenes tolerable to the viewer. Widescreen.

SHAWSHANK REDEMPTION

TIM ROBBINS, MORGAN FREEMAN, JAMES WHITMORE

FRANK DARABONT

USA (GUILD) 1994

131m   (15)

Lengthy but always amusing version of a Stephen King novelette *(Rita Hayworth and the Shawshank Redemption)* about a wrongly imprisoned man who overcomes a brutal regime to change his own life and those of the men around him. It may not be a believable or serious prison picture, but it makes for a truly pleasurable and uplifting couple of hours. Nominated for a gallery of Oscars.

SHINE

GEOFFREY RUSH, ARMIN MUELLER-STAHL, LYNN REDGRAVE, JOHN GIELGUD

SCOTT HICKS

AUSTRALIA (BUENA VISTA) 1996

101m   (15)

Moving story of disturbed, brilliant pianist, David Helfgott, from sad childhood to the success and relative happiness of today. Excellent central performance by Rush as the adult Helfgott. Some critics carp about the pianist's odd style of playing, which often also involves singing or humming along to the music, but audiences have taken him (and the film) to their hearts. Oscar: best actor for Geoffrey Rush.

CLASSIC 1000 VIDEOS

SID AND NANCY [3]

GARY OLDMAN, CHLOE WEBB, DAVID HAYMAN, EDWARD TUDOR-POLE

ALEX COX

UK (BMG) 1986

109m (18)

Oldman is a reasonable facsimile of that most self-destructive member of the Sex Pistols, Sid Vicious, in this biopic about his doomed, heroin-fuelled romance with the disturbed American groupie Nancy Spungen. He was charged with murder when she was found stabbed to death beside him in their New York hotel room, but died of an overdose before he could be tried. Many who knew them doubt his guilt and there were rumours of a frame-up by unpaid drug dealers, but the film doesn't solve the mystery.

SMOKE [3]

HARVEY KEITEL, WILLIAM HURT, STOCKARD CHANNING, FOREST WHITAKER

WAYNE WANG

USA (HOLLYWOOD) 1995

108m (15)

Intricate tale of cigar-seller and pals scripted by Paul Auster. Harvey Keitel's cigar store is the focal point for various characters to meet, talk, interact and philosophise. Note: there is a companion piece of sorts, *Blue In The Face*, with Keitel, Lou Reed and others delivering monologues and stories direct to camera. Interesting.

THE SWEET SMELL OF SUCCESS [4]

BURT LANCASTER, TONY CURTIS, MARTIN MILNER, SUSAN HARRISON

ALEXANDER MacKENDRICK

USA (WARNER) 1957 B&W

96m (PG)

Brit MacKendrick helmed this sewer-level study of a pompous USA gossip columnist (Lancaster) and the PR who runs in his gilded heels (Curtis). Their grimy pact goes horribly awry when Curtis bungles his assignment to snuff the romance between Lancaster's sister and a young jazz musician. Sparklingly vicious script by Clifford Odets.

A TIME TO KILL [3]

MATTHEW McCONAUGHEY, SAMUEL L JACKSON, SANDRA BULLOCK, KEVIN SPACEY

JOEL SCHUMACHER

USA (WARNER) 1996

143m (15)

Author John Grisham criticised *Natural Born Killers* for inciting violence – strange, then, that this faithful retelling of his novel suggests that it's okay to spray bullets around if your child is raped, and that even if you cripple an innocent bystander, heck, he'll forgive you. And then you'll be let off anyway. We all might, of course, do what the 'hero' does here – but that's why trials are conducted by impartial juries. Manipulative but well made. Grisham really has a cheek.

DRAMA

THE TOWERING INFERNO

STEVE McQUEEN, PAUL NEWMAN, WILLIAM HOLDEN, FAYE DUNAWAY

JOHN GUILLERMIN, IRWIN ALLEN

USA (WARNER) 1974

158m (15)

Hacked together from a couple of forgettable pulp stories, this tale of a burning skyscraper set the style for disaster movies to come: endanger a lot of famous faces with big bangs while they bicker about love and survival. So-so.

TRAINSPOTTING

EWAN McGREGOR, EWAN BREMNER, JONNY LEE MILLER, ROBERT CARLYLE

DANNY BOYLE

SCOTLAND (POLYGRAM) 1995

93m (18)

This serio-comic version of Irvine Welsh's acclaimed novel of episodes in the lives of a group of Edinburgh heroin addicts may disgust some, but, bolstered by fantasy sequences (such as a headlong dive into 'the worst toilet in Scotland' in search of lost morphine suppositories) and a great music soundtrack, there's no denying its ingenuity and raw power. The title derives from drug deals being made in an old railway station, though this isn't made clear in the film version.

TREES LOUNGE

STEVE BUSCEMI, ANTHONY LA PAGLIA, CHLOE SEVIGNY

STEVE BUSCEMI

USA (BMG) 1996

91m (15)

Directorial stint for actor Buscemi, revolving around the clientèle of the cruddy bar of the title. No great story; just the pleasure of watching some fine thespians doing their stuff and making it all look deceptively easy. Catch it – it's worth watching.

THE USUAL SUSPECTS

GABRIEL BYRNE, STEPHEN BALDWIN, CHAZZ PALMINTERI, PETER POSTLETHWAITE, KEVIN SPACEY

BRYAN SINGER

USA (POLYGRAM) 1995

101m (18)

Byzantine complexity abounds in this story of crooks in search of the criminal mastermind who appears to be controlling their lives and dogging their steps. Subtle acting from a brilliant cast. Oscar: best screenplay. Available in widescreen, also in pan-scan on a two-for-one tape with *Mulholland Falls*.

WALL STREET [4]

MICHAEL DOUGLAS, CHARLIE SHEEN, DARYL HANNAH, TERENCE STAMP, SEAN YOUNG

OLIVER STONE

USA (FOX) 1987

120m (15)

One of Stone's more commercial efforts, this look at big-business corruption won an Oscar for Douglas as the devilish Gecko: a boss wearing loud braces who spouts sayings like, 'Greed is good' and 'Lunch is for wimps' as he seduces eager young Sheen into his wicked ways. See this before you get carried away by free windfall shares from your building society!

WHO'S AFRAID OF VIRGINIA WOOLF? [3]

ELIZABETH TAYLOR, RICHARD BURTON, SANDY DENNIS, GEORGE SEGAL

MIKE NICHOLS

USA (WARNER) 1966

124m (15)

Richard Albee's classic American play is presented here as a soused slanging match between sour, middle-aged college prof and his missus, conducted in front of an embarrassed younger couple. A bit of a downer, but both ladies won Oscars, as did Haskell Wexler's camera work, the sets and costumes. A Liz 'n' Dick *tour de force*, with the famous couple firing on all cylinders from start to finish.

WILDE [3]

STEPHEN FRY, JUDE LAW, VANESSA REDGRAVE, JENNIFER EHLE

BRIAN GILBERT

UK (POLYGRAM) 1997

112m (15)

Somewhat overpraised biopic on *fin de siècle* Irish writer Oscar Wilde and his fatal attraction for the handsome but petulant Lord Alfred Douglas, which led to his ruin and imprisonment for then-illegal sodomy. It has been said that the multi-talented Fry was born to play the role of Wilde but, though he looks the part, his delivery is altogether too languid when it should be vigorous and sharp. A lovely film to look at, with an imaginative opening set during Wilde's trip to the Wild West, it doesn't match up to the 60s pic *The Trials Of Oscar Wilde*, starring Peter Finch.

WITNESS [4]

HARRISON FORD, KELLY McGILLIS, LUKAS HAAS, DANNY GLOVER

PETER WEIR

USA (CIC) 1985

108m (15)

Detective Ford hides out in Amish religious town to protect the small boy who witnessed a murder while on a trip to the city. He also finds time to attempt a doomed romance with the lad's mother. An excellent blend of thoughtful drama and shoot-'em-up. Oscars for script and editing.

EPICS

Epics are notoriously hard to define: to some, an epic is any 70mm movie which is long enough to merit an intermission or a trip to the lavatory. *How The West Was Won* would probably, on that basis, qualify – if it wasn't already in the Westerns section. Ditto *2001*, which is in the Science Fiction chapter. To many, the only true epics were made in the USA and invariably set in ancient Rome. Others favour the old Italian sword-and-sandal pix (or 'peplums', from the short skirts worn by the male gladiator-types therein). I've tried to be fair to all these notions, but I accept that some may baulk at my inclusion of Shakespearean and other historical films. I've only included those works which seem to me to have a genuine epic quality to them. Sadly, however, the day of the real epic seems to have gone. The odd anomaly nothwithstanding (such as *Braveheart*), the classics of the genre were all produced in the 50s and 60s, when producers were showmen and budgets were for true spectacle, not just special effects explosions.

THE 10 COMMANDMENTS

CHARLTON HESTON, YUL BRYNNER, EDGAR G ROBINSON, ANNE BAXTER

CECIL B DeMILLE

USA (CIC) 1956

219m (U)

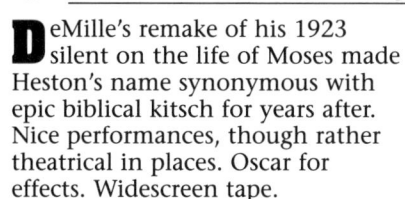

DeMille's remake of his 1923 silent on the life of Moses made Heston's name synonymous with epic biblical kitsch for years after. Nice performances, though rather theatrical in places. Oscar for effects. Widescreen tape.

55 DAYS AT PEKING

CHARLTON HESTON, DAVID NIVEN, AVA GARDNER, FLORA ROBSON

NICHOLAS RAY

USA/SPAIN (VIDEO COLLECTION) 1962

147m (U)

One of a series of epics made in the 60s in Europe by USA showman Sam Bronston, this is set in the period of the Chinese Boxer Rebellion of 1900. Gardner as a Russki Countess is stiff, but the rest of the cast are on top form, especially Robson as the wily Dowager Empress. Ray quit through ill health and the film was finished without him.

BARABBAS

ANTHONY QUINN, JACK PALANCE, SILVANO MANGANO, ARTHUR KENNEDY

RICHARD FLEISCHER

ITALY/USA (HOLLYWOOD COLLECTION) 1962

127m (PG)

'**B**egins where the other big ones leave off' – so ran the ads. True enough, as this is the story of the bandit the mob chose to free instead of Jesus – and an engrossing tale it is too, aided by a top-notch bit of scenery-chewing (overacting) from Quinn. Rather diminished in this pan-scan version.

THE BARBARIAN

JACK PALANCE, RICHARD WYLER, MILLY VITALE

RUDOLPH MATE

ITALY/USA (WARNER) 1961

84m (18)

Palance is good value, but this is pretty average sword-and-sandal territory.

BECKET

RICHARD BURTON, PETER O'TOOLE, DONALD WOLFIT, MARTITA HUNT

PETER GLENVILLE

UK (ODYSSEY) 1964

142m (PG)

Tale of the martyred archbishop (Burton) from his early days as chum-in-ribaldry of Henry II (O'Toole, a role he reprised in *The Lion In Winter*) to later life as a genuinely pious priest. Fab cast of UK thesps. The sets were re-used for the horror film classic *The Masque Of The Red Death*. The screenplay, based on Jean Anouilh's play, won an Oscar.

BEN-HUR

CHARLTON HESTON, STEPHEN BOYD, JACK HAWKINS, HUGH GRIFFITHS

WILLIAM WYLER

USA (MGM/UA) 1959

209m (PG)

This is *the* epic, for many. Woven around the story of Christ, it is a remake of the silent classic based on Lew Wallace's novel about a Jewish lord betrayed by his Roman friend – he survives slavery to return for vengeance via a stunningly lensed chariot race. Widescreen and boxed-set available. Won a staggering 11 Oscars, including best picture, direction, actor (Heston) and music.

EPICS

THE BIBLE

GEORGE C SCOTT, PETER O'TOOLE, AVA GARDNER, RICHARD HARRIS

JOHN HUSTON

ITALY/USA (FOX) 1966

155m (U)

Who knows what hubris led the great Huston to attempt this guff? It was soon apparent that this was a doomed enterprise and only early parts of the film were completed, necessitating a subtitle of *In The Beginning...* – which didn't save the pic from disaster, or from the joke, 'Never read the book. Saw the film, though!'. Cut from 174m.

BRAVEHEART

MEL GIBSON, PATRICK McGOOHAN

MEL GIBSON

USA/SCOTLAND (FOX) 1995

170m (15)

This Oscar-winning story of Scots patriot William Wallace's fight against English tyrant Edward Longshanks is a wonderful piece of film-making by star/director Gibson. Pity that foolish 'love interest' was added, but he doesn't shirk the hero's sad end – even if history is twisted to add glory. Although I'm a Scot, I'm no fan of the 'Scotia Nostra' of expats who revel in all things tartan – but this is such bravura stuff I'll make an exception. The Scottish baring behinds at the English army is a historical truth, as anyone who has been to a Scotland-England football match at Wembley can attest.

CALIGULA

MALCOLM McDOWELL, TERESA ANN SAVOY, PETER O'TOOLE, JOHN GIELGUD, HELEN MIRREN, LORI WAGNER

TINTO BRASS, BOB GUCCIONE

ITALY/USA (ELECTRIC) 1979

90/156m (18)

Much-maligned epic penned by Gore Vidal, about a mad, perverted Roman emperor. Financed by *Penthouse* magazine with no expense spared, and featuring amazing sets, the film was remarkable for being the first hard-core sex movie to star respected actors. The magazine's boss, Bob Guccione, shot more sex footage himself and added it to the director's work. The times given are for the shortest and longest versions available worldwide. The UK 90m tape is unlikely to include the incredible scenes of cruelty and orgies present in the print I saw in America on first release. There is rumoured to be a German cut with even more barbarous stuff, but I can't say if this is true. An experience, to say the least. Inspired several fake sequels, rip-offs, etc., including *Caligula II – The Untold Story*, in which a woman has sex with a horse!

125

CLASSIC 1000 VIDEOS

THE CHARGE OF THE LIGHT BRIGADE 🎬4

DAVID HEMMINGS, TREVOR HOWARD, HARRY ANDREWS, JOHN GIELGUD

TONY RICHARDSON

UK (CONNOISSEUR) 1968

⏱ 141m (PG)

Revisionist look at the legendary British heroic disaster. A political antidote to the Errol Flynn version, brimming with great UK acting talent. This tape is slightly cut by the censor due to alleged cruelty to horses – but not in the manner of *Caligula II* (see page 125).

CLEOPATRA 🎬4

ELIZABETH TAYLOR, RICHARD BURTON, REX HARRISON, GEORGE COLE

JOSEPH L MANKIEWICZ

USA (FOX) 1963

⏱ 248m (PG)

The film which ruined two marriages, got executives sacked and nearly destroyed a studio. Various stars and directors were on and off at various times, but it has to be said that in spite of the length this is a literate and engaging film and one can't imagine anyone being better than Taylor and Burton. Incredibly, the present four-hours-plus version is missing some two hours of original footage! The director intended to issue two films, but was overruled though there is a project underway with the aim of convincing the studio to restore the missing footage. Widescreen tape available. Oscars for cinematography, effects, art/sets, costumes. (And yes, that *is* George Cole who starred in TV's *Minder*!)

CROMWELL 🎬4

RICHARD HARRIS, ALEC GUINNESS, ROBERT MORLEY, DOROTHY TUTIN

KEN HUGHES

UK (VIDEO COLLECTION) 1970

⏱ 134m (PG)

Somewhat wordy tale of Cromwell and his politicking with King Charles, but it has the virtue of a solid lead performance by Harris to commend it. This is a cut version, apparently, also now in widescreen at full price from Columbia TriStar.

DANTON 🎬3

GERARD DEPARDIEU, PATRICE CHEREAU

ANDRZEJ WADJA

FRANCE/POLAND (ARTIFICIAL EYE) 1983

⏱ 130m (PG)

Danton versus Robespierre, 1793, political terror. An allegory for Poland? Perhaps, but it's too long and flabby to have any real impact. Depardieu is watchable as always, though. Talky is the word for it.

126

EPICS

DEMETRIUS AND THE GLADIATORS [3]

VICTOR MATURE, SUSAN HAYWARD, MICHAEL RENNIE

DELMER DAVES

USA (FOX) 1954

97m (PG)

Western ace Daves was perhaps not the man to helm this sequel to *The Robe* (see page 135), with crazed Caligula going spare in search of Christ's garment which he thinks is magically endowed. Widescreen tape available.

DOCTOR ZHIVAGO [4]

OMAR SHARIF, JULIE CHRISTIE, ROD STEIGER, ALEC GUINNESS

DAVID LEAN

UK (MGM/UA) 1965

185m (15)

Epic of romance and Russian revolution based on Boris Pasternak's novel. A love story with an end that would wrench the heart – if only one felt anything for the characters. Several Oscars, including the hit music score. Widescreen and boxed edition.

EL CID [4]

CHARLTON HESTON, SOPHIA LOREN, HERBERT LOM, HURD HATFIELD, JOHN FRASER

ANTHONY MANN

SPAIN/USA (VIDEO COLLECTION) 1961

172m (U)

This was one of several classic epics made in Spain in the 60s by Samuel Bronston, an American producer who used Europe as a base. Mann was equally adept at Westerns and epics, and he handles with style the story of the eleventh-century Spanish patriot's battles with the Moors. The love angle is laboured in the extreme, but the cast disport themselves well and the spectacle is tops. The newly restored print has not yet emerged on video.

EXCALIBUR [4]

NICOL WILLIAMSON, NIGEL TERRY, HELEN MIRREN, CHERIE LUNGHI

JOHN BOORMAN

UK/USA (WARNER) 1981

140m (15)

Boorman's dream of a definitive version of the Arthurian legends is realised here in a glowing, golden vision. Williamson is remarkable as a slightly seedy Merlin with an impenetrable accent. Lots of armour and blood and sunsets.

THE FALL OF THE ROMAN EMPIRE [4]

STEPHEN BOYD, SOPHIA LOREN, JAMES MASON, ALEC GUINNESS

ANTHONY MANN

SPAIN/USA (4-FRONT) 1964

172m (U)

Another Mann-Bronston film, severely underrated critically – perhaps due to the lack of a Heston for the lead. Some awesomely beautifully scenes of snowy landscapes and huge armies, but these will be diminished here due to a) incorrectly letterboxed print, and b) only cut versions being available. A sad fate for an interesting movie. Restoration, anyone?

FELLINI SATYRICON [3]

MARTIN POTTER, HIRAM KELLER, CAPUCINE

FEDERICO FELLINI

FRANCE/ITALY(WARNER) 1969

124m (18)

Fellini's interpretation of Petronius – sex shenanigans of a boy in ancient Rome amid a gallery of grotesques. Fun frolic.

A FISTFUL OF DYNAMITE [4]

JAMES COBURN, ROD STEIGER, ROMOLO VALLI

SERGIO LEONE

ITALY (WARNER) 1971

132m (18)

Original title in Italy was *Giu La Testa* (*Duck, You Sucker*), but in France it was *Once Upon A Time ... The Revolution* – a more pleasing notion, as the film is the centrepiece of a sort of trilogy with *Once Upon A Time In The West* and *... In America*. This was a problematic film: the stars went to Italy thinking they were to make a film with Leone, as original director Peter Bogdanovich's contract had fallen through. They arrived to find they were expected to work with an Italian protégé of the great man – and refused. Leone finally reluctantly helmed this tale of an IRA man (Coburn) and a bandit (Steiger) confronting political realities in the Mexican revolution, but the complete 158m widescreen cut is tragically rare. Worth seeing, however, even in this mutilated format. (Full print now on USA laserdisc.)

EPICS

FLAVIA THE HERETIC 🎬4

FLORINDA BALKAN, MARIA
CASARES, CLAUDIO CASSINELLI

GIANFRANCO MINGOZZI

ITALY/FRANCE (REDEMPTION) 1974

86m (18)

Naughty-nun flicks are a popular subgenre in Italy. This tells the story of an oppressed girl who sides with the invading infidels to take revenge on her Christian abusers – but in the end they prove treacherous, too. Widescreen. Shocking imagery, cut by the BBFC.

GANDHI 🎬4

BEN KINGSLEY, CANDICE BERGEN,
JOHN MILLS, MARTIN SHEEN,
JOHN GIELGUD

RICHARD ATTENBOROUGH

UK/INDIA (CINEMA CLUB V) 1982

188m (PG)

Eight Oscars for this epic account of Gandhi's life, including best actor for Kingsley and best picture. We follow Gandhi as he quits his life in the legal profession to fight for peace, becomes a world statesman and is finally martyred for his beliefs. There were complaints that only someone of pure Indian blood ought to have played the role, but one can't imagine Kingsley's work being bettered and this is surely the sort of racial pedantry which Gandhi himself would have deplored. Other Oscars include best director, screenplay, cinematography and costumes. Also available in widescreen on the Columbia Tristar label at a higher price.

GENGHIS KHAN 🎬3

OMAR SHARIF, STEPHEN BOYD,
JAMES MASON, ELI WALLACH

HENRY LEVIN

UK/USA/WEST GERMANY
(VIDEO COLLECTION) 1965

119m (PG)

Sprightly and spectacular story of a very bad barbarian who is painted as not-quite-so-bad in this version of his life. Mason has a bizarre cameo role as a Chinese diplomat. Boyd snarls superbly as evil Jamuga, GK's arch-enemy.

GONE WITH THE WIND 🎬5

CLARK GABLE, VIVIEN LEIGH,
OLIVIA DE HAVILLAND, LESLIE HOWARD

VICTOR FLEMING

USA (MGM/UA) 1939

240m (PG)

One of the most popular movies of all time, based on Margaret Mitchell's blockbuster novel of the old South and the American Civil War. Leigh was signed only after a massive search to find the right actress to play the heroine – and she won an Academy Award. The film has undergone negative-cleaning and other restoration techniques and looks great. Won eight Oscars in all, including best picture.

CLASSIC 1000 VIDEOS

GREYSTOKE

CHRISTOPHER LAMBERT, IAN HOLM, RALPH RICHARDSON, ANDIE McDOWELL

HUGH HUDSON

UK (WARNER) 1984

129m (PG)

This attempt at a literate version of the 'Tarzan' story is only partly a success as some of the scenes of the return to England, notably when Tarzan meets an ape in a cage and calls it 'Daddy' (!), aim for pathos but only provoke laughter. McDowell (as Jane) was dubbed by Glenn Close. A laudable, beautifully-shot try at doing something different with the Edgar Rice Burroughs hero. The print shown on TV is longer than the one released to UK cinemas.

HAMLET

MEL GIBSON, GLENN CLOSE, ALAN BATES, PAUL SCOFIELD

FRANCO ZEFIRELLI

USA (COLUMBIA TRISTAR) 1990

129m (PG)

Don't laugh – Mel holds his own as the troubled Dane in this epic version of Shakespeare's tragedy. At least, unlike so many other attempts, it doesn't come over as a filmed stage play. Full of sparks.

HENRY V

KENNETH BRANAGH, EMMA THOMPSON, DEREK JACOBI, PAUL SCOFIELD

KENNETH BRANAGH

UK (COLUMBIA TRISTAR) 1989

137m (PG)

Branagh does the impossible and outdoes Olivier's version of the Bard's play; curiously, both films are exactly the same length. If the previous film was taken as wartime patriotism, this one shows the horrors and muddy exhaustion of war. Every Brit actor of merit seems to be here. The definitive version – for now. Oscar for costumes.

HENRY VIII AND HIS SIX WIVES

KEITH MICHELL, CHARLOTTE RAMPLING, DONALD PLEASENCE

WARIS HUSSEIN

UK (WARNER) 1972

120m (PG)

Film remake of the TV show, which also starred Michell. Entertaining, but inevitably taken at a clip compared to the more leisurely BBC series.

EPICS

HERCULES CONQUERS ATLANTIS 🎬4

REG PARK, FAY SPAIN, ETTORE MANNI

VITTORIO COTTAFAVI

FRANCE/ITALY (PARAGON) 1961

80m (PG)

Classic peplum by master of the genre Cottafavi, starring Brit muscleman Park, the man who inspired Arnold Schwarzenegger to pump iron. Widescreen, though not indicated on box, as the ratio is somewhat cropped. It's possible this title may be (technically) deleted, but I've seen enough copies around in stores to indicate you should be able to find it if you look. Sadly, the same cannot be said of Mario Bava's companion piece, *Hercules In The Centre Of The Earth*, starring Park and Christopher Lee, which was available on the same label. If any reader knows where I can find a copy, I'll be eternally grateful!

THE HINDENBURG 🎬3

GEORGE C SCOTT, ANN BANCROFT, BURGESS MEREDITH

ROBERT WISE

USA (CIC) 1975

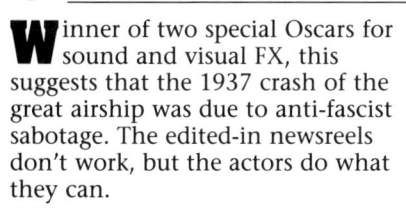

110m (PG)

Winner of two special Oscars for sound and visual FX, this suggests that the 1937 crash of the great airship was due to anti-fascist sabotage. The edited-in newsreels don't work, but the actors do what they can.

IVAN THE TERRIBLE 🎬4

NIKOLAI CHERKASSOV, SERAFIMA BIRMAN, ERIC PYRIEV

SERGI EISENSTEIN

USSR (TARTAN) 1944/6 B&W/COL

185m (PG)

Although the third section was never finished, the two completed parts of this Russian epic tell the story of the great tyrant's life from childhood to encroaching old age. A marvellous piece of cinema by any standard. Parts 1 and 2 are available separately. The third section was never completed due to Stalin's interference.

JUDGMENT AT NUREMBERG 🎬4

SPENCER TRACY, JUDY GARLAND, BURT LANCASTER, MONTGOMERY CLIFT

STANLEY KRAMER

USA (WARNER) 1961

178m (PG)

Movingly-acted story of the trials of Nazis at the end of World War Two. Lancaster is powerful as a man who realises the enormity of his crimes, while Clift as a witness gives a performance that is searing and painful to watch. The sad fact, though, is that at the same time as the Allies were trying big-name Nazis they were protecting others (scientists and so forth) who they felt were 'useful'. Never again? Don't you believe it. Two Oscars, one for Abby Mann's screenplay (based on his TV play), the other for Maximilian Schell as a defence lawyer.

KHARTOUM

CHARLTON HESTON, LAURENCE OLIVIER, RICHARD JOHNSON, RALPH RICHARDSON

BASIL DEARDEN

UK (WARNER) 1966

127m (PG)

Heston is magisterial as General Gordon, as is Olivier as the Mahdi. The two enemies never met, but for dramatic purposes such a scene is absolutely essential. Olivier is as over-the-top as Heston is restrained. Excellent. Pan-scan only.

KING DAVID

RICHARD GERE, EDWARD WOODWARD, ALICE KRIGE, DENIS QUILLEY

BRUCE BERESFORD

USA (CIC) 1985

109m (PG)

Tedious version of the life of the Jewish leader. Panned by the critics on release and rightly so. How this highly regarded director and cast managed to botch such a potentially exciting story is a mystery, but botch it they did. Avoid.

THE LAST EMPEROR

JOHN LONE, JOAN CHEN, PETER O'TOOLE, VICTOR WONG

BERNARDO BERTOLUCCI

ITALY/CHINA/UK (COLUMBIA TRISTAR) 1987

156m (15)

Winner of nine Oscars (including best picture), this is the epic account of Pu Yi, final emperor of China. We see him develop from child to playboy wastrel to just another face in the communist crowd. I know it got all those awards, but it's hard to see what got everyone so het up. Glacial and overlong.

THE LAST OF THE MOHICANS

DANIEL DAY-LEWIS, MADELEINE STOWE, MAURICE RÖEVES, WES STUDI

MICHAEL MANN

USA (WARNER) 1992

122m (PG)

Arousing version by Mann, one of the best action directors working today, of James Fenimore Cooper's 'Hawkeye' novel. Day-Lewis makes a good square-jawed hero, battling his arch-enemy (Studi) to save Stowe. An amazing-looking pic. Widescreen tape available. Thrilling battle sequences.

THE LAST TEMPTATION OF CHRIST

WILLEM DAFOE, HARVEY KEITEL, HARRY DEAN STANTON, DAVID BOWIE

MARTIN SCORSESE

USA (CIC) 1988

156m (18)

Ignore the ridiculous and unjustified controversy about this film of Nikos Kazantzakis's novel on the life of Jesus – there is little to shock here. Sadly, there's little to entertain, either. It's a worthy enough project, but stars and director seem just too 'modern' to be at home with this genre. Worth seeing, though, just to check out a good cast and to see what all the fuss was about.

LAWRENCE OF ARABIA

PETER O'TOOLE, OMAR SHARIF, ALEC GUINNESS, ANTHONY QUINN, JACK HAWKINS, CLAUDE RAINS, DONALD WOLFIT, ARTHUR KENNEDY, ANTHONY QUAYLE

DAVID LEAN

UK (COLUMBIA TRISTAR) 1962

217m (PG)

Winner of seven Oscars, and perhaps the best epic of all, Lean's 70mm story of TE Lawrence and the First World War desert campaign was nibbled away over the years. In 1989, restorer Robert Harris completed the near-impossible task of putting back the cuts, re-doing lost soundtrack, etc., and then allowed Lean to fine-tune the material. This version was issued on tape with musical overture and intermission music, properly letterboxed. Now Columbia have put out a '35th Anniversary' tape: the widescreen image is altered, the music has been cut, over two minutes of footage discovered by Harris are still not included, and Michael Wilson is denied his co-writing credit with Robert Bolt as per the Academy ruling, which ought to have been included in 1989 prints. Try to find the earlier widescreen tape if you can – you'll recognise it by the full-length drawing of O'Toole as Lawrence on the box. NB: After I alerted them, the company found the overture had been omitted in error. All praise to them for recalling the master tapes and fixing the problem. New copies are stickered 'Includes the overture' and the company *will* swap your old copies on request!

LORD JIM

PETER O'TOOLE, JAMES MASON, CURT JURGENS, ELI WALLACH, JACK HAWKINS

RICHARD BROOKS

UK (ENCORE) 1964

148m (PG)

Undervalued film version of Conrad tale. After *Lawrence*, O'Toole found himself temporarily typecast as an enigmatic, flawed anti-hero – but he makes a bloody good job of it in this outing. You can almost smell the jungle rot, the indecision and the fear before our boy redeems himself.

MACBETH [4]

JON FINCH, FRANCESCA ANNIS, MARTIN SHAW, JOHN STRIDE

ROMAN POLANSKI

UK (COLUMBIA TRISTAR) 1971

134m (15)

Gory, epic version of Shakespeare's tale of witchery and dark ambition. Plenty of weird scenes and outdoor footage, with not a whiff of theatrical boards, make this a better bet than most other movie versions. Sadly not out in widescreen.

A MAN FOR ALL SEASONS [4]

PAUL SCOFIELD, WENDY HILLER, ROBERT SHAW, LEO McKERN

FRED ZINNEMANN

UK (COLUMBIA TRISTAR) 1966

116m (U)

Beautifully acted version of Robert Bolt's play about the trial of Sir Thomas More, who would not swear an oath that the divorce and new marriage of Henry VIII was legal. Pretty unimpeachable, but I will now commit heresy and say that I find Charlton Heston's cable TV remake a far, far better thing. So throw me in the tower!

MUTINY ON THE BOUNTY [4]

MARLON BRANDO, TREVOR HOWARD, TARITA, RICHARD HARRIS

LEWIS MILESTONE

USA (MGM/UA) 1962

177m (15)

One of several versions of the classic tale of the shipboard revolt. Brando's accent is a hoot, but Trevor Howard is suitably vile. The trouble is that this reading of the events has since been shown to be rather skewed – apparently Cap'n Bligh was not as nasty as we've been led to believe. This is the most epic and visual version, for sure. Widescreen.

QUO VADIS [3]

ROBERT TAYLOR, DEBORAH KERR, PETER USTINOV, LEO GENN

MERVYN LEROY

USA (MGM/UA-WARNER) 1951

162m (PG)

Feisty, randy Roman (Taylor) gets converted to Christianity by his girlfriend (Kerr). Slow tosh, saved by the wonderfully camp capering of Ustinov as Nero. What a crooner!

EPICS

THE RIGHT STUFF 🎬4

⭐ SAM SHEPARD, DENNIS QUAID, SCOTT GLEN, ED HARRIS

🎬 PHILIP KAUFMAN

USA (WARNER) 1983

⏱ 185m   (15)

Epic recounting of the American space race and the astronauts involved, warts and all. Based on the book by Tom Wolfe. Gripping for the whole ride. Won Oscars for SFX, sound and others.

THE ROBE 🎬3

⭐ VICTOR MATURE, RICHARD BURTON, JEAN SIMMONS, MICHAEL RENNIE

🎬 HENRY KOSTER

USA (FOX) 1953

⏱ 129m   (U)

Christians and Romans fight over the robe of Jesus. Leaden, but won Oscars. See *Demetrius And The Gladiators* (page 127). Shot in widescreen and TV-shaped versions simultaneously.

SAMSON AND DELILAH 🎬4

⭐ VICTOR MATURE, HEDY LAMARR, ANGELA LANSBURY, GEORGE SANDERS

🎬 CECIL B DeMILLE

USA (CIC) 1949

⏱ 122m   (U)

Biblical tale of the man who needed no more than the jawbone of an ass to slay his enemies. He offends Delilah by preferring her sister, and so she contrives to chop off his strength-giving locks and have him enslaved by the ruling race to which she belongs. You know the rest. Recently remade for TV with Liz Hurley as Big D.

SOLOMON AND SHEBA 🎬3

⭐ YUL BRYNNER, GINA LOLLOBRIGIDA, GEORGE SANDERS

🎬 KING VIDOR

USA (MGM/UA-WARNER) 1959

⏱ 139m   (PG)

Filming on this biblical love story had to be scrapped when star Tyrone Power suddenly died of a heart attack, and the movie was begun again with Brynner replacing him. Was it worth it? Well, it looks pretty good, but it's really a very melodramatic trek to no great purpose.

135

SPARTACUS

KIRK DOUGLAS, LAURENCE OLIVIER, TONY CURTIS, JEAN SIMMONS, CHARLES LAUGHTON, PETER USTINOV, HERBERT LOM

STANLEY KUBRICK

USA (CIC) 1960

188m (PG)

Producer Douglas fired director Anthony Mann and brought in Kubrick to helm this film, based on Howard Fast's self-published novel about the illiterate slave who led a failed revolt against the might of ancient Rome. It won four Oscars (including a supporting actor award for Ustinov) but was cut by the censors. The full version, with some mild sex and violence restored, is now available on widescreen tape, with the overture music included. (For one scene the sound has been lost, so Tony Curtis had to re-do his dialogue with Sir Anthony Hopkins standing in for the late Laurence Olivier. The scene had been cut due to implied homosexual desire for Curtis's character by Olivier's.) A sombre epic – no happy endings here, but plenty of great performances.

THRONE OF BLOOD

TOSHIRO MIFUNE, ISUZU YAMADA, MINORU CHIAKI

AKIRA KUROSAWA

JAPAN (CONNOISSEUR) 1957 B&W

105m (PG)

Macbeth transposed to ancient Japan. More visual than literary, with eerie atmospherics and spirits calling for much blood. A bit of a masterwork, really.

THE VIKINGS

KIRK DOUGLAS, TONY CURTIS, JANET LEIGH, ERNEST BORGNINE

RICHARD FLEISCHER

USA (WARNER/ELITE) 1958

116m (PG)

Cruel story of two half-brothers who don't know they're related. One loses an eye, the other a hand, one's a Viking, the other a slave, but both are in love with the same girl. Lots of raping and pillaging and a real swashbuckling showdown. Produced by Douglas, this was a big hit and much imitated. Often shown on afternoon TV, with the brutality snipped out. Uncut on tape, and in widescreen.

EPICS

WAR AND PEACE 🎬 4

⭐ HENRY FONDA, AUDREY HEPBURN, HERBERT LOM, MEL FERRER

🎬 KING VIDOR

ITALY/USA (CIC/4-FRONT) 1956

⏱ 211m (U)

Even at this length, this is a condensed version of Tolstoy's epic story of war between France and Russia. The stars do their best but it doesn't fully come together.

WAR AND PEACE 🎬 4

⭐ LUDMILA SAVELYEVA, SERGEI BONDARCHUK, VASILY LANOVOI

🎬 SERGEI BONDARCHUK

USSR (TARTAN) 1967

⏱ 403m (PG)

Now, if you're truly a glutton for the real thing, try this! This three-tape boxed set is the longest version of this epic so far issued in the UK, costing more than the $40 million of *Cleopatra* (see page 126) and taking five years to film. S-l-o-w, but worthy, well-made and spectacular, it won the Oscar for best foreign picture - but that may have been an award for sheer tenacity of spirit. Seriously, this has got to be the ultimate version of Tolstoy's classic.

WATERLOO 🎬 3

⭐ ROD STEIGER, CHRISTOPHER PLUMMER, ORSON WELLES, JACK HAWKINS

🎬 SERGEI BONDARCHUK

ITALY/USSR (COLUMBIA TRISTAR) 1971

⏱ 128m (U)

Seriously confused (as you'd expect, with the film being cut to half the length of the original 240 m Russian print) movie version of Napoleon's big defeat at the hands of the Brits. Based on part of Tolstoy's novel *War and Peace* – does Bondarchuk never get tired of adapting this book, or what?

ZULU 🎬 5

⭐ STANLEY BAKER, MICHAEL CAINE, JACK HAWKINS, NIGEL GREEN

🎬 CY ENDFIELD

UK (CIC) 1963

⏱ 135m (PG)

Baker produced this story of a Brit regiment's fight against an overwhelming force of Zulu warriors at Rorke's Drift, a tiny outpost in Natal in 1879. The small band of men won several Victoria Crosses between them, and the tale has passed into legend. For all its imperialist, gung-ho gloss, the film tells a neat story. Well worth seeing. Available at last in a widescreen tape.

Family Entertainment

Films that young kids and parents can watch comfortably together are not as rare as moral campaigners would have us believe. Despite the howlings of American politicians about sex and violence on-screen, Hollywood knows that a solid family movie will always do good business in the multiplexes and on video. So here's a selection of the best, ranging from Disney classics right up to modern smashes such as *Free Willy* and *Home Alone*.

13 GHOSTS

CHARLES HERBERT, JO MORROW, MARTIN MILNER, MARGARET HAMILTON

WILLIAM CASTLE

USA (ENCORE) 1960 B&W

79m (PG)

Who'd-a-thunk-it? A horror film for kids! When I saw this back in 1960 in the cinema, viewing aids were handed out (a typical William Castle gimmick) so that when the ghosts appeared you could choose to see them or not, depending on which bit you looked through. Sadly, this trick has not been included on the video release, making the ghosts pretty hard to see and depriving the movie of its selling point. Still, it's fun – and it won't scare the toddlers.

THE ADVENTURES OF PINOCCHIO

MARTIN LANDAU, JONATHAN TAYLOR THOMAS, GENEVIEVE BUJOLD, UDO KIER, DAWN FRENCH

STEVE BARRON

UK/FRANCE/GERMANY/CZECH REPUBLIC/USA (POLYGRAM) 1996

94m (U)

Imaginative version of the classic tale of the puppet who comes to life. Brilliant cast and visuals make it worthy of comparison with the Disney cartoon (see page 58). Kids will love it and adults can enjoy the top cast hamming it up gloriously.

BABE

JAMES CROMWELL (AND LOTS OF TALKING ANIMALS!)

CHRIS NOONAN

USA (CIC) 1995

89m (U)

Charming fable about a runty piglet saved from the chopping block when it reveals an unprecedented talent for herding sheep. The mix of FX and real animals is wonderful, and the personalities given the various farmyard creatures all seem believable and never twee, in spite of the mid-Atlantic accent of the star piglet. The way the sheep huddle and bleat 'Wooo-ooolllf!' whenever the grumpy sheepdog hoves into view is especially sharp. A sardonic edge undercuts any tendency to sickliness, but kids'll still love it.

BIG

TOM HANKS, ELIZABETH PERKINS, ROBERT LOGGIA, JOHN HEARD

PENNY MARSHALL

USA (FOX) 1988

100m (PG)

Another variation on the common-or-garden body-swap theme, in which a kid achieves his wish of overnight adulthood. Works due to a typically smooth performance from Hanks. A good fun film.

BORN FREE

VIRGINIA MCKENNA, BILL TRAVERS, GEOFFREY KEEN, PETER LUKOYE

JAMES HILL

UK (CINEMA CLUB V) 1966

91m (U)

Joy Adamson's book about rearing and releasing lion cub Elsa back into the wild is the basis for this lovely hit movie, sure to please kids who care for animals. Oscars: score and song. Sequel: *Living Free*.

THE BOYS CLUB

CHRIS PENN, DOMINIC ZAMPROGNA, STUART STONE, DEVON ZAWA

JOHN FAWCETT

CANADA (HIGH FLIERS) 1996

87m (15)

One for older kids only. A man hiding out in the forest convinces local lads who find him that he's an undercover cop in this intriguing drama reminiscent of the old Hayley Mills vehicle *Whistle Down The Wind* (now a stage musical). Well acted, especially by Penn.

FAMILY ENTERTAINMENT

CHITTY CHITTY BANG BANG

DICK VAN DYKE, LIONEL JEFFRIES, SALLY ANN HOWES, BENNY HILL

KEN HUGHES

UK (WARNER) 1968

145m (U)

Based on Ian (James Bond) Fleming's fantasy about a flying car. Fun and a good cast will help keep the little ones amused for a time, but the excessive length defeats all the efforts in the end. The beauty of video is that at least you can watch it in segments!

DALEKS – INVASION EARTH 2150 AD

PETER CUSHING, JILL CURZON, RAY BROOKS, ANDREW KEIR

GORDON FLEMYNG

UK (WARNER/BEYONDVISION) 1966

84m (U)

When the roll of actors who've played Dr Who is called, people always forget the best of them: Peter Cushing. He never took the part on TV, but appeared in two spin-off movies made to cash in on the popularity of the villains of the series, the Daleks. This is the second and best of those films, and despite the cheap 'n' cheerful effects work it benefits from lush colour and a widescreen transfer to tape. Brats raised on digital animation may need reminding that this is an old film: please treat it gently!

DANNY THE CHAMPION OF THE WORLD

JEREMY IRONS, SAMUEL IRONS, ROBBIE COLTRANE, CYRIL CUSACK, MICHAEL HORDERN

GAVIN MILLAR

UK (BMG) 1989

99m (U)

Feisty Roald Dahl tale about a lad who fights off property developers intent on taking over the land where his caravan is parked. Kids never fail to respond to Dahl's stories of vile adults and resourceful sprogs. Try it.

DRAGONHEART

SEAN CONNERY (voice of Draco), DENNIS QUAID, DAVID THEWLIS

ROB COHEN

USA (CIC) 1996

103m (PG)

Massively entertaining fantasy film featuring an animated dragon named Draco, with the droll voice of Sean Connery. It forms a relationship with Quaid in a movie which rather lampoons the notion of the heroic days of yore. The effects are marvellous in the extreme, but never overwhelm the plot.

EDWARD SCISSORHANDS [4]

JOHNNY DEPP, VINCENT PRICE, WINONA RYDER, DIANNE WIEST

TIM BURTON

USA (FOX) 1990

98m (PG)

Typically dark modern myth from Burton. An elderly inventor dies before finishing work on his creation and as a result, the bizarre punk-like boy is left with scissors for hands. Rescued from the inventor's expressionist mansion by a kindly housewife and transplanted to suburbia, USA, the lad tries to make use of his mechanical mitts, but has trouble fitting in. Might be seen as a parable on how society treats those who are 'different' – the disabled, etc. – but all but the youngest kids ought to enjoy it even if they miss the message. Widescreen available.

FLY AWAY HOME [4]

ANNA PAQUIN, JEFF DANIELS, DANA DELANEY

CARROLL BALLARD

USA (COLUMBIA TRISTAR) 1996

103m (U)

Based on a true story, this is about a little girl who adopts a family of baby geese and helps them fly home. Manages to avoid ickyness and the Canada geese (so hated by London park keepers) prove themselves natural actors.

FREE WILLY [3]

JASON JAMES RICHTER, LORI PETTY, MICHAEL MADSEN, JAYNE ATKINSON

SIMON WINCER

USA (WARNER) 1993

112m (U)

While cleaning up his graffiti from a crappy seaquarium, a troubled lad makes pals with a (supposedly) untrainable Orca. Realising that the killer whale is miserable in captivity, the kid plots to arrange its freedom. As a movie it works – but ecologically-concerned punters should know that there was widespread outrage when it was found that there had been no happy ending for the creature in real life. Unlike the film's climax, 'Willy' was still living in crummy quarters. A lot of fuss was made about improving conditions – I confess I don't know the outcome, but I'd be very much surprised if the Orca is (as in the flick) out cruising the ocean with his 'pod'. Two sequels so far.

THE GOONIES [3]

COREY FELDMAN, JOSH BROLIN, SEAN AUSTIN, ROBERT DAVI

RICHARD DONNER

USA (WARNER) 1985

109m (PG)

Noisy movie about kids who find pirate treasure and do some community good at the same time. From the Steven Spielberg stable. A perennial hit with yobby lads of a certain age.

HOME ALONE [4]

MACAULAY CULKIN, JOE PESCI, DANIEL STERN, JOHN HEARD, JOHN CANDY

CHRIS COLUMBUS

USA (FOX) 1990

98m (PG)

Virtually a live action cartoon, with brattish Culkin using increasingly violent methods to repel the sleazy burglars trying to invade his house. Charmless, but fast-and-furious and a massive hit all over the globe.

HOME ALONE 2 [3]

MACAULAY CULKIN, JOE PESCI, DANIEL STERN, JOHN HEARD, CATHERINE O'HARA

CHRIS COLUMBUS

USA (FOX) 1992

120m (PG)

This time Culkin is left in the big city by his forgetful parents only to be menaced once more by the same thugs as in the first film, of which this is a virtual retread. Critics were concerned by the escalation of violence, which is never shown to have consequences. You'd be better off ignoring BBFC certifications and running *The Wild Bunch* (see page 309) for your children – at least it has the message that violent acts hurt people.

HOME ALONE 3 [2]

ALEX D LINZ, HAVILAND MORRIS

RAJA GOSNELL

USA (FOX) 1997

98m (PG)

Third in the brat-in-peril series. Macaulay Culkin was too old and his Dad too obnoxious for the studio execs to deal with, so Linz takes over. There's a new director too, but the package is as appetising as flat soda pop. I doubt if even the kids will find this acceptable entertainment.

HONEY, I BLEW UP THE KID

RICK MORANIS, LLOYD BRIDGES, MARCIA STRASSMAN, AMY O'NEILL

RANDAL KLEISER

USA (DISNEY) 1992

89m (U)

Sequel to *Honey, I Shrunk The Kids* (see below): this time Moranis enlarges his two-year-old son via a raygun and has mucho SFX fun trying to corral him and get him back to scale.

HONEY, I SHRUNK THE KIDS

RICK MORANIS, MATT FREWER, MARCIA STRASSMAN

JOE JOHNSTON

USA (DISNEY) 1989

101m (U)

Classic family entertainment in the Disney style of old: scientist Moranis reduces offspring and they face myriad dangers in their garden, which now seems like a jungle filled with most upsetting creatures! Huge hit. See above for the sequel – another has recently emerged. Superb FX.

IN SEARCH OF THE CASTAWAYS

HAYLEY MILLS, MAURICE CHEVALIER, WILFRED HYDE-WHITE, GEORGE SANDERS

ROBERT STEVENSON

UK/USA (DISNEY) 1961

94m (U)

This mesmerisingly spectacular film will be undoubtedly diminished on the small screen, but it remains a rollercoaster ride of hugely enjoyable proportions. The title pretty much gives away the plot which is based on the Jules Verne story *Captain Grant's Children*. Must-see: even the most sophisticated toddler will not remain unmoved.

INNERSPACE

DENNIS QUAID, MEG RYAN, MARTIN SHORT, KEVIN McCARTHY

JOE DANTE

USA (WARNER) 1987

116m (PG)

Spoof on the theme of *Fantastic Voyage* (see page 246), with a scientist accidentally injected into the bloodstream of someone after being miniaturised. Won a deserved Oscar for special effects. Available in widescreen.

FAMILY ENTERTAINMENT

JUMANJI

ROBIN WILLIAMS, JONATHAN HYDE, KIRSTEN DUNST, BRADLEY PIERCE

JOE JOHNSON

USA (COLUMBIA TRISTAR) 1995

104m (PG)

Demented story concerning a malevolent boardgame that conjures up all manner of traps and dangerous wildlife each time the dice are thrown. Williams is fine as a previous victim, unlocked from his purgatory when someone else continues his interrupted game of years before, but his normally ebullient style is swamped by the amazing FX work. Children will love it, though it might be too scary for little 'uns.

THE KARATE KID

RALPH MACCHIO, NORIYUKI 'PAT' MORITA, MARTIN KOVE, ELISABETH SHUE

JOHN G AVILDSEN

USA (COLUMBIA TRISTAR) 1984

122m (15)

The old theme of wimpy kid learning self-defence at the hands of a master and settling scores with his new skills. The '15' certificate seems harsh – the sequels (the first of which is available on a two-for-one tape with this film) were rated 'PG' which seems more apt.

MARY POPPINS

JULIE ANDREWS, DICK VAN DYKE, GLYNIS JOHNS, DAVID TOMLINSON

ROBERT STEVENSON

USA (DISNEY) 1964

133m (U)

Twee but amusing adaptation of PL Travers's novel about a magical nanny: Van Dyke has the worst cock-er-nee accent in movie history, but the film is lovely to look at and quite rightly won Oscars for music, special effects, etc. Best suited to younger kids.

MATILDA

MARA WILSON, DANNY DeVITO, RHEA PERLMAN, PAM FERRIS

DANNY DeVITO

USA (COLUMBIA TRISTAR) 1996

98m (PG)

Aka *Roald Dahl's Matilda*, this is the usual wonderful Dahl mix of swinish adults and smart kids: our heroine is a bright gal with dumb folks and a dastardly headmistress to contend with, and naturally she trashes the lot of 'em. DeVito handles the direction with aplomb as well as appearing as Matilda's awful dad. Grrrrreat stuff!

THE NEVERENDING STORY [4]

NOAH HATHAWAY, BARRETT OLIVER, PATRICIA HAYES, MOSES GUNN

WOLFGANG PETERSEN

UK/WEST GERMANY (WARNER) 1984

90m (U)

Michael Ende's novel is the source of this fable about a boy who runs from bullies into an old bookshop, where he finds a magic tome that catapults him into a delightful world so different from the one he knows. There is a sequel, and both are available together on a two-for-one tape if you prefer. Younger kids should love this movie.

THE PRINCESS BRIDE [5]

CARY ELWES, PETER FALK, MANDY PATINKIN, BILLY CRYSTAL

ROB REINER

USA (CINEMA CLUB V) 1987

94m (PG)

Lovely movie for adults and children alike, based on William Goldman's novel. Grouchy kid doesn't fancy having Gramps read him a soppy book about princesses and brides, but as the tale gets under way he (and we) soon warm to it. A knowing and delicious revamp of the swashbuckler genre, with some smashing cameos from fine performers. If you've never heard of this movie, let alone seen it, you are in for a treat.

THE RAILWAY CHILDREN [3]

JENNY AGUTTER, DINAH SHERIDAN, WILLIAM MERVYN, IAIN CUTHBERTSON

LIONEL JEFFRIES

UK (WARNER) 1970

104m (U)

E Nesbit novel provides the basis for a simple story of children's lives beside a railway as they wait to hear if their father is to be found guilty of spying. It's a pity Lionel Jeffries only directed a few films, especially on this showing.

RICHIE RICH [2]

MACAULAY CULKIN, JOHN LARROQUETTE, EDWARD HERRMANN, CHRISTINE EBERSOLE

DONALD PETRIE

USA (WARNER) 1994

94m (PG)

Another Culkin star vehicle, but it lacks the visceral comic feel of *Home Alone*. Here he plays a wealthy brat who saves his family from schemers. At least one critic lambasted the movie for portraying capitalists as good guys who care about the world. Still, fans of Culkin should enjoy it – if there are any left.

FAMILY ENTERTAINMENT

RING OF BRIGHT WATER

BILL TRAVERS, VIRGINIA McKENNA, PETER JEFFREY, RODDY McMILLAN

JACK COUFFER

UK (ODYSSEY) 1969

102m (U)

Making *Born Free* (see page 140) seems to have been a turning point in the lives of husband-and-wife Travers and McKenna – even when they weren't making films about wildlife, like this one, they were campaigning to help endangered species. This is an enjoyable, simple story about friendship between man and otter, based on Gavin Maxwell's book.

SWISS FAMILY ROBINSON

JOHN MILLS, DOROTHY McGUIRE, JAMES MacARTHUR, TOMMY KIRK

KEN ANNAKIN

USA (DISNEY) 1960

126m (U)

Second of three filmed versions of the Johann Wyss novel about a shipwrecked family, and definitely the best. Not really in the same class as *In Search Of The Castaways* (see page 144) but guaranteed to appease the younger thrill-seekers amongst you.

TEENAGE MUTANT NINJA TURTLES

ELIAS KOTEAS, JUDITH HOAG, JAMES SAITO, MICHAEL TURNEY

STEVE BARRON

USA (4-FRONT) 1990

87m (PG)

First of the films based on the cult comics about the martial arts amphibians. The fan mania seems to have died away, so kids may turn up their noses at this these days. Plus the BBFC are still obsessed with the supposed danger of martial arts weapons, and even though the turtle here was using a string of sausages instead of real rice-flails in a fight they insisted on cuts! Aren't you glad your kids are being protected from frankfurter brutality, folks?

THOSE MAGNIFICENT MEN IN THEIR FLYING MACHINES (Or How I Flew From London To Paris In 25 Hours And 11 Minutes)

ROBERT MORLEY, SARAH MILES, TERRY-THOMAS, STUART WHITMAN

KEN ANNAKIN

UK (FOX) 1965

138m (U)

Spiffingly silly-ass stuff about the early days of manned flight. The late Terry-Thomas all but steals the show as an out-and-out bounder up to all manner of dastardly deeds. In July 1998, director Annakin was given a retrospective at the NFT.

TIMEMASTER

JESSE CAMERON-GLICKENHAUS, NORIYUKI 'PAT' MORITA, DUNCAN REGEHR

JAMES GLICKENHAUS

USA (FIRST INDEPENDENT) 1995

95m (12)

Time lords play human pinball by zooming our young hero back-and-forth through the temporal streams in a daft but sporadically engrossing confection.

THE WIND IN THE WILLOWS

STEVE COOGAN, TERRY JONES, ERIC IDLE, STEPHEN FRY, JOHN CLEESE

TERRY JONES

UK (GUILD) 1996

87m (U)

Excellent version of the Kenneth Grahame classic about the adventures of Toad, Ratty, Mole and their neighbours. The only thing missing, as usual, is the yearning, mystical quality of the book – but that would (sadly) be lost on most kids anyway. It's certainly super to look at, at any rate.

GANGSTERS

Gangsters first became a staple of movies with the prohibition-inspired 1930s classics from Warner Brothers, starring the likes of Humphrey Bogart and James Cagney. They enjoyed something of a rebirth with the 1970s success of Francis Ford Coppola's *The Godfather*, and as I write the genre is taking off once again as young writers and directors follow the lead of Quentin Tarantino's violent classics *Reservoir Dogs* and *Pulp Fiction* with films such as the UK hit *Lock, Stock And Two Smoking Barrels*. While all of these forms, as well as offshoots such as black 'gangsta' movies and the dark, often literary-inspired *film noir* genre, are well covered on video, there is one area that remains in need of rediscovery: in the wake of the 'Godfather' films, Italian directors made a series of ultra-violent Mafia thrillers, often with middle-ranking American players in the lead. Few of these are available, yet a considerable cult has built up around them. To name just one, Damiano Damiani's *Confessions Of A Police Captain*, starring Martin Balsam, thoroughly deserves to be reissued on video. Any enterprising video tycoons reading this, please take note!

AL CAPONE [4]

ROD STEIGER, FAY SPAIN, NEHEMIAH PERSOFF, MARTIN BALSAM

RICHARD WILSON

USA (FOX) 1959 B&W

104m (15)

Violent, flashy account of the rise and fall of the legendary Chicago hoodlum. Steiger gives a showy, mesmerising performance in the lead, ably supported by a cast which includes Martin Balsam as a corrupt journalist in the gang lord's employ. Lensed by Lucien Ballard in sharp-edged, gritty monochrome. Remains one of the best Capone movies in spite of many later big-budget versions of the story.

THE ASPHALT JUNGLE [4]

STERLING HAYDEN, SAM JAFFE, JAMES WHITMORE, MARILYN MONROE

JOHN HUSTON

USA (MGM/UA) 1950 B&W

108m (PG)

Classic heist picture elevated by Huston's unsentimental direction and fine ensemble playing by a superb cast. Hayden is suitably tough, and Jaffe excels as the old-timer finally brought down through lingering too long over the suggestive dancing of a sexy teenager in a bar. A landmark film. There have been three remakes, none of which remotely approaches the intelligence and quality of the original.

BAD LIEUTENANT [5]

HARVEY KEITEL, ZOE LUND, FRANKIE THORN, ANTHONY RUGGIERO

ABEL FERRARA

USA (GUILD) 1992

96m (18)

Cult director Ferrara (who started out as the maker of banned horror flick *The Driller Killer*) relies on Keitel to carry this picture, which has little plot and is mainly a character study of a crooked, drugged-up cop as bad as the gangsters he chases. Keitel gives a stunning performance as the cop, investigating the rape of a nun and being so moved by her forgiveness of the rapists that he releases them, sealing his own fate at the same time. The UK video was heavily cut by the censor, and the music is not that on the cinema version due to legal problems. Nevertheless, worth watching in any form.

GANGSTERS

BILLY BATHGATE

DUSTIN HOFFMAN, NICOLE KIDMAN, BRUCE WILLIS, LOREN DEAN

ROBERT BENTON

USA (TOUCHSTONE) 1991

102m (15)

Based on a novel by EL Doctorow and scripted by Tom Stoppard, this is the story of an ambitious youngster who gets involved with gang-leader Dutch Schultz (Hoffman, on good form) and falls in love with his girlfriend. A fair story, with Willis excellent as a hit man, but at the end one is left feeling that the title character is one whom things simply happen around rather than to.

BLACK RAIN

MICHAEL DOUGLAS, ANDY GARCIA, KATE CAPSHAW, KEN TAKAKURA

RIDLEY SCOTT

USA (CIC) 1989

120m (18)

Two cops deliver a Japanese hoodlum back to his homeland from the USA, but lose him at the last moment. Determined to make good, they stay on in Japan and get involved in more murky matters than they can handle. The mood of cultural dislocation between the Yanks and the Japs is well handled, and Douglas is believable as the mildly corrupt copper who returns to the straight-and-narrow after his partner is killed. Not one of Ridley Scott's best, but it looks nice and rattles along at a cracking pace. Oscar: sound.

BONNIE AND CLYDE

WARREN BEATTY, FAYE DUNAWAY, GENE HACKMAN, MICHAEL J POLLARD, ESTELLE PARSONS

ARTHUR PENN

USA (WARNER) 1967

106m (18)

Hugely influential film about two real-life 30s American rural thugs and their gang. The acting is fine, but the two stars are much too glamorous and in spite of the gory finale it tends to make violence seem exciting and fun at times. Oscars: best supporting actress (Parsons) and cinematography. Available in boxed set with book.

BRING ME THE HEAD OF ALFREDO GARCIA

WARREN OATES, ISELA VEGA, GIG YOUNG, KRIS KRISTOFFERSON

SAM PECKINPAH

USA (WARNER) 1974

108m (18)

A sleazy piano player in a Mexican bar learns that a local gang lord wants the head of the man who impregnated his daughter. Knowing the man is already dead, he accepts the contract and plans to simply dig up the grave and claim his prize. Things are not that simple, however. This nihilistic classic was initially seen as a decline for Peckinpah, and has only lately been given its critical due. The title has become a byword for nastiness in film and has been much parodied: *Bring Me The Head Of Dobie Gillis*, *Bring Me The Head Of Light Entertainment*, etc.

151

CLASSIC 1000 VIDEOS

BRONX WARRIORS [4]

VIC MORROW, MARK GREGORY, FRED WILLIAMSON, CHRISTOPHER CONNOLLY

ENZO G CASTELLARI

ITALY/USA (UNIQUE) 1982

82m (18)

Futuristic tosh set in a Manhattan which has become little more than territory fought over by rival garishly-clad youth gangs. A box-office hit and a major title in the early days of home video, it inspired sequels and rip-offs. Cut, but in widescreen format.

BUGSY [3]

WARREN BEATTY, ANNETTE BENING, HARVEY KEITEL, BEN KINGSLEY, JOE MANTEGNA

BARRY LEVINSON

USA (20/20) 1991

131m (18)

Star-studded story of the gangster who built Las Vagas into a gambling paradise. The actors are all fine but it seems too polished and glitzy for a mob story. Bugsy Siegel was a nasty piece of work, but he rates a better pic than this. Penned by James Toback, who has made some interesting films in his time. This isn't comparable with his low-budget Harvey Keitel vehicle *Fingers*, an amazing gangster pic about a pianist who doubles as a thug. Now *that* should be on tape.

CAPONE [3]

BEN GAZZARA, HARRY GUARDINO, JOHN CASSAVETES, SYLVESTER STALLONE

STEVE CARVER

USA (FOX) 1975

97m (18)

A gutsy Roger Corman production utilising stock footage from his own Capone effort *The St Valentine's Day Massacre*. Surprisingly top-notch cast for a cheapjack movie. Gazzara can't dispel memories of Rod Steiger's interpretation of Capone, however.

GANGSTERS

CARLITO'S WAY [5]

AL PACINO, SEAN PENN, PENELOPE ANN MILLER, VIGGO MORTENSEN

BRIAN DE PALMA

USA (CIC) 1993

145m (18)

De Palma's best gangland epic, on a par with his *Scarface* (also with Pacino, see page 163) and miles better than the over-polished *The Untouchables*, see page 165). Pacino is a heroin dealer who, released via a technicality found by his lawyer, resolves to go straight and wed the girl of his dreams – but the old life will not allow him to let go. Penn is marvellous as the crooked lawyer who both saves our anti-hero from jail and then seals his fate. It's truly remarkable, in the middle of today's war on drugs (which officials privately admit cannot be won as long as people want to take them), to see a mainstream Hollywood picture that accepts that someone who once dealt heroin is not necessarily a demon. Available in a perfect widescreen format.

CASINO [4]

ROBERT DE NIRO, SHARON STONE, JOE PESCI, JAMES WOODS

MARTIN SCORSESE

USA (CIC) 1995

178m (18)

Scorsese used to seem incapable of making a bad movie, but, in spite of a stellar cast and a gleaming credits sequence by the late Saul Bass, this tale of a mob-controlled gambling house feels rather like a re-run of the director's superior *Goodfellas* (see page 154). Widescreen available.

COLORS [5]

SEAN PENN, ROBERT DUVALL, MARIA CONCHITA ALONSO, RANDY BROOKS

DENNIS HOPPER

USA (4-FRONT) 1988

121m (18)

As Hopper is one of my heroes, my proudest moment during my tenure as *Penthouse* film critic was when I walked into Leicester Square tube station to see the walls plastered with posters for this flick – all bearing my name and the quote, 'A must-see film'. And so it is. The story is of an old cop (Duvall) and his young sidekick (Penn) patrolling the no-go areas of Los Angeles where gun-toting youth gangs rule the streets. The actors are entirely believable, and Hopper directed the film in real tough areas with real gangster extras. Fabulous. Apparently, this version has some footage not in the original cinema release.

153

THE CRIMINAL 🎬[4]

STANLEY BAKER, SAM WANAMAKER, MARGIT SAAD, PATRICK MAGEE

JOSEPH LOSEY

UK (LUMIERE) 1960 B&W

97m (PG)

Made in England by then-blacklisted American director Losey, this tough portrait of a career criminal who accepts jail as an occupational hazard is exciting yet grim, with a downbeat ending. Baker is all too real as the villain (in real life he was a pal of the Krays) and Magee is chilling as a cruel prison officer. A Brit crime classic.

DONNIE BRASCO 🎬[4]

AL PACINO, JOHNNY DEPP, MICHAEL MADSEN, ANNE HECHE

MIKE NEWELL

USA (ENTERTAINMENT) 1997

126m (18)

True story of an undercover cop who infiltrates a Mafia crew by befriending a lower-echelon hoodlum. An engrossing but somewhat downbeat tale from British director Newell, which nevertheless rated highly with critics. Pacino does well enough as the betrayed crook, but Depp seems a bit too young and pretty to be a top-rank copper. Give it a whirl.

FORCE OF EVIL 🎬[4]

JOHN GARFIELD, THOMAS GOMEZ, BEATRICE PARSON

ABRAHAM POLONSKY

USA (2ND SIGHT) 1948 B&W

78m (PG)

Moody piece about two brothers involved in the numbers racket, the illegal lottery run by the Mob. Lots of symbolism and allegorical flourishes don't overwhelm Garfield's powerful performance. A key film of the 1940s, its doomy feel no doubt influenced by the director's persecution in the McCarthy anti-communist witch-hunts.

GET SHORTY 🎬[4]

JOHN TRAVOLTA, GENE HACKMAN, RENE RUSSO, DANNY DE VITO

BARRY SONNENFELD

USA (MGM/UA) 1995

105m (15)

Based on Elmore Leonard's novel inspired by a real-life debt collector, this was Travolta's first big hit subsequent to his rediscovery at the hands of Quentin Tarantino in *Pulp Fiction* (see page 163). Travelling to Hollywood to get debts owed by director Hackman, Travolta gets involved in film-producing and other less salubrious pastimes. (Then again, film-producing ain't all that salubrious when you come to think of it.) Witty, sharp, and the cast look like they're having a ball. You will too.

THE GETAWAY

STEVE McQUEEN, ALI MacGRAW, BEN JOHNSON, SLIM PICKENS

SAM PECKINPAH

USA (WARNER) 1972

117m (18)

Scripted by Walter Hill from Jim Thompson's novel, this was a star vehicle with Peckinpah under no illusions but that he was simply a hired hand. Nevertheless, he still managed to inject his trademark concerns about loyalty and violence into the story about an ex-con and his wife. Even MacGraw, a woman who couldn't act if a gun was put to her head, can't slow the pace. Now available in widescreen. There was a recent remake, which you ought to avoid at all costs.

THE GODFATHER

MARLON BRANDO, AL PACINO, DIANE KEATON, JAMES CAAN, ROBERT DUVALL

FRANCIS FORD COPPOLA

USA (CIC) 1971

167m (18)

Classic Mafia dynastic epic based on the Mario Puzo novel, with Brando as the old boss under attack and Pacino as the 'clean' son forced to helm the family business. Oozes quality from every frame. Oscars for best picture, best actor (Brando) and best screenplay. Essential viewing.

THE GODFATHER PART II

AL PACINO, ROBERT DE NIRO, ROBERT DUVALL, DIANE KEATON

FRANCIS FORD COPPOLA

USA (CIC) 1974

190m (18)

That rarity, a sequel that improves on the original. The story is split between the early adventures of the Brando character (played here as a young man by Robert De Niro) and the further trials of Pacino as the new Don. Coppola has reworked the two films several times, adding extra footage, for video packages and TV airings. This film won Oscars for best picture, director, supporting actor (De Niro) and more.

THE GODFATHER PART III

AL PACINO, DIANE KEATON, ANDY GARCIA, ELI WALLACH, SOFIA COPPOLA

FRANCIS FORD COPPOLA

USA (CIC) 1990

163m (15)

This third part of the saga sees Pacino as an old guy trying to hold on to his empire. Most critics praised it, but to me it has a false feel, as if Coppola has lost the thread. Pacino is unconvincing as an aged man, Coppola's nepotism in casting his own daughter comes adrift as she simply cannot act, and the plot involving corrupt Vatican officials seems forced rather than an organic follow-on from previous events. The video apparently is a director's cut which includes nine minutes of scenes which were cut from the cinema release.

GOODFELLAS

RAY LIOTTA, ROBERT DE NIRO, JOE PESCI, LORRAINE BRACCO, PAUL SORVINO

MARTIN SCORSESE

USA (WARNER) 1990

139m (18)

Brutal true story of Henry Hill, a kid who joined the local Mob as a teenager, progressed to bigger things and ended up informing on his chums when caught dealing drugs. Scorsese dazzles with every cinematic trick in the book (including having the protagonist descend from the witness stand in court and directly address the cinema audience), and sets scenes of the most awful cruelty against a background of nostalgic rock songs. It's really an actors' film, though, with sterling work from all concerned, especially Liotta as Hill, De Niro as his thieving mentor and Pesci (who won an Oscar) as a cheerful psychopath.

GOTTI

ARMAND ASSANTE, ANTHONY QUINN, WILLIAM FORSYTHE

ROBERT HARMON

USA (HIGH FLIERS) 1996

117m (18)

Superior made-for-TV film about the downfall of John Gotti, USA Mafia boss once dubbed 'the teflon don' because no charge could stick to him. Award-winning star role for Assante, with top support from Quinn and Forsythe. Engrossing.

THE GRIFTERS

JOHN CUSACK, ANGELICA HUSTON, ANNETTE BENING, PAT HINGLE

STEPHEN FREARS

USA (POLYGRAM) 1990

105m (18)

Brit Frears attempts to interpret a Jim Thompson story of related professional criminals, but though widely praised I'm afraid it feels rather cold and empty to me. Pretty bleak and largely unsatisfying stuff, though the performers are all decent enough.

HEAT

ROBERT DE NIRO, AL PACINO, VAL KILMER, JON VOIGHT

MICHAEL MANN

USA (WARNER) 1995

171m (15)

This story of a top cop and head gangster stalking each other is unique for being the first time De Niro and Pacino acted together – the scene where they meet and discuss their lives is a tour de force of eyeball-to-eyeball acting genius. Mann is a master of the action film, and this is one of his best. The film is, interestingly enough, a large-scale reworking of a movie he made for TV, known variously as *LA Takedown* (see page 158), *LA Crimewave* and *Made In LA*, with lesser-known stars.

KEY LARGO

HUMPHREY BOGART, EDGAR G ROBINSON, LAUREN BACALL, LIONEL BARRYMORE, CLAIRE TREVOR

JOHN HUSTON

USA (WARNER) 1948 B&W

97m (??)

Thriller about a gangster hiding out during a storm in the Florida Keys and making life tough for the occupants of the sleazy hotel he picks as a bolthole. A bona fide legendary flick. Trevor won an Oscar for best supporting actress as a drunken gangster's moll.

THE KILLING OF A CHINESE BOOKIE

BEN GAZZARA, TIM CAREY, SEYMOUR CASSEL, ALICE FRIEDLAND

JOHN CASSAVETES

USA (ELECTRIC) 1976

113m (15)

As well as being a respected actor, Cassavetes was also a highly regarded independent director. This is a long, character-led story about a nightclub owner told the only way out of his big debt to the Mob is to shoot an aged Chinese bookmaker for them. It has an improvised feel and a seedy reality about it that make it a compelling experience. Apparently there are two different versions of the film in existence as the director re-edited the material at some point, but only this one is out on tape.

KING OF NEW YORK [4]

⭐ CHRISTOPHER WALKEN, LARRY FISHBURNE, WESLEY SNIPES, STEVE BUSCEMI

🎬 ABEL FERRARA

ITALY/USA (VIDEO COLLECTION) 1990

⏱ 100m (18)

The sinister, distracted Walken is super-cool in Ferrara's story of a drug lord, who is released from jail and plans to re-establish his supremacy in the narcotics trade in order to finance a hospital for the poor. Improbable, but amid the sex and violence Ferrara is asking the question: 'How do you decide who is good and who is evil?' At least, I think that's what it's about. Uncut. Not in widescreen format at present, but deserves to be as the present print is cropped on all four sides of the image.

THE KRAYS [3]

⭐ GARY KEMP, MARTIN KEMP, BILLIE WHITELAW, STEVEN BERKOFF

🎬 PETER MEDAK

UK (POLYGRAM) 1989

⏱ 115m (18)

The makers of this biopic on the notorious rulers of 60s London gangland claim they went out of their way not to glamorise the twins – but getting twin pop stars (ex-members of Spandau Ballet) to play the gangsters hardly supports the notion, especially as the pair are far more handsome than the thugs they're portraying. Nasty and violent, but saved somewhat by Jimmy Jewel as the pair's grandpa and Steven Berkoff as victim George Cornell. Billie Whitelaw pouts a lot as the matriarch of the clan, but one suspects that the real Violet Kray was a much nicer and far more interesting lady than she's portrayed as here. The film was mooted for some time before it was actually filmed, and the same seems to be happening with a proposed sequel. Available by itself or on a two-for-one tape with *McVicar* (see page 160).

LA TAKEDOWN [3]

⭐ SCOTT PLANK, ALEX McARTHUR, ELY POUGET

🎬 MICHAEL MANN

USA (MIA) 1989

⏱ 95m (15)

Interesting to see this early version of the film Mann later re-made as a big picture with De Niro and Pacino under the title *Heat* (see page 157), but the actors here are just too young for the parts. When one actor threatens 'I'll blow you outta your socks!' he is so wimpy in his delivery that it sounds like he's suggesting nothing more violent than handbags at ten paces. This is basically a sketch for *Heat*, of interest to scholars of Mann's filmic techniques but not a patch on the later film.

LAST MAN STANDING 4

BRUCE WILLIS, BRUCE DERN, CHRISTOPHER WALKEN, ALEXANDRA POWERS

WALTER HILL

USA (ENTERTAINMENT) 1996

101m (18)

Latest version of a movie that has been a samurai pic (*Yojimbo*), then a Western (*A Fistful Of Dollars*, see page 297) – and now a gangster film, but the story is basically the same: a stranger arrives in a town ruled by two gangs, and proceeds to sell his gun to both sides. Clint Eastwood's 'Man with No Name' is now the equally anonymous 'John Smith' (Willis), but he's still after a fistful of cash. Christopher Walken is creepy as an evil killer. Even if you've seen the other versions, this is first rate fun. Widescreen available.

LE SAMOURAI 4

ALAIN DELON, NATHALIE DELON, FRANCOIS PERIER, CATHY ROSIER

JEAN-PIERRE MELVILLE

FRANCE (ARTIFICIAL EYE) 1967

95m (PG)

A classic, stripped-to-essentials story of a hitman by the great Melville, with icy Alain Delon living in a bare apartment with only a caged bird for company. Caught between pursuing *flics* and treacherous hoods with only his girl on his side, Delon is impassive and menacing. In the correct ratio and subtitled.

LEPKE 3

TONY CURTIS, ANJANETTE COMER, MICHAEL CALLAN, MILTON BERLE

MENAHEM GOLAN

USA (WARNER) 1974

105m (18)

Cheap pic about the man who started Murder Incorporated. Curtis tries hard but he is simply too old for the scenes where Lepke is shown as a promising young thug. Directed sluggishly by Golan, who later became one of the men behind Cannon Films, purveyors of much cinematic drivel.

LITTLE CAESAR 4

EDGAR G ROBINSON, DOUGLAS FAIRBANKS Jnr, SIDNEY BLACKMER, GLENDA FARRELL

MERVYN LE ROY

USA (WARNER) 1930 B&W

76m (PG)

Stonking tale, loosely based on the rise and fall of Al Capone. Only the names have been changed to protect the guilty. An absolute stone classic, though it may look rather theatrical and dated to today's younger viewers.

McVICAR

ROGER DALTREY, ADAM FAITH, GEORGINA HALE, STEVEN BERKOFF

TOM CLEGG

UK (POLYGRAM) 1980

107m (18)

Biog of McVicar, a hardened British criminal who studied in prison and is now a respected journalist. Gimmicky, with Who vocalist Daltry's sloppy music heavily featured. And if you doubt my charge of frivolity, I can tell you that the original preview for journos had bread and water instead of the usual refreshments! With another ex-singer, Adam Faith, featured, it's perhaps suitable that this is on a two-for-one tape with *The Krays* (see page 158), starring ex-members of Spandau Ballet. No glamorising of crime of course, oh no indeed! Also available by itself on 4-Front.

MEAN STREETS

HARVEY KEITEL, ROBERT DE NIRO, DAVID PROVAL, AMY ROBINSON

MARTIN SCORSESE

USA (ELECTRIC) 1973

108m (18)

Early hit from Scorsese, with Keitel as a young 'connected' chap torn between loyalty to his Mafia family, love for his girl and the need to help his feckless, troublesome pal Johnny Boy (De Niro). His indecision finally results in tragedy. All the Scorsese stylistic trademarks are here, set to the usual nostalgic pop beat. Invigorating.

MEN OF RESPECT

ROB STEIGER, JOHN TURTURRO, PETER BOYLE, DENNIS FARINA, STANLEY TUCCI

WILLIAM REILLY

USA (CINEMA CLUB V) 1990

109m (18)

In essence, this is *Macbeth* updated to modern Mafia environment. Doesn't come off in spite of a respectable cast, including the excellent Tucci, so memorable as the sybaritic tycoon in TV's *Murder One*.

MIAMI BLUES

FRED WARD, ALEC BALDWIN, JENNIFER JASON LEIGH, CHARLES NAPIER

GEORGE ARMITAGE

USA (VISION) 1989

92m (18)

Bizarre crime thriller based on one of the late Charles Willeford's novels about sleazy cop Hoke Mosely. Ward makes a great Mosely, out to catch a just-freed psycho who has stolen his false teeth and badge. Shame it wasn't a hit, as it would be nice to see Ward reprise the role.

GANGSTERS

MILLER'S CROSSING

GABRIEL BYRNE, JOHN TURTURRO, ALBERT FINNEY, FRANCES McDORMAND

JOEL COEN

USA (FOX) 1990

110m (18)

Classy gangsterism with Gabriel Byrne oozing charisma, but it's not in the same league as Coen's later thriller *Fargo* (see page 104). Shot by Barry Sonnenfeld, who went on to direct *Get Shorty* (see page 154).

MOBSTERS

CHRISTIAN SLATER, PATRICK DEMPSEY, F MURRAY ABRAHAM, MICHAEL GAMBON, ANTHONY QUINN

MICHAEL KARBELNIKOFF

USA (CIC) 1991

116m (18)

A Brat Pack-type gangster film. Just as the 'Young Guns' movies portrayed cowpoke-era baddies as fresh-faced kids, this tries to do the same for Lucky Luciano and cronies in 20s New York. It doesn't always work but hardly deserves the slagging it got on first release. The violent story is attention-holding, and Quinn and Gambon excel as old hoods reluctant to give up their empires.

NEW JACK CITY

WESLEY SNIPES, ICE-T, MARIO VAN PEEBLES, JUDD NELSON

MARIO VAN PEEBLES

USA (WARNER) 1991

96m (18)

Black hoods take over the city's drugs trade in this amoral, violent thriller. Enjoyable, but the sort of movie that community leaders are always complaining about for giving negative images of black kids. The trouble is, it was made by black film-makers.

ONCE UPON A TIME IN AMERICA

ROBERT DE NIRO, JAMES WOODS, ELIZABETH McGOVERN, BURT YOUNG

SERGIO LEONE

USA (WARNER) 1984

228m (18)

The third Leone film with 'Once Upon A Time ...' in the title, and his final picture. It's a complex, multi-flashback/forward structured epic about a bunch of gangsters and their lives together. Great score by Ennio Morricone. Cut to 144m in the USA and re-edited into a dull, linear form, but public demand led to this long version being issued. Apparently there is a 250m European print but it is not available on tape. A moving piece of cinema from a film-making genius.

ORIGINAL GANGSTAS 🎬3

⭐ FRED WILLIAMSON, JIM BROWN, PAM GRIER, RON O'NEAL, RICHARD ROUNDTREE

🎬 LARRY COHEN

USA (FIRST INDEPENDENT) 1996

⏱ 99m (18)

Cult director Cohen brings together the stars of the 'blaxploitation' movies of the 70s for a sort of class reunion, which is apt as he made his name in the genre. A deliberate 'B' movie, with the old-timers fighting the new breed of Uzi-toting twerps. Wild fun.

THE PUBLIC ENEMY 🎬4

⭐ JAMES CAGNEY, JEAN HARLOW, JOAN BLONDELL, MAE CLARKE

🎬 WILLIAM WELLMAN

USA (WARNER) 1931 B&W

⏱ 80m (PG)

Though cut down from 96m, this is still a powerhouse story of two gangsters, and it made Cagney a star. Connoisseurs of classic scenes will recall the moment when a grumpy Cagney shoves half a grapefruit into Mae Clarke's face over breakfast.

POINT BREAK 🎬3

⭐ KEANU REEVES, PATRICK SWAYZE, LORI PETTY, GARY BUSEY

🎬 KATHRYN BIGELOW

USA (FOX) 1991

⏱ 117m (18)

Improbable rubbish about a young FBI man set the task of infiltrating a hedonistic gang of surfers and skydivers who finance their lifestyle by bank robberies. Bigelow overcomes the silliness by virtue of exhilaratingly-lensed action sequences, though the idea that the cop would let his prey go off and attempt suicide-by-surfboard after all the abuse he'd suffered from the man pushes belief-suspension a notch too far.

GANGSTERS

PULP FICTION 🎬 5

⭐ JOHN TRAVOLTA, SAMUEL L JACKSON, BRUCE WILLIS, UMA THURMAN, HARVEY KEITEL, TIM ROTH, CHRISTOPHER WALKEN

🎬 QUENTIN TARANTINO

USA (TOUCHSTONE) 1994

⏱ 148m   (18)

Wunderkind Tarantino's follow-up to *Reservoir Dogs* (see opposite) is a multi-layered story involving several interconnected plot threads too unremittingly bizarre to explain in the space available. The film revitalised Travolta's career and is full of actors pulling together rather than competing. This is the latest version to be made available, a widescreen print with a bonus of two cut scenes revealed for the first time with an intro by Tarantino. The censor has optically enlarged scenes of heroin injection so that the point of the needle can't be seen penetrating the skin – apparently he thinks no one will know how to take drugs if they don't see the skin being broken! Weird. Oscar: best screenplay. (Note: the brand of heroin Travolta buys in the film is called 'Bava', after one of Tarantino's heroes, late Italian director Mario Bava, who made a multi-story film called *Black Sabbath*.)

RESERVOIR DOGS 🎬 5

⭐ HARVEY KEITEL, TIM ROTH, MICHAEL MADSEN, STEVE BUSCEMI, CHRIS PENN, LAWRENCE TIERNEY, QUENTIN TARANTINO

🎬 QUENTIN TARANTINO

USA (POLYGRAM) 1992

⏱ 99m   (18)

The film that catapulted Tarantino from the guy who used to rent videos to an old girlfriend of mine in her local Californian store to one of the world's top directors – I guess it really *can* happen to anybody. It's the story of a heist gone wrong and its aftermath, with undercover cop Roth bleeding to death and a patrolman having his ear severed by sadist Madsen. Hilarious dialogue and tense ensemble acting and action make this a sledgehammer debut. The title appears to be meaningless. Widescreen available. Also in pan-scan on a two-for-one tape with the excellent *Killing Zoe*.

SCARFACE 🎬 4

⭐ PAUL MUNI, GEORGE RAFT, BORIS KARLOFF, ANN DVORAK

🎬 HOWARD HAWKS

USA (CIC) 1932 B&W

⏱ 86m   (15)

This Hawks classic has Muni as a fictional version of Capone, manically discovering the joys of the machine-gun and wasting all in his path. Cut from 99m. A piece of cinema history that still thrills.

SCARFACE

AL PACINO, STEVEN BAUER, MARY ELIZABETH MASTRANTONIO, MICHELLE PFEIFFER

BRIAN DE PALMA

USA (CIC) 1983

162m (18)

Less a remake of the Hawks film than an update of its themes. Instead of an Italian exploiting the prohibition of booze in the 20s, we have a Cuban in 70s Miami tearing up the cocaine business. Ultra-violent with absurd amounts of coke being snorted, the film explores the greed of the 'Me, me me' 70s and one man's downfall. Magnificent stuff, scripted by Oliver Stone. This new widescreen print has restored a 25-second cut to the scene of a man being tortured with a chainsaw which was made to the original movie release. I guess the censor feels we have stronger stomachs these days!

SHARKY'S MACHINE

BURT REYNOLDS, RACHEL WARD, BRIAN KEITH, VITTORIO GASSMAN

BURT REYNOLDS

USA (WARNER) 1981

118m (18)

One of Burt's last major hits before his career began to nosedive, this is about a tough cop who sets out to protect the discarded moll of a Mob boss. Predictably, soppy romance gets in the way of the action, but not for too long. Spectacular stunts and gunplay.

STATE OF GRACE

SEAN PENN, ED HARRIS, GARY OLDMAN, BURGESS MEREDITH

PHIL JOANOU

USA (VISION) 1990

109m (18)

Uncompromising epic of Irish gangs in New York. Extremely nasty in places – many people have their civil rights most egregiously violated, I can assure you. A sadly underrated film that deserves your attention far more than most of the rubbish that fills our multiplexes week after week. Some stylish acting on display, notably from Penn and Oldman.

TRUE ROMANCE 🎬 5

CHRISTIAN SLATER, PATRICIA ARQUETTE, DENNIS HOPPER, CHRISTOPHER WALKEN, VAL KILMER, GARY OLDMAN, BRAD PITT

TONY SCOTT

USA (WARNER) 1993

⏱ 121m (18)

Tarantino-scripted thriller about a comic-store assistant who falls in love with a hooker, kills her pimp and steals a suitcase full of cocaine before they high-tail it to California with the Mob on their trail. Cameos include a great two-hander from Hopper and Walken. Beware: this uncut version is an already-censored American print that was submitted to the BBFC. The full version, out on USA laserdisc, is considerably more violent. The cuts don't detract from the picture too much, however. Widescreen available in a special box.

THE UNTOUCHABLES 🎬 3

KEVIN COSTNER, ROBERT DE NIRO, SEAN CONNERY, ANDY GARCIA

BRIAN DE PALMA

USA (CIC) 1987

⏱ 115m (15)

Glossy, entertaining, but vastly overpraised story of Eliot Ness and his battle against Al Capone. In spite of a pounding score by Ennio Morricone and some fine set pieces (such as a finale that replays the classic *Battleship Potemkin* scene of a pram bouncing down steps amid violence) this doesn't quite work. Costner and pals are too nicey-nice and the story is wildly inaccurate, with such non-historical absurdities as Ness hurling Capone henchman Frank Nitti off a roof while making quips worthy of Schwarzenegger at his worst. Connery is the exception, and deservedly won an Oscar for his role as an Irish cop with an inexplicable Scots accent. Widescreen available.

VILLAIN 🎬 3

RICHARD BURTON, IAN McSHANE, NIGEL DAVENPORT, FIONA LEWIS

MICHAEL TUCHNER

UK (WARNER) 1971

⏱ 93m (18)

Burton is a nasty piece of work as a brutish homosexual crime boss in London's underworld. A neglected bit of cinematic grime 'n' crime that shows what Burton could do when he was firing on all cylinders and committed to a role.

YEAR OF THE DRAGON 🎬 4

MICKEY ROURKE, JOHN LONE, ARIANE, LEONARD TERMO

MICHAEL CIMINO

USA (4-FRONT) 1985

⏱ 129m (18)

Hurrah! A Michael Cimino film that isn't boring! Over-the-top violence in New York's Chinatown as a cop fights his own drug war. Rourke seems to have faded from view of late, but he is blistering here. Written by Oliver Stone. Maybe that's why it's worth watching!

HONG KONG

Although the 1970s fad for martial arts movies died down after the tragic death of kung fu superstar Bruce Lee, a vogue for all manner of commercial Hong Kong cinema has grown by leaps and bounds in recent years. Take a look in any major video store and you'll see a large section devoted to these movies, stacked with tapes from specialist labels such as Missing In Action's 'Hong Kong Classics' subsidiary and 'Eastern Heroes'. The reason for fan enthusiasm isn't hard to fathom: Hong Kong film folk seem to be completely free of the genre restraints of their western counterparts – they'll remix plot elements with abandon and incorporate ideas that USA directors would reject as smashing the bounds of credibility. A film about a true-life serial killer will have scenes of incongruous slapstick comedy, flying ghosts indulge in sexy pursuits, there are hopping vampires and sobbing hitmen ...

Some of the former colony's top stars, such as comic martial arts stunt genius Jackie Chan and gunplay-actioner director John Woo, have already made inroads into the American industry. With Hong Kong now handed back to China, the fate of those back home remains to be seen, but in the meantime here is a small sampling of some of the better videos currently on offer.

ANGEL ENFORCERS 🎬 3

SHARON YOUNG, RON VAN LEE, DAISY MAN

GODFREY HO

HONG KONG (HONG KONG CLASSICS/MIA) 1991

87m (18)

Flashy girly/gunfire hokum, a weird oriental version of TV's *Charlie's Angels*. Too much blah-blah, but there are some stunning stunts mixed with nudity, gay rape and all the cheerfully offensive muddle one expects from Hong Kong cinema. Widescreen.

ANGELS 🎬 2

MOON LEE, HIDEKO SAIJO, ALEX FU

TERESA WOO

HONG KONG (HONG KONG CLASSICS/MIA) 1988

88m (18)

More girls with guns! This time battling the dastardly Madam Sue and her fiendish torture-chamber, our heroines never take a hit or so much as smudge their mascara. Amiably mindless widescreen fun, badly dubbed.

A BETTER TOMORROW 🎬 5

CHOW YUN FAT, LESLIE CHEUNG, LEE CHE HUNG

JOHN WOO

HONG KONG (HONG KONG CLASSICS/MIA) 1986

92m (18)

This was the movie which began Woo's rise as the master of the 'heroic bloodshed' genre, where black-suited cops and hitmen indulge in excessive shoot-outs and smouldering glances. A big influence on Quentin Tarantino, and highly charged entertainment in its own right. Subtitled and widescreen. Boxed set available too.

A BETTER TOMORROW 2 🎬 4

CHOW YUN FAT, LESLIE CHEUNG, TONY LEUNG

JOHN WOO

HONG KONG (MADE IN HONG KONG) 1987

100m (18)

Serviceable follow-up to Woo's earlier shoot-'em-up. Star Chow Yun Fat is reduced to playing his own identical twin (!) as his character was snuffed in the previous outing – see what I mean about Hong Kong's disregard for plot conventions? Starts slowly but soon erupts in balletic bullet mayhem. Many prefer this to the first film. Subtitled and widescreen. A third segment was helmed by producer Tsui Hark in the director's chair.

EASTERN CONDORS

SAMMO HUNG, YUEN BAIO, JOYCE GODENZI

SAMMO HUNG

HONG KONG
(MADE IN HONG KONG) 1986

93m (18)

Director/star Sammo Hung is one of the leading lights of the Hong Kong action scene, and this is something of a legendary film. It's rather like *The Dirty Dozen* (see page 283) in conception, with a motley band being sent to capture an enemy base (in Vietnam this time). Huge, explosive nonsense. Subtitled and widescreen.

ENCOUNTERS OF THE SPOOKY KIND

SAMMO HUNG, CHUNG FAT, CHAN LUNG

SAMMO HUNG

HONG KONG
(MADE IN HONG KONG) 1981

98m (18)

Cuckolded hubby invokes demons to revenge himself on cheating wife. Typically mad HK movie from the prolific Hung. Silly, with wacky special effects to goggle over. Subtitled and widescreen.

ENTER THE DRAGON

BRUCE LEE, JOHN SAXON, JIM KELLY

ROBERT CLOUSE

USA/HONG KONG (WARNER) 1973

93m (18)

The charismatic Lee died just as this breakthrough kung fu epic was being released. It's a sort of James Bond type effort, with Lee enlisted by secret agents to attend a martial arts tournament held by a shady businessman on his private isle – though he has personal reasons for accepting. Not much of a story but the battles are top-notch. Though this is a remastered widescreen edition, there are problems: on the copy I saw, the upper matte-line crashed down for several seconds during a fight scene, ruining the picture. Why wasn't this noticed before copies were run off? And the fight with a rice-flail removed by the censor back in 1973 remains cut from this print. Still a must-see, however! A version with extra scenes is out on import Digital Versatile Disc, or DVD as it's known.

FISTS OF FURY [3]

BRUCE LEE, JAMES TIEN, MARIA YI

LO WEI

HONG KONG (POLYGRAM) 1971
99m (18)

Bruce Lee is the only good thing about his early films, frankly. Bad dubbing, shoddy sets, poor direction: and yet they cannot detract from the man's electric screen presence and dynamic skills. Not a great movie, but certainly a great star.

FIVE VENOMS [3]

CHIANG SHENG, LU FENG, WEI PAI

CHANG CHEH

HONG KONG (MADE IN HONG KONG) 1978
98m (18)

Classic 70s kung fu epic from the legendary Shaw Studios, with typical plotline about a dying master who wants his star pupil to check that other students are not betraying the rules they were taught. Dubbed, but the superb stunt work is shown to advantage in this widescreen presentation.

HAND OF DEATH [2]

JACKIE CHAN, SAMMO HUNG, JOHN WOO

JOHN WOO

HONG KONG (HONG KONG CLASSICS/MIA) 1976
92m (18)

Very early work from Chan, Hung and Woo, made before any of the three had developed a distinctive style. Really just a messily dubbed and rather average kung fu pic, but interesting to see these artists in their formative days.

HEROES SHED NO TEARS [3]

EDDY KO, LAM CHING YING, LAU CHAU SANG

JOHN WOO

HONG KONG (HONG KONG CLASSICS/MIA) 1986
81m (18)

Extremely violent John Woo flick. Like Sammo Hung's *Eastern Condors* (see page 169) it's a variant on *The Dirty Dozen* (see page 283), but with an odd atmosphere all its own and some brutal scenes of impalement and dismemberment. Lacks the style of Woo's later pix.

THE HOT, THE COOL AND THE VICIOUS 🎬3

⭐ WONG TAO, TOMMY LEE, GEORGE WANG

🎬 LEE TSO NAM

HONG KONG (HONG KONG CLASSICS/MIA) 1979

⏱ 89m (18)

Impressively subtitled and widescreen martial arts film of the old school, with a clever plot and dazzlingly staged action scenes.

ISLAND ON FIRE 🎬2

⭐ JACKIE CHAN, SAMMO HUNG, JIMMY WANG YU, TONY LEUNG, ANDY LAU

🎬 CHU YEN PING

HONG KONG (HONG KONG CLASSICS/MIA) 1991

⏱ 92m (18)

A veritable roll-call of HK stars should guarantee solid fun, but apparently many of the actors were filmed separately and the footage flung together later on. Some good scenes in this revenge saga but, as you'd expect, it isn't really a coherent package.

THE KILLER 🎬5

⭐ CHOW YUN FAT, SALLY YEH, DANNY LEE

🎬 JOHN WOO

HONG KONG (MADE IN HONG KONG) 1989

⏱ 106m (18)

Considered by many to be Woo's best film, *The Killer*, a dizzying blend of romance, sentiment and gunplay, was first showcased at London's Institute of Contemporary Arts. The story concerns a gunman who accidentally blinds a cabaret singer and takes on a final hit to raise money for an operation on her eyes – but meanwhile the law is on his trail. Beautiful visuals and staggering shoot-outs, far beyond anything Hollywood could dream of, made this a *cause célèbrè* among action fans. I believe the longest version ran 135m. Widescreen.

NAKED KILLER

- CHINGAMY YAU, SIMON YAM, CARRIE NG
- CLARENCE FORD
- HONG KONG (HONG KONG CLASSICS/MIA) 1992
- 96m (18)

Crazy dyke hitwoman is pursued by a cop who thinks he knows her from another life. Described by some as a HK blend of *Vertigo* (see page 276), *Basic Instinct* (see page 258) and *Nikita* (see page 317), this is a stylishly lensed erotic thriller. Avoid the dubbed/pan-scan version and go for the subtitled/widescreen print. Boxed set also available.

ONE-ARMED BOXER

- WANG YU, MA CHI, LUNG FEI
- WANG YU
- HONG KONG (HONG KONG CLASSICS/MIA) 1972
- 88m (18)

Cheesy-but-cheerful early kung fu classic, with the star/director battling an Indian yogi and magic monks on behalf of his martial arts school. Cheaply done but never less than breathtaking in enthusiasm and audacity.

PROJECT A

- JACKIE CHAN, SAMMO HUNG, YUEN BAIO
- JACKIE CHAN
- HONG KONG (IMPERIAL) 1985
- 100m (PG)

One of Chan's best, with early 1900s marines sent to fight pirates on the high seas. Spectacular and such a hit that it spawned a sequel. Highly recommended as a starter if you have yet to have the Chan experience.

SATAN'S RETURN

- CHINGAMY YAU, DONNIE YEN, YUEN KING DAN
- AH LUN
- HONG KONG (HONG KONG CLASSICS/MIA) 1996
- 95m (18)

Supernatural cop thriller which has been compared to *Se7en* (see page 119). Ends with gunfire, crucifixion and chainsaw violence, with humour and a convoluted plot bunged in – just the type of excess which HK cinema excels at producing. Subtitled and widescreen.

SNAKE IN THE EAGLE'S SHADOW

JACKIE CHAN, YUEN SIU TIEN, HWANG JANG LEE

YUEN SIU TIEN

HONG KONG (MADE IN HONG KONG) 1978

97m (18)

Early Chan flick in which he plays a bullied youngster fed up with being a dogsbody at his kung fu school – so he takes instruction from the old master of the 'Snake Fist' style of the art, combines it with his own 'Cat Claw' style and manages to defeat the 'Eagle Claw' master who threatens the school (don't worry, you'll pick it up as you go along). Naff dubbing, but in widescreen.

THE TIGERS

ANDY LAU, TONY LEUNG, MIU KI WAI

ERIC TSANG

HONG KONG (EASTERN HEROES) 1992

110m (18)

Relatively serious actioner about current Hong Kong, strongly directed and with a powerful cast. If you find much of the HK stuff too frivolous, this may just be up your street. Subtitled and widescreen.

HORROR

The horror genre is a problematic one in the UK. Whatever your views on moral panics and censorship – and I'm agin 'em – the BBFC bans and demands cuts in many films, large numbers of which are horror movies freely available in Europe and the USA. Video firms are not bothered by this as they're not legally obliged to inform potential buyers that the product has been butchered – but they have been forced by the advent of specialist labels like Redemption and Encore to rethink unadventurous releasing policies. Look at it this way: for horror fans things can only improve! *The Exorcist* can't stay banned forever. Can it?

THE ADDICTION

CHRISTOPHER WALKEN, ANNABELLA SCIORRA, LILI TAYLOR

ABEL FERRARA

USA (POLYGRAM) 1995 B&W

79m (18)

A rainy, gritty vampire story from cult director Ferrara, about a newly infected lady bloodsucker who is rampaging all over the city until a wise elder vamp (the fabulously ethereal Walken) tries to counsel her. The drug-problem parallels are obvious from the title. Quite shocking in places – as Hitchcock found in *Psycho*, blood can look even more upsetting in monochrome.

AN AMERICAN WEREWOLF IN LONDON

DAVID NAUGHTON, GRIFFIN DUNNE, JENNY AGUTTER

JOHN LANDIS

USA (ENTERTAINMENT) 1981

97m (18)

Comedy and horror are notoriously difficult to mix, but Landis hits just the right note from the opening scenes where two Yank backpackers stray into a pub full of nattering, threatening rural types and occult symbols. One boy is slaughtered by a werewolf, only to return from the dead (in increasingly decayed form) to urge his injured buddy to top himself before he too becomes a lycanthrope. So far, so funny – but the ensuing transformations (by Rick Baker) are grisly and convincing in equal measure, as are the monsters in a shock dream sequence. Scary and irreverent – do see it.

ANGEL HEART

ROBERT DE NIRO, MICKEY ROURKE, LISA BONET, CHARLOTTE RAMPLING

ALAN PARKER

USA (POLYGRAM) 1987

109m (18)

Rourke is great as a private detective stumbling into an occult conspiracy in Brit Parker's film of William Hjortsberg's novel *Falling Angel*, but as in the book the devilish clues are blindingly obvious to anyone with even a passing interest in black magic: for instance, De Niro's character is named Louis Ciphre – Lucifer, geddit? The print may be slightly cut as there was a lot of huffing at the time of release over the sex scene between Bonet and Rourke.

ARACHNAPHOBIA

JEFF DANIELS, JULIAN SANDS, JOHN GOODMAN, HARLEY JANE KOZAK

FRANK MARSHALL

USA (TOUCHSTONE) 1990

105m (PG)

Playing on the widespread primal fear of spiders, this family-oriented scare ride features a virulent, hairy monster that comes to America from the tropics in the body of its victim, only to mate with the domestic article in the barn of arachnaphobe Daniels. Plenty of shrieks, and laughs are provided by bug-killer Goodman. Decent SFX.

THE AWFUL DOCTOR ORLOF

HOWARD VERNON, PERLA CRISTAL, CONRADO SAN MARTIN

JESS FRANCO

SPAIN (REDEMPTION) 1962 B&W

88m (15)

In the manner of Franju's *Les Yeux Sans Visage* (see *Eyes Without A Face*, page 185), Franco's sex 'n' surgery opus deals with a nutty doc intent on grafting stolen faces in place of that of his badly disfigured daughter. Orlof(f) became a pivotal figure in Franco's career as a director, and his *Faceless* and *Jack The Ripper* are virtual remakes (the latter nearly shot-for shot) of this movie. Franco has undergone a critical re-evaluation of late; formerly seen as a hack with a zoom-lens fetish, he's now accepted as the master of Spanish weirdness and perversity, a man with a mania for film-making regardless of budgetary constraints. This is well made 'grue', boasting luminous black and white photography – it can hardly be chance that the great Orson Welles thought Franco good enough to shoot the acclaimed battle footage for his *Chimes At Midnight* and to take charge of the second unit on that picture. This is Jess at his best. Presented in the correct aspect ratio.

HORROR

BLOOD FOR DRACULA

UDO KIER, JOE DALLESANDRO, ROMAN POLANSKI

PAUL MORRISSEY

ITALY (FIRST INDEPENDENT) 1974

99m (18)

Mad, gory, sexy flick about Drac (Kier) leaving home in search of 'wirgins' to exsanguinate, but finding only whores (a houseful) whose blood makes him 'womit', he finally succumbs to the axe of priapic, commie, anti-aristo handyman Dallesandro in a climax which the censor has thankfully left intact. There has been much debate over who directed this and its companion piece *Flesh For Frankenstein* (they were made back-to-back), Morrissey or the man credited for tax reasons on Italian prints, Antonio Margheriti. The truth appears to be that the Italian (a fine horror/action director) helped with both films, less so on this one. This is hilarious and over-the-top, often billed as an Andy Warhol film – but in reality he did nothing. Morrissey made other Warhol movies, like *Heat* and *Trash*. (*Flesh For Frankenstein* is available, but in a cut version.)

BRAM STOKER'S COUNT DRACULA

CHRISTOPHER LEE, HERBERT LOM, KLAUS KINSKI, SOLEDAD MIRANDA

JESS FRANCO

SPAIN/ITALY/WEST GERMANY (4-FRONT) 1970

96m (12)

Not to be confused with Lee's Hammer classics or Coppola's film with (almost) the same title. Cheaply shot but with a good showing by Lee as Dracula (growing gradually younger as in the novel), ably supported by a fine cast and some dodgy plastic bats. Cult director Franco could undoubtedly do better given a decent budget, but this rarely-seen version of the vampire tale is deserving of a look, especially on this budget-priced tape.

BRAM STOKER'S DRACULA [4]

GARY OLDMAN, RICHARD E GRANT, WINONA RYDER, ANTHONY HOPKINS, KEANU REEVES

FRANCIS FORD COPPOLA

USA (COLUMBIA TRISTAR) 1992

130m (18)

Hailed as a big-budget version of the classic vampire tale, this was actually shot for a relatively modest amount compared to most Hollywood films, with director Coppola eschewing computer FX and returning to some of the oldest and simplest cinematic tricks in the book: for example, an entire battle is suggested using nothing more than red lights and a few shadows. In trying to recapture the sense of wonder engendered by such early versions as the silent German *Nosferatu*, Coppola drew giggles from some critics, who paradoxically found the camerawork so tricksy that they dubbed it a horror film for MTV pop video fans, but even if only partially successful it's a brave attempt. Gary Oldman makes a spooky Dracula in the early scenes, but as he grows younger as he feeds on blood he starts to look like Screaming Lord Sutch! The author's proprietorial credit in the title is supposed to imply that we are seeing the first movie completely faithful to the book – we're not, though it's a claim many makers of Drac flicks have made. Anyway: beautiful to look at, especially in the widescreen version.

THE BROOD [4]

SAMANTHA EGGAR, OLIVER REED, ART HINDLE

DAVID CRONENBERG

CANADA (ARROW) 1979

91m (18)

More thought-provoking sick images from Cronenberg: oddball doctor Reed treats Eggar with his therapy, urging her to give shape to her inner rage. Soon she's developing womb-like sacs outside her body – her husband isn't amused, but we are. Wonder what's in there? Yuk. Fab. Not for pregnant female viewers.

HORROR

CEMETERY MAN [4]

RUPERT EVERETT, ANNA FALCHI, FRANCOIS HADJI-LAZARO

MICHELE SOAVI

ITALY (ENTERTAINMENT) 1993
99m   (18)

Lambasted and lauded in equal measure, Soavi's adaptation of the novel *Dellamorte Dellamore* (the film's Italian title) and the comic it inspired, *Dylan Dog*, is about a reclusive graveyard keeper troubled by lively corpses, a slobby assistant who keeps the talking severed head of his lady love in his room, and the problem that every girl he fancies looks the same. The story veers from macabre to madcap and back rather alarmingly, the rug being constantly yanked from under our feet as we're bombarded by some of the densest, most lovely imagery ever seen in a horror movie. Admired and loathed by opposing fan bases, it ends with a Wellesian flourish. A remarkable piece of cinema. Note: Everett got the title part because the face of the comic character is based on his own. (And Martin Scorsese apparently hailed it as the best film of 1993!)

THE CHURCH [5]

HUGH QUARSHIE, TOMAS ARANA, BARBARA CUPISTI, ASIA ARGENTO

MICHELE SOAVI

ITALY (FIRST INDEPENDENT/ REFLECTIVE) 1989
98m   (18)

Soavi's second film after the slasher *Stagefright* is a visually overloaded gothic jaunt about evil from the past taking over in a sealed cathedral, and is full of historical allusions to the likes of the Knights Templar and Fulcanelli. Allegedly planned as just another in the 'Demons' series – which also involve monsters in locked buildings – but Soavi expands the idea from a tired sequel to an epic that should satisfy those who look for mystery and intelligence in horror as well as gorehounds after more visceral thrills. Despite packaging which suggests producer Dario Argento is the director, Soavi stands on his own as a unique talent for those who thought Italian horror was kaput. Slightly letterboxed, though this is not noted on the box.

CRONOS

FEDERICO LUPPI, CLAUDIO BROOK, RON PERLMAN

GUILLERMO DEL TORO

MEXICO (TARTAN) 1992

91m (18)

Nifty debut from the Mexican director, about an old antique dealer who finds an odd occult device which grants eternal youth – at a price. While coming to terms with the fact that he's a vampire (the scene of him lapping the residue of someone's nosebleed off the floor in a men's room is not for the squeamish) he has also to contend with the brutal son of a fading millionaire who is desperate to get his hands on the clockwork nasty. The eagle-eyed cineastes among you may detect references to other classic horror films, but that doesn't detract from the pleasure to be had from being in the hands of a genuine talent. He's now made a big American film, *Mimic*.

THE CROW

BRANDON LEE, ERNIE HUDSON, ANGEL DAVID, DAVID PATRICK KELLY

ALEX PROYAS

USA (EIV) 1994

113m (18)

Zombie rocker comes back from the grave a year after his Hallowe'en demise to tackle those who did the deed and raped and murdered his girl. Dark and weird, with cult status boosted by the eerily tragic death during filming of starring actor Lee in a gun accident on set. He was the son of the late Bruce Lee, who also died young and who believed his whole family was doomed to be stalked by a demonic entity.

HORROR

CURSE OF THE DEMON 🎬 5

DANA ANDREWS, PEGGY CUMMINS, NIALL MacGINNIS, ATHENE SEYLER

JACQUES TOURNEUR

UK (ENCORE) 1957 B&W

91m (12)

It's a mystery why the ghost stories of MR James have not been used in more movies – perhaps they're just too subtle to translate into a hit. Which brings us to critical debate over this film, based on MRJ's *Casting The Runes*, about an Aleister Crowley-type, black-tinged cult leader who disposes of his enemies by passing them, by trickery, runic curses which summon a denizen of hell to rend them in pieces. Since the film version centres on a sceptic (Andrews) gradually being convinced that he truly is in supernatural danger, many feel that it was a mistake to let us actually see the demon. I don't agree; however, the monster's inclusion in the first death scene *was* a mistake. If it had been cut, we would, like Andrews, be close to the finale before we were sure of what was going on. The cast is superb, notably MacGinnis as the evil magus, Julian Karswell, and Athene Seyler as his doting mother. This print bears the title of the shortened USA release (the picture was issued in Britain as *Night Of The Demon*, where it ran 13 minutes longer) but it has been taken from a complete master tape of the full-length version.

DAUGHTERS OF DARKNESS 🎬 4

DELPHINE SEYRIG, JOHN KARLEN, DANIELE OUIMET

HARRY KUMEL

BELGIUM (TARTAN) 1971

97m (18)

Disturbing and sensuous arthouse horror from cult hero Kumel. In an off-season seaside hotel, two slinky lesbian babes (supposedly the undead Countess Bathory, historical blood-drinker who has inspired several movies, and her amour) seduce a young couple into kinky games – much talk of red-hot pokers and so forth. You just know it'll all end in tears, don't you? Seyrig is icily sexy, while the young hubby (Karlen) is the actor who went on to become Harvey the husband in TV's girlcop shop *Cagney and Lacey*. If you're hung up on chainsaws and such, this may be a bit slow for you, but the vivid colours of the interiors contrast startlingly with the muted outdoor sequences to make cinema that glows like an accursed jewel.

DEMENTIA 13

WILLIAM CAMPBELL, LUANA ANDERS, PATRICK MAGEE, BART PATTON

FRANCIS FORD COPPOLA

USA (SCREEN MULTIMEDIA) 1963 B&W

75m (15)

This is the full version of future *Godfather* helmsman Coppola's atmospheric cheapie, shot for producer Roger Corman (who has helped many get a foot in the door, including Martin Scorsese and Jack Nicholson) on the trip to Europe that spawned Corman's *The Young Racers*. Axe-pocalypse naff? No, just lots of hatchet killings, family secrets and spooky locations. It's the sort of thing they don't do these days, the sort that was very popular in the wake of Hitchcock's *Psycho*. With the great Magee in ham mode, Coppola makes the most of the tiny budget – check out the startling shot of a radio burbling to the bottom of a corpse-filled lake. The only thing missing here is the short intro by psychiatrist Dr William J Bryan Jnr (shot by Monte Hellman) which was shown on some American prints. Released to UK cinemas in heavily cut form as *The Haunted And The Hunted*.

DEMONS

NATASHA HOVEY, FIORE ARGENTO, URBANO BARBERINI

LAMBERTO BAVA

ITALY (SPEARHEAD) 1985

93m (18)

Directed by the son of the late, great Mario Bava (who has not inherited his pop's genius) and produced by Dario Argento, this concerns a bunch of nerds locked in a cinema while watching a movie on prophet-of-doom Nostradamus. Suddenly, audience members turn into nasties of the title and decimate the rest. Illogical, gory and quite scary, it nevertheless runs out of steam quite soon. Sequel: *Demons 2*. (See review of *The Church*, page 179.)

DON'T LOOK NOW

JULIE CHRISTIE, DONALD SUTHERLAND, HILARY MASON, CELIA MATANIA

NICOLAS ROEG

UK (WARNER) 1973

105m (18)

Short story by Daphne du Maurier inspires this creepy film about an architect who thinks he sees visions of his dead child while on a trip to Venice, with horrific results. One of Roeg's better efforts, made before his weird and dislocated style got too garbled for its own good. Contains a controversial sex scene, in which Christie and Sutherland were rumoured to be having intercourse for real.

HORROR

DRACULA

CHRISTOPHER LEE, PETER CUSHING, MELISSA STRIBLING, MICHAEL GOUGH

TERENCE FISHER

UK (WARNER/TERRORVISION) 1958

78m (15)

This is the first time Hammer's classic version of the famed vampire story has been available on tape in Britain. Lee makes a dashing, romantic Dracula, seducing his female victims through the sheer physicality of his presence, with Cushing as his implacably decent adversary Van Helsing. This, the first colour version, draws parallels between vampirism and drug addiction in the same way that more recent vampire films – such as Abel Ferrara's *The Addiction* (see page 175) – have done. A landmark in the horror genre. Note: this is actually the USA print (on-screen title *Horror Of Dracula*) and – in spite of the reduced running time due to the faster PAL projection speed – is longer by a few fleeting seconds of gore cut by the BBFC back in 1958. It does not, however, have the uncut version of Lee's final disintegration, which is extant only in some obscure foreign-language prints.

DRACULA

BELA LUGOSI, HELEN CHANDLER, EDWARD VAN SLOAN, DWIGHT FRYE, DAVID MANNERS

TOD BROWNING

USA (CIC) 1931 B&W

75m (PG)

This first sound version of the vampire story is dated and theatrical, though Lugosi's performance and a certain weird atmosphere carry it off. This remastered version restores some censored sound effects and presents the full image, which was slightly cropped years ago when the sound (originally on discs) was added to prints which had to have the track printed on to the film stock. It's a pity that the far superior Spanish-language version, shot on the same sets at night with a different cast and crew and recently restored in the USA, is still not available here.

DRACULA – PRINCE OF DARKNESS 🎬4

CHRISTOPHER LEE, BARBARA SHELLEY, ANDREW KEIR, FRANCIS MATTHEWS

TERENCE FISHER

UK (LUMIERE) 1965

⏱ 87m (15)

For me, Chris Lee is the best screen Count ever, though his Hammer outings in the role diminished in quality (through no fault of his own) as they went along. Once again directed by the elegant yet robust Terence Fisher, the film-maker with the most coherent career in the genre, it has a simple yet effective plot about some silly-ass English tourists who ignore warnings and become fang-fodder for the Count's resurrection. Lee is mute, as though his bloody rejuvenation has left him in spectral form, but Barbara Shelley is outstanding as a stuffy matron transformed by Drac's bite into a bisexual babe. Sadly, this is a cut print. Original trailer included.

DRIPPING RED WAX 🎬3

VIRGINIA STELLAR, UGO RODOLFO, GIAN MARIA TOGNAZZI

SERGIO ROSSO

ITALY/SWITZERLAND (ARZ) 1971

⏱ 110m (18)

Rarely seen *giallo* (the Italian slasher/mystery genre) of legendary status among the chosen few now turns up in a severely truncated print from this small label. Nevertheless, the insane psychedelic party sequences, with drug abuse and goat-sex amid the wildly fruggin' satanists, make this oddity a must-see in any version. Catch it while you can.

THE EVIL DEAD 🎬4

BRUCE CAMPBELL, ELLEN SANDWEISS, BETSY BAKER

SAM RAIMI

USA (4-FRONT) 1982

⏱ 86m (18)

Acclaimed but controversial gorefest which got caught up in the moral panic which led to the Video Recordings Act – the result was that the version available had to have numerous small cuts made in order that the BBFC could legally pass it. It's a mix of gore and frantic excess that has more in common with Raimi's beloved *Three Stooges* than with most horror pix – crazy kids in a cabin accidentally evoke demons and – whooooaaarggh! – that's it. Many directors launch a career on the back of a cheap horror film, but Raimi's only subsequent hits have been the other two 'Evil Dead' films – and the first of those wasn't even a sequel, just a bigger budget revision! Most mainstream critics didn't even notice. See the book *Seduction of the Gullible* by John Martin (Procrustes Press) for the VRA story. Raimi now produces the tackily fun *Xena* and *Hercules* TV shows. *The Evil Dead* is available in a boxed set with its two sequels which are also sold separately on the 4-Front label. The third film (*Army Of Darkness – The Medieval Dead*) is presented with two different endings.

EYES WITHOUT A FACE

PIERRE BRASSEUR, ALIDA VALLI, EDITH SCOB

GEORGES FRANJU

FRANCE (CONNOISSEUR) 1959 B&W

87m (18)

Arthouse maverick Franju provoked outrage with this tale of a mad surgeon abducting girls in order to graft their skin on to his daughter's face, disfigured in a car crash caused by him. Like Michael Powell's career-derailing *Peeping Tom* and Terence Fisher's *The Curse Of Frankenstein*, the film outlived and outlasted its critics and retains its power and poetry. Stunningly lensed by Eugen Shuftan, the movie influenced a whole surgical-horror genre including films like *Corruption* and Jess Franco's *Faceless* and *The Awful Dr Orlof* (see page 176). French title: *Les Yeux Sans Visage*. This is the first time the full version has been available in the UK. Subtitled and correct aspect ratio.

THE FEARLESS VAMPIRE KILLERS

SHARON TATE, ROMAN POLANSKI, FERDY MAYNE, JACK MacGOWRAN

ROMAN POLANSKI

UK (WARNER/TERRORVISION) 1967

107m (18)

Polanski's wry tribute to Hammer is here presented in the long version and in widescreen. It has a genuine beauty amid the slapstick and gags about gay vampires, only slightly diminished on the TV screen. Original title: *Dance Of The Vampires*. Fantastic score by Krzysztof Komeda.

FEMALE VAMPIRE 🎬

☆ LINA ROMAY, ALICE ARNO, JACK TAYLOR

🎬 JESS FRANCO

FRANCE (REDEMPTION) 1973

⏱ 94m (18)

With a director like Franco, who recycles footage and issues his films with titles and versions which vary from territory to territory to take account of censorship problems and ethnic preferences, it's hard to speak of a definitive print. This picture has been seen as *Erotikill*, *The Bare Breasted Countess*, *La Comtesse Noire*, etc., etc., some versions accenting horror while others insert hard-core sex shots. This seems to be the longest cut, though unsurprisingly it has been shorn of some six minutes of sex and sado-masochism by the BBFC. Franco's partner and muse Romay (who named herself after the singer of the same name from way back) appears as a nude vampire who sucks her lovers to death. And you can read that any way you wish. Falling in love with one victim, she elects to drown in a bath of blood. Much hypnotic wandering and softcore fondling in this lovely widescreen print. I like it, but then I'm a weirdo.

THE FOG 🎬

☆ ADRIENNE BARBEAU, HAL HOLBROOK, JANET LEIGH, JAMIE LEE CURTIS

🎬 JOHN CARPENTER

USA (4-FRONT) 1979

⏱ 86m (15)

One of Carpenter's lesser scarejobs, but offers some ghostly shivers for all that. Spectres of old seadogs take revenge on a town where the people lured their ship to a rocky doom a century before. Much more whimsical and less shocking than the same director's classic *Halloween* (see page 189).

FRANKENSTEIN

BORIS KARLOFF, COLIN CLIVE, MAE CLARKE, EDWARD VAN SLOAN, DWIGHT FRYE

JAMES WHALE

USA (CIC) 1931 B&W

71m (PG)

The classic first sound version of Mary Shelley's novel of a man who makes a monster from graveyard detritus and electricity has never been surpassed, and is at last available on video once more – this time in a digitally remastered print with a full restoration of all the censored snippets, most importantly the usually truncated scene where the creator (Karloff) kills a child by drowning her, albeit through ignorance rather than malice. Karloff's mute performance is deeply moving as well as scary, but the shock power of the film is obviously diminished in the light of the gorier efforts of today. Although made in the USA, the director and stars are (almost) all British.

FRANKENSTEIN MUST BE DESTROYED

PETER CUSHING, VERONICA CARLSON, SIMON WARD, FREDDIE JONES

TERENCE FISHER

UK (WARNER/TERRORVISION) 1969

97m (18)

As with Dracula, I've chosen not to fill these pages with numerous films based on Frankenstein; I must, however, include one from Terence Fisher's wonderful series for Hammer. And why not? Peter Cushing was a better Baron than Colin Clive, and the chosen film illustrates the way the character deepened as the series went on (a characteristic that is maintained even in a film not helmed by Fisher, Freddie Francis's *Evil Of Frankenstein*). *Frankenstein Must Be Destroyed* has a tragic tone, with Freddie Jones excellent as a man who finds his brain in a body his wife fails to see as his. Ignoring Jimmy Sangster's ribald remake of *The Curse of Frankenstein* (the first in the series, which he wrote and which is also out on video at long last) as *Horror Of Frankenstein*, Fisher brought the epic to a dark close in 1973's *Frankenstein And The Monster From Hell*, his last, underrated film.

FREAKS [4]

HARRY EARLES, OLGA BACLANOVA, WALLACE FORD

TOD BROWNING

USA (VISIONARY) 1932 B&W

64m (15)

This pic outraged MGM when they saw it – they disowned it and director Browning was toppled from the big time, the film being cut, retitled and sold cheap to sideshow exploitation operators. Unseen for years, it is now perhaps a tad overrated. Still, Browning knew the carnie world, and the compassionate yet unsentimental use of real freaks in a tale where they take horrible revenge on a woman who marries one of them for his money is a brave move that results in an honest film.

FROM DUSK TILL DAWN [3]

GEORGE CLOONEY, QUENTIN TARANTINO, HARVEY KEITEL, JULIETTE LEWIS

ROBERT RODRIGUEZ

USA (BUENA VISTA) 1996

104m

Hotshot Tarantino dusts off one of his early efforts at scriptwriting to star with heart-throb George (*ER*) Clooney in this madcap story, which is like two different films cobbled together. First half is a heist tale, as two robber brothers kidnap a widowed preacher and his kids and force them to drive to Mexico. Once there we veer into horror as the group are trapped by vampires in a sleazy bar. Good SFX. Available in widescreen. A documentary, *Full Tilt Boogie*, has been made about the film's production.

THE FURY [4]

KIRK DOUGLAS, AMY IRVING, FIONA LEWIS, JOHN CASSAVETES, CARRIE SNODGRESS, DARYL HANNAH

BRIAN DE PALMA

USA (FOX) 1978

113m (18)

Semi-forgotten De Palma classic about a secret agent (Douglas) who has to call upon all his skills when his son, who has telekinetic powers, is kidnapped for shady experiments. Wildly gory for the time, especially a great 'exploding head' sequence which drew gasps from the audience when I was fortunate enough to attend a preview introduced by De Palma at the time of its first release. Best on a big screen, but survives on video rather well. Script by John Farris from his novel.

HORROR

GOTHIC

GABRIEL BYRNE, JULIAN SANDS, NATASHA RICHARDSON, TIMOTHY SPALL

KEN RUSSELL

UK (VISION) 1986

83m (18)

Typically frantic and gleefully excessive visual feast from Ken Russell about the night in nineteenth-century Switzerland when debauched, druggy Byron, his doctor/opium supplier and Mr and Ms Shelley had a spook-story session which inspired Dr Polidori's tale *The Vampyre* and started Mary Shelley off on *Frankenstein*. Narrative flow is sacrificed to imagery which, to be fair, is often rooted in fact: for example, anti-Russellites may go spare at the sight of a woman with eyes in her nipples, but this is based on a hallucination which Shelley experienced and thoughtfully described for posterity. The four stars have gone on to bigger things. Oddly enough, two other versions of the same story were made almost simultaneously: *Haunted Summer* and *Rowing Against The Wind*.

HALLOWEEN

JAMIE LEE CURTIS, DONALD PLEASENCE, PJ SOLES

JOHN CARPENTER

USA (MIA) 1978

91 m (18)

So much better than the slasher flix it inspired – and we can at last see why, as *Halloween* is made available in this full widescreen print. Carpenter is a master of the Panavision frame, painting with light and inky darkness to make the viewer jump out of his/her skin. The story is nothing: a young child commits bloody murder, grows more evil in captivity, then flees the asylum to menace babysitter Curtis. Pleasence is the shrink in hot pursuit. Works best on a big screen, but this print is the next best option. There are sequels, which are the usual training-grounds for new directors. Ignore them.

CLASSIC 1000 VIDEOS

THE HAUNTING 5

JULIE HARRIS, CLAIRE BLOOM, RICHARD JOHNSON, RUSS TAMBLYN

ROBERT WISE

UK (WARNER/TERRORVISION) 1963 B&W

112m (12)

Parapsychologists check out a haunted house in Wise's adaptation of a literary ghost story by Shirley Jackson, though the film seems less concerned with revenants than the kinks of the living members of the company. As at least one critic has noted, the flick seems to suggest that Bloom's lesbianism is as monstrous as any ghost – still, the actors are fine and it's a fabulous late-night, lights-out chiller. Widescreen print.

HELLRAISER 3

ANDREW ROBINSON, CLAIRE HIGGINS, ASHLEY LAURENCE

CLIVE BARKER

UK (CINEMA CLUB) 1987

93m (18)

Writer/director Barker spins a neat yarn about a man who solves an occult version of Rubik's Cube, unleasing S&M-obsessed demons who torture him down to his bare bones. To revive he needs blood – and who better to get it for him than the sister-in-law he was having an affair with before things went pear-shaped. At one time Barker was thought to be the future of both horror fiction and films, but now he pens fat fantasy epics, has adopted a mid-Atlantic accent and spends his time developing movie projects that are supposed to be 'the next big thing' but which invariably flop. This one still packs a punch, but the body-piercing imagery has become rather *passé* over the last decade and has lost the ability to shock. Avoid the sequels: the first changes the location of the house in the story from the UK to the USA with no explanation at all. The critics didn't notice, or care.

THE HITCHER 4

RUTGER HAUER, JENNIFER JASON LEIGH, C THOMAS HOWELL, BILL GREEN BUSH

ROBERT HARMON

USA (WARNER/TERRORVISION) 1986

97m (18)

Cat-and-mouse game between a murderous drifter of seemingly supernatural abilities and the hapless boy who gives him a ride only to be blamed for his crimes. Requires massive suspension of belief, but it's an extremely scary and competently made horror romp with a better-than-average cast. Available in widescreen.

HORROR

THE HOWLING [4]

DEE WALLACE, PATRICK MACNEE, ELISABETH BROOKS, JOHN CARRADINE

JOE DANTE

USA (ENTERTAINMENT) 1980

90m (18)

If *An American Werewolf in London* (see page 175) wasn't enough, there's an equally wild comedy lycanthrope film for you. Scripted by arthouse man John Sayles, it mixed outstanding effects by Rob Bottin with a plot about a therapy retreat where our furry friends are rehabilitated for return to society. Characters are named after famous horror directors. Dante is a Roger Corman-protégé who went on to greater things, but this remains one of his best efforts. Avoid the sequels like the plague.

THE HUNGER [3]

SUSAN SARANDON, CATHERINE DENEUVE, DAVID BOWIE, CLIFF DE YOUNG

TONY SCOTT

USA (WARNER) 1983

92m (18)

Female vampire takes mates for centuries at a time – but the gift of extended youth she brings is not quite eternal, so she has to keep previous crumbling lovers suffering in coffins in the attic! Gory horror from the brother of director Ridley Scott, based on Whitley Streiber's novel. Available in widescreen.

INFERNO [4]

LEIGH McCLOSKEY, DARIA NICOLODI, ALIDA VALLI

DARIO ARGENTO

ITALY (FOX/WORLD) 1980

107m (18)

In spite of serious critical acclaim, Argento's films are still mainly available here in cut, censored, cropped, dubbed forms – and that's when they're released at all. *Inferno* follows *Suspiria* (see page 201) as the second part of the not-yet-complete 'Three Mothers' trilogy, and though slightly less amazing than its predecessor, it still weaves a distinctly strange vision of occultism and violence in Manhattan. This print does not appear to be in full widescreen, and the BBFC have been at work with the scissors again.

INTERVIEW WITH THE VAMPIRE [3]

☆ TOM CRUISE, BRAD PITT, CHRISTIAN SLATER, ANTONIO BANDERAS

🎬 NEIL JORDAN

USA (WARNER) 1994

⏱ 117m (18)

Though the hugely popular sequels stink, Anne Rice's original source novel of a sad vampire telling all is the best bloodsucker yarn since *Dracula* – and she was wary of Tom Cruise playing her evil, manipulative anti-hero Lestat when a film version finally got the green light. She changed her mind after seeing the movie, and though not as bad as most of these un-scary big studio horrors (and fairly faithful to the book) this is rather a cold, empty spectacular.

ISLAND OF LOST SOULS [3]

☆ CHARLES LAUGHTON, RICHARD ARLEN, BELA LUGOSI, KATHLEEN BURKE

🎬 ERLE C KENTON

USA (VISIONARY) 1932 B&W

⏱ 72m (12)

Forget the more recent two versions of HG Wells' *Island Of Dr Moreau*, for in spite of the great man's dislike this is the definitive movie interpretation of the tale of the mad scientist who grafts human and animal flesh in his 'House of Pain'. Despite a great performance from Brit Laughton in the main role of the nut who wants to mate Arlen with panther woman Burke, the pic was banned in UK until 1958. Apart from the 1977 and 1997 versions, the Aurum Film Encyclopedia states that the story also inspired films in 1913 and 1959. (See how daft censorship is – banned for 26 years, yet this film is now considered okay for 12-year-olds!)

LA VAMPIRE NUE [5]

☆ OLIVER MARTIN, MAURICE LEMAITRE, CAROLINE CARTIER

🎬 JEAN ROLLIN

FRANCE (REDEMPTION) 1969

⏱ 82m (18)

For years we could only read about Rollin's surreal vampire films – now, thanks to the efforts of Redemption (and writers Cathal Tohill and Pete Tombs, who ran a season at the NFT), we can see them. This is just one of several titles issued lately, a bizarre, fetishistic effort in the manner of a comic or an old serial. And yet it's very French, which makes it sad that his homeland – which has done so much for neglected film-makers – still refuses to salute Rollin's genius.

THE LOST BOYS [3]

KIEFER SUTHERLAND, JASON PATRIC, DIANNE WIEST, COREY HAIM

JOEL SCHUMACHER

USA (WARNER/TERRORVISION) 1987

97m (15)

This rather lame attempt at a modern rock 'n' roll/comic vampire fantasy for teens has inexplicably become something of a cult film. A woman and her kids move to a small Californian town only to find it infested by blood-sucking yobs battling it out with local lads who are in-the-know because they've perused the horror section in the comix store they run. Stupid, but boasts sporadic bursts of fun. Available in a widescreen special edition.

MANIAC COP [3]

TOM ATKINS, BRUCE CAMPBELL, SHEREE NORTH, RICHARD ROUNDTREE

WILLIAM LUSTIG

USA (POLYGRAM) 1988

81m (18)

Jokey slash-'em-up about a monstrous vigilante policeman is quite a neat little effort from cult horror director Lustig, and inspired a series of sequels which don't match up to the original. Also available, at least for a time, on a two-for-one tape with *Maniac Cop 2*.

THE MARK OF THE DEVIL [2]

HERBERT LOM, UDO KIER, REGGIE NALDER, GABY FUCHS

MICHAEL ARMSTRONG

W GERMANY (REDEMPTION) 1969

90m (18)

I include this only as a warning. This excellent witch-finding story would have been rated 'four' had it not been cut to shreds by the BBFC, who still gave it an '18' cert! Redemption occasionally bite the bullet and do what very few companies do by indicating that the censor may have cut the product, but on the copies of this title I've seen I can find no such notice. I know they have to balance the war against censorship with the need to sell tapes, but if any tape needs a 'butchered' sticker, it's this one! Uncut version available from Holland.

MARY SHELLEY'S FRANKENSTEIN

ROBERT DE NIRO, KENNETH BRANAGH, TOM HULCE, HELENA BONHAM CARTER, IAN HOLM, JOHN CLEESE, AIDAN QUINN

KENNETH BRANAGH

USA/UK (COLUMBIA TRISTAR) 1994

123m (15)

The author's name in the title marks this as an attempt to replicate the success of the studio's *Bram Stoker's Dracula* (see page 177), but this is a less successful enterprise altogether. Critics ignorant of the genre praised the scenes set in icy wastes as being both innovative and uniquely true to the book – but this aspect, and the 'birthing' of the monster, cannot be said to be any different (or indeed any better) than amazingly similar material in a TV version of the story starring Randy Quaid which was made shortly before Branagh's film. It all looks very picturesque, but horror (even with a literary pedigree) is meant to be nasty, upsetting and transgressive, and big studios trying to make 'respectable' horrors will inevitably fail, because the one thing horror should never be is respectable. De Niro is awful as the creature, and the make-up isn't a patch on the old classic look Jack Pierce did on Boris Karloff. Any of Karloff's performances as the Frankenstein monster beat this hands down. Widescreen available.

MASK OF SATAN

BARBARA STEELE, JOHN RICHARDSON, IVO GARRANI, ANDREA CECCHI

MARIO BAVA

ITALY (REDEMPTION) 1960 B&W

84m (15)

Issued under many names, this Bava masterpiece (better known as *Black Sunday*) was banned in the UK for some years for being too horrific – but it's actually an atmospheric, ghostly story that started the career of Steele as a horror icon and is rightly regarded as a classic today. It's a tale of an evil witch who comes back from the dead after she and her man have had spiked masks hammered on to their faces – wow! This print is in the correct ratio and has the original music plus the few moments of graphic gore which were removed for USA audiences.

MR SARDONICUS

OSCAR HOMOLKA, RONALD LEWIS, AUDREY DALTON, GUY ROLFE

WILLIAM CASTLE

USA (ENCORE) 1961 B&W

87m (12)

Gimmick-master Castle is in his element with this version of Ray Russell's story about a surgeon summoned to a scary castle by his ex-girlfriend, now married to a cruel noble who threatens dire vengeance on both if the doc can't cure his frozen grimace caused by – well, see it for yourselves! This print happily retains the cinematic pause where the audience is asked to vote on a happy or sad ending for the beastly Baron – but don't fret, there only ever was the one climax and the baddy gets his come-uppance. Great fun.

MYSTERY OF THE WAX MUSEUM

LIONEL ATWILL, FAY WRAY, GLENDA FARRELL

MICHAEL CURTIZ

USA (VISIONARY) 1933

78m (PG)

Early, lovingly restored, two-strip Technicolor horror from the team that made *Doctor X* in the same process. Atwill is great and the colour is eerily rich given its technical limitations. Only the typical period humour jars. Remade as *House Of Wax* in 1953.

NEAR DARK

ADRIAN PASDAR, JENNY WRIGHT, LANCE HENRIKSEN, BILL PAXTON

KATHRYN BIGELOW

USA (ENTERTAINMENT) 1987

94m (18)

New slant on the vampire myth sees them as a sort of addict-breed, roving the land rather like an unwashed sub-species of the Manson Family. A lad is bitten by the befanged gal he lusts after, and the film gets to explore the moral dilemma of a new vampire reluctant to kill but having to in order to survive – nearly a decade before *Interview With The Vampire* (see page 192), too. No Tom Cruise in this one, okay?

NIGHT OF THE LIVING DEAD [5]

DUANE JONES, JUDITH O'DEA, KARL HARDMAN

GEORGE A ROMERO

USA (TARTAN) 1968 B&W

96m (18)

Radical reworking of zombie lore as the dead suddenly come to life for no known reason and attack the living, and we follow a group of survivors holed up in a house under siege. This unbelievably nihilistic pic shocks right up to the final moment, and was the first breakthrough 'indie' horror. It inspired other young directors to take a chance on low-budget shockers. Romero made two interesting sequels, *Dawn Of The Dead* and *Day Of The Dead*, which may be more gory and fun but will never be as historically important. There have been offshoots, like the *Return Of The Living Dead* films, and clever Italian rip-offs, while the original has been colourised and even re-made. But after years of fuzzy prints we now have a video release from the new materials used for the recent pristine USA laserdisc release. Enjoy. If that's the right word.

NOSFERATU THE VAMPYRE [4]

KLAUS KINSKI, BRUNO GANZ, ISABELLE ADJANI, ROLAND TOPOR

WERNER HERZOG

WEST GERMANY (FOX) 1979

107m (15)

Arty genius Herzog's remake of Murnau's silent classic was shot in English and German versions. The Anglo print was deemed too naff to release to cinemas – so why is that the only version on tape? Hypnotic moments, but the subtitled print is much superior.

HORROR

PEEPING TOM [5]

CARL BOEHM, ANNA MASSEY, MOIRA SHEARER, SHIRLEY ANNE FIELD

MICHAEL POWELL

UK (WARNER/TERRORVISION) 1960

97m (18)

The film that virtually destroyed the revered Powell's career. A horror pic from the company that released stuff like *Horrors Of The Black Museum* and *Circus Of Horrors* in tatty, lurid colour was not what the critics wanted from the director of *The Red Shoes*. Thanks to the efforts of Martin Scorsese and others, this is now seen as a brilliant work by a master craftsman. The story of a young focus-puller who, frightened and then filmed by his mad doctor dad, goes on to impale women on a sharpened tripod as he lenses their agony. Scoptophilia (the morbid desire to watch) didn't make for big box office in 1960 – Powell was snubbed and Boehm (aka Karl Bohm) wasn't seen again much until Fassbinder cast him years later in *Fox*. Wrongly stated in film references to be 109m, this is (allowing for the faster PAL speed) the full version. Atone for our fathers' sins and see it.

POLTERGEIST [3]

JO BETH WILLIAMS, CRAIG T NELSON, ZELDA RUBINSTEIN

TOBE HOOPER

USA (WARNER) 1982

114m (15)

Producer Spielberg (that's Steve to you) is given (by some) as much credit for this gory, ghostly story of spooks and a missing child as nominal director Hooper, one critic condemning it as a 'Walt Disney horror movie'. Well, you will not be able to compare it with ol' Tobe's best work – because that's *The Texas Chainsaw Massacre* and we in the UK are not considered mature enough to see that by the powers-that-BBFC. It's certainly better than most of either man's recent stuff. Forget the sequels, though.

197

PSYCHO

ANTHONY PERKINS, JANET LEIGH, VERA MILES, MARTIN BALSAM

ALFRED HITCHCOCK

USA (CIC) 1960 B&W

109m (15)

Shot low-budget with the crew of his TV show, Hitch's film of Robert Bloch's novel had a unique twist – you follow this gal who has nicked some money, she's played by a big star. Then, suddenly, the carpet is whisked away and the tale takes a left turn! It hadn't been done before and it still works a treat if you don't know the film. Sick, black comedy and genius film-making. Bloch's novel was inspired by the real-life killer, Ed Gein, who was also the basis for films like *The Texas Chainsaw Massacre* and *Deranged*. *Psycho*'s sequels are not quite as naff as you might expect, but I'll say no more than that for them. A restored, widescreen edition of *Psycho* (with extras including a version of the famous shower scene *sans* music) has just been released on the new DVD (Digital Versatile Disc) format.

RABID

MARILYN CHAMBERS, FRANK MOORE, JOE SILVER, SUSAN ROMAN

DAVID CRONENBERG

CANADA (ARROW) 1976

90m (18)

Porn star Chambers takes the lead in this typical Cronenberg body horror epic about a girl who develops a vampiric, penis-like underarm appendage after being treated in a clinic for injuries from a road crash. Soon all in her path are foaming at the mouth. Lovely jubbly.

RASPUTIN THE MAD MONK

CHRISTOPHER LEE, BARBARA SHELLEY, RICHARD PASCO, FRANCIS MATTHEWS

DON SHARP

UK (LUMIERE) 1965

92m (15)

Shot back-to-back with *Dracula – Prince of Darkness*, and for legal reasons only loosely based on the real death of Rasputin (the murderer of the Russian mystic was alive at the time and had sued MGM years before). Quite why the law should protect a self-confessed murderer is beyond me, but there it is. A great, thoroughly trashy piece of nonsense, with Lee in fine form. Sadly, as is so often the case, not in widescreen ratio unless you plump for the US laserdisc and even that is cropped for technical reasons.

HORROR

ROSEMARY'S BABY 5

MIA FARROW, JOHN CASSAVETES, RUTH GORDON, SIDNEY BLACKMER, MAURICE EVANS

ROMAN POLANSKI

USA (CIC) 1968

137m (18)

Prestige production by shlock-meister William Castle, with Polanski helming a chilling version of Ira Levin's novel about an actor who signs on with some satanic cultists to have his wife give birth to the son of the horned one himself. Filmed in the apartment building where John Lennon was later murdered, it has an errie, disturbing, claustrophobic feel and the coven are disturbingly mundane and believable. There's a nice joke where actress Angela Dorian (as a previous candidate for devil-birthing) agrees that she resembles 'Victoria Vetri' – this was a name she appeared under in other movies! A great book of photographs shot during production has just come out.

THE SECT 5

HERBERT LOM, KELLY LEIGH CURTIS, TOMAS ARANA

MICHELE SOAVI

ITALY (MARQUEE) 1991

115m (18)

A Manson-style murder in the desert. Gore in the subway. Global cults. Soavi mixes a compellingly mysterious brew that, like most of his work, will delight some and bore others. Lustrously lensed and let down only by a silly ending.

SCREAM 3

DAVID ARQUETTE, NEVE CAMPBELL, DREW BARRYMORE, COURTENEY COX

WES CRAVEN

USA (BUENA VISTA) 1996

107m (18)

An attempt to vary the standard slasher movie by having the cast say droll, knowing things to let the audience understand that they dig just what a silly film they're in. For some reason this has been hailed as a major breakthrough and the pic has been a runaway hit. I'm not convinced, but you might enjoy it. Sequel: *Scream 2*.

199

THE SHINING 🎬4

JACK NICHOLSON, SHELLEY
DUVALL, DANNY LLOYD, SCATMAN
CROTHERS

STANLEY KUBRICK

UK (WARNER) 1980

119m   (18)

Overrated but still interesting epic version of Stephen King's novel about a half-crazed writer and family snowed in for the winter in a haunted hotel. Kubrick, as with his *2001*, cut nearly 30 minutes after the American opening and only the short print is on tape. A longer cut has been seen on UK TV. (Full version runs 146m approx.)

SPIRITS OF THE DEAD 🎬4

JANE FONDA, PETER FONDA,
ALAIN DELON, BRIGITTE BARDOT,
TERENCE STAMP

ROGER VADIM, LOUIS MALLE,
FEDERICO FELLINI

FRANCE/ITALY (ARROW) 1967

121m   (18)

Three Poe tales adapted by arthouse directors: Vadim's *Metzengerstein* uses the pervy idea of casting brother/sister Fondas as lovers; Malle's *William Wilson* has two Alain Delons mixing it up with Bardot; and Fellini has Stamp being pursued by the Devil (in the form of a little girl, an idea nicked from Mario Bava): *Toby Dammit* is the title of his segment. Elegant and worthy of critical reappraisal.

THE STRANGLERS OF BOMBAY 🎬5

ALLAN CUTHBERTSON, ANDREW
CRUICKSHANK, GEORGE PASTELL,
MARIE DEVEREUX, GUY ROLFE

TERENCE FISHER

UK (ENCORE) 1959 B&W

80m   (15)

Controversial and Sadian Hammer horror about murders in the Raj period by the Thugees of India – cultists who worship Kali, a goddess who wears a necklace of skulls. She is incarnated in the flesh by the busty Devereux, a devotee who salivates as various gougings, tongue-pullings and other tortures are inflicted on hapless victims. Curiously for such a supposedly vile movie, I recall that it only rated the old 'A' certificate, which admitted youngsters when with an adult. Not in widescreen, unfortunately.

A STUDY IN TERROR 🎬3

JOHN NEVILLE, DONALD
HOUSTON, JOHN FRASER,
ANTHONY QUAYLE, JUDI DENCH

JAMES HILL

UK (ARTHOUSE) 1965

95m   (15)

Oodles of top thesps in this rather lurid and tatty film which pits Sherlock Holmes against Jack the Ripper. The theme was handled better in *Murder By Decree*.

HORROR

SUSPIRIA [4]

★ JESSICA HARPER, UDO KIER, ALIDA VALLI, JOAN BENNETT

🎬 DARIO ARGENTO

ITALY (NOUVEAUX) 1976

⏱ 95m   (18)

Argento's supernatural classic, for years only available here in a censored print, has at last been passed in this uncut widescreen version by the BBFC. It's a psychedelically-coloured tale of a ballet school mixed up in witchy doings, with Harper making a good showing as the menaced student up to her ears in gore and mystery. The first part of Argento's unfinished 'Three Mothers' trilogy. *Inferno* (see page 191) forms the second episode.

THE TERROR OF DR HICHCOCK [4]

★ BARBARA STEELE, ROBERT FLEMYNG, HARRIET WHITE

🎬 RICCARDO FREDA

ITALY (MOVIELAND) 1962

⏱ 88m   (18)

Seminal necrophiliac sleaze from one of the masters of the golden age of Italian horror. Steele looks haunting, glowering in morbid colour through the glass lid of her coffin. Not widescreen, but still a must. Box incorrectly spells the Doc's name as 'Hitchcock', like the great Alfred.

THEATRE OF BLOOD [4]

★ VINCENT PRICE, DIANA RIGG, CORAL BROWNE, JACK HAWKINS

🎬 DOUGLAS HICKOX

UK (MGM/UA-WARNER) 1973

⏱ 104m   (18)

Stuffed with famous Brit thespians, this is a must-see for any actor who has wanted to waste his critics. An old Shakespearean barnstormer named Lionheart (cast in the Donald Wolfit, 'Sir', mode) takes to snuffing out hacks who did him down – each murder being based on a scene by the Bard. Price is wonderful, as are the supporting cast. Funny. Bloody.

THE THING [5]

★ KURT RUSSELL, WILFORD BRIMLEY, RICHARD DYSART, TK CARTER

🎬 JOHN CARPENTER

USA (CIC) 1982

⏱ 109m   (18)

Spirited remake of the Hawks/Nyby classic about a monster thawed from an ice-bound flying saucer. Modern SFX enable Carpenter to go back to the source story's premise about a creature that can shapeshift to mimic any living … er … thing. Bleak ending. Wonderful film. Not letterboxed. Underrated when released, ripe for re-evaluation.

TOMBS OF THE BLIND DEAD

CESAR BURNER, MARIA SILVA, JUAN CORTES

AMANDO DE OSSORIO

SPAIN/PORTUGAL (REDEMPTION) 1971

93m (18)

First of a series about nasty corpses of Templars coming back to life to abuse the populace. Overrated through non-availability. Letterboxed. Cut.

THE VAMPIRE BAT

LIONELL ATWILL, FAY WRAY, MELVYN DOUGLAS, DWIGHT FRYE

FRANK STRAYER

USA (REDEMPTION) 1993 B&W

67m (PG)

Mad-scientist stuff, with Atwill escaping suspicion for a time as the crimes of his creation are blamed on vampires by superstitious locals. Neat early indie horror.

VAMPIRE CIRCUS

ADRIENNE CORRI, LAURENCE PAYNE, THORLEY WALTERS, LYNNE FREDERICK

ROBERT YOUNG

UK (CINEMA CLUB) 1971

87m (18)

Circus relatives of slaughtered vampire take revenge on the village that done the dirty deed. A genuine late-Hammer gem with a large cast in the manner of the old gothic novels so beloved of critic of the genre Montague Summers. The seductive-yet-menacing air that carnivals and circuses seem to exude is here in spades.

VIDEODROME

JAMES WOODS, DEBBIE HARRY, LYNNE GORMAN

DAVID CRONENBERG

CANADA (CIC) 1982

89m (18)

Surreal trip in typical Cronenberg body-loathing style, about cancers inflicted by watching oddball S&M 'snuff' videos. Marvellous but confusing – it comes as no surprise to learn it was begun without a finished script. Cut for tape during the moral panic of the early 80s, but the full theatrical print is now on video. A slightly longer director's cut is on laserdisc. There is also a USA TV print which replaces violence and/or sex with dialogue out-takes.

HORROR

WHITE ZOMBIE 🎬 4

⭐ BELA LUGOSI, MADGE BELLAMY, ROBERT FRAZER

🎬 VICTOR HALPERIN

USA (ReVISION) 1932

⏱ 73m   (PG)

Atmospheric early indie zombie flick set in Haiti, with clever use of sound as well as visuals. Lugosi is a treat as zombie-master Murder Legendre. Also available on Redemption.

THE WICKER MAN 🎬 5

⭐ EDWARD WOODWARD, CHRISTOPHER LEE, BRITT EKLAND, DIANE CILENTO, INGRID PITT

🎬 ROBIN HARDY

UK (WARNER/TERRORVISION) 1973

⏱ 102/87m   (18)

Heavily cut and stuck on a double bill under *Don't Look Now*, this creepy story of pagan worship and human sacrifice on a Scottish island gained a cult rep over the years: *Cinefantastique* dubbed it 'the Citizen Kane of horror films', and it was partly restored by the BBC. Recently, in spite of all the odds, a print of the full, supposedly lost, version turned up – so why have Warners, even on a specialist label, put out the old cut-to-shreds copy once again? It's tapes like this that have led some to dub the new label, perhaps unfairly, 'TerribleVision'.

Try and get hold of a copy of the uncut USA tape – it really makes all the difference. But this little classic, with Edward Woodward as the unwitting copper who thinks he's a hunter when he's really the prey, is a must-see in any version. Note: Star Lee says even the longest version is not the full film he made. Times stated are for longest and shortest extant versions.

WITCHFINDER GENERAL 🎬 5

⭐ VINCENT PRICE, IAN OGILVY, HILARY DWYER, RUPERT DAVIES, PATRICK WYMARK

🎬 MICHAEL REEVES

UK (REDEMPTION) 1968

⏱ 84m   (18)

It was a loss to cinema when Reeves died while still in his twenties, but now we have this, his best work, in its full version at last. Loosely based on a real-life character, it concerns Price's sanctimonious and hypocritical witchfinder and his assistant in the time of Cromwell, and the way in which righteous revenge can become almost as bad as the wrongs it seeks to stop. Redemption have restored violence previously cut by the BBFC, as well as nudity previously only seen in European prints. Print is rather scratchy. Box says the print is letterboxed at 1.66, but on my copy this is virtually unnoticeable.

WOLF 🎬2

⭐ JACK NICHOLSON, MICHELLE PFEIFFER, CHRISTOPHER PLUMMER, JAMES SPADER

🎬 MIKE NICHOLS

USA (COLUMBIA TRISTAR) 1994

⏱ 125m (15)

Slow horror-comedy about a businessman revitalised but troubled after being infected by lycanthropy. This old tale has been done better in *An American Werewolf In London* (see page 175).

WOLFEN 🎬4

⭐ ALBERT FINNEY, GREGORY HINES, DIANE VENORA, EDWARD JAMES OLMOS

🎬 MICHAEL WADLEIGH

USA (WARNER/TERRORVISION) 1981

⏱ 115m (18)

Ecological fable from *Woodstock* director Wadleigh, about a pack of wolves living in cities and preying on vagrants. Plenty of psychedelic animal-point-of-view shots. Letterboxed.

ZOMBIE FLESH EATERS 🎬3

⭐ RICHARD JOHNSON, TISA FARROW, IAN McCULLOCH, AL CLIVER

🎬 LUCIO FULCI

ITALY (VIPCO) 1979

⏱ 91m (18)

The recently-deceased Fulci directed this pseudo-sequel to Romero's *Dawn Of The Dead* (an alternative, Dario Argento-edit of that film was issued in Italy as *Zombi*, so this version was known as *Zombi 2* over there) and it was passed by the BBFC for UK cinemas with cuts. Then came the moral scare of the 80s which led to the VRA, and video copies of this film – exactly the same as in the cinema version – were seized! Laughably, after all that carry-on, that same version is now out on video with a BBFC cert! So what was all the fuss about? You tell me. Vipco are one of the few firms to indicate on their box that films have been cut – it may not help sales but you have to admire them. They issue an uncut version of this movie in Holland. This UK version is available letterboxed. Note: Vipco seem to have stopped trading in Britain but copies of their tapes are stll found in many stores. The uncut and letterboxed print of this film is also an import disc, on DVD, under the name *Zombie*.

MUSICALS

To most people, movie musicals mean only one thing: big-budget, colour extravaganzas from the heyday of the MGM studios. But the films of rock stars like the Beatles, Prince and Elvis Presley are musicals too, as are dramas such as *A Star Is Born* and *Absolute Beginners*. Whether your taste runs to golden oldies like *High Society* and *Showboat* or something a little more up-to-date such as *The Commitments*, there is a rich vein here for the viewer to mine. Best of all, somehow the addition of a few classic songs and dazzling dance routines makes even the most slender plot worth viewing over and over again, so the titles in this section are well worth adding to your permanent video collection.

7 BRIDES FOR 7 BROTHERS

HOWARD KEEL, JANE POWELL, RUSS TAMBLYN, JULIE NEWMEYER

STANLEY DONEN

USA (MGM/UA) 1954

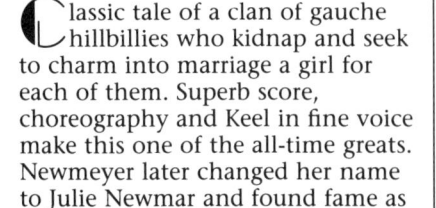

104m (U)

Classic tale of a clan of gauche hillbillies who kidnap and seek to charm into marriage a girl for each of them. Superb score, choreography and Keel in fine voice make this one of the all-time greats. Newmeyer later changed her name to Julie Newmar and found fame as Catwoman in the 60s TV series *Batman*. Available in a widescreen transfer.

ABSOLUTE BEGINNERS

EDDIE O'CONNELL, PATSY KENSIT, JAMES FOX, DAVID BOWIE, RAY DAVIES

JULIEN TEMPLE

USK (VISION) 1986

107m (15)

Ambitious musical adaptation of Colin McInnes' 1959 novel set amidst Notting Hill's racial mix. A major flop and often abused by critics, yet hardly as bad as is suggested. Though the two juvenile leads, Kensit and O'Connell, are weak in the extreme (director Temple described Kensit as having 'ankles like milk bottles') there are some grand set-pieces, particularly those featuring Bowie and Kinks' singer Davies.

CLASSIC 1000 VIDEOS

ALL THAT JAZZ 🎬3

⭐ ROY SCHEIDER, JESSICA LANGE, JOHN LITHGOW, CLIFF GORMAN

🎬 BOB FOSSE

USA (FOX) 1979

⏱ 118m (15)

Autobiographical fantasy by Fosse about a choreographer who relives his life of sex and excess as he lies ill in hospital and indulges fantasies of his wildest dance concepts. Not a big hit, but won several Oscars including one for best score. Inspired a porn version, *All That Jizz* (!).

AN AMERICAN IN PARIS 🎬4

⭐ GENE KELLY, LESLIE CARON, NINA FOCH, OSCAR LEVANT

🎬 VINCENTE MINELLI

USA (MGM/UA) 1951

⏱ 108m (U)

American soldier lingers in Paree after World War Two and finds himself in love with two gals. No big surprises but a classic of sorts and satisfying entertainment. Six Oscars including best picture, score and cinematography. Highly recommended. Available on a two-for-one tape with *Gigi* (see page 211).

BLUE HAWAII 🎬2

⭐ ELVIS PRESLEY, ANGELA LANSBURY, JOAN BLACKMAN, NANCY WALTERS

🎬 NORMAN TAUROG

USA (4-FRONT) 1961

⏱ 101m (PG)

Neither the nadir nor the zenith of Presley's numerous pix. Despite the non-existent plot, it's saved (just) by the lush locations and some reasonable tunes.

THE BOYFRIEND 🎬4

⭐ TWIGGY, CHRISTOPHER GABLE, MAX ADRIAN, TOMMY TUNE

🎬 KEN RUSSELL

UK (MGM/UA) 1971

⏱ 125m (U)

This film, inspired by Sandy Wilson's musical show, was a radical departure for the controversial Russell, with its air of naive flapperism and choreography in the manner of Busby Berkeley. Twiggy is okay, but is outshone by Gable and the fancy footwork of young American Tune. Running time quoted is for the full version, but the current print may be cut.

MUSICALS

BREAKING GLASS 🎬3

HAZEL O'CONNOR, PHIL DANIELS, JON FINCH, JONATHAN PRYCE

BRIAN GIBSON

UK (ENTERTAINMENT) 1980

104m (15)

Seedy drama of the neuroses of punky girl singer on her way to the top – and back down again. Overrated. Fictional rock stories, in my experience, rarely match up to the crazed outrageousness of the real thing. O'Connor was widely promoted but did not become a major actress (or singer, for that matter). Daniels is always worth a look, though.

BRIGADOON 🎬3

GENE KELLY, CYD CHARISSE, VAN JOHNSON, ELAINE STEWART

VINCENTE MINELLI

USA (MGM/UA) 1954

103m (U)

Film version of the Lerner/Loewe musical about Yanks who stumble upon a ghostly Scottish hamlet that only comes to life once in an age. Top-notch dancing and songs make it a treat for addicts of this classic Hollywood genre.

THE BUDDY HOLLY STORY 🎬4

GARY BUSEY, DON STROUD, CHARLES MARTIN SMITH, MARIA RICHWINE

STEVE RASH

USA (GUILD) 1978

110m (PG)

Inspired biopic of the short-lived 50s singer/songwriter. Oddly enough, I first saw this pic about a man who dies at the climax in a plane crash during a transatlantic flight! Cheered me up no end. Busey really lived the part, and after the movie he embarked on gigs with his own band. When I worked for the original publisher of Holly's music (before the songs were sold to fan Paul McCartney) I met Holly's widow – it was odd to see this middle-aged lady living in the shadow of a man who would be a teenager for evermore. Wonderful songs, played 'live' by Busey and pals. Note: the name of Will Jordan appears twice in the credits – you're not seeing double, there are two actors with the same name!

207

CABARET 🎬 5

LIZA MINNELLI, JOEL GREY, MICHAEL YORK, HELMUT GRIEM, MARISA BERENSON

BOB FOSSE

USA (CINEMA CLUB V) 1972

123m (15)

Christopher Isherwood's tales of decadent American Sally Bowles in Berlin during the rise of Nazism, transformed into a stunning musical piece set in the sleazy cabaret of the title. All the actors perform with brio, especially Minnelli and nimble Grey as the MC. They both won Oscars, as did the score and the director. Not to be missed on any account – even if you hate musicals! Music by Ebb and Kander.

CALAMITY JANE 🎬 3

DORIS DAY, HOWARD KEEL, ALLYN ANN McLERIE, PHILIP CAREY

DAVID BUTLER

USA (WARNER) 1953

97m (U)

Doris Day was once considered the epitome of homely womanhood, but in recent years she has been hailed as a pre-feminist icon – and it's not too hard to see why from viewing her in this tale (highly fictionalised, of course) of the rootin', tootin', buckskin-clad Wild West gal. Great fun, and the memorable song 'Secret Love' won an Oscar.

CAMELOT 🎬 4

RICHARD HARRIS, VANESSA REDGRAVE, DAVID HEMMINGS, FRANCO NERO

JOSHUA LOGAN

USA (WARNER) 1967

175m (U)

Adaptation of the Lerner/Loewe stage musical based on the myths about the *ménage-à-trois* of King Arthur, Guinevere and Sir Lancelot. Spectacular and with a fine score, though musical form is perhaps not best served by being stretched to epic length and the actors don't entirely convince. Impressive for all that. Oscars for score, costumes and art direction.

CAN-CAN 🎬 3

FRANK SINATRA, SHIRLEY MacLAINE, MAURICE CHEVALIER, JULIET PROWSE

WALTER LANG

USA (FOX) 1960

131m (U)

Set in 90s Paris (1890s, that is) the story concerns a nightspot hassled by the police over its supposedly risqué dance routine of the title. In real life when the girls threw up their skirts their bottoms were bare, but you mustn't hope for such thrills hereabouts, I'm afraid! Saved by a good cast, especially Sinatra and MacLaine.

MUSICALS

THE COMMITMENTS ▣4

ANGELINE BALL, BRONAGH GALLAGHER, ROBERT ARKINS, MICHAEL AHERNE

ALAN PARKER

USA/EIRE (FOX) 1991

113m (15)

Roddy Doyle's novel is the basis for this funny, moving and hugely appealing little pic about the adventures of a nascent soul band in Dublin. The only sad thing is that the talented cast of new faces have either returned to obscurity or have so far been given no more than cameo stints in subsequent movies, which seems a waste. A box set with documentary was available but appears to have been deleted.

CRY-BABY ▣3

JOHNNY DEPP, AMY LOCAINE, IGGY POP, RICKI LAKE, TRACI LORDS

JOHN WATERS

USA (CIC) 1990

81m (15)

Waters has moved increasingly away from wildly inspired filth like *Pink Flamingos* into commercially safer kitsch teen parodies of 50s trash, such as *Hairspray* and this effort. Lovingly crafted tat, with an interesting cast: Depp is now a major star, Lords is an ex-hard-porno player and Pop is the former leader of the Stooges, a genius rock and roll group with self-destruct tendencies.

DADDY LONG LEGS ▣3

FRED ASTAIRE, LESLIE CARON, FRED CLARK, THELMA RITTER

JEAN NEGULESCO

USA (FOX) 1955

126m (U)

'Something's Gotta Give' indeed, when Astaire fancies Caron in yet another of the many Paris-set musicals on offer. Debonair hoofing, and songs by the great Johnny Mercer. Not a great movie, but Astaire is on form.

DOCTOR DOOLITTLE ▣3

REX HARRISON, SAMANTHA EGGAR, RICHARD ATTENBOROUGH, ANTHONY NEWLEY

RICHARD FLEISCHER

USA (FOX) 1967

138m (U)

Colour abounds in this misguided attempt to make a musical version of Hugh Lofting's stories about a zany doc who studies animal languages. It may even soon lose novelty value as I saw a woman on TV the other day who claims to speak fluent 'cat'! And *The Horse Whisperer* is said to be based on truth, too! Oscars: SFX and best song for Bricusse's 'Talk to the Animals'. Now a London stage hit. 1998 non-musical remake with Eddie Murphy.

EXPRESSO BONGO 〖4〗

☆ LAURENCE HARVEY, SYLVIA SYMS, CLIFF RICHARD, YOLANDE DONLAN

🎬 VAL GUEST

UK (VISION) 1959 B&W

⏱ 101m (PG)

Impressive monochrome version of a Wolf Mankowitz play about Soho and its denizens. The young, not yet 'Sir', Cliff Richard is pretty insipid as are the songs, but Harvey is able as a husting wide-boy. A cult movie nowadays, yet it gets by on more than mere camp appeal.

FAME 〖4〗

☆ IRENE CARA, LEE CURRERI, GENE ANTHONY RAY, DEBBIE ALLEN

🎬 ALAN PARKER

USA (MGM/UA) 1980

⏱ 128m (15)

Brit Parker's second musical foray (the first was the kiddy gangster pic *Bugsy Malone*) is the now somewhat dated, yet still exuberant, story of youngsters desperate to 'make it' (in both senses of the phrase) as they attend New York's real-life performing arts high school and cope with personal traumas. The dancing is still explosive, though the songs feel stuck in the disco era. Inspired a TV series also called *Fame*, so the film is sometimes billed as *Fame – The Movie* to differentiate. Ironic note: when the film first came out I went along to a preview with a bunch of hopeful youngsters of the type the movie was both about and aimed at, only to hear an old dear in a fur coat whisper to her pal: 'I've never seen so many dead-beats at a premiere, dear!' Some folks never get the message.

FIDDLER ON THE ROOF 〖4〗

☆ TOPOL, NORMA CRANE, MOLLY PICON, PAUL MICHAEL GLASER

🎬 NORMAN JEWISON

USA (MGM/UA) 1971

⏱ 172m (U)

Over-long but well-crafted film of the Broadway show about life for poor rural Jews in pre-Communist Russia. Serious themes but memorable tunes like *If I Were a Rich Man* helped make Topol an international star. Oscars for best score, cinematography and sound. Available in widescreen.

FLASHDANCE 〖3〗

☆ JENNIFER BEALS, MICHAEL NOURI, LILIA SKALA, BELINDA BAUER

🎬 ADRIAN LYNE

USA (CIC) 1983

⏱ 91m (15)

Inspirational tale of female welder (!) who wants to be a dancer. Beals is great but I understand some of the dancing was doubled by a male hoofer – don't ask me how they managed it! Oscar: best song (*What a Feeling*). Not available in widescreen. Not bad, but I got tired just watching the dance sequences.

MUSICALS

FUNNY GIRL

BARBRA STREISAND, OMAR SHARIF, ANNE FRANCIS, WALTER PIDGEON

WILLIAM WYLER

USA (CINEMA CLUB V) 1968

141m (U)

Streisand before her ego went crazy is brimming with star quality in this biopic of stage legend Fanny Brice. She won an Oscar for her performance, though she had to share the award with Katharine Hepburn in *The Lion In Winter*. This would seem to be a cut print as the original was listed on release as some ten minutes longer.

GIGI

LESLIE CARON, MAURICE CHEVALIER, LOUIS JOURDAN, HERMIONE GINGOLD

VINCENTE MINNELLI

USA (MGM/UA) 1958

111m (PG)

Colourful Parisian (again!) froth about a boyish cutie who grows up to be a courtesan but opts for romance in this adaptation of the Colette story. Caron is perfect as the ingenue, though I personally find the crooning of Chevalier (*Thank Heaven for Little Girls, I Remember It Well*) sickly sweet. A weighty nine Oscars (best picture, director, cinematography, editing, sets, script, costumes, score and song – 'Gigi' – plus a special award for Chevalier). Available on a two-for-one tape with *An American In Paris* (see page 206).

GREASE

JOHN TRAVOLTA, OLIVIA NEWTON-JOHN, SID CAESAR, STOCKARD CHANNING

RANDAL KLEISER

USA (CIC) 1978

105m (PG)

Nauseating film version of ersatz rock 'n' roll teen romance musical. Cloying songs, wimpy 'Ms Neutron-Bomb' and vulgar hip-thrusting from Travolta, yet it does have the undeniable drive and catchy songs to account for its hit status. Atrocious sequel, *Grease 2*, has nothing to commend it at all. Available in widescreen.

THE GREAT ROCK 'N' ROLL SWINDLE

THE SEX PISTOLS, MALCOLM McLAREN, RONNIE BIGGS, IRENE HANDL, LIZ FRASER

JULIEN TEMPLE

UK (POLYGRAM) 1980

100m (18)

It's hard to believe over 20 years have passed since the manufactured punk outrage of The Sex Pistols caused so much fuss in the UK press – spawning a movement that was the most exciting youth cult since the hippy daze of 1967. Svengali manager Malcolm McLaren originally planned a Pistols flick – *Who Killed Bambi?* – to be helmed by soft-core sex maestro Russ Meyer, but it fell through and this project was cobbled together in the aftermath. It has, in addition to the group, a bizarre cast of everyone from train-robber Ronnie Biggs to tragic sex star Mary Millington, plus under-age nudes, dwarfs and obscene cartoon footage in a wry comment on the way the hype was created and sold. For a darker view of the band, take a look at Alex Cox's *Sid And Nancy* (see page 120).

GYPSY

ROSALIND RUSSELL, NATALIE WOOD, KARL MALDEN, PAUL WALLACE

MERVYN LEROY

USA (ENTERTAINMENT) 1962

149m (PG)

Sondheim/Styne stage musical adapted for the screen, telling the story of stripper Gypsy Rose Lee. A fizzing cast give it all they've got, but as *Radio Times* critic Derek Winnert has noted, one of the film's best tunes, 'Together Wherever We Go', has been cut out so poorly that the music trails over into the next scene. Still worth catching.

MUSICALS

HAIR

JOHN SAVAGE, TREAT WILLIAMS, BEVERLY D'ANGELO, ANNIE GOLDEN, ELLEN FOLEY

MILOS FORMAN

USA (MGM/UA) 1979

121m (15)

Forman is a Euro director who has made a career out of films giving his outsider's view of the USA. The problem with hit hippy show *Hair* was that it was neither filmed soon enough to be contemporary or late enough to have nostalgia value, but lensed in the wake of the punk era when the anti-war, flower-power ethos that fills the score was firmly out of favour. It's hard to trash work that involves people you know, but I have to say that two girl singers I became friends with in my rock-hack days, Annie Golden and Ellen Foley, have no chance to shine here: Golden has the bigger part, but her considerable vocal prowess isn't really used – she went on to good non-singing roles in TV's *Miami Vice* and the recent sci-fi film *12 Monkeys* (see page 238). Foley has only one song 'n' dance, but had a better acting part in *Fatal Attraction* (see page 104). As for *Hair*, you'll hardly notice the Twyla Tharp choreography and the good songs are badly sung.

A HARD DAY'S NIGHT

THE BEATLES, WILFRID BRAMBELL, NORMAN ROSSINGTON

RICHARD LESTER

UK (VIDEO COLLECTION) 1964 B&W

83m (U)

A veritable time-capsule of the initial excitement of the early 60s fan mania surrounding the emergence of the Beatles. Grainy, documentary feel, merged with Lester's choreographing of silent-movie-styled antics to the group's hits which set the style for pop-promo video for many years to come. Inevitably a bit dated and occasionally embarrassing, it is nevertheless filled with its share of fresh and amusing moments. For instance, Brambell was gay in real life and George Harrison at one point comments slyly on the fact that he's pictured reading a copy of *Queen* magazine! This is the best of the Fab Four's films.

HELLO, DOLLY! [3]

BARBRA STREISAND, WALTER MATTHAU, MICHAEL CRAWFORD, LOUIS ARMSTRONG

GENE KELLY

USA (FOX) 1969

146m (U)

Lengthy film of stage show based on Thornton Wilder's play *The Matchmaker*, pulled off via Streisand's remarkable vocals and stack of memorable songs. Oscars for best score, sets and sound. Available at the time of writing in a widescreen transfer video.

HELP! [3]

THE BEATLES, LEO McKERN, ELEANOR BRON

RICHARD LESTER

UK (VIDEO COLLECTION) 1965

92m (U)

The second Beatles movie isn't a patch on *A Hard Day's Night* (see page 213), despite the addition of colour and exotic locations. The basic concert-based plot of the first pic has been replaced by absurdist hi-jinks about a mysterious jewel, but the songs carry the day due to the compositional genius of Lennon and McCartney at their creative peak. A 60s antique.

HIGH SOCIETY [4]

FRANK SINATRA, BING CROSBY, GRACE KELLY, CELESTE HOLM

CHARLES WALTERS

USA (MGM/UA) 1956

103m (U)

Musical reworking of earlier play and film *The Philadelphia Story* is a light and sophisticated confection about romantic entanglements among the socialite set. This was Grace Kelly's final film before she became Princess Grace of Monaco. Great fun.

KING CREOLE [4]

ELVIS PRESLEY, CAROLYN JONES, DEAN JAGGER, WALTER MATTHAU, VIC MORROW

MICHAEL CURTIZ

USA (4-FRONT) 1958 B&W

116m (PG)

Presley's best film. He turns in a fair acting stint as a rebellious young would-be singer mixed up with New Orleans hoodlum Matthau, and both plot and tunes are way above average – not to mention a support cast of superb quality. Based on Harold Robbins's trashy novel *A Stone for Danny Fisher*.

MUSICALS

NEW YORK, NEW YORK 🎬 4

ROBERT DE NIRO, LIZA MINNELLI, LIONEL STANDER, DICK MILLER

MARTIN SCORSESE

USA (WARNER) 1977

164m (PG)

Scorsese's loving tribute to the kind of glitzy musical turned out in the heyday of the form by star Minnelli's dad Vincente was savaged by critics until it was reissued in this uncut version. A simple story of the on/off love of two musical stars, but the sheer scale and style will blow you away.

OLIVER! 🎬 5

RON MOODY, OLIVER REED, SHANI WALLIS, MARK LESTER, JACK WILD

CAROL REED

UK (COLUMBIA TRISTAR) 1968

146m (U)

Lionel Bart's evergreen fave based on *Oliver Twist* by Charles Dickens is seen here in its incarnation as the greatest Brit movie musical of all time. A raft of classic songs ('Food Glorious Food', 'Who Will Buy?', 'As Long as He Needs Me', etc.) and a perfect Fagin in Moody combine in a sumptuous treat for eye and ear. Sullen Ollie Reed, nephew of director Carol, proves that it wasn't mere nepotism that got him the part of evil Bill Sikes. Oscars: best picture, director, score, sets and more. Available in widescreen.

PAINT YOUR WAGON 🎬 2

CLINT EASTWOOD, LEE MARVIN, JEAN SEBERG, HARVE PRESNELL

JOSHUA LOGAN

USA (CIC) 1969

167m (PG)

S-l-o-w and misguided film of Lerner/Loewe stage success about two Californian goldrush pards who share a wife bought in an auction. Only proves the obvious: that neither Clint ('I Talk to the Trees') or Marvin ('Wandrin' Star') can sing worth a damn. However, the latter's gruff talk-a-long proved a surprise hit single. Available in widescreen.

PAL JOEY 🎬 4

FRANK SINATRA, RITA HAYWORTH, KIM NOVAK, BOBBY SHERWOOD

GEORGE SIDNEY

USA (COLUMBIA TRISTAR) 1957 B&W

105m (PG)

A crooner in San Francisco finds himself torn between two women in this musical by Rodgers and Hart based on material by John O'Hara. Includes the legendary songs 'My Funny Valentine' and 'The Lady is a Tramp'. Sinatra at his peak.

PENNIES FROM HEAVEN [2]

STEVE MARTIN, CHRISTOPHER WALKEN, BERNADETTE PETERS, JESSICA HARPER

HERBERT ROSS

USA (MGM/UA) 1982

103m (15)

Pointless transposition into an American setting of Dennis Potter's UK TV series starring Bob Hoskins, with Martin miscast as the music seller with a life sadly at odds with the world portrayed in the songs he loves. The original worked precisely because of the downbeat Brit locale being a world away from the Yank-style fantasy of the music, something this air-headed remake misses. Beautiful photography by Gordon Willis, though.

PINK FLOYD – THE WALL [2]

BOB GELDOF, JAMES LAURENSON, CHRISTINE HARGREAVES, BOB HOSKINS

ALAN PARKER

UK (POLYGRAM0 1982

92m (15)

Ever since the early departure of founder Syd Barrett, rock experimenters Pink Floyd have become more and more obsessed with overblown, crowd-pleasing bombast, and this movie is no exception: live performance, cartoons by Gerald Scarfe and pretentious thesping derail this whiny tale of the sufferings of a poor rocker, based on the smash hit album of the same name.

PURPLE RAIN [2]

PRINCE, APPOLLONIA KOTERO, MORRIS DAY, OLGA KARLATOS

ALBERT MAGNOLI

USA (WARNER) 1984

107m (15)

Prince – or whatever name he is now going by – was once an innovative artist, blending soul with guitar antics and sex-driven rock, but success has led him to change his name to a symbol and to indulge in ever-madder schemes. This was his debut flick, made when the foolishness was still amusing and the man was obsessed with the colour of the title – the story of a pop muso's efforts to make it isn't much, but the songs are ace. Oscar: best score. Also available on a two-for-one tape with Prince's subsequent, but less satisfying, *Graffiti Bridge*.

MUSICALS

QUADROPHENIA [3]

PHIL DANIELS, MARK WINGETT, LESLIE ASH, STING

FRANC RODDAM

UK (FEATURE FILM CO) 1979

120m (15)

I remember this one – not because I liked it, but because the scene where a scooter breaks down was filmed opposite my flat one night in 1979 and required endless takes which kept me awake. It's a decent enough little story, based on the concept album by The Who, about the lives of mod Jimmy (Daniels) and his pals led by Ace Face (Sting). Tries for poignancy but doesn't always manage it. Daniels remains a seriously undervalued talent, but many of the cast members are now quite well known, including Mark Wingett, a staple on TV's *The Bill*. Newly reissued.

THE ROCKY HORROR PICTURE SHOW [4]

TIM CURRY, SUSAN SARANDON, BARRY BOSTWICK, RICHARD O'BRIEN, CHARLES GRAY

JIM SHARMAN

UK (FOX) 1975

99m (15)

Cult film of the long-running stage show which is a daft homage to trashy rock 'n' roll and tacky 50s science-fiction flicks. A young couple stranded in the mansion of randy transvestite Curry are molested by all manner of singin', dancin' weirdos. Sick, hilarious romp, now such a cult item that some people watch it once a week and go along dressed as their favourite characters in order to shout out the dialogue along with the actors. Composer O'Brien has tried to duplicate the show's success several times but has yet to succeed.

SHOWBOAT [2]

AVA GARDNER, HOWARD KEEL, JOE E BROWN, KATHRYN GRAYSON

GEORGE SIDNEY

USA (MGM/UA) 1951

103m (U)

Hardly the best version of the Jerome Kern musical about life on a riverboat in the Deep South, but Howard Keel sings up a storm. The perfect interpretation remains James Whale's 1936 film. Based on the Edna Ferber novel.

SILK STOCKINGS [3]

FRED ASTAIRE, CYD CHARISSE, PETER LORRE, JANIS PAIGE

ROUBEN MAMOULIAN

USA (MGM/UA) 1957

114m (U)

Hollywood innovator Mamoulian's musical remake of *Ninotchka*, about a Russki politico babe in Paris, with a fine Cole Porter soundtrack. Based on the hit stage musical version, Astaire and leggy Charisse are hot, but it goes on too long.

217

CLASSIC 1000 VIDEOS

SINGIN' IN THE RAIN [5]

☆ GENE KELLY, DONALD O'CONNOR, CYD CHARISSE, RITA MORENO, DEBBIE REYNOLDS

🎬 GENE KELLY, STANLEY DONEN

USA (MGM/UA) 1952

⏱ 98m   (U)

Set in Hollywood during the advent of sound film, this is a deservedly legendary picture containing one of the most famous scenes in all of motion pictures, when Kelly splashes his way through a street set in a rainstorm while performing the title song. Magical, memorable, sheer bliss. They don't make musicals like this any more.

A STAR IS BORN [5]

☆ JUDY GARLAND, JAMES MASON, CHARLES BICKFORD, JACK CARSON

🎬 GEORGE CUKOR

USA (WARNER) 1954

⏱ 181m   (U)

Cukor's film, which functions as a drama as well as a musical, is the best of several versions of the story of a drunken star who sacrifices himself to save the career of his talented wife. Heavily cut after initial release, it was restored in 1983 to something close to original length – though in some cases only the soundtrack could be found and this had to be played back with stills replacing the missing footage on screen. It is a testament to the power of Cukor's direction, the Arlen/Ira Gershwin songs and the performances of Garland and Mason that audiences were willing to accept this. Running time given is for the original but the restoration runs to 176m. For the full story of the film's loss and rebirth, read Ronald Haver's book *A Star is Born*. Astonishingly, this 'scope classic is not out on a widescreen tape.

SWEET CHARITY [4]

☆ SHIRLEY MACLAINE, RICARDO MONTALBAN, CHITA RIVERA, JOHN McMARTIN

🎬 BOB FOSSE

USA (CIC/4-FRONT) 1969

⏱ 142m   (PG)

Fosse's first pic is a version of the Broadway hit about a bar-room tart in search of true love. Lots of pizzazz. Neil Simon's story is based on Fellini's 1957 flick *Nights of Cabiria*. No widescreen available.

THAT'LL BE THE DAY [3]

☆ DAVID ESSEX, RINGO STARR, KEITH MOON, BILLY FURY

🎬 CLAUDE WHATHAM

UK (WARNER/LUMIERE) 1973

⏱ 87m   (15)

Real-life rock stars in this story of a singer's crawl up the greasy pole of pop success. Nice work from Essex and some okay tunes. The story was continued in the follow up, *Stardust*, and the films are available on a two-for-one tape.

218

MUSICALS

THAT'S ENTERTAINMENT [4]

FRED ASTAIRE, GENE KELLY, FRANK SINATRA, DEBBIE REYNOLDS, MICKEY ROONEY

JACK HALEY Jnr

USA (MGM/UA) 1974

122m (U)

Compilation of classic moments from hit musicals of yore. A good idea that proved a hit with a nostalgic public. Original running time was allegedly 137m, so this appears to be a cut version. Followed by Parts 2 and 3, though by the third effort there were definite signs of barrel-scraping.

TOMMY [2]

OLIVER REED, ROGER DALTREY, ANN-MARGRET, JACK NICHOLSON, TINA TURNER

KEN RUSSELL

UK (POLYGRAM) 1975

111m (18)

Russell's bloated and vulgar adaptation of rock band the Who's pop opera about a psychosomatically sense-impaired boy who triumphs over his abused childhood to become a messiah. Stupid and garish and the songs were performed to better effect on the group's original album version. Still, if you need to see busty Ann-Margret lolling in a sea of baked beans, this is your chance!

THE UNSINKABLE MOLLY BROWN [2]

DEBBIE REYNOLDS, HARVE PRESNELL, ED BEGLEY, MARTITA HUNT

CHARLES WALTERS

USA (MGM/UA) 1964

128m (U)

Based on the rags-to-riches story of a woman who survived the *Titanic* disaster, with Reynolds as the Denver girl who seeks her fortune and escape from rural isolation. Too long by half.

WEST SIDE STORY [5]

NALALIE WOOD, RUSS TAMBLYN, GEORGE CHAKIRIS, RITA MORENO, RICHARD BEYMER

ROBERT WISE, JEROME ROBBINS

USA (MGM/UA) 1961

155m (PG)

Classy musical version of the plot of Shakespeare's *Romeo and Juliet* transposed to the tough, gang-ridden streets of New York. Great Leonard Bernstein music, Sondheim lyrics and Robbins choreography make it work. Oscars include: best picture, direction, cinematography, supporting actor (Chakiris) and supporting actress (Moreno). Available in widescreen. A classic.

WHITE CHRISTMAS

BING CROSBY, DANNY KAYE, ROSEMARY CLOONEY, DEAN JAGGER

MICHAEL CURTIZ

USA (CIC) 1954

115m (U)

Winter Wonderland nonsense set in a holiday resort run by ex-GIs. Some decent Irving Berlin tunes. Available in widescreen.

THE WIZARD OF OZ

JUDY GARLAND, BERT LAHR, RAY BOLGER, JACK HALEY, MARGARET HAMILTON

VICTOR FLEMING

USA (WARNER) 1939 COL/B&W

102m (U)

The 'Oz' tales of L Frank Baum have been the subject of several films: silent, cartoon, Disney ... even a Michael Jackson vehicle. This, however, remains the classic interpretation: the glowing colour is nicely contrasted with the monochrome of 'real life' in Kansas before the young Garland is transported to the land of the Tin Man, Cowardly Lion, Wicked Witch *et al*. Enjoyable tunes and an indefinable magical quality make it a must-see for all ages. Oscars: best song ('Over the Rainbow') and score.

YANKEE DOODLE DANDY

JAMES CAGNEY, JOAN LESLIE, WALTER HUSTON, EDDIE FOY Jnr

MICHAEL CURTIZ

USA (MGM/UA) 1942 B&W

126m (U)

Biopic of songwriter/performer George M Cohan, with Cagney showing his prowess as a hoofer. Those who have only ever seen him in gangster parts will be pleasantly surprised. Oscars: best actor (Cagney), best score and sound, all well deserved.

ROMANCE

A romantic video can provide the perfect finishing touch for your cosy evening in *à deux* – and there seems to have been an upsurge of romantic movies of late, from the 'odd couple' of *The Piano* to street-smart stories like *Sleepless in Seattle*. But we mustn't forget that romance has always been part of film-making: the numerous versions of classics such as *Romeo and Juliet* and *Wuthering Heights* are testament to that.

ABOUT LAST NIGHT

ROB LOWE, DEMI MOORE, JAMES BELUSHI, ELIZABETH PERKINS

EDWARD ZWICK

USA (CINEMA CLUB V) 1986

102m (18)

Hip romantic comedy, based on David Mamet's play *Sexual Perversity in Chicago*, and emblematic of the modern genre. Debut for Perkins, with nice work from Lowe and Moore. Original running time listed at 113m in some sources.

THE ACCIDENTAL TOURIST

WILLIAM HURT, KATHLEEN TURNER, GEENA DAVIS, BILL PULLMAN

LAWRENCE KASDAN

USA (WARNER) 1988

116m (PG)

Travel writer rebuilds his life via an affair after his child dies in an accident – but then his estranged wife returns. What to do? Based on a novel by Anne Tyler, this romantic comedy hit won an Oscar for Geena Davis.

AN AFFAIR TO REMEMBER

CARY GRANT, DEBORAH KERR, CATHLEEN NESBITT, RICHARD DENNING

LEO McCAREY

USA (FOX) 1957

115m (U)

Weepy remake of the same director's 1939 film *Love Affair*. Two people, both engaged to others, test the strength of the shipboard romance by agreeing to meet in six months – but fate takes a hand. Engaging.

AGE OF CONSENT 🎬2

JAMES MASON, HELEN MIRREN, FRANK THRING, JACK MacGOWRAN

MICHAEL POWELL

AUSTRALIA (TARTAN) 1969

⏱ 95m (15)

Rare turkey for Powell, about a painter's love for his young model. Based on a story by Norman Lindsay. Beautiful-looking photography of the Great Barrier Reef. Widescreen available.

THE AGE OF INNOCENCE 🎬3

DANIEL DAY-LEWIS, MICHELLE PFEIFFER, WINONA RYDER

MARTIN SCORSESE

USA (COLUMBIA TRISTAR) 1993

⏱ 138m (U)

Lives and loves of posh folk in New York of the 1870s. Not Scorsese's usual turf, but a sumptuously shot (if ennui-inducing) version of Edith Wharton's Pulitzer Prize-winning novel. Previously filmed in 1934. Widescreen available.

THE AMERICAN PRESIDENT 🎬3

MICHAEL DOUGLAS, ANNETTE BENING, MARTIN SHEEN, MICHAEL J FOX

ROB REINER

USA (CIC) 1995

⏱ 109m (15)

Topical tale of love in the White House. Slender stuff, but with a good cast of attractive professionals and craftsman-like direction from the ever-reliable Rob Reiner it makes for an amusing evening's entertainment.

ANNE OF THE THOUSAND DAYS 🎬3

RICHARD BURTON, GENEVIEVE BUJOLD, ANTHONY QUAYLE, IRENE PAPAS

CHARLES JARROTT

USA (CIC) 1969

⏱ 140m (PG)

Maxwell Anderson's stage play provides the basis for this gloomy tale of one of Henry VIII's doomed wives, Anne Boleyn. Solid fare for those who dote on these historical romances. Oscar for costumes; nine nominations in all.

BLOOD AND SAND 🎬4

TYRONE POWER, LINDA DARNELL, RITA HAYWORTH, LAIRD CREGAR

ROUBEN MAMOULIAN

USA (FOX) 1941

⏱ 120m (PG)

Richly coloured remake of the classic Valentino silent. As handsome Tyrone Power fights his way to the top of the bullfighting world, he is pursued by women and praised by camp critic Cregar. Made once more in 1989, with Sharon Stone the only notable name in the cast.

ROMANCE

THE BLUE LAGOON [2]

BROOKE SHIELDS, CHRISTOPHER ATKINS, LEO McKERN

RANDAL KLEISER

USA (MIA) 1980

104m (15)

Sexier re-make of 1949 Brit flick about two stranded kids growing to randy maturity on a tropical isle. I met Ms Shields around the time this was made, and her mom (with commendable honesty) told me that all her daughter's pix were dire. No one seeing this is likely to argue with that opinion, unless skinny-dipping footage is the sole criterion for top marks. (See page 229, *Pretty Baby*.)

THE BODYGUARD [2]

KEVIN COSTNER, WHITNEY HOUSTON, GARY KEMP

MICK JACKSON

USA (WARNER) 1993

130m (15)

Over-long tale of ex-secret service bodyguard who falls for his pop singer charge while protecting her from a killer. Formulaic guff, with crooner Houston dreadful – mugging and grimacing in an embarrassing display of what she evidently believes constitutes 'acting'. An inexplicable hit. Widescreen available.

BREATHLESS [4]

RICHARD GERE, VALERIE KAPRISKY, ART METRANO

JIM McBRIDE

USA (4-FRONT) 1983

96m (18)

Cult director McBride's remake of Godard's 1959 *A Bout De Souffle*, with Gere on top form as the young crook on the run with the gorgeous Kaprisky, living for the amoral moment with no care for future conseuences. Much praised by Quentin Tarantino. The censor cut a few seconds that showed how to break into a car.

THE BRIDGES OF MADISON COUNTY [3]

CLINT EASTWOOD, MERYL STREEP

CLINT EASTWOOD

USA (WARNER) 1995

129m (12)

Brief romance between photographer Eastwood and Ms Streep ensues after they meet when he asks directions to the famous wooden bridges of Madison County while on a photographic shoot. Not for those who like action in their movies – there isn't any. I found it turgid and dreary but others might find themselves reaching for the Kleenex as Streep chooses between passion and loyalty.

223

CASTAWAY

OLIVER REED, AMANDA DONOHOE, GEORGINA HALE, FRANCES BARBER

NICOLAS ROEG

UK (WARNER) 1986

112m (15)

True story of a young girl who signed up for a stay on a deserted island with an older man, with Donohoe stripping off a lot and inflaming Ollie Reed's lust before it all comes to an acrimonious end. (In real life the old gent is still taking women for island jaunts, it seems.) It's amazing to see Donohoe's confident showing (!) here – I remember when she was the quiet young girlfriend of pop singer Adam Ant, was known as 'Mandy' and wouldn't say 'Boo' to a goose. A rather straightforward story for the usually convoluted-minded Nic Roeg to have handled.

CHILDREN OF A LESSER GOD

WILLIAM HURT, MARLEE MATLIN, PIPER LAURIE, PHILIP BOSCO

RANDA HAINES

USA (4-FRONT) 1986

118m (15)

Mark Medoff's hit play about a deaf girl's romance with her teacher provided the vehicle for real-life deaf actress Matlin to score a richly deserved Oscar. There are some awkward moments but the film never descends to maudlin sentiment, which would have been the easy option.

COMING HOME

JON VOIGHT, JANE FONDA, BRUCE DERN, ROBERT CARRADINE

HAL ASHBY

USA (WARNER) 1978

122m (18)

Love-triangle in the time of the Vietnam War, with Fonda as the wife who falls for paralysed veteran while hubby is overseas doing his bit. Based on the book by Nancy Dowd, who helped pen the Oscar-winning script. Oscars too for Voight and Fonda.

FALLING IN LOVE

ROBERT DE NIRO, MERYL STREEP, HARVEY KEITEL, DIANNE WIEST

ULU GROSSBARD

USA (CIC) 1984

102m (PG)

A pair of upmarket New York commuters fall madly in love in spite of the fact that they're both married. Glitzy and tiresome, but undeniably well acted by the principals.

ROMANCE

FAR AND AWAY [2]

TOM CRUISE, NICOLE KIDMAN, ROBERT PROSKY, THOMAS GIBSON

RON HOWARD

USA (CIC) 1992

140m (12)

Bloated epic romance typical of the American love affair with their (imagined) roots in nineteenth-century Ireland. Cruise and Kidman, the world's most famous Scientologists, play a lout and a lady who flee trouble and emigrate to the USA, scrapping and spitting all the while, but finally going gooey-eyed at the end. Nice to look at, but this is really for fans of the two leads only.

A FAREWELL TO ARMS [3]

ROCK HUDSON, JENNIFER JONES, VITTORIO DE SICA, OSCAR HOMOLKA

KING VIDOR

USA (FOX) 1957

146m (15)

Big-scale re-make of the Oscar-winning 1932 film based on Ernest Hemingway's novel about an injured World War One ambulance driver and his love for the nurse who tends him. Hudson is wooden and the movie is simply too long, but it all looks pretty and impressive.

FOR THE BOYS [3]

BETTE MIDLER, JAMES CAAN, GEORGE SEGAL, PATRICK O'NEAL

MARK RYDELL

USA (FOX) 1991

139m (15)

Romance following Midler as she struts her stuff to entertain American 'boys' in the forces through the country's varied wars: World War Two, Korea, Vietnam. Starts off okay, but soon succumbs to dreariness and overstays its welcome.

FOREVER YOUNG [3]

MEL GIBSON, JAMIE LEE CURTIS, ELIJAH WOOD

STEVE MINER

USA (WARNER) 1992

102m (PG)

Gibson is a test-pilot in 1939. Believing his girlfriend is dying, he agrees to an experiment where he'll be frozen in suspended animation – but he is forgotten and left in a warehouse until being accidentally awakened in 1992. Finding his lover is still alive and now an old woman, the rapidly ageing Mel gets assistance from Curtis and her son to track her down before it's too late. Silly, but improbably moving if you're prepared to go along for the ride.

FORREST GUMP

TOM HANKS, ROBIN WRIGHT,
GARY SINISE, SALLY FIELD

ROBERT ZEMECKIS

USA (CIC) 1994

137m (12)

'Life is like a box of chocolates. You never know what you're gonna get.' Hmmm ... Oscar-laden film about a man too stupid to read the menu on a choc box might not seem romantic, but America is ever-ready to take the dumb and disabled to its heart (on film, at least) and *Gump* was a smash. Simple Forrest overcomes childhood disability with the aid of his can-do mom (Field), becomes a war-hero, a business success and a national icon. Love, however eludes him as his hippy girlfriend (Wright) wants to live life to the full. She makes mistakes (shame on her) while Forrest can do no wrong – even when his mind snaps and he runs the highways of the USA sporting an ever-larger beard. Despite the dubious 'stupid-is-good' message, Oscar-winning Hanks is truly mesmerising and the ending will bring a lump to the unjaundiced throat. Widescreen.

FOUR WEDDINGS AND A FUNERAL

HUGH GRANT, ANDIE McDOWELL,
SIMON CALLOW, KRISTIN SCOTT THOMAS

MIKE NEWELL

UK (POLYGRAM) 1994

117m (15)

Brit romantic comedy which was staggeringly financially successful especially in the USA where the folks are always keen to revel in the eccentricities of us madcap limeys. For me it's vastly overrated, with Hugh Grant perfecting his gauche, twitching twit routine and Andie McDowell, lovely though she is, having little of substance to do. Try it and see what you think.

THE FRENCH LIEUTENANT'S WOMAN

JEREMY IRONS, MERYL STREEP,
DAVID WARNER, LEO McKERN

KAREL REISZ

UK (WARNER) 1981

119m (15)

Based on John Fowles' novel via a script by Harold Pinter about a doomed Victorian love affair mirrored by that of the couple playing the protagonists in a modern movie. Arty and wet but proved a box-office hit with those up for a weepy. Streep is eminently watchable, as ever.

ROMANCE

GHOST

DEMI MOORE, PATRICK SWAYZE, WHOOPI GOLDBERG

JERRY ZUCKER

USA (CIC) 1990

121m (15)

Romantic fantasy about the spook of a murder victim who tries to protect his girl through a medium. Much parodied and spoofed, and has inspired the filming of other ghostly love tales. Oscars for screenplay and for supporting actress Goldberg as the dodgy spiritualist.

THE GREAT GATSBY

ROBERT REDFORD, MIA FARROW, BRUCE DERN, SAM WATERSTON, SCOTT WILSON

JACK CLAYTON

USA (CIC) 1974

135m (PG)

Second movie attempt at F Scott Fitzgerald's story of mysterious 1920s Gatsby and his tragic love. Redford is perfect as the glowingly handsome tycoon, and Waterston is wonderful as the young observer. All the cast are on form with the unfortunate exception of the insipid Farrow – in these pre-Woody Allen days one simply can't imagine a guy of Jay Gatsby's clout getting his Y-fronts in a twist over her. Patsy Kensit makes an early screen appearance as a kiddy. Oscars for score and costumes. Script by Francis Ford Coppola.

THE HUNCHBACK OF NOTRE DAME

CHARLES LAUGHTON, MAUREEN O'HARA, CEDRIC HARDWICKE, EDMOND O'BRIEN, THOMAS MITCHELL, GEORGE ZUCCO

WILLIAM DIETERLE

USA (4-FRONT) 1939 B&W

112m (PG)

Laughton stars as Quasimodo, the deformed cathedral bell-ringer, in the best-ever version of Victor Hugo's tale. His unrequited love for the gypsy girl, Esmeralda, spurs him to protect her from the lust of his master, who has commanded him to kidnap her. Criticised for sentimental style, but the compassion for the title character never bogs down the story or action. Dizzying camera-work and fantastic sets, but the crux of the film is love: those who love Esmeralda and those she loves.

227

INDECENT PROPOSAL [4]

ROBERT REDFORD, DEMI MOORE, WOODY HARRELSON

ADRIAN LYNE

USA (CIC) 1993

119m (15)

A young couple fail to gamble themselves out of a hole in Las Vegas until rich smoothy Redford takes a shine to the wife and offers a million dollars for a night of sex. Acceptance should bring relief, but the trouble is only beginning – hubby can't handle it and the rich man starts using all his wiles to obtain second helpings. An intriguing premise, let down only by an unrealistic ending.

LOVE FIELD [3]

MICHELLE PFEIFFER, DENNIS HAYSBERT, BRIAN KERWIN

JONATHAN KAPLAN

USA (CINEMA CLUB V) 1992

104m (15)

Dallas wife takes off for the funeral of JFK despite husband's objections. En route she meets a black man and his kid, inadvertently causing them a heap of trouble. Touching in places, but it's a rather flimsy piece.

LOVE IS A MANY- [2]
SPLENDORED THING

WILLIAM HOLDEN, JENNIFER JONES, TORIN THATCHER

HENRY KING

USA (FOX) 1955

120m (U)

Based on Han Suyin's novel *A Many Splendoured Thing*, this tells of a mixed-race female doc's affair with an American correspondent during the Korean War. Oscars for title-tune, score and costumes, but it's a so-so movie with the usual tearjerker ending one would expect.

ROMANCE

A MATTER OF LIFE AND DEATH [5]

☆ DAVID NIVEN, KIM HUNTER, ROGER LIVESY, MARIUS GORING

🎬 MICHAEL POWELL, EMERIC PRESSBURGER

UK (RANK) 1941 COL/B&W

⏱ 104m (U)

Mooted as a World War Two propaganda piece calling for USA/UK co-operation, but in the hands of Powell and Pressburger became a classic of screen imagination. Niven is a pilot who escapes certain death only because the angel (Goring) assigned to conduct him to heaven misses him in the fog. Having fallen in love in the meantime, he's allowed to argue his case for extra life before an angry Yank prosecutor from the American War of Independence while his body undergoes a kill-or-cure op down on earth. Heaven is depicted as silvery monochrome: 'One is starved for Technicolor up there!' sighs the angel. A truly magical picture in all departments: acting, ideas, effects, design. See it again and again. American title: *Stairway To Heaven*.

MAYERLING [2]

☆ OMAR SHARIF, JAMES MASON, CATHERINE DENEUVE, AVA GARDNER

🎬 TERENCE YOUNG

FRANCE/UK (LUMIERE) 1968

⏱ 135m (PG)

Slushy remake of 1936 effort, based on a Claude Anet novel about real-life tragic love of Euro royals. Good cast is wasted, particularly Sharif who is simply wrong for the part.

MOONSTRUCK [3]

☆ CHER, NICOLAS CAGE, VINCENT GARDENIA, OLYMPIA DUKAKIS

🎬 NORMAN JEWISON

USA (MGM/UA) 1987

⏱ 98m (PG)

Brooklyn babe Cher gets the naughty hot-to-trots for the brother of her intended. Amusing piece of froth with some good dialogue and an ace supporting cast. Cher and Dukakis both won Oscars, as did writer John Patrick Shanly. Perennially popular with romance buffs, though I personally feel it's somewhat overrated. Worth renting.

CLASSIC 1000 VIDEOS

AN OFFICER AND A GENTLEMAN [4]

RICHARD GERE, DEBRA WINGER, DAVID KEITH, LOUIS GOSSETT Jnr

TAYLOR HACKFORD

USA (CIC) 1981

119m (15)

Wide-boy Gere joins US Navy to train as an officer and has the naughtiness knocked out of him by instructor Gossett Jnr (in an Oscar-winning performance). Romance and tragedy intrude when the lad and his pal take up with two slutty gals, but our hero makes good in the end. Theme tune ('Up Where We Belong') also snared an Oscar and – like the movie – was a massive hit.

OUT OF AFRICA [3]

MERYL STREEP, ROBERT REDFORD, KLAUS MARIA BRANDAUER, MICHAEL KITCHEN

SYDNEY POLLACK

UK/USA (CIC) 1985

115m (PG)

Inspired by the life in Africa of Danish lady Karen Blixen (who wrote books as Isak Dinesen) and her romance with a white hunter, this smash hit picture is ace to look at but slow as treacle. Streep passes the accent test, but Redford is badly miscast as a stiff upper Brit. Seven Oscars: best picture/director/ cinematography/script/art direction/sound/score.

PEYTON PLACE [2]

LANA TURNER, HOPE LANGE, ARTHUR KENNEDY, RUSS TAMBLYN

MARK ROBSON

USA (FOX) 1957

152m (15)

The Grace Metalious potboiler inspired both this movie and a TV series. Soap opera trash about the steamy goings-on beneath the prim facade of a small New England town. David Lynch ought to do a remake – after all, what was *Blue Velvet* (see page 260) but a wilder *Peyton Place* for the 80s?

THE PIANO [3]

HARVEY KEITEL, HOLLY HUNTER, SAM NEILL, ANNA PAQUIN

JANE CAMPION

NEW ZEALAND (ENTERTAINMENT) 1983

121m (15)

Tale of a woman and child landed with an arranged marriage. When hubby leaves her precious piano on the beach she makes a deal with the estate manager to give him piano lessons in exchange for saving it. Soon the lessons are in love, rather than music. Critics have noted flaws – Keitel (as the manager) is illiterate, yet he reads a message at one point! Affecting, nevertheless. Widescreen. Highly acclaimed both at Cannes and the Academy Awards.

ROMANCE

PRETTY BABY 🎬4

BROOKE SHIELDS, KEITH CARRADINE, SUSAN SARANDON, BARBARA STEELE

LOUIS MALLE

USA (CIC) 1978

106m (15)

Photographer is obsessed with 12-year-old hooker in a New Orleans brothel. Controversial films usually lose their edge with time, but, in the current climate of hysteria about child abuse, this movie (though relatively innocuous) would probably never get a studio green light were it to be proposed today. Shields is amazing: though she cannot act for toffee (see *The Blue Lagoon*, page 223), she has the body of a child and the face of a Vogue model, making her perfect for the part.

PRETTY IN PINK 🎬3

MOLLY RINGWALD, HARRY DEAN STANTON, ANDREW McCARTHY

HOWARD DEUTCH

USA (CIC) 1986

93m (15)

Rich boy and poor girl fall for each other, with all the problems one might expect from such a relationship. Plenty of teenage angst and Ringwald displays real talent as the sweet young thing.

PRETTY WOMAN 🎬4

RICHARD GERE, JULIA ROBERTS, RALPH BELLAMY, ALEX HYDE-WHITE

GARRY MARSHALL

USA (TOUCHSTONE) 1990

115m (15)

Prostitute is hired by a rich businessman to escort him round town, but in the process of making her socially acceptable (à la *My Fair Lady*) he falls in love with her. Lightweight fun, but much-lambasted by feminists for making prostitution appear glam and a viable career opportunity – after all, most runaway girls who become hookers end up on drugs and/or in thrall to a pimp, not as the babe of a millionaire!

THE PRINCE OF TIDES 🎬2

BARBRA STREISAND, NICK NOLTE, BLYTHE DANNER, KATE NELLIGAN

BARBRA STREISAND

USA (COLUMBIA TRISTAR) 1991

128m (15)

Based on a novel of the same name by Pat Conroy, this is a dreary story of a failed football boss who falls for the lady shrink he has hired to help his suffering sister. With the psychiatrist already wed and the lover being no barrel of laughs himself, this too-long tale is no fun at all.

231

ROMAN HOLIDAY [4]

☆ GREGORY PECK, AUDREY HEPBURN, EDDIE ALBERT

🎬 WILLIAM WYLER

USA (CIC) 1953 B&W

⏱ 113m (U)

S velte Hepburn won an Oscar as the princess who tires of official duties while in Rome and falls for reporter Peck. Light comedy/romance which also garnered Oscars for story and Edith Head's costumes. Remade for TV in 1987 to no great purpose.

THE ROMANTIC ENGLISHWOMAN [3]

☆ GLENDA JACKSON, MICHAEL CAINE, HELMUT BERGER, KATE NELLIGAN

🎬 JOSEPH LOSEY

FRANCE/UK (ODYSSEY) 1975

⏱ 112m (15)

Though I've grown to see his merits, Joseph Losey made so many downbeat movies that my teenage pals and I used to call him 'Joseph Lousy' in honour of the boredom he inflicted on us. In truth, this is one of his lesser works – but with Glenda Jackson (in pre-MP days) as the spouse of a writer who gets the gibbering hots for Helmut Berger (we called him 'German Helmet') the story is an entertaining *ménage-à-trois* piece. Penned by Tom Stoppard (now Sir Tom) and Thomas Wiseman, from the latter's novel.

ROMEO AND JULIET [3]

☆ LEONARD WHITING, OLIVIA HUSSEY, MILO O'SHEA, ROBERT STEPHENS

🎬 FRANCO ZEFFIRELLI

ITALY/UK (CIC) 1968

⏱ 133m (PG)

This star-studded version of Shakespeare's play has the virtue of players who are closer to the correct ages for the parts of the young lovers than most who have undertaken the roles – Whiting was 17 and Hussey 15 when the film was made. Captures the essence of the play. Oscars for cinematography and costumes. Some sources list an original running time of 152 m. There are numerous other versions, of course, including a hard-porn one and trash expert Troma's *Tromeo and Juliet*!

SCENT OF A WOMAN [3]

☆ AL PACINO, GABRIELLE ANWAR, CHRIS O'DONNELL, RICHARD BRADFORD

🎬 MARTIN BREST

USA (CIC) 1992

⏱ 151m (15)

A lcoholic ex-army man blinded when horsing about with grenades decides to get his young minder to take him out for one last wild binge before killing himself – but things don't go as planned. A feel-good picture which, though it may not be Pacino's best, won the star an Oscar which was long overdue.

ROMANCE

SLEEPLESS IN SEATTLE [5]

TOM HANKS, MEG RYAN, BILL PULLMAN, ROSIE O'DONNELL

NORA EPHRON

USA (COLUMBIA TRISTAR) 1993

105m (PG)

Classic 'girly' movie about a man left with a child after his wife dies, the girl who's unsure about her impending marriage, and how fate brings them together via a radio show shrink. Charming, endearing, feel-good movie magic that has become something of a legend. Romance fans will not have to fake any orgasms over this one.

SOMEWHERE IN TIME [4]

CHRISTOPHER REEVE, JANE SEYMOUR, CHRISTOPHER PLUMMER, TERESA WRIGHT

JEANNOT SZWARC

USA (CIC) 1980

98m (PG)

Based on Richard Matheson's novel *Bid Time Return*, this is a romantic fantasy about a man who becomes so enraptured by the picture of an actress in an old locket that he wills himself back to 1912 to meet with her. It's never quite explained just how he manages this, but in truth you'll hardly care. Time-travel tales are always fascinating – who would not love to be free of the here-and-now? – and this is no exception. Great.

SOMMERSBY [3]

RICHARD GERE, JODIE FOSTER, BILL PULLMAN, JAMES EARL JONES

JON AMIEL

USA (WARNER) 1993

114m (15)

A man comes back from the American Civil War – but instead of the ogre who went off to fight he's now a caring chappie. His wife is well pleased, but soon begins to doubt if this is really her husband at all. Implausible (who wouldn't know their own husband, even after six years?) but engrossing reworking of the French movie *The Return Of Martin Guerre*.

STANLEY AND IRIS [3]

ROBERT DE NIRO, JANE FONDA, SWOOSIE KURTZ

MARTIN RITT

USA (WARNER) 1989

100m (15)

Widow teaches an illiterate male workmate to read, but finds that they are growing attracted to each other. Simple tale, warmly told and considerably elevated by the power of the two leads. Based on the book *Union Street* by Pat Barker.

SUMMER OF '42

JENNIFER O'NEILL, GARY GRIMES, LOU FRIZELL, JERRY HOUSER

ROBERT MULLIGAN

USA (WARNER) 1971

98m (15)

Herman Raucher's World War Two novel is the basis for this lovely-looking movie. A young woman (played by the beautiful former model O'Neill) gets news that her husband has been killed and takes a teenage boy who has been mooning after her to bed in an act of mutual consolation. There's not much more to it than that – it's an atmosphere piece all the way. Michel Legrand's music won an Oscar.

TENDER MERCIES

ROBERT DUVALL, TESS HARPER, ELLEN BARKIN, WILFORD BRIMLEY

BRUCE BERESFORD

USA (WARNER) 1982

88m (PG)

Country singer is helped to reconstruct his life by a lonely widow and her boy. Unremarkable, but Duvall's Oscar-winning performance carries the film. Oscar for original screenplay, too.

TERMS OF ENDEARMENT

SHIRLEY MacLAINE, DEBRA WINGER, JACK NICHOLSON, DANNY DeVITO

JAMES L BROOKS

USA (CIC) 1983

126m (15)

Maudlin film about a feuding mother and daughter, their romance, and how they finally come together when the girl contracts cancer. Oscars for pic, director, actress (MacLaine), supporting actor (Nicholson), script. Based on the Larry McMurtry novel. A sequel of sorts was attempted recently, but it sank without trace.

THREE COINS IN THE FOUNTAIN

CLIFTON WEBB, DOROTHY McGUIRE, JEAN PETERS, LOUIS JOURDAN

JEAN NEGULESCO

USA (FOX) 1954

98m (U)

Based on the novel by John B Secondari, this tells of three American girls who toss coins into the Trevi in Rome and get their wish for love with hunky locals. The same director remade the same story in 1964 with the action shifted to Spain, as *The Pleasure Seekers*. Oscars for hit title tune and cinematography.

TORN BETWEEN TWO LOVERS

LEE REMICK, GEORGE PEPPARD, JOSEPH BOLOGNA

DELBERT MANN

USA (ODYSSEY) 1979

97m (PG)

Airport romance between married lady and handsome guy. Dreadfully sluggish eye-dabber. Save your Kleenex for a better film.

VALENTINO

RUDOLPH NUREYEV, LESLIE CARON, MICHELLE PHILLIPS, ANTON DIFFRING

KEN RUSSELL

USA (WARNER) 1977

123m (18)

Competently-told story of the great silent star's loves, with the imaginative stroke of casting sex-god dancer Nureyev in the lead. Not our Ken's greatest moment, but there are enough visual fireworks and lusty episodes to satisfy.

THE WAY WE WERE

ROBERT REDFORD, BARBRA STREISAND, BRADFORD DILLMAN, LOIS CHILES

SIDNEY POLLACK

USA (CINEMA CLUB V) 1973

113m (PG)

Story of love over many years betwixt straight-ahead guy and leftie lady. Insipid. Oscars for title song and score.

WHEN HARRY MET SALLY

BILLY CRYSTAL, MEG RYAN, CARRIE FISHER, LISA JANE PERSKY

ROB REINER

USA (ENTERTAINMENT) 1989

91m (15)

Smash hit scripted by Nora Ephron, the creator of *Sleepless In Seattle* (see page 233) with nice performances by Crystal and Ryan as two antagonistic old pals who gradually fall in love. Orgasm-faking gals of the world will love this one for its honesty and sensitivity about human relationships. Salty, smart dialogue.

WHITE PALACE

SUSAN SARANDON, JAMES SPADER, KATHY BATES, EILEEN BRENNAN

LOUIS MANDOKI

USA (CIC) 1990

99m (18)

Glenn Savan's novel is the basis for this love story of a shy guy who falls for an older woman from a working-class background, only to realise that love doesn't automatically conquer all. Subtle characterisation makes it come alive.

WILD AT HEART

NICOLAS CAGE, LAURA DERN, WILLEM DAFOE, DIANE LADD

DAVID LYNCH

USA (ELECTRIC) 1990

119m (18)

Lynch's typically crazed adaptation of Barry Gifford's book. Just out of jail for murder, Cage takes to the road with sexy Dern only to have her demented mama (played by Ladd, her real-life mom) send a thug on their trail. Flawed portrait of American misfits in love, and very violent. Widescreen.

WOMEN IN LOVE

ALAN BATES, GLENDA JACKSON, OLIVER REED, JENNIE LINDEN

KEN RUSSELL

UK (WARNER) 1970

125m (18)

Russell's flamboyant version of the DH Lawrence novel, famous for its groundbreaking male nude wrestling scene. Jackson scored the best actress Oscar for her work here. One of Ken Russell's best movies.

WUTHERING HEIGHTS

LAURENCE OLIVIER, MERLE OBERON, DAVID NIVEN, FLORA ROBSON, DONALD CRISP

WILLIAM WYLER

USA (CINEMA CLUB V) 1939 B&W

104m (U)

Still the best of several film versions of the Emily Brontë story of brooding love between a high-spirited girl and the orphan boy her father adopted. Olivier and Oberon run away with the picture, and Gregg Toland's photography deservedly bagged an Oscar. Stands repeated viewings. Classic? Undoubtedly. Romantic? Definitively.

Science Fiction

Science Fiction has been an important facet of cinema from its earliest days; audiences over 60 years ago were as delighted by the unsophisticated silent capers of Méliès and the American Edison company's *A Trip To Mars* as we are by the hi-tech mega-bucks-budget films of today.

But in the 1990s, with special effects stretching both our imaginations and the studios' budgets almost beyond belief, it is the plots and underlying messages that are looking worryingly trite, if not downright suspect. I've no complaints about the films such as the 'Star Wars' or 'Star Trek' series: these offer pure fantasy in the best style of Flash Gordon and still manage to show that ray-guns and serious ideas need not be mutually exclusive. But when the multi-million-dollar budget of a film like *Independence Day* produces nothing more than a piece of jingoistic 'Planet USA' guff, that does make me somewhat uneasy.

Mind-boggling SFX do, without doubt, play a great part in good sci-fi films but the best should also have a few thought-provoking ideas. I am happy to say that there is enough of both in my selection in this chapter for me to have some optimism for the future of the genre. *Mars Attacks!* may be full of self-indulgent star cameos, but for me it is still great to see the best of hi-tech used to make SFX in the style of a set of bubble-gum cards I remember collecting in the 1960s. If your preference is for entertainment with a more philosophical bent, try *Bladerunner* or *12 Monkeys*. Whatever your taste, there are plenty of worthwhile titles out there for the discerning video-viewer.

12 MONKEYS [5]

	BRUCE WILLIS, MADELEINE STOWE, BRAD PITT, FRANK GORSHIN, ANNIE GOLDEN
	TERRY GILLIAM
	USA (POLYGRAM) 1995
	128m (15)

Inspired by Chris Marker's experimental short *La Jetée* (made in 1962), this complex film involves a man being sent back in time to avert the events that led to global disaster. Sent to the wrong point in the past, he's judged to be mad – and that's only the start of his troubles. To explain the whole plot of this marvellous movie would take too long and would only spoil the fun for you. Suffice to say it deals with the possibility of time travel and the problems of same in a sophisticated, moving way. Willis is on top form. Gilliam's best movie since the dark *Brazil* (see page 243). Widescreen and special boxed edition available.

2001 – A SPACE ODYSSEY [4]

	KEIR DULLEA, GARY LOCKWOOD, DOUGLAS RAIN, LEONARD ROSSITER
	STANLEY KUBRICK
	UK (MGM/UA-WARNER) 1968
	141m (U)

Kubrick's controversial epic (based on a story by Arthur C Clarke) was nevertheless praised for its stunning visuals of ships spinning and planets rising via Oscar-winning SFX handmade in those far-off pre-digital days, all accompanied by the grand strains of classical music. The story starts with a monolithic slab which mesmerises a group of apemen; a similar object is found on the moon by mankind in 2001; it emits a signal that points us to Jupiter's moons, and a ship is sent to investigate – but the ship's talking computer (HAL, voiced by Douglas Rain, one of the movie's best features) has other ideas ... It was the one surviving astronaut's psychedelic 'stargate' trip and the ending that confused the critics – it's certainly open to many interpretations about birth, death and eternity. Does not appear to be available in widescreen, which is crazy. I saw it on one of the original Cinerama playdates and it was awesome. Cut by the director by some 20m to 141m after those dates, and now seen in 70mm or 35mm cinema prints (widescreen), it is inevitably a somewhat diminished experience. If we have to see it on TV, at least we should have it in the right ratio! The classical score was used because some of the director's co-workers, who heard the music being used temporarily during editing, said they preferred it to Alex North's original score – which is available for the curious on CD. There is a sequel to 2001, titled *2010 – The Year We Make Contact* (see right).

SCIENCE FICTION

2010 – THE YEAR WE MAKE CONTACT ▦4

ROY SCHEIDER, HELEN MIRREN, KEIR DULLEA, BOB BALABAN, JOHN LITHGOW

PETER HYAMS

USA (MGM/UA-WARNER) 1984

116m   (PG)

Any sequel to Kubrick's *2001* was going to be on a hiding to nothing from day one, and any solution to the questions posed by the original were certain to annoy those who delighted in the enigmatic qualities of the first film. It's hardy surprising then that *2010* is not highly regarded, and it has to be admitted that the functional Hyams is no Kubrick, but the pic has a lot going for it: a fine cast (including Dullea, reprising his role from *2001*); the use of Arthur C Clarke's own sequel novel as basis for the script; and meticulous recreation of sets and costumes seen in the first film – even HAL comes back-on-line, voiced once more by Douglas Rain. If you can put your preconceptions away, this much-maligned piece may entertain you, even if there are no ultimate answers or surprises. Like *2001*, the film got several Oscar nominations. It won none, while *2001* won only one, for effects.

THE ABYSS ▦4

ED HARRIS, MARY ELIZABETH MASTRANTONIO, MICHAEL BIEHN

JAMES CAMERON

USA (FOX) 1989

140/171m   (15)

This underwater epic seemed overlong when I first saw it in 1989. After being trapped while trying to locate a missing sub, our heroes suddenly discover that the aliens causing all the trouble never meant any harm in the first place! It felt like a rushed and most unsatisfying close to a claustrophobic two hours plus, and this wasn't helped by rumours that major SFX had been cut from the troubled $50 million production. The director later admitted that the film was hindered by time constraints, and he assented to a special version on laserdisc and video. Made more coherent by the extra half-hour of material, the movie paradoxically feels shorter. Both versions are available in pan-scan or widescreen, and the special edition was issued in a limited-edition box with booklet and documentary footage. For me, the letterbox version is always the preferred option, but – incredibly – in the booklet director Cameron disagrees. He claims that because a letterbox print has half or so of the TV screen masked-off, this makes the picture lose quality. As *Video Watchdog* critic Tim Lucas has pointed out, it is simply wrong to state that the letterbox copy is any less clear – the same part of what was shot is occupying the same part of your TV whichever version you pick. Of course, with a movie that was actually shot in widescreen ratio, pan-scan does bring things up close – but you lose nearly half the picture. Make your choice, but be informed. *The Abyss* won an Oscar for sound. The censor cut a shot of a rat being submerged in a 'breathable liquid'. Cameron went on to make that other watery effort, *Titanic*.

239

ALIEN [3]

SIGOURNEY WEAVER, JOHN HURT, IAN HOLM, TOM SKERRITT

RIDLEY SCOTT

UK (FOX) 1979

117m (18)

As much a horror film as it is SF, this involves a dark scruffy spaceship invaded by an organism which grows parasitically in the body of one of the crew, only to burst forth and stalk the remaining humans. Weaver's feisty female survivor and artist HR Giger's creature ensured a cult following, leading to three sequels so far and lots of merchandising opportunities. Widescreen available.

ALIENS [4]

SIGOURNEY WEAVER, MICHAEL BIEHN, LANCE HENRIKSEN, BILL PAXTON

JAMES CAMERON

USA (FOX) 1986

137m (18)

Sequel sees Weaver awakened from the suspended-animation pod she escaped in at the climax of *Alien*. Over 50 years have passed, but the creatures are still out there. She returns to do battle with a monstrous egg-laying queen in a movie that is both a gung-ho Vietnam-in-space and a reprise of the earlier film. Henriksen is superb as a tough android who fights back even when cut in two! Oscars: sound effects and visual effects. Widescreen available, and in an extended version with 17m more footage.

ALIEN³ [3]

SIGOURNEY WEAVER, CHARLES DANCE, BRIAN GLOVER

DAVID FINCHER

USA (FOX) 1992

115m (18)

Weakest of the series. Weaver has escaped again, only to land on a prison planet full of rapists and murderers where women are not welcome. The only ally she has is the resident medic (Dance), the one man who believes that she may be telling the truth about the aliens. Despite her suicide dive at the end – in order to kill the creature spawning inside her – Weaver's Ripley character is back in yet another sequel, believe it or not! Widescreen available.

SCIENCE FICTION

ALIEN RESURRECTION

SIGOURNEY WEAVER, WINONA RYDER, DAN HEDAYA, RON PERLMAN

JEAN-PIERRE JEUNET

USA (FOX) 1997

104m (18)

Desperate fourth continuation of the 'Aliens' franchise: Ripley (a zonked-out Weaver) topped herself at the end of the last movie, so we have to swallow the idea that they clone her using her DNA! After that it's business as usual – all the trademark surprises have turned to cliché, so we get the 'It's inside you ... splat!' bit, the 'White blood? You're an android!' moment, the 'I'm gonna whup yer alien butt!' battle and the last-minute escape, plus the usual selection of nerds who think they can handle the monsters until it all goes pear shaped and they end up as cinematic cannon-fodder. All quite entertaining. Director Jeunet was hired on the strength of his work on *The City Of Lost Children* (see page 314) and he gives the pic some of that film's odd visual style and dreamlike quality – I especially enjoyed the underwater sequence with aliens zipping around like sharks. Fox have also issued a boxed set, comprising the previous three 'Aliens' pix and a documentary tape.

ALPHAVILLE

EDDIE CONSTANTINE, ANNA KARINA, AKIM TAMIROFF, HOWARD VERNON

JEAN-LUC GODARD

FRANCE/ITALY (CONNOISSEUR) 1965 B&W

98m (PG)

Delirious mix of art movie/*film noir*/SF, with Paris standing in for Saris, the computerised city of the future where a private eye tries to rescue a boffin. Call it brilliant or pretentious, it's never boring. Godard claimed it was actually about a man from the 40s in the Paris of the 60s. Was originally to be called *Tarzan Versus IBM*.

ALTERED STATES 🎬5

⭐ WILLIAM HURT, BLAIR BROWN, BOB BALABAN, CHARLES HAID

🎬 KEN RUSSELL

USA (WARNER) 1980

⏱ 102m   (18)

Troubled movie based on Paddy Chayevsky novel. Russell replaced Arthur Penn, Chayevsky retreated behind a pseudonym. The story involves a scientist combining drugs, mysticism and flotation-tank experiments to the point where his psychedelic regression to apeman days begins to take hold physically as well as mentally. Can love save him? Much panned by critics, but stunning on a big screen. No letterbox version available.

BARBARELLA 🎬4

⭐ JANE FONDA, DAVID HEMMINGS, ANITA PALLENBERG, MILO O'SHEA, JOHN PHILLIP LAW

🎬 ROGER VADIM

FRANCE/ITALY (CIC) 1967

⏱ 97m   (15)

Part of the plan by Fonda's then-spouse Vadim to make her another of his sex-symbol stars in the Bardot manner, this adaptation of an adult comic strip (with the accent on strip) about a naive-but-cute astronaut boasts lovely fetishistic art direction and some overripe acting. Scientist Duran Duran (from whom the pop group took their name) tries to kill Barbarella with his orgasm machine, but the oversexed minx blows its fuses. You get the picture. There's actually very little bare flesh on show, and the opening anti-gravity striptease was rejigged in the USA in order to obscure a glimpse of Fonda's pubic hair. Not released on tape in widescreen.

BLADE RUNNER 🎬5

⭐ HARRISON FORD, RUTGER HAUER, SEAN YOUNG, DARYL HANNAH

🎬 RIDLEY SCOTT

USA (WARNER) 1982

⏱ 117m   (15)

This film of Philip K Dick's novel *Do Androids Dream Of Electric Sheep?* is now regarded as one of the most influential SF movies of all time, with its drab, realistic look and philosophical questioning about what constitutes humanity. Ford plays a detective hunting down 'replicants', androids who've escaped. He reluctantly terminates them – until he falls in love with one and we are left to consider whether he may be a replicant himself. The world-weary voice-over was hated by many fans, and a version without it was issued recently as a 'director's cut'. In Paul M Sammon's book on the film, director Scott confesses that this new version (with a few visual changes and slightly shorter than the original) is *not* a 'director's cut', as he was not given the time he wanted to complete it. There are, it appears, several versions of the film in existence, including a more violent print and a radically different work-print. Widescreen versions are available and Sammon's book is highly recommended.

SCIENCE FICTION

BRAZIL 🎬4

JONATHAN PRYCE, KIM GREIST, ROBERT DE NIRO, IAN HOLM

TERRY GILLIAM

UK (WARNER) 1985

142m (15)

Gilliam's epic of a daydreaming everyman (Pryce) trapped in a surreal, Kafka-esque bureaucracy of the future was hampered in the USA when bosses delayed release, prompting a war of words between director and studio. While the Yanks had to suffer cut prints that destroyed the meaning of the piece, we Brits got the whole thing. Pryce tries to save the girl he loves from afar as the machinery of the law (literally) accidentally names her as a terrorist. Mad sets, great performances and just when you think everything's okay, Gilliam destroys the happy ending with a stab to the heart.

CLOSE ENCOUNTERS OF THE THIRD KIND 🎬3

RICHARD DREYFUSS, FRANCOIS TRUFFAUT, TERRI GARR, MELINDA DILLON

STEVEN SPIELBERG

USA (COLUMBIA) 1977

135m (PG)

More a film about the search for meaning in life than an effects romp, this is quintessential Spielberg. Magical intimations of alien existence are intercut with the effects these have on the lives of several people. It's a moving film, but works best the first time you see it. In 1980 the director re-edited the material and added new footage to create a 'special edition', but in this hack's opinion it did not make for a significantly better movie. The original is the one I would recommend though you may want to rent the other out of curiosity. Widescreen available. Oscars: cinematography, sound effects editing.

COCOON 🎬3

DON AMECHE, HUME CRONYN, JESSICA TANDY, WILFORD BRIMLEY

RON HOWARD

USA (FOX) 1985

117m (PG)

Whimsical piece about old folk stumbling upon a rejuvenating pool created by aliens for the purpose of rescuing stranded compadres. Starts well but turns silly, remaining amusing for all that. A sequel exists: *Cocoon 2: The Return*, made in 1988. Oscars: Ameche (supporting actor), SFX.

243

CONTACT

JODIE FOSTER, JAMES WOODS, MATTHEW McCONAUGHEY, JOHN HURT, TOM SKERRITT

ROBERT ZEMECKIS

USA (WARNER) 1977

143m (PG)

This moving, low-key and thoroughly believable story about the search for extraterrestrial life was a flop at the box office, probably due to the length and the lack of flashy FX, but hopefully it'll find its audience on video. Foster is a scientist who battles against all the odds to continue her project to contact other planets, pooh-poohed by sceptics and aided only by ailing mega-rich mogul John Hurt. Just when it looks like she's on the brink of success, her place on the trip of a lifetime is nabbed by the very guy who refused to credit her theories all along! But the lady ain't about to give up that easily. Some will say this is a film for airheads who need to believe in little green men, but it has a message about hanging on to your ideals and, yes, your faith. Do see it.

THE DAY THE EARTH STOOD STILL

MICHAEL RENNIE, PATRICIA NEAL, SAM JAFFE

ROBERT WISE

USA (FOX) 1951 B&W

92m (U)

Landmark SF about an alien who comes to warn earth to abjure war or face heavy measures for its own good. Naturally, he is not welcomed. Fatally wounded but temporarily revived, he leaves behind his robot (Gort) and others as planetary policemen. Well directed by Jack-of-all-genres Wise, it was a major influence on *The Abyss* (see page 239) and many other SF films. The alien catch-phrase 'Klaatu Barada Nikto' has entered into pop culture to emerge in albums by Ringo Starr of the Beatles and Beatles-imitators Klaatu and in various movies. Now available in a digitally remastered edition.

DEMON SEED

JULIE CHRISTIE, FRITZ WEAVER, GERRIT GRAHAM

DONALD CAMMELL

USA (WARNER/BEYONDVISION) 1977

95m (15)

Cammell was the son of occultist Aleister Crowley's first biographer, and appears in Kenneth Anger's Crowleyan film *Lucifer Rising*. He died recently, having made only a handful of movies, one of which was his debut directorial effort *Performance* (see page 116), on which he shared credit with the equally radical but more commercially successful Nicolas Roeg. *Demon Seed* is about a huge, house-running computer imprisoning and impregnating the wife of its creator. Only partly a success, it's still a testament to its creator's audacious style. He will be sadly missed by fans of wild cinema. Widescreen.

SCIENCE FICTION

DUNE

KYLE MacLACHLAN, STING, DEAN STOCKWELL, MAX VON SYDOW

DAVID LYNCH

USA (POLYGRAM) 1984

136m (15)

This is a brave attempt to get the images and plot of Frank Herbert's epic novel on film, but it tries too hard. We open with an incomprehensible spoken prologue to tell us what's going on, but it confuses rather than illuminates. Beautiful to look at, however. A TV version of longer duration exists, but Lynch asked for it to be credited to Alan Smithee, the standard director-pseudonym used when a film-maker is unhappy with a product. A Japanese import laserdisc set exists containing the TV version and the widescreen cinema print.

THE EMPIRE STRIKES BACK

HARRISON FORD, MARK HAMILL, CARRIE FISHER

IRVIN KERSHNER

UK/USA (FOX) 1980

124m (U)

Second in the hugely successful 'Star Wars' trilogy with more adventures of galactic rebellion. Confusingly, the films' storylines are not always in sequence and one is into the action from the word go. Great effects but not much of a story in this one. As a prelude to a new trilogy, the first three flicks are being reissued with new SFX. Widescreen. Oscars: SFX and sound.

ENEMY MINE

DENNIS QUAID, LOU GOSSETT Jnr, BRION JAMES

WOLFANG PETERSEN

USA (FOX) 1985

93m (15)

Begun by another director (Richard Loncraine) whose footage was junked, this troubled production was cut outside the USA. It is like a space version of the war film *Hell In The Pacific*, with two enemies stranded and forced to come to terms. It also bears similarities to the 60s SF classic *Robinson Crusoe On Mars*, another butchered epic. Plot twists include the fact that one protagonist is a unisexual alien lizard who is about to give birth(!) Interesting.

ET – THE EXTRA-TERRESTRIAL

HENRY THOMAS, DEE WALLACE, DREW BARRYMORE, PETER COYOTE

STEVEN SPIELBERG

USA (CIC) 1982

115m (U)

Disneyesque fantasy about a cuddly alien stranded on earth and rescued by kids. Spielberg remembers to instil a sense of evil in the threat posed by government men who want to experiment on the creature. Weird to see sex-symbol Barrymore and *Playboy* centrefold/actress Erika Eleniak as innocent kiddies. A classic. Oscars: SFX, sound effects editing, sound and score.

FANTASTIC VOYAGE 🎬5

STEPHEN BOYD, RAQUEL WELCH, DONALD PLEASENCE, ARTHUR KENNEDY

RICHARD FLEISCHER

USA (FOX) 1966

100m (U)

Mad but watchable. Scientists are shrunk and injected into the bloodstream of an injured genius with the task of piloting their submarine to a blood clot and eliminating it. Pleasures include staggering (for that time) art direction depicting human insides, and Raquel Welch's bust straining at her white rubber diving suit. Parodied in *Innerspace* (see page 144). Oscars: SFX, art and set direction.

THE FIFTH ELEMENT 🎬5

BRUCE WILLIS, IAN HOLM, GARY OLDMAN, MILLA JOVOVICH, CHRIS TUCKER

LUC BESSON

FRANCE/USA (FOX) 1997

121m (PG)

Delirious feast for the eyes in this mad SFX romp in which Willis has to rescue an alien girl who holds the secret of world salvation. If this all sounds tired and predictable, you are in for a surprise: the visuals are wildly imaginative and so are the characters – a blue-skinned, multi-tentacled diva, Oldman's drawling killer and Tucker's camp TV host to name but three. Available in widescreen and in a hideously expensive boxed set with book.

FIRST MEN IN THE MOON 🎬4

EDWARD JUDD, MARTHA HYER, LIONEL JEFFRIES

NATHAN JURAN

UK (COLUMBIA) 1964

104m (U)

Written by Nigel Kneale and based on an HG Wells novel, this has American astronauts going to the moon only to find a faded Brit flag. Absurd fun. Turns out some mad Victorians got there first! (Tape also includes *Earth Vs The Flying Saucers* (1956). Great FX by Ray Harryhausen. Would benefit from a reissue in its widescreen form.

FLASH GORDON 🎬3

SAM JONES, MELODY ANDERSON, TOPOL, ORNELLA MUTI, MAX VON SYDOW, TIMOTHY DALTON, BRIAN BLESSED, PETER WYNGARDE

MIKE HODGES

UK (POLYGRAM) 1980

115m (PG)

Revamp, *Barbarella*-style, of the old comic-based serials, with a rock score by the group Queen, uncredited script input by philosopher Colin Wilson, and cameos from everyone from Bond-actor Dalton to some guy who used to be on *Blue Peter*! Panned on release, but much fun. Available in widescreen, though if it's the same as the USA laser disc it may be 'blown-up' within the frame.

SCIENCE FICTION

THE FLY 🎬4

⭐ JEFF GOLDBLUM, GEENA DAVIS, JOHN GETZ, DAVID CRONENBERG

🎬 DAVID CRONENBERG

USA (FOX) 1986

⏱ 92m (18)

Update of the 50s chiller about a scientist who invents a matter teleporter and tests it on himself with horrific results. In the first version he ended up with a fly's head and the unfortunate insect got a tiny human head. Cronenberg adapts the story into his own *oeuvre* of genetic rebellion by having the man gradually mutate in vile ways after he and a housefly are transported together. Goldblum is his usual eccentric self and the yukky makeup FX won an Oscar. Sequel: *The Fly 2* (1989), directed by make-up man Chris Walas, was less fun.

FORBIDDEN PLANET 🎬5

⭐ WALTER PIDGEON, ANNE FRANCIS, LESLIE NIELSEN, JACK KELLY

🎬 FRED M WILCOX

USA (MGM/UA-WARNER) 1956

⏱ 98m (U)

Shakespeare's *The Tempest* as SF. Earthmen visit planet inhabited only by scientist and his daughter. But something else stalks unseen ... Scenes of the invisible 'Id' monster caught in electric rays are legendary, and Robby the Robot was revived for a film called *The Invisible Boy* – but not, as some say, for the TV show *Lost in Space*, though the robot in the show is obviously inspired by Robby. Now in a special widescreen edition.

THE ILLUSTRATED MAN 🎬2

⭐ ROD STEIGER, CLAIRE BLOOM, ROBERT DRIVAS

🎬 JACK SMIGHT

USA (WARNER/BEYONDVISION) 1968

⏱ 103m (15)

Interesting but unsuccessful attempt to bring to the screen Ray Bradbury's tales told by a tattoo-covered man. Steiger gives a fine performance but the film fails to hang together, due in part to the random and episodic nature of the (rather unexciting) tales included. Widescreen.

INDEPENDENCE DAY 🎬3

⭐ JEFF GOLDBLUM, RANDY QUAID, WILL SMITH, BILL PULLMAN

🎬 ROLAND EMMERICH

USA (FOX) 1996

⏱ 139m (12)

Admittedly visually impressive, but vastly overpraised America-saves-the-world-from-bad-aliens tripe. Goldblum coasts along in his bumbling-genius autopilot mode but is always watchable. Nice explosions. A film to sell toys by – but less than a year after release I note they are being sold off cheap in shops. Widescreen available, in fancy hologram box.

247

INVASION OF THE BODY SNATCHERS

DONALD SUTHERLAND, BROOKE ADAMS, LEONARD NIMOY, VERONICA CARTWRIGHT

PHILIP KAUFMAN

USA (WARNER) 1978

115m (15)

Second of three extant versions of this scary story about alien seed pods which duplicate humans and take over the persona of the originals. The 1956 version may well be the one to beat, but this has superior SFX and is a laudable attempt. The director and star of the original, Don Siegel and Kevin McCarthy, have cameo parts. The third version was Abel Ferrara's more recent *Body Snatchers*. Available in widescreen.

LOGAN'S RUN

MICHAEL YORK, JENNY AGUTTER, PETER USTINOV

MICHAEL ANDERSON

USA (MGM/UA-WARNER) 1976

118m (PG)

The story is set in a future where people are 'snuffed' at the age of 30. York is assigned to stop escapees – but he escapes himself with his gal and finds it's all a riot after 30. So unlike the lives of our own dear selves. Spawned a TV series. Now in widescreen special edition.

MARS ATTACKS!

JACK NICHOLSON, GLENN CLOSE, PIERCE BROSNAN, DANNY DeVITO, ANNETTE BENING

TIM BURTON

USA (WARNER) 1996

101m (12)

Based on a gory series of bubblegum cards I recall collecting back in the 60s, this science fiction comedy employs state-of-the-art technology to replicate the cheesy SFX of cheapo classics of yore. Pop-eyed, skull-faced aliens proclaim peace and then frazzle everything in sight with happy cries of 'Ack-ack-ack-ack!' The cast appear to enjoy themselves immensely, but audiences seem not to have surrendered to the mood and the pic was not the hit expected. Should find its true home on video. Good, light-hearted entertainment! Available in widescreen.

SCIENCE FICTION

MEN IN BLACK [4]

TOMMY LEE JONES, RIP TORN, WILL SMITH, LINDA FIORENTINO

BARRY SONNENFELD

USA (COLUMBIA TRISTAR) 1997

94m (PG)

Based on a comic-strip (themed around the rumour that mysterious dark-clad fellows are always seen in the wake of UFO activity), this hilarious SFX-fest has cop Smith being inducted into a secret agency that polices the myriad of galactic aliens apparently already living among us. They go around keeping a lid on things by blanking people's memories of bizarre encounters while tracking renegade weirdos. Humour and science fiction don't often blend well but this is an exception: the FX, acting and Danny Elfman's score are all superb.

THE MESA OF LOST WOMEN [3]

JACKIE COOGAN, RICHARD TRAVIS, ALLAN NIXON

HERBERT TEVOS

USA (KILLER Bs) 1953 B&W

70m (15)

Former child star Coogan is a mad doctor conducting pervy experiments to create a breed of angry gals. Daft, but preferable to much big-budget hokum. Coogan also appeared as Fester in TV's *The Addams Family*.

THE OMEGA MAN [4]

CHARLTON HESTON, ANTHONY ZERBE, ROSALIND CASH

BORIS SAGAL

USA (WARNER/BEYONDVISION) 1971

98m (PG)

Hammer planned a version of Richard Matheson's SF vampire novel in the 1960s – the book, *I Am Legend*, was ripe for filming, but the BBFC said any movie version would be banned. Much to their annoyance, the ditched project was made as *The Last Man On Earth* by another company in Italy with Vincent Price and passed by the censor with no trouble! This stylised 1970s version sees Heston roaming around empty shops and battling with the undead, but softens the book's punchline. Apparently a new version is soon to be made. Widescreen tape.

249

OUTLAND

SEAN CONNERY, PETER BOYLE, FRANCES STERNHAGEN

PETER HYAMS

USA (WARNER/BEYONDVISION) 1981

109m (15)

This is *High Noon* in space, with Connery as cussed lawman probing amphetamine-style psychosis and corporate drug-dealing in the environment of a mine on one of Jupiter's moons. Great stuff – sort of 'Io-silver'! Some gruesome FX, especially when a man explodes in a decompressed airlock.

PLAN 9 FROM OUTER SPACE

BELA LUGOSI, VAMPIRA, GREGORY WALCOTT, TOR JOHNSON

EDWARD D WOOD

USA (CARLTON) 1956 B&W

79m (PG)

Ed Wood has become a cult figure as (allegedly) the worst film-maker ever, due to the recent biographical volume (Richard Grey's *Visions of Ecstasy*, published by Faber) and Tim Burton's movie based on it. Actually, Wood was like many people who want to be creative – except that in his case the *outré* ideas were matched by a fierce dedication which led to him managing to get books published and movies made, however trying his personal circumstances. If you want to see how an alcoholic, transvestite *auteur* forged a film around a couple of minutes of footage of Bela Lugosi, look no further. Cheap and amateurish it may be, but *Plan 9* is enjoyable for all that.

PLANET OF THE APES

CHARLTON HESTON, RODDY McDOWALL, KIM HUNTER

FRANKLIN J SCHAFFNER

USA (FOX) 1968

102m (PG)

Based on a book by the man who wrote *The Bridge On The River Kwai*, scripted by Michael Wilson (uncredited co-writer of *Lawrence Of Arabia*) and TV series *Twilight Zone*'s creator Rod Serling, this is an intelligent effort about astronauts who find themselves on a planet where apes rule and men are subservient. Makes a salient point about animal rights and racism, and the wonderful make-up (which got a special Oscar) still looks good today. Sequels followed, but couldn't match the shock ending of this film. A remake is mooted.

SCIENCE FICTION

RETURN OF THE JEDI 🎬 4

☆	HARRISON FORD, MARK HAMILL, CARRIE FISHER
🎬	RICHARD MARQUAND
	UK/USA (FOX) 1983
⏱	132m (U)

Third of the 'Star Wars' films. The Ewoks are a bit too cuddly, but there is some nice creature make-up and the pace never slackens. The Ewoks, as befits cute little teddybears, appeared in spin-off TV fare. Widescreen. Reissued with the other two instalments in 1997, with new SFX, as an appetiser for the next trilogy.

ROBOCOP 🎬 5

☆	PETER WELLER, NANCY ALLEN, DAN O'HERLIHY
🎬	PAUL VERHOEVEN
	USA (ENTERTAINMENT) 1987
⏱	102m (18)

Dutch director Verhoeven uses this story of a blown-apart policeman (mutilated by gunfire in a shocking sequence) who is rebuilt as the title character to make acid comment on the state of the USA. Spoof commercials abound, and the RoboCop's have-a-nice-day demeanour as he blows away baddies is hilarious. Spawned sequels and a TV series. This first movie can be found on a tape from budget label 4-Front as well, coupled with the film *RoboCop 2*. The dark side of TV's *Six Million Dollar Man*.

ROLLERBALL 🎬 3

☆	JAMES CAAN, JOHN HOUSEMAN, MAUD ADAMS, RALPH RICHARDSON
🎬	NORMAN JEWISON
	USA (WARNER/BEYONDVISION) 1975
⏱	125m (15)

Prophetic and much-copied film about future sport becoming more violent and gladiatorial. The trouble is, while it sets out to condemn the sport and those who watch it, we are at the same time being given our own thrills by watching the on-screen brutality – a common contradiction in films seeking to critique spectacle. Dull apart from the rollerball sequences. Widescreen special edition is now available.

SOLARIS 🎬 4

☆	NATALYA BONDARCHUK, DONATAS BANIONIS, YURI JARVET
🎬	ANDREI TARKOVSKY
	USSR (CONNOISSEUR) 1971
⏱	167m (PG)

Splendid visuals in the Kubrick manner, but preferred by arthouse fans as it's by a Russian. Planet has the power to affect the minds of those in an orbiting space laboratory to bad ends. Widescreen.

SOYLENT GREEN [5]

CHARLTON HESTON, LEIGH TAYLOR-YOUNG, EDGAR G ROBINSON

RICHARD FLEISCHER

USA (WARNER/BEYONDVISION) 1973

97m (15)

Set in a future where the rich live in fortresses and the poor starve, this dark film has Heston as a cop who finds out just what's in the popular new nutritious stuff being offered – and not liking it. Based on the novel *Make Room, Make Room* by Harry Harrison, it offers Robinson's final, moving performance. Widescreen.

STALKER [3]

ALEKSANDR KAIDANOVSKY, NIKOLAI GRINKO, ANATOLY SOLONITSYN

ANDREI TARKOVSKY

USSR (CONNOISSEUR) 1979

161m (PG)

A guide takes the curious to a forbidden zone in an industrial wasteland, searching for a room that makes dreams come true. Pessimistic arthouse stuff from Tarkovsky, one of Russia's greatest exponents of serious SF.

STAR TREK – THE MOTION PICTURE [3]

WILLIAM SHATNER, LEONARD NIMOY, JAMES DOOHAN

ROBERT WISE

USA (CIC) 1979

132m (U)

Dull film based on short-lived TV series that became a cult via re-runs. Made long after the series had ended, this nevertheless spawned better sequels on film and TV.

STAR TREK II – THE WRATH OF KHAN [4]

WILLIAM SHATNER, LEONARD NIMOY, RICARDO MONTALBAN

NICHOLAS MEYER

USA (CIC) 1982

113m (15)

This, the second film for the Trekkers, sees Montalban reprise his role of Shatner's enemy from an episode of the TV show, spitting quotes from *Moby Dick* and torturing good guys by inserting centipedes in earholes. Nice.

SCIENCE FICTION

STAR TREK III – THE SEARCH FOR SPOCK ④

WILLIAM SHATNER, LEONARD NIMOY, JAMES DOOHAN

LEONARD NIMOY

USA (CIC) 1984

105m (PG)

Nimoy directs himself as Spock in this daft 'Trek' entry, a film about the reincarnation (or whatever) of the pointy-eared hero who gave his life heroically at the climax of the previous flick.

STAR TREK IV – THE VOYAGE HOME ②

WILLIAM SHATNER, LEONARD NIMOY, JAMES DOOHAN, CATHERINE HICKS

LEONARD NIMOY

USA (CIC) 1986

119m (PG)

Dull, ecological, supposed comedy-romp, where the space heroes spend too much time on the earth of the past in search of whales. Boring.

STAR TREK V – THE FINAL FRONTIER ④

WILLIAM SHATNER, LEONARD NIMOY, DAVID WARNER

WILLIAM SHATNER

USA (CIC) 1989

106m (PG)

The boys meet God – honest. Absurd, but fun, like it should be. Also available is *Star Trek – The Undiscovered Country*. This was followed by *Star Trek – Generations*, in which the old-timers hand over the reins of the filmic 'Trek' to the stars of the superior TV offshoot, *The Next Generation*. The cast of the latter, which blends serious philosophical questions with hokum far better than the originals ever did, have since appeared in the first of their own movies (see below).

STAR TREK – FIRST CONTACT ④

PATRICK STEWART, ALICE KRIGE, BRENT SPINER, LEVAR BURTON

JONATHAN FRAKES

USA (CIC) 1996

106m (12)

Superb big-screen outing for the *Next Generation* team, with Captain Picard (Stewart) matching wits with a slinky Krige as the nasty alien queen. Few TV shows transfer well to the cinema as punters are often unwilling to shell out for characters they're used to seeing free, but the Trekkers are the exception. As befits a movie, the FX are bigger/better, but they work just as well on video.

STAR WARS [5]

MARK HAMILL, HARRISON FORD, CARRIE FISHER, PETER CUSHING, ALEC GUINNESS

GEORGE LUCAS

UK/USA (FOX) 1977

121m (U)

First and best of Lucas's *Flash Gordon*-inspired ray-gun romps. Currently on show in revamped form to herald a new series. Oscars: sets, editing, effects, costumes, sound, score and sound effects.

STARMAN [3]

JEFF BRIDGES, KAREN ALLEN, CHARLES MARTIN SMITH, RICHARD JAECKEL

JOHN CARPENTER

USA (VIDEO COLLECTION) 1984

110m (PG)

Delightful, if slender, tale of an alien who assumes the form of a dead man and cajoles his wife into helping him escape nasty secret-agent types. Oddly touching, with a fine performance from Bridges. Inspired a flop TV series.

STARSHIP TROOPERS [4]

CASPER VAN DIEM, MICHAEL IRONSIDE, JAKE BUSEY, NEIL PATRICK HARRIS

PAUL VERHOEVEN

USA (BUENA VISTA) 1997

124m (15)

Space-opera based on (allegedly fascist) Robert Heinlein novel about gung-ho astronautical grunts battling giant alien insects is turned into a blend of *Aliens* (see page 240) and *Beverley Hills 90210* as director Verhoeven attempts, with limited success, to repeat the outsider critique of America of his original *RoboCop* (see page 251). Super digital SFX, though the actors are bronzed ciphers – but maybe that's the whole idea. A Chinese takeaway accompaniment supreme.

THX 1138 [3]

ROBERT DUVALL, DONALD PLEASENCE

GEORGE LUCAS

USA (WARNER/BEYONDVISION) 1970

95m (15)

Nice widescreen tape of Lucas's debut, based on a film he made as a student. A *1984*-derived story about a man determined to escape from a restrictive underground society of the future where men have numbers instead of names. Allegedly, the title number was the registration of the director's first car – it appears in most of his films and THX is also the name of his sound-system for cinemas, laserdiscs, etc.

SCIENCE FICTION

THE TIME MACHINE 🎬 5

ROD TAYLOR, ALAN YOUNG, YVIETTE MIMIEUX, WHIT BISSELL

GEORGE PAL

USA (WARNER/BEYONDVISION) 1960

103m (PG)

My favourite SF film, from the marvellous score to the robust playing of Taylor. A fine version of HG Wells' story of a man who invents a device for time travel, only to find a future where lotus-eating wimps are preyed on by cannibals. Inevitably simplified – when our hero helps the good guys (Eloi) destroy a few cannibal (Morlock) tunnels, we're expected to accept that the war is over. Yet surely the whole world is supposed to be full of the devils? The SFX were Oscar-winners and are excellent, apart from an atomic war sequence which seems to be made from custard and Dinky toys. A hugely enjoyable film and stunning to look at.

TOTAL RECALL 🎬 4

ARNOLD SCHWARZENEGGER, RACHEL TICOTIN, SHARON STONE

PAUL VERHOEVEN

USA (GUILD) 1990

113m (18)

Complex spectacular with Oscar-winning effects about a man who has been having dreams of Mars. He can't afford a holiday, so 'buys' someone else's memories. This brings on the realisation that he's an agent who has been submerged into a boring everyday life ... The sequence where he is told to kill himself in order to prove that he is only dreaming is particularly unnerving. Well, would *you* do it? The only flaw is that it's hard to accept Arnie as an ordinary guy in the first place. Based on a crazed PK Dick tale.

WAR OF THE WORLDS 🎬 4

GENE BARRY, ANN ROBINSON, ROBERT CORNTHWAITE

BYRON HASKIN

USA (CIC) 1953

85m (PG)

SFX Oscar-winner which updates HG Wells' story of Martian invaders to modern times. The Martians are bizarre in the extreme, and the film had an 'X' certificate on first UK release. Great, though let down by actors. Narration by Sir Cedric Hardwicke.

WARLORDS OF ATLANTIS 🎬 2

DOUG McCLURE, PETER GILMORE, SHANE RIMMER, CYD CHARISSE

KEVIN CONNOR

USA (WARNER/BEYONDVISION) 1978

96m (PG)

Fast moving adventure about Victorians battling Atlantis, let down by cheesy effects work. McClure was in a run of such medium-budget epics.

WESTWORLD

- YUL BRYNNER, RICHARD BENJAMIN, JAMES BROLIN
- MICHAEL CRICHTON
- USA (WARNER/BEYONDVISION) 1973
- 89m (15)

Now a hit novelist and filmmaker, Crichton made his directorial debut with this story of a futuristic Disneyland where several eras are recreated and guests can kill and have sex with realistic robots. It all goes wrong and the robot underclass fights back; Brynner in particular as a killer gunslinger just will not lie down. A duff sequel entitled *Futureworld* was made in 1976.

XTRO

- BERNICE STEGERS, PHILIP SAYER
- HARRY BROMLEY DAVENPORT
- UK (FIRST INDEPENDENT) 1982
- 80m (18)

Raped by an alien? I don't belieeeeve it! Neither will you when you see this. Silly fun, but suffers from tedious sections and naff effects. On tape with *Xtro 2*. A further sequel is available if you are mad enough. Owes a visual debt to *Alien* (see page 241).

YOU ONLY LIVE TWICE

- SEAN CONNERY, DONALD PLEASENCE, AKIKO WAKABAYASHI
- LEWIS GILBERT
- USA (MGM/UA-WARNER) 1967
- 116m (PG)

Many James Bond films qualify as science fiction and none more so than this, with mini-copters and stolen spaceships, the SPECTRE (ha) of World War Three and a mechanical volcano. Connery is still the best Bond ever in my book. Script by Roald Dahl.

ZARDOZ

- SEAN CONNERY, CHARLOTTE RAMPLING, JOHN ALDERTON
- JOHN BOORMAN
- UK (FOX) 1974
- 105m (15)

Stunning visuals in Boorman's idea of a future world rather like that of The Time Machine (see page 255), with wimpy lotus-eaters in protected zones being attacked by thuggish killers on the prowl. Things get interesting when Connery and Rampling, members of opposing factions, get involved and attempt to solve the mystery at the heart of their society and (ultimately) their god. Boorman's script doesn't really gel, but it's a dazzling curio and a real cult gem.

THRILLERS

Video fans in search of a true 'thrill' might profitably investigate several other sections of this book – Gangsters (see pages 149–66) and Horror (see pages 175–204) should prove especially fruitful. For many, the pinnacle of the genre is the work of Alfred Hitchcock, movies which prove that art and entertainment need not be mutually-exclusive cinematic notions; but in recent years the thriller has come to be defined by the sleazy psychosexual whodunnit as purveyed by writer Joe Eszterhas in pix such as *Jagged Edge* (see page 269) and *Basic Instinct* (see page 258) – films which provide a momentary frisson but offer little depth. A friend of mine dubs them 'hamburger movies': enjoyable products, but instantly forgotten the moment you step out into the real world. Pay your money and take your choice ...

10 RILLINGTON PLACE 🎬3

RICHARD ATTENBOROUGH, JUDY GEESON, JOHN HURT, ISOBEL BLACK

RICHARD FLEISCHER

UK (CINEMA CLUB V) 1970

110m (15)

Ludovic Kennedy's book on the Christie case provides the groundwork for USA director Fleischer's surprisingly able grasp of post-war London *mis-en-scène*. Christie (Attenborough) was a serial killer who eluded capture for years, even giving evidence against simpleton Tim Evans (Hurt) in order to see him hung (for allegedly murdering his wife and baby) before the truth about his own guilt came to light too late. There is still much debate about what Evans did or didn't do, but there's no doubt that he should never have hung. Attenborough gives a creepy portrayal of a seedy, weedy monster.

ANGEL OF VENGEANCE 🎬4

ZOE TAMERLIS, STEVE SINGER, JACK THIBEAU, PETER YELLEN

ABEL FERRARA

USA (WARNER) 1980

78m (18)

Long-banned female revenge flick from cult director Ferrara, also known by the title *Ms 45*. It's about a mute seamstress who goes over the edge after being raped twice in one day. She kills the second assailant, chops his body into bits, then proceeds to use his gun to blow away every leering male she encounters. Teenage Tamerlis, who went on to script later films for the director under the name Zoe Lund, gives a powerful performance, all the more remarkable given her age (16) and the fact that she has no dialogue. This is a pristine print, though cut by the BBFC. Note: the tape was issued then withdrawn for remastering, due to what a Warner's source (who refused to give his name) calls 'technical problems' – in fact, the first copies shipped in early September 1997 were accidentally issued *sans* cuts! If your copy has the number 082897 on the side of the tape, it is uncut. Even in censored form, though, this is a gripping picture.

BASIC INSTINCT 🎬4

MICHAEL DOUGLAS, SHARON STONE, JEANNE TRIPPLEHORN, GEORGE DZUNDZA

PAUL VERHOEVEN

USA (GUILD) 1992

128m (18)

Improbable hooey about a bisexual thrill-killing babe who enjoys writing novels which tease the cops by mirroring her real-life crimes. Tacky visual popcorn. There's lots of sex and slashing, with Douglas plodding along as the infatuated policeman and Stone uncrossing her legs in the no-panties scene which made her a star (and which she later implausibly claimed she didn't realise was being shot). Picketed by gays in the USA for suggesting that lesbianism and murder go hand-in-hand. Widescreen available.

THE BIG SLEEP

HUMPHREY BOGART, LAUREN BACALL, JOHN RIDGELY, ELISHA COOK Jnr

HOWARD HAWKS

USA (WARNER) 1944 B&W

110m (PG)

Raymond Chandler's first hard-boiled novel makes a compelling *noir* with gumshoe Philip Marlowe up to his eyes in incomprehensible intrigues. It is pretty much accepted – even by those who made it – that the film makes little sense. That doesn't stop it being a wonderfully atmospheric classic. The pic wasn't issued to the public until 1946, but a simpler version with explanatory scenes was shown to USA troops abroad in 1944.

THE BIRDS

ROD TAYLOR, TIPPI HEDREN, SUZANNE PLESHETTE, JESSICA TANDY

ALFRED HITCHCOCK

USA (CIC) 1963

113m (15)

Based on the Daphne du Maurier tale of the same name, this Hitchcock oddity has the amorous desires of a spoiled rich girl (Hedren) and a smart lawyer (Taylor) upset by the intrusion of the irrational forces of nature, incarnated here by the sudden revolt of all avian life against humankind. The aura of dislocation is aided by composer Bernard Herrmann, who eschews a conventional score and instead supplies a soundtrack of unsettling bird-like noises.

BLACK WIDOW

DEBRA WINGER, THERESA RUSSELL, DENNIS HOPPER, NICOL WILLIAMSON

BOB RAFELSON

USA (FOX) 1986

97m (15)

Hot-blooded, sleazy thriller from cult director Rafelson about two opposed women – one who marries men, then bumps them off for their money, the other an FBI agent tracking her down. The two leads (Russell and Winger respectively) work hard but it's all rather unmoving.

BLOOD SIMPLE

FRANCES McDORMAND, JOHN GETZ, DAN HEDAYA, M EMMET WALSH

JOEL COEN

USA (POLYGRAM) 1983

95m (18)

Breakthrough pulp fiction from the brothers Coen. Sleazy bar boss hires a detective to murder his cheating wife and her lover, but with everyone concerned either misunderstanding or double-crossing at every twist it turns into a sick, funny rollercoaster of trashy Texas malice in blunderland. Walsh is marvellous as the bent detective. Also sold in a boxed set with Coen's *Fargo* (see page 104).

BLOW OUT 🎬 4

JOHN TRAVOLTA, NANCY ALLEN, JOHN LITHGOW, DENNIS FRANZ

BRIAN DE PALMA

USA (FOX) 1981

108m (18)

Clever variation of the theme of *Blow Up* – instead of spotting a murder in a snap, however, Travolta is a sound engineer who accidentally records the gunshot that causes a car to smash, plunging him into a maelstrom involving a hooker, a politician and a psycho hitman. One of De Palma's best, working on many levels and constantly undermining audience perceptions as to what is really happening.

BLUE STEEL 🎬 4

JAMIE LEE CURTIS, RON SILVER, CLANCY BROWN, LOUISE FLETCHER

KATHRYN BIGELOW

USA (FIRST INDEPENDENT) 1989

97m (18)

Unlikely story of a rookie policewoman involved in a relationship with a seemingly respectable chap who goes off the rails when he stumbles upon a robbery and picks up a gun dropped at the scene. Starts off well, but gradually becomes more and more unbelievable as it rolls along, though Ron Silver as the killer compels attention right to the very end.

BLUE VELVET 🎬 5

KYLE MacLACHLAN, LAURA DERN, DENNIS HOPPER, ISABELLA ROSSELLINI, DEAN STOCKWELL

DAVID LYNCH

USA (ELECTRIC) 1986

115m (18)

Weirdo Lynch's masterful exploration of the corruption behind the white-picket-fence image of small-town America, with MacLachlan and Dern as the two kids who come up against a bunch of ambisexual, druggy, violent pervos in the oddest rite-of-passage ever lensed. One of those films which scholars love to discuss in terms of symbolism and metaphor, but don't let that put you off. Seriously strange. Widescreen available.

THRILLERS

BODY DOUBLE

CRAIG WASSON, DEBORAH SHELTON, MELANIE GRIFFITH, DENNIS FRANZ

BRIAN DE PALMA

USA (CINEMA CLUB V) 1984

109m (18)

One of De Palma's numerous reworkings of Hitchcockian themes – this time both *Rear Window* and *Vertigo* are thrown into the mix, with Wasson as a jobbing actor afflicted by claustrophobia who witnesses sexy goings-on from the vantage point of a pal's apartment. (The film also uses themes alleged to be based on Hitch's own life, since biographers have stated that Grace Kelly once agreed to strip naked while he spied on her from his house by telescope.) Often dismissed by critics, this is one of De Palma's best. Slightly cut by the BBFC for gore content, which is actually minimal.

THE BOYS FROM BRAZIL

GREGORY PECK, LAURENCE OLIVIER, JAMES MASON, LILLI PALMER

FRANKLIN J SCHAFFNER

USA (4-FRONT) 1979

120m (18)

Absurd version of an Ira Levin novel, with caricatures of Nazi scientist Josef Mengele (Peck) and nemesis Simon Wiesenthal (Olivier) battling over a plot to create a race of Hitler clones. It remains bizarre fun, but one can't avoid the niggling feeling that men who were involved in such terrible and serious recent historical events in the holocaust ought not to be seen as comic-strip characters, lest today's kids fail to realise that Hitler's ideas of racial purity were not only dangerous but deadly serious.

BRUBAKER

ROBERT REDFORD, YAPHET KOTTO, JANE ALEXANDER, M EMMET WALSH

STUART ROSENBERG

USA (FOX) 1980

130m (15)

Oscar-nominated script about a young prison governor who sets out to reform the rural penitentiary he's appointed to run, by pretending to be an inmate in order to unearth murder and corruption in the system. The kind of over-worthy pic Hollywood likes to applaud itself for undertaking, but well-honed and featuring a decent, understated star turn from Redford as the tow-headed zealot.

BULLITT

STEVE McQUEEN, ROBERT VAUGHN, JACQUELINE BISSET, ROBERT DUVALL

PETER YATES

USA (WARNER) 1969

109m (15)

Classic San Francisco car-chase flick features McQueen as a wooden-faced cop battling intrigue and gunshots in the hands of former 'Man from UNCLE' Vaughn. Undemanding, fast and just a bit too good to be a mere hamburger movie. Based on the hard-boiled novel *Mute Witness* by Robert L Pike. Oscar for best editing.

CAPE FEAR

ROBERT MITCHUM, GREGORY PECK, MARTIN BALSAM

J LEE THOMPSON

USA (CIC) 1961 B&W

106m (15)

Evil ex-convict stalks the family of the lawyer who put him in jail in this taut, grim adaptation of a novel *(The Executioner)* by John D MacDonald. Mitchum is downright scary as the sadistic, misogynistic criminal and Peck his usual upright self in an unusual thriller dealing with the (now topical) theme of the cops being powerless to stop stalkers. The original cinema release back in 1961 was cut by the BBFC as the violence was extreme for the time, but this appears to be the full print.

CAPE FEAR

ROBERT DE NIRO, NICK NOLTE, JESSICA LANGE, JULIETTE LEWIS

MARTIN SCORSESE

USA (CIC) 1991

122m (18)

Interesting reworking of the 1961 thriller. Scorsese makes the film morally ambiguous – this time the lawyer who sent the crook to jail was not the prosecutor but his own defence attorney, who thought he was 'doing the right thing' in betraying his evil client. Stalked by the baddy (an impressively mad De Niro) the lawyer adopts equally unlawful methods to see him off. Not quite in the same class as the original, but still powerful stuff. Features cameo appearances by Mitchum, Peck and Balsam in parts different from the ones they played in the first version.

COMA

MICHAEL DOUGLAS, GENEVIEVE BUJOLD, RICHARD WIDMARK, ED HARRIS, TOM SELLECK

MICHAEL CRICHTON

USA (WARNER) 1978

113m (15)

Written and directed by the author of *Jurassic Park* (see page 28) this is another of Crichton's effective technology-runs-rampant fancies, set in a hospital where a young doctor (Bujold) has difficulty convincing her associates she's not mad when she starts insisting that the bosses are killing healthy patients to run a lucrative spare-parts racket in organ transplants. Based on Robin Cook's novel of the same name, it manages to keep your attention, and has the bonus of sounding just plausible enough to be true.

COPLAND

ROBERT DE NIRO, HARVEY KEITEL, SYLVESTER STALLONE, RAY LIOTTA

JAMES MANGOLD

USA (BUENA VISTA) 1997

101m (18)

Highly praised cop story about a small town ruled by corrupt police, but I have to say I was slightly underwhelmed by the sluggish nature of the film which feels much longer than it actually is. Always a bad sign. Amid a raft of highly regarded thesps, most praise has surprisingly gone to Sylvester Stallone: in his first serious role for years he gained weight to play the local cop who finally rebels against his dodgy bosses. Worth a look for this aspect alone.

COPYCAT

SIGOURNEY WEAVER, HARRY CONNICK Jnr

JON AMIEL

USA (WARNER) 1995

118m (18)

Weaver battles a nutter, played by crooner Connick Jnr, who is copying the styles of famous serial killers of the past in this daft thriller. Note: in real-life the nemesis of anti-capital punishment campaigner Sister Helen Prejean (see *Dead Man Walking* on page 98) is Harry Connick Snr, who is a pro-death penalty prosecutor!

CRUISING

AL PACINO, PAUL SORVINO, KAREN ALLEN, JOE SPINELL

WILLIAM FRIEDKIN

USA (WARNER) 1980

102m (18)

Sleazoid epic about a cop who goes undercover to probe killings among New York's gay sadomasochist community, only to end up being corrupted by the fascinating, leather-clad milieu he is forced to inhabit. Controversial and sordid, but well made and featuring a compelling and powerful central performance by star Pacino. Cruising for a bruising! Cut on original release.

CUJO

☆	DEE WALLACE, CHRISTOPHER STONE, DANNY PINTAURO
🎬	LEWIS TEAGUE
	USA (MIA) 1983
⏱	87m (18)

Average adaptation of Stephen King novel about people trapped in a car by a rabid St Bernard. Not as silly as it sounds, but director Teague doesn't make as much of it as Hitchcock or De Palma would.

THE DAY OF THE JACKAL

☆	EDWARD FOX, ALAN BADEL, ERIC PORTER, DONALD SINDEN
🎬	FRED ZINNEMANN
	FRANCE/UK (CIC/4-FRONT) 1973
⏱	136m (15)

Methodical recounting of a lone assassin's preparations for the shooting of President de Gaulle, with Fox smooth and cold as a snake as the hitman of the title. Based on a smash novel of the same name by Frederick Forsyth. Loose update, *The Jackal*, released in 1998.

THE DEAD ZONE

☆	CHRISTOPHER WALKEN, MARTIN SHEEN, HERBERT LOM, BROOKE ADAMS
🎬	DAVID CRONENBERG
	USA (ENTERTAINMENT) 1983
⏱	99m (18)

A Stephen King story of a man who comes out of a coma to find he can tell the future, but also finds himself confronted by that age old problem: if you knew there was a future Hitler standing in front of you, but couldn't prove it, would you kill him? Director Cronenberg directs with his usual flair for plots dealing with bodies and minds rebelling against themselves, aided by a haunting turn from Walken as a man isolated by his unlooked-for psychic talents.

DIAL M FOR MURDER

☆	RAY MILLAND, GRACE KELLY, ROBERT CUMMINGS, ANTHONY DAWSON
🎬	ALFRED HITCHCOCK
	USA/UK (WARNER) 1954
⏱	100m (PG)

Originally shot in 3D (which accounts for the odd, intrusive close-ups of thrusting objects), this is a tight thriller about a man who plots to have his wife murdered by a down-at-heel crook. Full of ingenious, old-fashioned twists, it never quite manages to escape its stage-play origins – most of the action takes place in one room – though the cast give it their best shot. Remade for TV in 1981.

THRILLERS

DOA

EDMUND O'BRIEN, PAMELA BRITTON, NEVILLE BRAND

RUDOLF MATE

USA (2nd SIGHT) 1949 B&W

84m (PG)

Strange but effective tale of a man who is 'dead on arrival' – but still alive. He's been poisoned with a radioactive substance for which there's no cure, and decides to spend the last few hours of his life tracking down his killer. Remade in 1969 as *Color Me Dead* and again under the original title in 1988 (see below).

DOA

DENNIS QUAID, MEG RYAN, CHARLOTTE RAMPLING

ROCKY MORTON, ANNABEL JANKEL

USA (TOUCHSTONE) 1988

93m (15)

Reworking of the 1949 thriller about a man trying to catch the person who poisoned him before the drug takes effect. Motivation is reduced to the trivial, car chases and romance are added but it's all to no real gain. Kinetic and watchable, but the original remains your best bet. Cut.

ESCAPE FROM ALCATRAZ

CLINT EASTWOOD, PATRICK McGOOHAN, ROBERTS BLOSSOM, DANNY GLOVER

DON SIEGEL

USA (CIC/4-FRONT) 1979

112m (15)

Fact-based drama from Eastwood's long-time collaborator Siegel about an escape from the former USA island prison. No one knows what happened to the escapees – they were never heard of again – but the movie drops an optimistic (if unrealistic) hint that they got away and avoided the death by drowning that was said to await all in the dangerous waters off San Francisco. Tough entertainment with a typically stoic act from the star.

FLATLINERS

KIEFER SUTHERLAND, JULIA ROBERTS, KEVIN BACON, WILLIAM BALDWIN

JOEL SCHUMACHER

USA (CINEMA CLUB V) 1990

109m (15)

Bizarre tale of overweening medical students who hijack equipment and experiment with stopping their own hearts in order to explore near-death experiences. Interestingly, the film chooses to deal with matters of memory, guilt and personal conscience rather than crazy supernatural guff. Great effects.

FOREIGN CORRESPONDENT ⑤

JOEL McCREA, LARAINE DAY, HERBERT MARSHALL, GEORGE SANDERS

ALFRED HITCHCOCK

USA (VIDEO SPECIALS) 1940 B&W

115m (PG)

Spy 'meller' set in pre-war Europe of the 30s with McCrea as a hack caught up in intrigue and Nazi espionage. Hurtles to a great finale. Definitely one of Hitch's best, with a surprisingly gory (for its time) shooting scene in which a man is blasted in the face by an assassin posing as a cameraman.

FRENZY ④

JON FINCH, ALEC McCOWEN, ANNA MASSEY, BARRY FOSTER

ALFRED HITCHCOCK

UK (CIC) 1972

111m (18)

Another of Hitchcock's 'wrong man' thrillers in which a bumbling innocent is wanted for crimes he didn't commit. This time it's Finch being set up by his serial-killer pal Foster to take the rap for the latter's murderous spree. As always, Hitch isn't interested in concealing whodunnit but is relentless in making us identify (at different times) with both the dupe and the killer – check out the scene where Foster is in the back of a lorry trying to wrest an incriminating ring from the stiff fingers of a victim. Like *Psycho* (see page 198), in its time, this was much lambasted on release for being tasteless and too explicit. A few seconds were cut by the censor. Fine Covent Garden location filming.

THE FUGITIVE ④

HARRISON FORD, TOMMY LEE JONES, SELA WARD, JEROEN KRABBE

ANDREW DAVIS

USA (WARNER) 1994

131m (15)

Update of the 60s television series about an escaped prisoner on the trail of the one-armed man who killed his wife and left him to be wrongly convicted of the crime. Ford adopts the hesitant, stressed style of a man on the run to perfection and Tommy Lee Jones all but steals the show as a dogged cop who cares about the law, not justice. Begins with a magical piece of effects work in the best train crash ever seen on screen and zooms off from there. A real crowd-pleaser.

GET CARTER [4]

- MICHAEL CAINE, JOHN OSBORNE, IAN HENDRY, BRITT EKLAND
- MIKE HODGES
- UK (WARNER) 1970
- 112m (18)

Gutsy actioner about internecine warfare and revenge among northern England's criminal fraternity. Caine is believable as the implacable gangster, and there's a fine cameo performance from playwright Osborne as a local crime boss. Very violent and atmospheric and now something of a cult film.

THE HAND THAT ROCKS THE CRADLE [3]

- ANNABELLA SCIORRA, REBECCA DE MORNAY, JULIANNE MOORE, MATT McCOY
- CURTIS HANSON
- USA (TOUCHSTONE) 1992
- 106m (15)

In some ways slightly reminiscent of a Bette Davis film called *The Nanny*, this is a malevolent melodrama about a thoroughly nasty girl taken on as childminder by a young woman who is unaware of her secret agenda of revenge. Not quite as scary or jolting as the publicity suggests. Widescreen available.

HOMICIDE [4]

- JOE MANTEGNA, VING RHAMES, NATALIJA NOGULICH, WILLIAM H MACY
- DAVID MAMET
- USA (FIRST INDEPENDENT) 1991
- 97m (15)

Unusual film from writer/director Mamet, about a murder squad cop roped into a case which makes him question whether his loyalty to the law is more important than his Jewish heritage. Thought-provoking with a fine lead performance from Joe Mantegna and an odd (but plausible) plot. Mamet also wrote *The Untouchables* (see page 165).

HOUSE OF GAMES [5]

- JOE MANTEGNA, LINDSAY CROUSE, LILIA SKALA, STEVE GOLDSTEIN
- DAVID MAMET
- USA (CONNOISSEUR) 1987
- 98m (15)

Mamet's masterpiece, concerning a psychologist who is drawn into the world of a group of conmen only to have her illicit fascination with, and complicity in, their crimes lead to tragedy. The 'cons' are lovingly staged and played out and the actors (particularly Mantegna) first-rate. Do not miss.

I WAKE UP SCREAMING

BETTY GRABLE, CAROLE LANDIS, VICTOR MATURE, LAIRD CREGAR

BRUCE HUMBERSTONE

USA (FOX) 1941 B&W

79m (PG)

It was a great loss to cinema when plump, lisping, character actor Laird Cregar died after completing only a handful of films. Here he plays a slimy, nasty cop determined to frame Mature for the murder of a beautiful girl. He spits out insane dialogue while creepily toying with a miniature hangman's noose to taunt his victim. One of the best *noirs*, and an essential part of cinema's soft, white underbelly. Wild.

IN THE HEAT OF THE NIGHT

SIDNEY POITIER, ROD STEIGER, WARREN OATES, SCOTT WILSON

NORMAN JEWISON

USA (WARNER) 1967

95m (15)

Landmark 1960s thriller about a black policeman wrongly arrested while waiting for a train in America's Deep South. When his identity is proven, white police chief Steiger calls him in to solve a local murder. The interplay and gradually-increasing respect between Steiger and the detective (Poitier) is well handled, and the plot is engrossing. Steiger is careful to make his character more than a comic-book racist and the southern atmosphere feels authentic. Oscars for best picture, script, actor (Steiger) and more. There was a lacklustre sequel, *They Call Me Mr Tibbs*, with Poitier investigating another case.

IN THE LINE OF FIRE

CLINT EASTWOOD, RENE RUSSO, JOHN MALKOVICH, DYLAN McDERMOTT

WOLFGANG PETERSEN

USA (COLUMBIA TRISTAR) 1993

127m (15)

Eastwood is a secret service man haunted by guilt because he failed to stop the assassination of President Kennedy in 1963, who hopes to redeem himself when a dangerous loony challenges him to a battle of wits with the life of the current incumbent of the White House as prize. Great action sequences, including an edge-of-the-seat rooftop chase, and Eastwood (unlike many other stars) never tries to hide his age – in fact he makes it an important part of the plot. Malkovich is unsettling as the nut-case and Russo makes a good love interest – check out the scene where she and Clint have to divest themselves of all manner of hardware before they can get into a clinch. Petersen came to the attention of Hollywood with his submarine picture *The Boat* (see page 280). Widescreen available.

THRILLERS

INTERNAL AFFAIRS 🎬 4

⭐ RICHARD GERE, ANDY GARCIA, NANCY TRAVIS, WILLIAM BALDWIN

🎬 MIKE FIGGIS

USA (CIC/4-FRONT) 1990

⏱ 110m (18)

Gere is a crooked cop under investigation by internal affairs detective Garcia, who pushes him into more and more acts of violence and corruption. Tough, rough atmosphere and heavyweight acting from the two leads make for a gruelling, uncompromising picture. This film proved that Gere could still deliver the goods when given the right material to work with.

JAGGED EDGE 🎬 4

⭐ JEFF BRIDGES, GLENN CLOSE, PETER COYOTE, ROBERT LOGGIA

🎬 RICHARD MARQUAND

USA (VCI CINEMA CLUB) 1985

⏱ 105m (18)

A good example of writer Joe Eszterhas's sleaze thriller style. Lawyer Close defends smoothie Bridges on a charge of brutally butchering his wife. She gets him off and falls for him in the process. Ah, but was he guilty after all? Jumpy, fraught 'meller', with a lovely hard-boiled performance by Robert Loggia as Close's private investigator buddy. Eszterhas's best effort.

JENNIFER EIGHT 🎬 3

⭐ ANDY GARCIA, UMA THURMAN, LANCE HENRIKSEN, JOHN MALKOVICH

🎬 BRUCE ROBINSON

USA (CIC) 19920

⏱ 124m (15)

Complicated story from *Withnail And I* (see page 86) director Robinson. Despite an all-star cast, this convoluted tale of a cocky young copper never got a cinema release in the UK due to studio intransigence – which is a great shame. It may tend to ramble towards the end but it has a great deal to commend it. Worth renting, at least.

KALIFORNIA 🎬 3

⭐ BRAD PITT, JULIETTE LEWIS, DAVID DUCHOVNY, MICHELLE FORBES

🎬 DOMINIC SENA

USA (COLUMBIA TRISTAR) 1993

⏱ 118 (18)

The trend a while back was for fraught domestic situations: the nanny from hell (*The Hand That Rocks The Cradle* see page 267), the tenant from hell (*Pacific Heights* see page 115), the flatmate from hell (*Single White Female* see page 275), the lover from hell (*Fatal Attraction*, see page 104), etc. This one might be subtitled the car-sharers from hell: disgusting slob Pitt and his trailer-trash girlfriend (Lewis). Violent but very well acted, especially by Lewis and Pitt.

CLASSIC 1000 VIDEOS

KLUTE 4

DONALD SUTHERLAND, JANE FONDA, ROY SCHEIDER, CHARLES CIOFFI

ALAN J PAKULA

USA (WARNER) 1971

109m (18)

Oscar-winning role for Fonda as a disturbed prostitute involved with a detective on the track of a maniacal killer. Depressing and dark atmosphere, but the actors force you to keep looking.

LEON 4

JEAN RENO, GARY OLDMAN, NATALIE PORTMAN, DANNY AIELLO

LUC BESSON

FRANCE/USA (TOUCHSTONE) 1995

106m (18)

Wonderfully off-beat thriller about a lonely hitman (Reno), and his relationship with a neglected little girl who helps him deal with corrupt cop Oldman and shifty boss Aiello. Also in widescreen. A laserdisc director's cut extends the film with more detail on the friendship of the child and the killer. A neat film in any version.

THE LONG GOOD FRIDAY 4

BOB HOSKINS, HELEN MIRREN, EDDIE CONSTANTINE, DAVE KING

JOHN MacKENZIE

UK (CIC) 1980

109m (18)

Already a legendary pic, this stars Hoskins as cockney criminal Harold Shand. On the eve of a lucrative deal with the American Mafia, he finds himself under attack from unknown forces. Explosively violent, but Hoskins has a sort of crude dignity – when the Mafia are scared off by trouble, he delivers a paean to the greatness of criminal Britain that mirrors the xenophobic speeches of 'respectable' politicians defending Little England, raising cheers in London cinemas by describing the Yank boss as 'a long streak of paralysed piss'! Unlovely he may be, but you can't take your eyes off Mr Shand.

THE MANCHURIAN CANDIDATE 4

LAURENCE HARVEY, FRANK SINATRA, JANET LEIGH, ANGELA LANSBURY

JOHN FRANKENHEIMER

USA (WARNER) 1962 B&W

126m (15)

Based on a novel by Richard Condon, this cold war epic, about a soldier returned to the USA by the Commies as a brainwashed assassin, was out of circulation for many years at the behest of Sinatra, who felt it paralleled too strongly the murder of his friend President Kennedy which occurred the year after it was released. The right-wing mater of the killer as portrayed by Lansbury provides a sardonic swipe at Mom and apple pie. Harvey does his best-ever work as the disturbed assassin. Sinatra made another assassination film, *Suddenly*, also rarely seen.

MANHUNTER

BRIAN COX, WILLIAM PETERSEN, KIM GREIST, TOM NOONAN, DENNIS FARINA

MICHAEL MANN

USA (FOX) 1986

115m (18)

Marvellous film based on Thomas Harris's novel *Red Dragon*. It concerns a weird FBI agent who is called out of retirement because he has the ability to track serial sex killers by identifying with their thoughts. It wasn't a hit but has attained cult status as it has an appearance by Brian Cox as imprisoned murderer Hannibal 'The Cannibal' Lecter – the character who became much talked-about when portrayed by Anthony Hopkins in the movie of the sequel novel, *The Silence Of The Lambs* (see page 275). Cox's version of the character is very different, and – in spite of Hopkins winning an Oscar – critically preferred. A beautifully-shot film which will make your skin crawl. Not out in widescreen. A 124m version was prepared in 1996 by Mann, but is unavailable.

MARATHON MAN

DUSTIN HOFFMAN, LAURENCE OLIVIER, ROY SCHEIDER, MARTHE KELLER

JOHN SCHLESINGER

USA (CIC/4-FRONT) 1976

119m (18)

Vastly over-praised by mainstream critics, this is the story of a young guy (Hoffman) unwittingly dragged into trouble by the death of his secret agent brother. The most talked-about scene is the one where Nazi Olivier uses crude dental skills to torture Hoffman in the hope of making him divulge important information. Solid hokum, but no more. Olivier was obviously saving up for his pension by appearing in this one.

MARNIE

SEAN CONNERY, TIPPI HEDREN, BRUCE DERN, DIANE BAKER

ALFRED HITCHCOCK

USA (CIC) 1964

130m (15)

Over-long melodrama about a thieving girl and her husband (Connery), who naturally wants to find out just why she's a frigid kleptomaniac. Trite and dreary, but Hitchcock films it lovingly and there's a dreamy score by his fave composer Bernard Herrmann.

MISERY

KATHY BATES, JAMES CAAN, FRANCES STERNHAGEN, LAUREN BACALL

ROB REINER

USA (CINEMA CLUB V) 1990

102m (18)

This version of Stephen King's novel is mainly a two-hander between Caan and Bates. He's a novelist injured in a car crash, she's the obsessive fan who finds him. She happens to be a nurse and is delighted to have him recuperate in her isolated home – but when she finds he has killed off her favourite romantic character, Misery Chastain, to write serious books, she goes off the rails in a big way. Sadistic and unnerving. Oscar: best actress (Bates).

MISSISSIPPI BURNING

GENE HACKMAN, WILLEM DAFOE, FRANCES McDORMAND, BRAD DOURIF

ALAN PARKER

USA (ENTERTAINMENT) 1988

121m (18)

Fact-based thriller about FBI investigations into the murder of civil rights workers in America's Deep South, with sterling acting all round – notably from McDormand as the wife of a guilty man. The film was criticised for concentrating on white characters as the 'saviours' of black victims, but it still works as a thriller and the cinematography rightly won an Oscar.

MONA LISA

BOB HOSKINS, CATHY TYSON, MICHAEL CAINE, ROBBIE COLTRANE, SAMMI DAVIS

NEIL JORDAN

UK (CIC) 1986

104m (18)

Hoskins impresses as an ex-con driving tart Tyson to her clients – but then he falls for her. Gritty story with a theme suitable only for adults, carried by good performances from Hoskins, Tyson and the ever-reliable Caine. Widescreen available.

NIGHT MOVES

GENE HACKMAN, JENNIFER WARREN, JAMES WOODS, MELANIE GRIFFITH

ARTHUR PENN

USA (WARNER) 1975

96m (18)

Dark detective thriller with characters whose lives suggest the unravelling of 70s American society. Early appearances from James Woods and Melanie Griffith, daughter of Tippi Hedren. Her part here, as a sexually-precocious teenager, mirrored her real-life antics at the time. Sloppily directed by Penn, with boom mikes occasionally intruding into the top of the frame, but an effective picture for all that. Special edition available.

NIGHTWATCH

NIKOLAJ WALDAU, SOFIE GRAABOEL, KIM BODNIA, ULF PILGAARD

OLE BORNEDAL

DENMARK (TARTAN) 1994

104m (18)

Acclaimed creepy thriller about evil goings-on in a mortuary. As is often the case with foreign thrillers, the director is has been wooed into making an English-language version with USA and UK stars voices. They usually turn out to be inferior to the originals, so if you can cope with subtitles this is for you. Issued in widescreen.

NO WAY OUT

KEVIN COSTNER, GENE HACKMAN, SEAN YOUNG, HOWARD DUFF

ROGER DONALDSON

USA (SPEARHEAD) 1987

110m (15)

Loosely based on *noir The Big Clock*, this is a tricksy double-agent story with sex and violence thrown in for bad measure. Costner proves he can act as well as look handsome, and while hardly an important film it'll provide a decent night's entertainment.

NORTH BY NORTHWEST

CARY GRANT, EVA MARIE SAINT, JAMES MASON, LEO G CARROLL, MARTIN LANDAU

ALFRED HITCHCOCK

USA (WARNER) 1959

131m (PG)

The pinnacle of Hitch's 'wrong man' epics, with Grant charming as the playboy fated to be drawn into a spy chase – the scene where he's pursued in a field by a crop sprayer plane is a classic sequence, and modern audiences always howl with laughter at the final shot: after we see Grant and Eva Marie Saint embrace in a railway carriage, there's a Freudian cut to the train roaring into a tunnel.

POINT BLANK

LEE MARVIN, ANGIE DICKINSON, KEENAN WYNN, CARROL O'CONNOR

JOHN BOORMAN

USA (WARNER) 1967

92m (18)

Based on a pulp character created by Richard Stark, this is a merciless revenge thriller about a hood (Marvin) stoically demanding the return of money given to the Mob by a bent accomplice, but finding modern gangland is run by men in suits with wallets full of nothing but credit cards. He responds by stealing from their illegal operations in a one-man war of attrition. Brutal and brilliantly directed by Brit Boorman. Recently revived in cinemas.

PRIMAL FEAR 4

	RICHARD GERE, FRANCES McDORMAND, EDWARD NORTON, LAURA LINNEY
	GREGORY HOBLIT
	USA (CIC) 1996
	124m (18)

Gripping story about the sleazy underbelly of the USA legal system. Gere is a flashy lawyer defending a seemingly feckless kid (the wonderful Norton) accused of murdering a top churchman. The lawyer appears to know all the tricks – but who is really manipulating whom? Somewhat underrated on cinema release, this nifty thriller ought to find its audience on video.

RAISING CAIN 3

	JOHN LITHGOW, LOLITA DAVIDOVICH, STEVEN BAUER, FRANCES STERNHAGEN
	BRIAN DE PALMA
	USA (CIC) 1992
	92m (15)

De Palma descends to self-parody with this story of a fractured persona at the mercy of his crazy child-psychologist dad. Not content with borrowing from Hitchcock, the theme of Michael Powell's *Peeping Tom* (see page 197) is added to the witch's brew. Critics chuckled at press screenings, but there's no denying the director's skill or John Lithgow's talent as an actor.

RANSOM 4

	MEL GIBSON, RENE RUSSO, GARY SINISE, DELROY LINDO
	RON HOWARD
	USA (TOUCHSTONE) 1996
	116m (18)

Fine update of the 1955 thriller. Wealthy Gibson gets fed up of being messed about when his child is kidnapped and goes on TV to announce (much to the horror of his wife) that he will not pay the ransom, but will give the cash to anyone who grasses the baddies up. Pulse-pounding stuff, with real emotion rather than big bangs.

REPULSION 3

	CATHERINE DENEUVE, IAN HENDRY, PATRICK WYMARK, YVONNE FURNEAUX
	ROMAN POLANSKI
	UK (ODYSSEY) 1965 B&W
	104m (18)

Dank story of a disturbed girl and her murderous assaults. There's a great surreal scene of hands coming out of walls in a corridor, but it has too much of the 'art-film' about it to really hold the viewer's attention to the end.

SEA OF LOVE

AL PACINO, ELLEN BARKIN, JOHN GOODMAN, MICHAEL ROOKER

HAROLD BECKER

USA (CIC) 1989

108m (18)

Gripping thriller about a cop investigating a chain of murders linked to 'lonely hearts' adverts who finds himself involved with a woman who may be the killer. Not as luridly satisfying as its rep suggests, but driven along neatly by a taut Richard Price screenplay and a good Pacino performance.

THE SILENCE OF THE LAMBS

JODIE FOSTER, ANTHONY HOPKINS, SCOTT GLENN, TED LEVINE

JONATHAN DEMME

USA (COLUMBIA TRISTAR) 1991

113m (18)

Gory version of Thomas Harris's novel about a caged serial killer (Hopkins) and his relationship with FBI rookie Foster as they track down another murderer. The pic won several Oscars, including best actor for Hopkins, but many feel his stint as Hannibal Lecter is inferior to that of Brian Cox in *Manhunter* (see page 271). There's a cameo performance from director/producer Roger Corman, who gave the pic's director Jonathan Demme his start years before. The film was condemned for equating transsexuality with murderous deviance, leading Demme to make the sympathetic AIDS drama *Philadelphia* (see page 116) to silence his critics.

SINGLE WHITE FEMALE

BRIDGET FONDA, JENNIFER JASON LEIGH, STEVEN WEBER

BARBET SCHROEDER

USA (CINEMA CLUB V) 1992

108m (18)

Flatmate from hell movie. Revenge, rage and lunacy abound, but I find it to be the least thrilling of the '… from hell' genre which was in vogue some years ago. The two leads are decent actresses but it's all a bit tired.

SLEEPERS

ROBERT DE NIRO, DUSTIN HOFFMAN, BRAD PITT, KEVIN BACON, JASON PATRIC

BARRY LEVINSON

USA (POLYGRAM) 1996

141m (18)

Controversial movie about boys abused in a kids' home who grow up and go separate ways until two of them, now gangsters, meet and kill one of their molesters. Another boy who has become a lawyer takes on the defence. It's allegedly all true, but investigating journalists could find no record of the case. And much as we all loathe child abuse, it's worrying to see a supposedly quality pic suggesting it's okay to take the law into your own hands and then lie and cheat (with the help of your priest!) in order to get away with it. It'd be all right if some doubt were voiced, but this never happens. All the more disturbing for being so well acted. Available in widescreen.

SLEUTH

	LAURENCE OLIVIER, MICHAEL CAINE
	JOSEPH L MANKIEWICZ
	UK/USA (MIA) 1972
	132m (15)

Anthony Shaffer's play makes a fine two-handed duel for Olivier and Caine as rivals in love engaged in a class-based battle of wits and mutual humiliation. The trouble is that the central visual deception, which I can't reveal as it would spoil the plot for you, didn't fool me for a minute. On stage it would pass, but on the big screen I saw through it right off. But the actors make it worthwhile. Agreeably crisp and salty dialogue.

TAXI DRIVER

	ROBERT DE NIRO, JODIE FOSTER, HARVEY KEITEL, CYBILL SHEPHERD, PETER BOYLE, ALBERT BROOKS, JOE SPINELL, MARTIN SCORSESE
	MARTIN SCORSESE
	USA (COLUMBIA TRISTAR) 1976
	114m (18)

Those that love it call it a work of genius, those that hate it say it's just a big-budget exploitation movie. Both statements may be true. De Niro is Travis Bickle, a Vietnam veteran who can't sleep and takes a night job as a taxi driver. Horrified by the life he sees on the street, his inability to form a relationship with the girl he worships and his failure to persuade a child prostitute to quit, he embarks on an apocalyptic explosion of violence – with surprising results. Paul Schrader's screenplay is still as relevant as ever to our mad, sad world. Fine score from Bernard Herrmann. Recently reissued in a remastered widescreen edition.

VERTIGO

	JAMES STEWART, KIM NOVAK, BARBARA BEL GEDDES, TOM HELMORE
	ALFRED HITCHCOCK
	USA (CIC) 1958
	122m (PG)

Hitch was miffed to have missed out on the rights to the novel which inspired the French thriller *Diabolique*, so the author penned a book specially for him to adapt. The result was this classic about a man who attempts to remake his new gal in the image of the lady he failed to save due to his suffering from the affliction of the title, only to discover he's been duped. Music by Hitchcock's favourite composer Herrmann is a great part of the package. The film has recently been somewhat controversially restored and reissued in 70mm, so this tape may well have been superseded by the time you read this. Many critics say this original version is preferable.

WAR

War films can be crash, bang, smash-'em-up entertainment, patriotic propaganda, historical adventure or polemics on the futility of armed conflict and there are plenty of all kinds available on video. Strangely enough, though, in spite of the potential for both action and human interest, very few directors seem to specialise in the genre. The great maverick Sam Fuller made several low-budget classics, but the only one of his war pix I could find currently available is his mutilated masterpiece *The Big Red One*. Oliver Stone at one time looked to be making a career of modern war epics, with films such as *Born On The Fourth Of July*, *Platoon* and *Salvador*, but he's since moved on to more controversial political and social dramas. Spielberg has recently scored with *Saving Private Ryan*. It would be nice if we lived in a world where war films were invariably set in the distant past – but it looks as if mankind will go on providing movie-makers with up-to-the-minute genocidal storylines for the forseeable future. How sad.

633 SQUADRON

GEORGE CHAKIRIS, CLIFF ROBERTSON, MARIA PERSCHY

WALTER GRAUMAN

UK (WARNER) 1964

92m (PG)

Exciting World War Two story of preparation for and execution of an extremely difficult bombing raid. Thrill-a-minute and a rousing score combine with a good cast to create a picture that remains a perennial favourite. Also available on a two-for-one tape with *The Battle Of Britain* (see page 278). Note: this appears to be a cut print.

ALL QUIET ON THE WESTERN FRONT

LEW AYRES, LOUIS WOLHEIM, JOHN WRAY

LEWIS MILESTONE

USA (CIC) 1930 B&W

103m (PG)

Based on Erich Maria Remarque's anti-war novel, this is the tale of German kids who volunteer for World War One. They rapidly change from gung-ho patriots to sad and scared cynics. This is a heavily cut version. The film spawned a sequel and was remade in the 70s. Oscar: best picture.

APOCALYPSE NOW

MARLON BRANDO, MARTIN SHEEN, ROBERT DUVALL, FREDERIC FORREST, DENNIS HOPPER

FRANCIS FORD COPPOLA

USA (CIC) 1979

146m (18)

Coppola's multi-million dollar epic relocates the action of Joseph Conrad's novel *Heart Of Darkness* to the Vietnam conflict, with Sheen as a soldier sent on a mission into Cambodia in order to kill Kurtz (Brando), a high-ranking officer who has gone mad and is conducting his own war with the help of native tribesmen. The boat journey upriver in the company of LSD-taking troops has been said to parallel an acid trip (indeed, the film was allegedly at one point titled *The Psychedelic Soldier*), and the acting and images often border on the surreal. Brando's dialogue was improvised and sounds it. The production took a toll on the physical, mental and financial health of several of those involved, and while some dismiss it as pretentious twaddle it remains one of the most spectacular, audacious and talked-about films of all time. There is a fine documentary on the making of the movie, *Hearts Of Darkness*. Oscars: cinematography and sound. Note: widescreen available, but the ratio is badly cropped.

THE BATTLE OF BRITAIN

LAURENCE OLIVIER, ROBERT SHAW, MICHAEL CAINE, SUSANNAH YORK

GUY HAMILTON

UK (WARNER) 1969

110m (PG)

Worthy if leaden attempt to tell the story of the decisive World War Two fight between the RAF and the Luftwaffe. Great music and aerial dogfights but far too many stars popping up for stiff upper-lip cameos. This appears to be a cut print (down from 132m). Also available on two-for-one tape with *633 Squadron* (see page 277), another war-in-the-air showpiece.

THE BATTLE OF MIDWAY

CHARLTON HESTON, TOSHIRO MIFUNE, HENRY FONDA, ROBERT MITCHUM, GLENN FORD, JAMES COBURN

JACK SMIGHT

USA (CIC/4-FRONT) 1976

126m (PG)

Account of a 1942 Pacific ocean battle between Japanese and Yanks. Suffers from similar star overload to *The Battle Of Britain* (see above), but is a tad more coherent and gripping a prospect. Most of the star performers underplay to good effect. Convincing battle scenes.

WAR

BATTLE OF THE BULGE [3]

HENRY FONDA, ROBERT RYAN, ROBERT SHAW, CHARLES BRONSON

KEN ANNAKIN

USA (WARNER) 1965

132m (PG)

Yet another account of a decisive World War Two fight – this time the final German attack of 1944 in the Ardennes – finds itself smothered in heavyweight acting cameos. Saved by Fonda's measured performance. Available in widescreen, which is the only way to see it.

THE BIG RED ONE [5]

LEE MARVIN, MARK HAMILL, ROBERT CARRADINE, BOBBY DI CICCO

SAM FULLER

USA (WARNER) 1980

82m (15)

Sam Fuller's autobiographical masterpiece was cut by the studio but remains a powerful story of a World War Two infantry division. The title refers to the figure '1' on the soldiers' badges, but misinterpretation of this was no doubt the reason for the (hilarious) seizure of the video in the 'nasties' debacle of the early 1980s! Police were confounded to find that they'd seized a worthy war film and not a hard-core porno flick. This is one picture that merits rediscovery and restoration to full director's cut length.

THE BLUE MAX [5]

GEORGE PEPPARD, JAMES MASON, URSULA ANDRESS, JEREMY KEMP

JOHN GUILLERMIN

USA (FOX) 1966

146m (PG)

Excellently acted and visually thrilling tale of German World War One flying aces. Peppard is the working-class yob who causes offence when his aviation skills gain him entry into the aristocratic world of fighter pilots, while Kemp is his resentful comrade. By chasing after the coveted 'Blue Max' medal, seducing the wife of a senior officer and generally ignoring the rules of chivalry and gentlemanly behaviour, Peppard becomes a hero to the people and a thorn in the side of his bosses. One of the best air-war pix ever. Available in a widescreen version, but unfortunately from a cut print.

THE BOAT 🎬 5

⭐ JURGEN PROCHNOW, HERBERT GRONEMEYER, KLAUS WENNEMANN

🎬 WOLFGANG PETERSEN

WEST GERMANY
(COLUMBIA TRISTAR) 1981

⏱ 143m   (15)

This U-Boat adventure was the most expensive German film ever at the time it was made. The claustrophobic, sweaty, fear-inducing world of the cramped 'boat' is shown in a way that outdoes all the Hollywood submarine pix. The movie was shown in a dubbed 128m version outside Germany, but acclaim led to a subtitled 143m print being released as *Das Boot*, the German title. That is the print available on this widescreen tape, subtitles (ha ha) and all. An epic 300m German TV series version has been shown on BBC TV. Director Petersen and lead actor Prochnow have gone on to Hollywood success.

BORN ON THE FOURTH OF JULY 🎬 4

⭐ TOM CRUISE, WILLEM DAFOE, JOHN GETZ, STEPHEN BALDWIN, TOM BERENGER

🎬 OLIVER STONE

USA (CIC) 1989

⏱ 138m   (18)

Perhaps the best of director Stone's series of Vietnam movies is based on the autobiography of Ron Kovic, a young man who was an enthusiastic soldier but changed his mind (as you do) after coming home crippled. The film ably moves from mindless patriotism on Kovic's part through degradation of body and spirit until his final realisation that he's been duped. Cruise's finest acting role, which admittedly, isn't saying much. Oscars for direction and editing. Available in widescreen.

THE BRIDGE ON THE RIVER KWAI 🎬 4

⭐ ALEC GUINNESS, WILLIAM HOLDEN, JACK HAWKINS, SESSUE HAYAKAWA

🎬 DAVID LEAN

UK (COLUMBIA TRISTAR) 1957

⏱ 155m   (PG)

Based on a novel by Pierre Boulle, who wrote the source story for *Planet Of The Apes*, this factually-inspired story of Allied troops on the notorious Burma railway built at the behest of the Japanese in World War Two is not without problems. Essentially a chracter study of two stubborn men (Guinness as the Brit and Hayakawa as the Jap) with different ideas of 'honour', it actually soft-pedals the Japanese atrocities in an attempt at psychological analysis. Guinness wants to show Brit superiority, but actually ends up collaborating with the enemy. Flawed, but still won several Oscars, including best film, director, cinematography and actor (Guinness).

WAR

CASUALTIES OF WAR

MICHAEL J FOX, SEAN PENN, DON HARVEY, THUY THU LE

BRIAN DE PALMA

USA (CINEMA CLUB V) 1989

108m (18)

Based on a true story of a group of young American troops who kidnapped, sexually abused and shot a Vietnamese girl, and the one man who refused to be a party to the crime. Fox is believable as the lad who refuses to be pressured or threatened into burying the facts, proving that he's a capable actor when given something other than the usual comedy rubbish to work with. Often derided – maybe the Americans dislike the truth – this is one of De Palma's best and least showy pix. Quentin Tarantino rates it as a classic, if that helps. Cut from 120m.

THE COLDITZ STORY

JOHN MILLS, ERIC PORTMAN, BRYAN FORBES, LIONEL JEFFRIES

GUY HAMILTON

UK (WARNER) 1954 B&W

93m (U)

Classic escape story of Allied captives in World War Two, ingenious and full of famous British faces. Also available in a two-for-one tape with *Ice Cold In Alex* (see page 285), which also stars Mills. The two films complement each other nicely.

CROSS OF IRON

JAMES COBURN, MAXIMILIAN SCHELL, JAMES MASON, DAVID WARNER

SAM PECKINPAH

UK/WEST GERMANY (WARNER) 1977

127m (18)

Peckinpah's men-stick-together ethos transported from the West to a wild bunch of German soldiers on the Russian front in World War Two. Coburn is the cynical leader, Schell the idiot desperate for the Iron Cross medal of the title. Solidly anti-war, though Peckinpah's version was undercut by his being forced to quit shooting before he had all the material he needed. Richard Burton took the Coburn part in a sequel shot by another director.

THE CRUEL SEA

JACK HAWKINS, STANLEY BAKER, DENHOLM ELLIOTT, MOIRA LISTER

CHARLES FREND

UK (WARNER) 1953 B&W

121m (PG)

Nicholas Monsarrat's novel of the men aboard a Brit Corvette in World War Two, with understated playing from all concerned. Sentimental in parts, but much of its time is spent in unvarnished portrayal of life at sea.

D-DAY THE 6TH OF JUNE [2]

ROBERT TAYLOR, RICHARD TODD, DANA WYNTER, EDMOND O'BRIEN

HENRY KOSTER

USA (FOX) 1956

106m (PG)

Romantic guff about a Yank and a Brit who love the same gal. Not enough gunfire, too much sloppy sentiment. Definitely not my idea of what constituted a good war movie. Taylor is a real stuffed shirt.

THE DAM BUSTERS [3]

MICHAEL REDGRAVE, RICHARD TODD, NIGEL STOCK, JOHN FRASER

MICHAEL ANDERSON

UK (WARNER) 1954 B&W

120m (U)

Story of the invention by Barnes Wallis of the bouncing bomb, and its subsequent use against German dams on the Ruhr in 1943. While it was probably a necessary act of war, it's easy in the excitement of the piece to forget that many ordinary civilians lost their lives in the process. Fine acting from Redgrave as the boffin.

THE DEER HUNTER [3]

ROBERT DE NIRO, CHRISTOPHER WALKEN, JOHN SAVAGE, MERYL STREEP

MICHAEL CIMINO

USA (WARNER) 1978

175m (18)

Cimino is the master of the overblown, with this and *Heaven's Gate* (see page 299) his worst offences. This tale of friends and families torn by the Vietnam war certainly has some memorable sequences, but these are offset by stretches of sheer tedium. When I saw it on first release, the audience groaned and shifted in their seats throughout and at the point where the weeping family sit around the table crooning 'God Bless America' the woman seated next to me exclaimed 'Oh for God's *sake!*' and made a noisy exit. Nevertheless, it won Oscars for best film, director and supporting actor (Walken), amongst others. To my mind Cimino's best film remains his simple, effective debut, the Clint Eastwood vehicle *Thunderbolt And Lightfoot,* but he seems to prefer epic tedium.

THE DESERT FOX

JAMES MASON, CEDRIC HARDWICKE, JESSICA TANDY, RICHARD BOONE

HENRY HATHAWAY

USA (FOX) 1951 B&W

85m (PG)

Life of German World War Two Field Marshall Erwin Rommel, from his desert war with adversary Montgomery to his part in the plot to kill Hitler. Mason is on top form here. He played Rommel again two years later in *The Desert Rats*, made to cash in on the success of this film.

THE DIRTY DOZEN

LEE MARVIN, ROBERT RYAN, TELLY SAVALAS, DONALD SUTHERLAND, JOHN CASSAVETES, CHARLES BRONSON

ROBERT ALDRICH

USA (WARNER) 1967

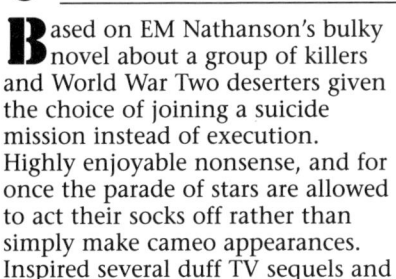

146m (15)

Based on EM Nathanson's bulky novel about a group of killers and World War Two deserters given the choice of joining a suicide mission instead of execution. Highly enjoyable nonsense, and for once the parade of stars are allowed to act their socks off rather than simply make cameo appearances. Inspired several duff TV sequels and not a few rip-offs. Widescreen tape is available. Aldrich has become something of a cult director in recent years, but somewhat unjustly this is not one of his more highly regarded pictures.

FULL METAL JACKET

MATTHEW MODINE, ADAM BALDWIN, LEE ERMEY, VINCENT D'ONOFRIO

STANLEY KUBRICK

USA/UK (WARNER) 1987

112m (18)

Late entry in the Vietnam movie stakes by the coldest of directors. Kubrick insisted on recreating Vietnam in London's docklands and it simply doesn't look believable. The movie follows the familiar pattern of showing a tough instructor training raw recruits, followed by a look at how the lads do in combat. The innovation here is that one bullied recruit loads his gun with real ammo (the full metal jacket of the title) and blows the bullying drill leader away! The Vietnam sequence which follows just seems to peter out. Perhaps war is like that but it doesn't make for great film-making. The last time I looked, some of the Vietnam sets could still be seen in docklands. They may even last longer than the film's inflated reputation.

GALLIPOLI 🎬3

| MARK LEE, MEL GIBSON, BILL HUNTER, BILL KERR |
| PETER WEIR |
| AUSTRALIA (CIC) 1981 |
| 106m (PG) |

Two pals tough it out in World War One Gallipoli landings. Decent acting and action. Available in widescreen. Note: one of Gibson's first big parts after the success of *Mad Max* (see page 30). He's now a major star, of course.

GLORY 🎬4

| MATTHEW BRODERICK, DENZEL WASHINGTON, MORGAN FREEMAN, CARY ELWES |
| EDWARD ZWICK |
| USA (COLUMBIA TRISTAR) 1989 |
| 117m (15) |

Black section of the Union army in the American Civil War. Well acted and beautifully shot (actor Washington won a best support Oscar and Freddie Francis was rewarded for his cinematography) but some of the sentiments are way off. It beggars belief how an actor of the calibre of Morgan Freeman could mouth dialogue about how whites had been doing all the fighting for blacks and that it was now time for them to pay back the debt – especially when we now know that the North's motives were as much economic as anything else. Some critics call *Glory* an anti-war film, but it seems (even in its title) to be gung-ho for battle. All that aside, a watchable piece. This appears to be a cut version, as sources list the original running time at 128m. Available in widescreen.

THE GREAT ESCAPE 🎬4

| STEVE MCQUEEN, JAMES GARNER, DONALD PLEASENCE, JAMES COBURN, RICHARD ATTENBOROUGH, CHARLES BRONSON, DAVID McCALLUM |
| JOHN STURGES |
| USA (WARNER) 1963 |
| 165m (PG) |

Detailed account of World War Two Allied escape from a German prison camp, the fun and games being undercut by a brutal ending. All the actors acquit themselves well. Remade for TV in 1988. A widescreen tape is now available. Note: the musical score has become as famous as the film due to the catchy theme tune.

THE GREEN BERETS 🎬2

| JOHN WAYNE, DAVID JANSSEN, JIM HUTTON, ALDO RAY |
| JOHN WAYNE, RAY KELLOGG |
| USA (WARNER) 1968 |
| 136m (15) |

Wayne's riposte to protests about USA's involvement in Vietnam, portraying all Commies as bad and Yanks as decent types doing the best they know how. Wayne is always entertaining, but with what we now know about the war in South East Asia this stuff rather sticks in the throat.

THE GUNS OF NAVARONE

GREGORY PECK, DAVID NIVEN, STANLEY BAKER, ANTHONY QUINN

J LEE THOMPSON

UK/USA (COLUMBIA TRISTAR) 1961

157m (PG)

Based on an Alistair MacLean novel, this lengthy adventure concerns a World War Two Allied team attempting to destroy German guns on a Greek island because they threaten shipping lanes. Performance-driven with much intrigue involving treacherous behaviour, the pic nevertheless won the Oscar for SFX. A lacklustre sequel was made many years later.

HAMBURGER HILL

ANTHONY BARRILE, MICHAEL PATRICK BOATMAN, TIM QUILL

JOHN IRVIN

USA (CINEMA CLUB V) 1987

110m (18)

True story with cast of unknowns, set in Vietnam during bloody attempt to secure the hill of the title. Irvin is always a dependable director, and it's a pity the film is not better known.

I WAS MONTY'S DOUBLE

JOHN MILLS, M.E. CLIFTON-JAMES, CECIL PARKER, MICHAEL HORDERN

JOHN GUILLERMIN

UK (WARNER/LUMIERE) 1958 B&W

96m (U)

Clifton-James plays himself in this true World War Two story of how he impersonated Field Marshal Montgomery to dupe the Nazis. The resemblance is uncanny, and as he is a professional actor he comes across well on-screen.

ICE COLD IN ALEX

JOHN MILLS, SYLVIA SIMS, ANTHONY QUAYLE, HARRY ANDREWS

J LEE THOMPSON

UK (WARNER) 1960 B&W

125m (PG)

World War Two desert trek by a varied group in a clapped-out ambulance. A neat little picture with some fine acting on display. Also on a two-for-one tape with *The Colditz Story* (see page 281), another Mills starrer.

IN HARM'S WAY 🎬3

	JOHN WAYNE, KIRK DOUGLAS, PATRICIA NEAL, HENRY FONDA
	OTTO PREMINGER
	USA (CIC/4-FRONT) 1965 B&W
⏱	167m (PG)

Bloated, star-laden romance set against the background of the World War Two Japanese attack on the American naval base at Pearl Harbor. Carried (just) by the star power on show. Dull.

KELLY'S HEROES 🎬3

	CLINT EASTWOOD, DONALD SUTHERLAND, CARROLL O'CONNOR
	BRIAN G HUTTON
	USA/YUGOSLAVIA (WARNER) 1970
⏱	143m (PG)

Silly story (in *M*A*S*H* style) of slovenly, rebellious US troops in World War Two deciding to go in for private enterprise by hijacking Nazi gold from bank vaults. Eastwood, Sutherland and O'Connor save the film, but it definitely overstays its welcome.

THE LONG AND THE SHORT AND THE TALL 🎬3

	RICHARD TODD, LAURENCE HARVEY, RICHARD HARRIS, RONALD FRASER
	LESLIE NORMAN
	UK (WARNER/LUMIERE) 1960 B&W
⏱	101m (PG)

World War Two conscience-drama set in Malaysia, where Brits have to decide whether to kill a captive. Based on the play by Willis Hall, directed by father of film critic Barry Norman. Good acting, especially from Ronald Fraser, who sadly passed away in 1997.

THE LONGEST DAY 🎬4

	JOHN WAYNE, ROD STEIGER, ROBERT RYAN, ROBERT MITCHUM, HENRY FONDA
	KEN ANNAKIN, ANDREW MARTIN, BERNARD WICKI
	USA (FOX) 1962 B&W
⏱	170m (PG)

Epic account of Normandy landings by the Allies in World War Two, recently shown more realistically in *Saving Private Ryan*. Someone once stated that black and white widescreen was the most redundant of filmic styles, and you can sample it for yourselves on this tape. Too many stars, too little story (or too much?), but it still won Oscars for cinematography and effects work. Colourised for TV showings in recent years.

WAR

MEMPHIS BELLE 4

- MATTHEW MODINE, ERIC STOLTZ, BILLY ZANE, TATE DONOVAN
- MICHAEL CATON-JONES
- USA (WARNER) 1990
- 103m (PG)

True tale of World War Two B-17 bomber crew previously told in a wartime documentary. A slow build-up to the final mission lets us get to grips with the featured characters. Well crafted and definitely worth seeing.

THE NAKED AND THE DEAD 3

- CLIFF ROBERTSON, ALDO RAY, RAYMOND MASSEY, RICHARD JAECKEL
- RAOUL WALSH
- USA (ODYSSEY) 1958
- 130m (PG)

Somewhat anodyne adaptation of Normal Mailer's novel of Americans versus Japanese in World War Two. The performers are up to scratch, but Mailer's gutsy prose doesn't get the translation it deserves. Still worth a glance, if only for Raymond Massey as a thoroughly nasty officer.

NIGHT OF THE GENERALS 4

- OMAR SHARIF, PETER O'TOOLE, TOM COURTENAY, JOANNA PETTET
- ANATOLE LITVAK
- FRANCE/UK (CINEMA CLUB V) 1967
- 138m (15)

Underrated and unusual war movie, with O'Toole as a German general in World War Two. He's also a serial killer, and when he's about to be found out he tries to implicate his underling in order to escape justice. Based on the novel by HH Kirst. This is a cut print, unfortunately, as far as I can determine.

PATTON 5

- GEORGE C SCOTT, KARL MALDEN, STEPHEN YOUNG, MICHAEL STRONG
- FRANKLIN J SCHAFFNER
- USA (FOX) 1970
- 169m (PG)

Magnificent epic on the life of flamboyant USA general Patton, with a mesmerising performance by Scott in the title role. Opens with a fantastic image of Patton addressing troops in front of a huge stars 'n' stripes and never pauses for breath. A real warts-and-all portrayal. Seven Oscars, including best picture, director, actor (Scott) and screenplay (Francis Ford Coppola and EH North). Widescreen edition available. Aka *Patton: Lust For Glory*. Scott refused his Oscar but reprised the role in a TV film on Patton's last years.

PLATOON

	TOM BERENGER, WILLEM DAFOE, CHARLIE SHEEN, KEVIN DILLON
	OLIVER STONE
	USA (CINEMA CLUB V) 1986
	115m (15)

Based on Stone's own experiences in Vietnam; he apparently drove the young stars hard to make them feel what soldiering is really like. Well acted. Oscars include best picture and director. No longer available in letterbox format since it was transferred to this budget label.

PT 109

	CLIFF ROBERTSON, TY HARDIN, JAMES GREGORY, ROBERT BLAKE
	LESLIE H MARTINSON
	USA (WARNER) 1963
	140m (U)

Flag-waving account of President John F Kennedy's wartime adventures. Well made but inevitably glamorised. Kennedy's assassination was a vile crime, but for me he was the son of a bootlegger who supported Hitler in World War Two and no mean sleazemonger in his own right. I mean, let's not get carried away here. A balanced portrait of his whole life would be of greater value.

RED DAWN

	CHARLIE SHEEN, PATRICK SWAYZE, POWERS BOOTHE, BEN JOHNSON
	JOHN MILIUS
	USA (WARNER) 1984
	109m (15)

High-school kids look out on the playing fields and see Commie troops landing by parachute in an invasion of the USA. They take to the hills and form guerilla bands, going so far as to court-martial and execute 'traitors'. Okay, so it's militaristic, right-wing guff, but I simply can't help liking John Milius and his pix. He's the last mad individualist of his kind in Hollywood-land and we must treasure him. Fun, and the young cast do a decent job, with help from seasoned performers such as Ben Johnson.

RUN SILENT, RUN DEEP

	CLARK GABLE, BURT LANCASTER, JACK WARDEN, BRAD DEXTER
	ROBERT WISE
	USA (WARNER) 1958 B&W
	89m (U)

Best of the old Hollywood submarine romps, with an all-star cast. However, I'm afraid after *The Boat* (see page 280), Germany's epic of claustrophobia and fear, films like this tend to pale into insignificance. Worth a look, though, as Wise is always a reliable purveyor of craftsman-like entertainment.

WAR

SALVADOR 4

| JAMES WOODS, JAMES BELUSHI, JOHN SAVAGE, MICHAEL MURPHY |
| OLIVER STONE |
| USA (VIDEO COLLECTION) 1986 |
| 117m (18) |

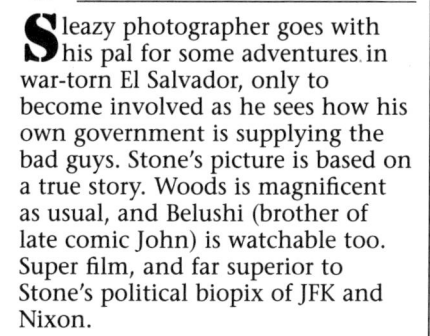

Sleazy photographer goes with his pal for some adventures in war-torn El Salvador, only to become involved as he sees how his own government is supplying the bad guys. Stone's picture is based on a true story. Woods is magnificent as usual, and Belushi (brother of late comic John) is watchable too. Super film, and far superior to Stone's political biopix of JFK and Nixon.

SANDS OF IWO JIMA 3

| JOHN WAYNE, JOHN AGAR, FORREST TUCKER, MARTIN MILNER |
| ALLAN DWAN |
| USA (4-FRONT) 1949 B&W |
| 108m (PG) |

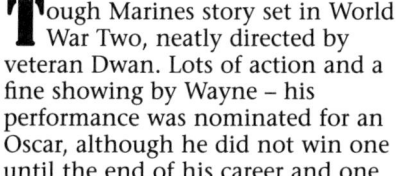

Tough Marines story set in World War Two, neatly directed by veteran Dwan. Lots of action and a fine showing by Wayne – his performance was nominated for an Oscar, although he did not win one until the end of his career and one of his last Westerns, *True Grit* (see page 309).

SERGEANT YORK 4

| GARY COOPER, WALTER BRENNAN, JOAN LESLIE, NOAH BEERY Jnr |
| HOWARD HAWKS |
| USA (WARNER) 1941 B&W |
| 129m (U) |

Classic World War One tale: true (if glamorised) story of a country hick who became an American legend. One of Hawks' best pictures. Cooper is delightful – he won an Oscar for best actor as the pacifist who captured 132 Germans all by himself.

SINK THE BISMARCK 3

| KENNETH MORE, DANA WYNTER, CARL MOHNER, LAURENCE NAISMITH |
| LEWIS GILBERT |
| UK (FOX) 1960 B&W |
| 97m (U) |

This story of the search for the Nazi battleship is saved from being a dry and impersonal saga by the moving acting of More as the navy's desk-man – the scene where we hear him crying behind closed doors when he learns his son has been rescued from the sea is powerful indeed. A British classic of the old school. Based on CS Forester's book.

STALAG 17 [3]

☆ WILLIAM HOLDEN, OTTO PREMINGER, PETER GRAVES, DON TAYLOR

🎬 BILLY WILDER

USA (CIC) 1953 B&W

⏱ 115m (PG)

Oscar-winning acting from Holden as the wiseguy in a World War Two POW camp, suspected of treachery by his compatriots because they can't manage to escape. An odd mix of laughs and drama, based on a hit play. Imperfect, but still considered an important movie in its day. Not one of Billy's best, I'm afraid.

TAPS [4]

☆ TIM HUTTON, SEAN PENN, GEORGE C SCOTT, TOM CRUISE

🎬 HAROLD BECKER

USA (FOX) 1981

⏱ 121m (PG)

Unusual story of students of a military academy who, faced by a closedown, start a small war by seizing control of the building. Veteran Scott is very nearly outshone by his youthful co-stars, especially Penn (in his screen debut) and Cruise. Do yourself a favour and get hold of a copy.

THEY WERE EXPENDABLE [3]

☆ JOHN WAYNE, ROBERT MONTGOMERY, DONNA REED, WARD BOND

🎬 JOHN FORD

USA (WARNER) 1945 B&W

⏱ 135m (U)

Beautifully shot story of torpedo crews in World War Two, with a bunch of believable actors and Ford's taut direction. A reminder that the great man did not only make Westerns. Wayne and Montgomery are especially credible here.

TOBRUK [3]

☆ ROCK HUDSON, GEORGE PEPPARD, NIGEL GREEN, GUY STOCKWELL

🎬 ARTHUR HILLER

USA (CIC/4-FRONT) 1967

⏱ 105m (PG)

Fanciful but fun rewrite of the raid on Tobruk – according to this movie the Yanks won the conflict and gave Rommel a pasting, etc. The stars are thoroughly enjoyable, but historical truth goes right out of the window.

WAR

TORA! TORA! TORA! [4]

★ MARTIN BALSAM, JOSEPH COTTEN, JASON ROBARDS, TAKAHIRO TAMURA

🎬 RICHARD FLEISCHER AND OTHERS

JAPAN/USA (FOX) 1970

⏱ 138m (U)

Pearl Harbor attack re-run in an epic that looks at both the Japanese and the American sides of the story. Legendary Japanese director Akira Kurosawa was contracted to do the non-American sequences, but was apparently so unfamiliar with this sort of stuff that he failed to notice when a full-size model of a battleship was built with guns facing the wrong way round! Fleischer finally did the film with the help of three other assistant directors, the result being explosive enough to win an Oscar for effects work. Available in a widescreen version.

THE TRAIN [4]

★ BURT LANCASTER, JEANNE MOREAU, PAUL SCOFIELD

🎬 JOHN FRANKENHEIMER

FRANCE/ITALY (WARNER) 1964 B&W

⏱ 128m (PG)

French resistance hijacks Nazi trainload of stolen art treasures. Lancaster is unmissable as the train driver and Scofield pulls considerable weight as the scheming German officer. This is a letterbox version but appears to be from a cut print. Still, it's nice to see a war movie that works because of character acting rather than lots of explosions.

VON RYAN'S EXPRESS [3]

★ FRANK SINATRA, TREVOR HOWARD, BRAD DEXTER, JOHN LEYTON

🎬 MARK ROBSON

USA (FOX) 1965

⏱ 112m (PG)

Slick World War Two caper. Sinatra is the new, top-ranking Yank officer in a POW camp hitherto dominated by the Brits. He rubs them up the wrong way and is accused of collaborating with the enemy commandant, but finally gains respect when he hijacks a German military train. Plenty of action.

THE WAY AHEAD [3]

★ DAVID NIVEN, STANLEY HOLLOWAY, WILLIAM HARTNELL, TREVOR HOWARD

🎬 CAROL REED

UK (BRITISH CLASSICS) 1944 B&W

⏱ 110m (U)

Penned by Peter Ustinov and Eric Ambler, this was intended as a training flick for raw recruits but worked so well that it was expanded to a cinema feature. Notable for Howard's first film appearance and an ace turn by Hartnell (the original TV *Dr Who*) as the tough-but-kindly sergeant who shapes the men into soldiers.

WHERE EAGLES DARE 🎬 4

RICHARD BURTON, CLINT EASTWOOD, PATRICK WYMARK, MARY URE

BRIAN G HUTTON

USA/UK (WARNER) 1969

148m (PG)

Far superior to Hutton's *Kelly's Heroes* (see page 286), which also featured Eastwood, this *Boy's Own*-style adventure was written for the screen by Alistair MacLean and later fashioned into a novel by him. It starts off reasonably simply, as what Quentin Tarantino has called 'a guys-on-a-mission movie' – but it soon gets unbelievably complex as it is revealed that the rescue attempt on a Nazi-occupied alpine castle is only part of the plan to unearth traitors at the heart of Allied command. It really has to be seen on a huge screen to appreciate the scale, but the currently available widescreen print is pretty good.

THE YOUNG LIONS 🎬 3

MARLON BRANDO, MONTGOMERY CLIFT, DEAN MARTIN, HOPE LANGE

EDWARD DMYTRYK

USA (FOX) 1958 B&W

167m (PG)

Based on Irwin Shaw's book, this looks at World War Two from the viewpoint of both German and American soldiers. Of course, Brando as a Nazi has to be seen doubting his ideals – he's a big star after all and we can't have him being all bad, can we? Clift is superb.

WESTERNS

The Western genre is undoubtedly one of the best-served on video. That being said, however, there are still some gaps: while huge numbers of John Wayne 'oaters' seem to be perennially available, some crucial work by directors like Sam Peckinpah and Budd Boetticher is missing from the shelves, as are many highly-regarded 'spaghetti' Westerns from Italian film-makers. Still, I had no trouble finding enough classics to fill this section; indeed, I could have filled it twice over ... which can only be good news for video viewers!

THE ALAMO

JOHN WAYNE, RICHARD WIDMARK, LAURENCE HARVEY, RICHARD BOONE, CHILL WILLS

JOHN WAYNE

USA (WARNER) 1960

192m (PG)

Star/director Wayne's dream project about Davy Crockett and pals holding off the Mexican army at the eponymous Texas mission was long considered a bit naff – but with the recent writing of a book on the picture and the restoration of this full-length widescreen version it is now being given its due. It's a bit like a Texas version of *Zulu* (three men and a dog against a howling mob) and with uncredited help from director John Ford, it's surely worth a look. Spectacular climax.

THE BALLAD OF CABLE HOGUE

JASON ROBARDS, STELLA STEVENS, DAVID WARNER, STROTHER MARTIN

SAM PECKINPAH

USA (WARNER) 1970

121m (PG)

Tragicomic tale of a loser left to die in the desert who finds water 'where it wasn't' – and with it love, friendship, compassion and death. Beautifully shot by Lucien Ballard and featuring some of Peckinpah's stock company of actors, it'll come as a surprise to those expecting another *The Wild Bunch* (see page 311). David Warner as a sleazy preacher is especially fine.

THE BIG COUNTRY 🎬 4

GREGORY PECK, CHARLTON HESTON, JEAN SIMMONS, CARROLL BAKER

WILLIAM WYLER

USA (WARNER) 1958

163m (PG)

Family-feud epic, with Peck as the seaman pitched into a battle for (ironically) water-rights when he leaves the ocean to marry. He rejects the macho posturing of his new environment to the dismay of all, but comes good in the end. A major hit, it remains a classic of big-style Hollywood movie-making. Great punch-up between Heston and Peck! And that theme ...

A BULLET FOR THE GENERAL 🎬 5

GIAN-MARIA VOLONTE, LOU CASTEL, KLAUS KINSKI, MARTINE BESWICK

DAMIANO DAMIANI

ITALY (AKTIV/4-FRONT) 1966

113m (18)

After the movies of Sergio Leone, this film is regarded as one of the best spaghettis ever. A meditation on revolution and corruption, it unfolds slowly as the bandit (Volonte, excellent as always) is tempted from the socialist path by Castel. Unfortunately this is a cut print. Nice mad-prophet antics from Kinski. Widescreen.

CHISUM 🎬 2

JOHN WAYNE, BEN JOHNSON, FORREST TUCKER

ANDREW V McLAGLEN

USA (WARNER) 1970

110m (PG)

Yet another version of the Billy the Kid legend (and his involvement in the Lincoln County Wars) this suffers from making the peripheral figure of Chisum (Wayne) the hero, and from sidelining the Kid (ineffectually played as a pretty boy by Geoffrey Deuel). Wayne is entertaining as usual, but the same story has been done better in films such as *Young Guns* (see page 312).

COMPAÑEROS 🎬 4

FRANCO NERO, TOMAS MILIAN, JACK PALANCE, FERNANDO REY

SERGIO CORBUCCI

ITALY/SPAIN/WEST GERMANY (AKTIV) 1970

110m (18)

Deliriously over-the-top political spaghetti Western by the other Sergio – Corbucci, creator of the notorious *Django* (see page 296). Mercenary Nero and revolutionary Milian unite to rescue the pacifist Rey. They are pursued by Palance, a dope-smoking nutter who has a wooden hand, gained when Nero left him crucified to a tree and his faithful pet hawk freed him by eating his hand off! Crazy and utterly marvellous – the only negative is that this is a faded, cut and crudely pan-scanned print.

DANCES WITH WOLVES 🎬 5

	KEVIN COSTNER, MARY McDONNELL, GRAHAM GREENE
	KEVIN COSTNER
	USA (GUILD) 1990
	173/225m (15)

Oscar-winning story of a cavalryman who is tired of war and gets himself posted to the limits of the frontier. There he makes a pet of a wolf and is initiated into Sioux tribal ways. Wonderful cinematography by Dean Semler, and Costner's confident acting and directing make this a magical film – though some have said it goes too far in its idealised portrait of the Native American. The movie was such a smash that a special version was issued with an extra 50 minutes or so of footage. Both versions are available on video. Widescreen.

DEAD MAN 🎬 4

	JOHNNY DEPP, GABRIEL BYRNE, ROBERT MITCHUM, GARY FARMER
	JIM JARMUSCH
	USA (POLYGRAM) 1996 B&W
	115m (18)

When Depp survives a bullet in this old West story, the fact that he's named William Blake leads injun Farmer to believe he's the immortal incarnation of the legendary visionary and poet of the same name. Strange stuff, shot in luminous monochrome, with a super cameo by Mitchum.

DEATH RIDES A HORSE 🎬 4

	LEE VAN CLEEF, JOHN PHILLIP LAW, ANTHONY DAWSON, LUIGI PISTILLI, MARIO BREGA
	GIULIO PETRONI
	ITALY (MGM/UA) 1967
	110m (12)

After his success in the Sergio Leone/Clint Eastwood films, American character actor Van Cleef became a star in his own right in several more spaghetti Westerns. This one, at long last available on video, reguraly features in critics' Top 20 lists for the genre: old gunhand Van Cleef teaches a young man how to shoot so he can revenge himself on those who slaughtered his folks – but what'll happen when he finds out his mentor was present at the massacre? Great stuff! Budget-price tape.

DJANGO [5]

FRANCO NERO, EDUARDO FAJARDO, JOSE BODALO

SERGIO CORBUCCI

ITALY/SPAIN (AKTIV/4-FRONT) 1966

95m (18)

Controversial spaghetti by Corbucci, which spawned a legion of dodgy sequels – often producers dubbing an Italian Western into English simply changed the title character's name to Django. Oddly enough, some of these *faux*-Djangos are better than the one official sequel (again with Nero), the 1980s sleazefest *Django Strikes Again* (see opposite). This first Django film begins with Nero dragging his gatling-gun (in a coffin) through the muddy streets of a hellish town, and doesn't let up until the final frames of cruelty and mutilation.

DJANGO THE BASTARD [4]

ANTHONY STEFFEN, PAOLO GOZLINO, LU KANANTE

SERGIO GARRONE

ITALY (AKTIV) 1969

95m (15)

Nice widescreen transfer of one of the 30 or so unofficial Django films. This one has a somewhat mysterious revenge theme that has led some critics to speculate that it inspired the USA Clint Eastwood hit *High Plains Drifter* (see page 299). Often appears on critical lists of the Top 20 spaghettis – and rightly so!

DJANGO STRIKES AGAIN [3]

FRANCO NERO, DONALD PLEASENCE, CHRISTOPHER CONNOLLY

TED ARCHER (NELLO ROSSATI)

ITALY (AKTIV/4-FRONT) 1987

88m (18)

Twenty years on and our gunfighter has become a monk – but he's lured out of retirement to rescue a daughter in some vile Amazonian jungle, where she's being held by a sadistic gunboat diplomatist with a passion for rare butterflies! Only Italians can make Westerns this insane. Pleasence plays a Scots entomologist (!) as he did in Dario Argento's horror flick *Phenomena* (aka *Creepers*).

EL DORADO [5]

JOHN WAYNE, ROBERT MITCHUM, JAMES CAAN

HOWARD HAWKS

USA (CIC/4-FRONT) 1967

127m (PG)

Rather a bleak re-run of his earlier *Rio Bravo* (see page 306), this is still Hawks at his very best. Wayne, Caan and boozy Mitchum fight for right against cattle king Ed Asner (TV's Lou Grant), and only the most mean-spirited churl will fail to enjoy being along for the ride. Admired as bravura movie-making by everyone from your grandad to Quentin Tarantino – and I should jolly well think so too!

FACE TO FACE

GIAN-MARIA VOLONTE, TOMAS MILIAN, WILLIAM BERGER

SERGIO SOLLIMA

ITALY/SPAIN (AKTIV) 1967

102m (15)

Unusual Euro-Western which sees ailing prof Volonte, in the west for his health, captured by bandit Milan only to use his brains to take over gradually as gang leader. Finally, it is the supposed bad guy who has to subdue the increasingly nasty professor. Entertainment with an anti-fascist message. This is a shortened print, but it is in widescreen.

A FISTFUL OF DOLLARS

CLINT EASTWOOD, GIAN-MARIA VOLONTE, MARIANNE KOCH

SERGIO LEONE

ITALY/WEST GERMANY/SPAIN (WARNER) 1964

94m (15)

The first in the 'Man With No Name' trilogy directed by Leone, which made Eastwood a star and caused spaghetti Westerns to be taken seriously when it was finally issued in English-speaking countries in 1967. It's a remake of Akira Kurosawa's samurai flick *Yojimbo* (which was itself said to be based on Budd Boetticher's oater *Buchanan Rides Alone*), with the same plot: a stranger rides into a corrupt town and sells his services to both sides in a gang feud. The laconic, poncho-clad Clint, Leone's delirious direction and Ennio Morricone's music make this an essential part of any Western fan's education. The film has recently been remade yet again, this time by Walter Hill, as the Bruce Willis gangster thriller *Last Man Standing* (see page 159).

FOR A FEW DOLLARS MORE

CLINT EASTWOOD, LEE VAN CLEEF, GIAN-MARIA VOLONTE

SERGIO LEONE

ITALY/WEST GERMANY/SPAIN (WARNER) 1965

128m (15)

The second 'Man With No Name' film (though he actually has a different name in each) boasts a much bigger budget and a rather more complex plot. Clint and rival Van Cleef cut up rough with each other and form an uneasy truce to snare the sadistic bandit Volonte. Be warned: the currently available print crops the widescreen image, and is in such bad shape that the video company have taken the unusual step of placing a warning sticker on the box.

FORT APACHE

	JOHN WAYNE, HENRY FONDA, WARD BOND
	JOHN FORD
	USA (4-FRONT) 1948 B&W
	127m (U)

Ford is the acknowledged master of the classic Western form, and this is one of his best. New commander Fonda blunders but Wayne covers up in the interests of the cavalry. A masterful film. Note: also available as a bargain two-in-one tape on the same label, coupled with Ford's *Stagecoach* (see page 309).

GERONIMO

	GENE HACKMAN, ROBERT DUVALL, WES STUDI, JASON PATRIC
	WALTER HILL
	USA (COLUMBIA) 1994
	111m (12)

With Peckinpah gone, Hill is the one man left making serious Westerns. This is an accurate version by John Milius of the tale of this famous Apache, but it lost out at the box office in the US when a simultaneous competing version was shown on TV. Then, in the UK, BBC TV critic Barry Norman wrongly told viewers Hill's movie was just a cut-down theatrical release of that TV film! Despite great reviews and a prestige London run it sank – don't miss it now. Wes Studi, villain of *The Last Of The Mohicans* (see page 133), is Geronimo.

THE GOOD, THE BAD AND THE UGLY

	CLINT EASTWOOD, LEE VAN CLEEF, ELI WALLACH
	SERGIO LEONE
	ITALY (WARNER) 1966
	161m (18)

The final part of Leone's Eastwood trilogy sees the three protagonists (and antagonists) of the title dodging through civil war lines in search of a coffin full of cash. It's a tragedy that these films have never been seen in their full length Italian versions over here, and that the videos available are not in widescreen. As with *For A Few Dollars More* (see page 297), this print is so rough there's a warning on the box. Restored version on import DVD.

THE GUNFIGHTER

	GREGORY PECK, MILLARD MITCHELL, KARL MALDEN
	HENRY KING
	USA (FOX) 1950 B&W
	84m (U)

Peck excels as the old gunfighter trying to settle down with the girl he loves but being forced into a final shoot-out be a glory-seeking punk. This may seem old hat now, but at the time the dark tone was something new. Nice performance from Karl Malden as the hero-worshipping bartender, and Peck is marvellously understated.

HANG 'EM HIGH

CLINT EASTWOOD, INGER STEVENS, ED BEGLEY, BEN JOHNSON

TED POST

USA (WARNER) 1967

114m (18)

Clint's first USA Western shows his determination not to forget the brutal realism of his Leone trilogy. In fact Leone was offered this film and refused. Although it is credited to Ted Post, a pal from his TV days, Eastwood, directed much of the picture. The opening scenes are shocking, as the ex-lawman turned cattle-rancher is hanged and left for dead by a posse of vigilantes who wrongly suspect him of rustling and murder. Saved by Ben Johnson, he takes up the badge again to hunt down his enemies with unflinching violence, while forming an odd relationship with a woman searching for those who killed her husband.

HEAVEN'S GATE

KRIS KRISTOFFERSON, CHRISTOPHER WALKEN, JOHN HURT, ISABELLE HUPPERT

MICHAEL CIMINO

USA (WARNER) 1980

205m (18)

Based on the Johnson County Wars, this is the film that infamously brought down a studio with its squandering of a reported $50 million budget. A flop with punters and critics on first release and then cut by over an hour, the full-length version has since come to be regarded as something of a masterwork of big-scale cinema. This is supposed to be the uncut print, but it emerged in 1997 that the initial release was actually longer still at 220m and a print was shown at the National Film Theatre. Beautiful but rather dull. For the full tale read the book *Final Cut*, and think of what you could have done with the money!

HIGH PLAINS DRIFTER

CLINT EASTWOOD, VERNA BLOOM, JACK GING, MITCHELL RYAN

CLINT EASTWOOD

USA (CIC) 1973

100m (18)

Eerie, strange Western about a gunman hired by a town to keep the baddies off – but his methods prove harsh and nearly as bad as the problem he's there to solve. Slowly we begin to wonder if he is not the ghost of a sheriff the town failed to help many years before. It doesn't entirely work but it has its moments. Some critics allege it was inspired by the Italian Western *Django The Bastard* (see page 296).

THE HORSE SOLDIERS [3]

JOHN WAYNE, WILLIAM HOLDEN, CONSTANCE TOWERS, HOOT GIBSON

JOHN FORD

USA (WARNER) 1959

119m (PG)

Perhaps this is one of Ford's lesser cavalry romps (I recall being bored by it as a child), but the friction between Wayne's soldier and Holden's medic is well handled and the film has a glorious look. Ripe for re-evaluation, methinks?

HOW THE WEST WAS WON [4]

SPENCER TRACY (narrator), HENRY FONDA, JAMES STEWART, JOHN WAYNE

HENRY HATHAWAY, JOHN FORD, GEORGE MARSHALL

USA (MGM/UA-WARNER) 1962

165m (PG)

An epic dealing with different parts of Western history (the rivers, the railroad, the plains, the outlaws, the Civil War) through one family's story. The first feature in the giant-screen Cinerama process, this patchy film has some spectacular scenes that are reduced in power on the small screen. Ford's Civil War bit works best, but the movie has always posed a problem on video as Cinerama involved three projectors side-by-side – leaving a pair of rather noticeable lines down the screen that are even more intrusive on video. Also available in a special edition.

JEREMIAH JOHNSON [4]

ROBERT REDFORD, WILL GEER

SIDNEY POLLACK

USA (WARNER) 1972

108m (PG)

This would have been a very different movie had it been made by the original choice for director, Sam Peckinpah – but it's still a wonderful picture about a man who rejects civilisation to become a mountain trapper, schooled in the ways of the wild by grizzled Will Geer. Written by the eccentric John Milius, last of the rugged individualists, it's a hauntingly shot tale of one man's battles with himself, the Crow tribe and nature itself. Worth several return visits.

JESSE JAMES [2]

TYRONE POWER, HENRY FONDA, RANDOLPH SCOTT, HENRY HULL

HENRY KING

USA (FOX) 1939

105m (U)

Idealised Hollywood biopic of the legendary outlaw and folk-hero. James is portrayed as a hero fighting injustice, emphasized by the casting of Power and Fonda – well loved stars – in the main outlaw parts. A smash hit, it spawned a sequel, *The Return Of Frank James* with Fonda returning in the title role. The James story has been more honestly told in other movies, notably Walter Hill's fabulous *The Long Riders* (see page 302).

KEOMA ... THE VIOLENT BREED [4]

FRANCO NERO, WOODY STRODE, WILLIAM BERGER, DONALD O'BRIEN

ENZIO G CASTELLARI

ITALY (AKTIV/4-FRONT) 1975

96m (15)

Released in some countries as yet another phoney 'Django' film (probably due to Nero's presence, he being the original), this powerful story with its nagging music certainly makes an impact. Nero is an alienated half-breed returning to clean up his racist home town. This is taken from a nicely restored and cleaned widescreen print. A sterling effort – if only all video firms would take such trouble over relatively minor releases like this.

THE LAST TRAIN FROM GUN HILL [2]

KIRK DOUGLAS, ANTHONY QUINN, EARL HOLLIMAN, CAROLYN JONES

JOHN STURGES

USA (4-FRONT) 1959

98m (15)

Tense thriller about a lawman who discovers that the boy who raped and killed his wife is the son of his best friend. The plot revolves around his determination to take the lad on a train to justice, in spite of the violent intrusion of his ex-pal. In the process he forms a friendship with the man's abused girlfriend. Well acted, but the empty characters preclude repeat attendance. One ride on this train will suffice.

THE LEFT-HANDED GUN [4]

PAUL NEWMAN, HURD HATFIELD, JOHN DEHNER

ARTHUR PENN

USA (WARNER) 1958 B&W

102m (PG)

Penn, who went on to make *Little Big Man* (see page 302) and *Bonnie and Clyde* (see page 151), got his movie break by directing this version of a Gore Vidal script he'd already made for TV – a gritty look at the Billy the Kid legend. Though Paul Newman is first-rate as the Kid, his movie-star handsomeness tends to undercut the realism the piece aims for. Still, this remains one of the best versions of the tale.

THE LIFE AND TIMES OF JUDGE ROY BEAN [3]

PAUL NEWMAN, STACY KEACH, AVA GARDNER, ANTHONY PERKINS

JOHN HUSTON

USA (WARNER) 1972

124m (15)

Derided upon first release, this has now been judged to be one of Huston's classics. Not by me, though! While the John Milius script is neat, the story of the half-mad Bean's obsession with law and order and Lillie Langtry (not necessarily in that order) is rather fragmented. A curiosity.

LITTLE BIG MAN

DUSTIN HOFFMAN, FAYE DUNAWAY, MARTIN BALSAM, CHIEF DAN GEORGE

ARTHUR PENN

USA (FOX) 1970

147m (15)

Penn seems to have fallen from favour – and this film shows why. Its jokey, debunking tone seems awfully dated (like that of *Butch Cassidy And The Sundance Kid*). It tells the reminiscences of a 121-year-old man who claims to be the one white survivor of Custer's Last Stand – great material, as the source novel proves to anyone who's read it – but what seemed gut-achingly wry in 1970 is just embarrassing today. You may well disagree.

THE LONG RIDERS

DAVID CARRADINE, KEITH CARRADINE, ROBERT CARRADINE, JAMES KEACH, STACY KEACH, DENNIS QUAID, RANDY QUAID, CHRISTOPHER GUEST, NICHOLAS GUEST

WALTER HILL

USA (WARNER) 1980

99m (18)

The Jesse James story has inspired great movies from directors such as Sam Fuller, Nicholas Ray and Philip Kaufman, but Walter Hill's piece takes some beating. It has an authentic, inbred, rural feel, helped by the inspired casting of several sets of real-life brothers as the siblings in the story, and we see how the James gang gets a somewhat undeserved Robin Hood image due to the old North/South hatreds and the accidental killing of an innocent boy by Pinkerton agents. Don't miss it, if only for the wonderfully staged bank robbery sequence.

THE MAGNIFICENT SEVEN

YUL BRYNNER, ELI WALLACH, STEVE McQUEEN, JAMES COBURN, HORST BUCHOLZ, CHARLES BRONSON, ROBERT VAUGHN

JOHN STURGES

USA (MGM/UA-WARNER) 1960

138m (PG)

Like *A Fistful Of Dollars* (see page 297), this is based on a Kurosawa samurai film. It replicates the plot of *Seven Samurai* precisely, with Brynner gathering together his group of violent men and convincing them uncharacteristically to 'do the right thing' and help run bandits out of a village for meagre pay. Spawned several sequels, but none of them came close to the original. Great score.

THE MAN WHO SHOT LIBERTY VALANCE [5]

- JOHN WAYNE, JAMES STEWART, LEE MARVIN, WOODY STRODE
- JOHN FORD
- USA (CIC) 1962 B&W
- 122m (U)

Pivotal Ford, undercutting the mythical West many of his earlier movies celebrated. Peaceable Stewart gets famous for shooting Valance (Marvin as a sleazy outlaw), only to find that things are not quite as they seem. But Stewart gets the girl they he and his friend love (Vera Miles) and becomes a senator, while his pal Wayne fades into the dark, just as he did on the night of the shooting. A dark and bittersweet film about the conflict between truth and legend.

THE MISSOURI BREAKS [4]

- MARLON BRANDO, JACK NICHOLSON, KATHLEEN LLOYD, RANDY QUAID
- ARTHUR PENN
- USA (WARNER) 1976
- 126m (15)

One of Penn's better works. Unlike *Little Big Man* (see page 320), the oddball tone hasn't dated: rustler Nicholson plays cat and mouse with weird hired killer Brando, who adopts strange accents and outfits (including a dress) to stalk his victims, at the same time as he romances the daughter of the man who is paying the 'regulator', Brando, to see him off. As bizarre as any spaghetti opus.

MY DARLING CLEMENTINE [4]

- HENRY FONDA, VICTOR MATURE, WALTER BRENNAN
- JOHN FORD
- USA (FOX) 1964 B&W
- 96m (U)

Ford actually knew Wyatt Earp (he lived until 1929) and so, while this may seem a mythologised version of his story, there are claims for the accuracy of the final shoot-out at the OK Corral. But it's the overall feel of the movie, filled with rich characters, that makes it work. It takes nothing away from *Clementine* if I say that other films about the lawman, like *Tombstone* (see page 309) and *Wyatt Earp* (see page 311) may well be more accurate. Whatever that means.

ONCE UPON A TIME IN THE WEST 5

	CHARLES BRONSON, HENRY FONDA, JASON ROBARDS, CLAUDIA CARDINALE
	SERGIO LEONE
	ITALY (CIC) 1968
	168m (15)

From the incredible credits sequence, where Bronson eliminates three killers at a train station, this is an unquestionable masterpiece from Leone. Casting the upright Fonda as a villain in the pay of the railroad trying to steal Cardinale's land was a clever bit of business, and the whole picture has an epic feel while never losing sight of the characters and their motives. This is the full-length print (though an even longer one is rumoured to exist) and is available in widescreen, which is the only way to see it. After the 'Man With No Name' films, this forms another trilogy of sorts with *Once Upon A Time ... The Revolution* (released here as *A Fistful Of Dynamite*) and *Once Upon A Time In America*.

ONE-EYED JACKS 4

	MARLON BRANDO, KARL MALDEN, BEN JOHNSON, KATY JURADO
	MARLON BRANDO
	USA (CIC) 1961
	141m (PG)

This was Brando's baby from the start, based on a novel (very) loosely inspired by Billy the Kid, and he soon got rid of proposed directors Sam Peckinpah and Stanley Kubrick – which certainly calls for some big ego! When it got out that the footage was cut down from a five-hour version critics expected the worst, but this is actually a pretty fine film. Brando tracks down his old outlaw buddy, who left him to be captured but is now a respected figure with a family, and it is only a matter of time before scores must be settled. A flawed but brilliant piece.

THE OUTLAW JOSEY WALES 4

	CLINT EASTWOOD, CHIEF DAN GEORGE, SONDRA LOCKE, JOHN VERNON
	CLINT EASTWOOD
	USA (WARNER) 1976
	134m (18)

When the Western was thought to be all but a dead form in the USA, along came Eastwood to give new life (once again) to the genre with this great picture. A farmer who becomes a killer after his family are slain in war, he gradually assembles a bunch of misfits around him and tries to make a new life for himself. Around this simple premise Eastwood weaves a film that is thoughtful, humorous and explosively violent.

WESTERNS

PALE RIDER 3

CLINT EASTWOOD, MICHAEL MORIARTY, CARRIE SNODGRESS, CHRIS PENN

CLINT EASTWOOD

USA (WARNER) 1985

115m ⓘ 15

Pale all right in my opinion – a pale imitation of the George Stevens 1953 Western classic *Shane* (see page 307), even down to certain shots and sequences: in *Shane*, a mystery man helps a young couple and their boy to fight nasty landowners who want to drive homesteaders out. He shows his strength by helping dig out a tree stump. In the end he leaves as he knows the wife fancies him and the kid likes him better than dad, and he doesn't want to cause trouble. In *Pale Rider*, a mystery man helps a couple and daughter fight mine owners, shows strength by smashing a huge rock, and he leaves because the woman and her daughter fancy him. (I haven't read AD Foster's source novel, so I can't say if it, too, rips off Jack Schaefer's novel *Shane*). All this apart, it's a well acted, entertaining Western and is now reissued in a widescreen version. Glowingly lensed by Bruce Surtees.

PAT GARRETT AND BILLY THE KID 5

JAMES COBURN, KRIS KRISTOFFERSON, BOB DYLAN, SLIM PICKENS

SAM PECKINPAH

USA (WARNER) 1973

122m ⓘ 18

Like much of his work, Peckinpah's version of the Billy the Kid story was mutilated by the studio that made it – but it remains an essential film. This version, though longer than the studio cut, is not perfect: touted as 'the director's cut', it is actually a work print, with one essential scene missing and many others lacking the fine-tuning present in the cut print's scenes. A proper restoration, presented in widescreen, would be most welcome, as this is one of Peckinpah's finest films. Coburn is magnificent as the regretful Garrett, doomed to kill his old pal just to keep his head above water. A stunning movie, both in its glowing look and in its performances.

305

RED RIVER [4]

JOHN WAYNE, MONTGOMERY CLIFT,
JOANNE DRU, WALTER BRENNAN

HOWARD HAWKS

USA (MGM/UA) 1948 B&W

125m (U)

Wayne is a ruthless rancher (we see him kill when his right simply to steal some land is challenged at the start of the film) who adopts Clift and begins a cattle dynasty. They fall out on a cattle-drive, and only Clift's gal (Dru) stops them killing each other at the climax. This ending has been rightly criticised as a cop-out, as it conflicts with all we've learned about Wayne's character up to that point. Nevertheless, this is one of Hawks' greats. Now available in a 'director's cut' version.

RIDE THE HIGH COUNTRY [7]

RANDOLPH SCOTT, JOEL McCREA,
MARIETTE HARTLEY, JAMES DRURY

SAM PECKINPAH

USA (MGM/UA) 1962

94m (15)

An object lesson in how to make the most of a simple story. Two old 'pards' take work carrying gold from a mining camp – but, saddled with a misguided young girl in search of love and a feisty young sidekick, they end up (not without conflict between themselves and with outsiders) having to decide whether cash or honour matters most. Treated as just one more oater by the studio and sold abroad as *Guns In The Afternoon* it still managed acclaim and is now considered a masterpiece. See it.

RIO BRAVO [5]

JOHN WAYNE, DEAN MARTIN,
RICKY NELSON, WALTER BRENNAN

HOWARD HAWKS

USA (WARNER) 1959

141m (PG)

First-rate Hawks, Wayne and assorted chums form a family to fight the encroaching baddies – a theme returned to in his *El Dorado* (see page 296) and *Rio Lobo* (see page 307), and perhaps inspiring Eastwood's *The Outlaw Josey Wales* (see page 304)? If you need any more nudging, it's one of Quentin Tarantino's fave flicks, okay? John Carpenter reworked it as *Assault On Precinct 13*.

RIO GRANDE [2]

JOHN WAYNE, MAUREEN O'HARA,
BEN JOHNSON, VICTOR McLAGLEN

JOHN FORD

USA (4-FRONT) 1950 B&W

105m (U)

Part of Ford's '7th Cavalry' trio, with *Fort Apache* and *She Wore A Yellow Ribbon*. Not his best – the hokey songs are off-putting – but even Ford at half-cock is not to be sniffed at.

RIO LOBO

JOHN WAYNE, JACK ELAM, JENNIFER O'NEILL

HOWARD HAWKS

USA (FOX) 1970

114m (PG)

Hawks' last film. Not in the league of *Rio Bravo* (see page 306) and *El Dorado* (see page 296), it's still an enjoyable romp with Wayne as an ex-army officer on the trail of traitors who sold him out in the Civil War – rather implausibly helped out by the southerners who dealt with the traitors during the conflict! Jennifer O'Neill is competent and beautiful, while Jack Elam is always good value.

THE SEARCHERS

JOHN WAYNE, JEFFREY HUNTER, VERA MILES, WARD BOND, NATALIE WOOD

JOHN FORD

USA (WARNER) 1956

119m (U)

A pristine widescreen print of Ford's epic about the quest for a girl kidnapped by Comanches. Wayne is like you've never seen him – a rootless man who, it's hinted, may be an outlaw, he embarks on a crazy search for the missing child. He's full of hate and anger throughout the picture, and we – along with Hunter at his side every step of the way – feel that he might as soon kill the girl as rescue her, when he finds her for the 'crime' of being defiled by the 'red men'. When he finally returns home he has completed his task, but the final image of a door closing while he remains outside shows that he is forever excluded from the inner circle. Much beloved of Martin Scorsese, and very influential: the NFT ran a season of films possibly inspired by *The Searchers*.

SHANE

ALAN LADD, VAN HEFLIN, JEAN ARTHUR, JACK PALANCE

GEORGE STEVENS

USA (CIC) 1953

118m (PG)

Loner Ladd (possibly a reformed bad man?) puts up his guns and helps a family of homesteaders – but when the local range king hires nasty Palance to slaughter the 'sodbusters' he's forced to pick up them shootin' irons again. Despite the admiration of the whole family, he has to ride off into the sunset – the implication being that, a) he may be dying of a bullet wound and doesn't want the boy who idolises him to see the end, and b) he likes the family too much to let the unspoken attraction between him and the woman of the house come to any kind of fruition. Clint Eastwood made a not entirely satisfactory unofficial remake: *Pale Rider* (see page 305).

THE SHOOTING [3]

⭐ JACK NICHOLSON, WARREN OATES, WILL HUTCHINS, MILLIE PERKINS

🎬 MONTE HELLMAN

USA (LABYRINTH MEDIA) 1966

⏱ 81m (PG)

Existential piece made by Hellman and Nicholson back-to-back with the equally bizarre *Ride In The Whirlwind* (82m), which is also on this budget tape which is marketed as 'The Jack Nicholson Westerns'. *Whirlwind* sees Nicholson and Cameron Mitchell accidentally being mistaken for outlaws to whom they've innocently given hospitality and chased endlessly through grim landscapes. *The Shooting* has a döppelganger theme, with a vengeful woman leading Oates to his twin brother in the final denouement. These two films show what can be done on a minuscule budget. Sadly, the prints used have seen better days.

THE SHOOTIST [5]

⭐ JOHN WAYNE, LAUREN BACALL, RON HOWARD, JAMES STEWART

🎬 DON SIEGEL

USA (CIC/4-FRONT) 1976

⏱ 100m (PG)

Bleak but satisfactory story of a gunman dying of cancer (as Wayne was when he made this, his last film) who chooses to go out in a blaze of glory rather than waste away. Wayne underplays beautifully, whether duelling verbally with landlady Bacall or educating her wild kid Howard in the ways of the world. Siegel chooses to have the boy reject violence at the end by throwing away the old man's gun, whereas in the source novel he struts off to become just another gunslinger (we are led to assume). Howard gave up acting and is now a top director – he recently made the Mel Gibson vehicle *Ransom* (see page 274).

SOLDIER BLUE [3]

⭐ CANDICE BERGEN, PETER STRAUSS, DONALD PLEASENCE

🎬 RALPH NELSON

USA (ENTERTAINMENT/4-FRONT) 1970

⏱ 114m (18)

Jobbing director Nelson attained a short-lived notoriety with this love story twixt feisty bitch and innocent cavalryman set amidst much gushing gore and severed limbs as soldiers massacre native Americans. See once for curiosity value – but the climax was heavily cut in Britain by the BBFC on initial release and probably remains so.

WESTERNS

STAGECOACH 🎬4

⭐ JOHN WAYNE, CLAIRE TREVOR, THOMAS MITCHELL, JOHN CARRADINE

🎬 JOHN FORD

USA (ENTERTAINMENT) 1939 B&W

⏱ 96m (U)

Also available on a two-film tape with Ford's *Fort Apache* (see page 298), this is the movie that made Wayne a star. Who today would risk appearing as 'The Ringo Kid' – those were the days. Savour them.

TOMBSTONE 🎬4

⭐ KURT RUSSELL, VAL KILMER, BILL PAXTON, CHARLTON HESTON

🎬 GEORGE P COSMATOS

USA (ENTERTAINMENT) 1993

⏱ 135m (15)

Made at the same time as the Kevin Costner epic *Wyatt Earp* (see page 311), which deals with Earp's whole life, this smaller reworking of the OK Corral tale was expected to be a box office joke ... but the laughs were on the big boys as Russell's superior, gutsy portrayal and Kilmer's dandyfied Doc proved to be a surprise hit. Works fine on tape too – but make sure you get the widescreen copy.

TRUE GRIT 🎬4

⭐ JOHN WAYNE, KIM DARBY, GLEN CAMPBELL, ROBERT DUVALL, DENNIS HOPPER

🎬 HENRY HATHAWAY

USA (CIC) 1969

⏱ 128m (PG)

Surprise Oscar-bestowing smash hit for Wayne as a gruff ruffian turned marshal, hired by a young girl to get the killer of her father and forced to take both her and a Texas Ranger along for the trip. The script and the photography of Lucien Ballard help make it a delight for eyes and ears. Do yourself a favour one wet afternoon and rent or buy this tape.

UNFORGIVEN

CLINT EASTWOOD, MORGAN FREEMAN, GENE HACKMAN, RICHARD HARRIS

CLINT EASTWOOD

USA (WARNER) 1992

131m (15)

Made from a script Eastwood had been saving until he felt he'd reached the right age for the part, this is a film about a reformed murderer and gunman living on a crappy farm with his kids. The wife who reformed him is gone, and he is tempted by the offer of money made by some whores to revenge one of their number who was slashed by a cowboy. It's a very dark movie, with no real good guys and no truly bad ones either. Gene Hackman's lawman tries to keep the peace, but is a cruel bully at heart. Richard Harris poses as a posh type, but turns out to be a cowardly cockney. And Eastwood is colder than we've ever seen him. 'For Sergio and Don' reads the dedication, for Clint's mentors Leone and Siegel. He learned from masters, and it shows. A cruel classic.

WILD BILL

JEFF BRIDGES, ELLEN BARKIN, BRUCE DERN, KEITH CARRADINE, DAVID ARQUETTE, DIANE LANE, JOHN HURT

WALTER HILL

USA (MGM/UA) 1995

94m (15)

Incredibly, Walter Hill's wonderful film about legendary gunfighter Wild Bill Hickok did not get a UK cinema release (apart from a short run at London's National Film Theatre) – outrageous, when you consider some of the drivel that fills our screens week after week. Depicting a series of episodes from Hickok's life, culminating in his death at the hands of a disturbed boy, it's perhaps the first Western since Peckinpah's *The Wild Bunch* (see page 311) to show the true horror and brutal unpredictability of gunfighting. Bridges makes a wild and woolly anti-hero, and the other actors are a match for him: Barkin as Calamity Jane (raunchier than Doris Day, that's for sure), Hurt as the archetypal Anglo-buddy, and Dern as a madman who challenges Hickok to a sit-down shoot-out after their earlier fight has confined him to a wheelchair! A masterful combination of sepia realism and elegaic myth, and a must-see for fans of Hill's earlier *Geronimo* (see page 298).

THE WILD BUNCH

WILLIAM HOLDEN, ROBERT RYAN, WARREN OATES, BEN JOHNSON, EDMOND O'BRIEN, ERNEST BORGNINE

SAM PECKINPAH

USA (WARNER) 1969

145m (18)

Sam Peckinpah's revisionist Western follows a gang of outlaws from when they're ambushed in a small town until they decide to go out in a final blast, fighting against impossible odds in support of one of their own, because they know that in 1912 men of their kind have outlived their usefulness. Both Holden as the boss outlaw and Ryan as the man he left to die (now his nemesis, not through choice but because it's the only way out of jail) are magnificent, as indeed are all the players. Derided for showing the effects of bullets on flesh at the time of release, it is now accepted as a classic. The recent restoration is problematic – it is relevant solely to the USA as that is the only place where the restored parts were cut! This means, sadly, that since the restored print is now used worldwide, the existing European print, which was always full-length and contained slight differences, is unlikely to be seen outside film archives. Peckinpah scholar Paul Seydor thinks that people like myself who mention this are nitpickers (see exchange of letters in *Sight and Sound* in late 1996) but many people agree with me. One good thing – at least the restoration means a widescreen print is now out on video. Masterful camera work yet again from Lucien Ballard. If you only see one Western, see this one.

WYATT EARP

KEVIN COSTNER, DENNIS QUAID, GENE HACKMAN, JEFF FAHEY

LAWRENCE KASDAN

USA (WARNER) 1994

183m (12)

This epic about frontier lawman Earp was overshadowed at the box-office by *Tombstone* (see page 309), which only deals with one part of the man's life and is all the better for it. Neither film managed to deflate the Earp myth, however, as the rather dubious character still retains his basically heroic image. Ambitious, but flawed, with Costner too lightweight for the role. Fine support cast, though.

CLASSIC 1000 VIDEOS

YOUNG GUNS

EMILIO ESTEVEZ, KIEFER
SUTHERLAND, CHARLIE SHEEN,
TERENCE STAMP, LOU DIAMOND
PHILLIPS, JACK PALANCE

CHRISTOPHER CAIN

USA (CINEMA CLUB) 1988

107m (18)

Denounced as a 'MTV-Western' on release, this is actually one of the better versions of the early part of Billy the Kid's career in the Lincoln County Wars – accurately told, with Stamp as his mentor Tunstall, taking a (gay?) interest in his young trail bums, and Palance as Murphy, the schemer who orders the man's death and provokes an explosion of revenge. The young cast are excellent to a man, or boy.

YOUNG GUNS II

WILLIAM PETERSEN, EMILIO
ESTEVEZ, KIEFER SUTHERLAND,
CHRISTIAN SLATER, LOU DIAMOND
PHILLIPS

GEOFF MURPHY

USA (FOX) 1990

104m (15)

Useful follow-up flick which completes the Billy the Kid story, with his supposed murder by Pat Garrett. Cleverly told in flashback by utilising the true tale of a man who, circa 1950, claimed to be the real Kid grown old. In real life the man's story was disbelieved, but for the purpose of this film ... well, it's intriguing, ain't it? It's not *The Left-Handed Gun* (see page 301) or *Pat Garrett And Billy The Kid* (see page 305), but it'll do.

WORLD GREATS

In recent years, ordinary film fans have been tempted in ever greater numbers to brace themselves and brave the world of dubbed or subtitled 'arthouse' films; they have not been disappointed. Popular hits, like the lavish Provence soap opera pairing of *Jean De Florette* and *Manon Des Sources* and the action-packed films of director Luc Besson, as well as the tendency of the USA studios to remake many French successes, have shown that international cinema is not all doom and gloom. What follows is a (very) short selection of world cinema films available on videotape. It's not possible to include swathes of Bergman and Kurosawa reviews, but if these examples tempt you then those classics are out there for rental or purchase.

AGUIRRE, THE WRATH OF GOD

KLAUS KINSKI, HELENA ROJO, CECILIA RIVERA, RUY GUERRA

WERNER HERZOG

WEST GERMANY (TARTAN) 1972

94m (15)

The late Kinski (dad of pouting Nastassja) had a great face and used it to perfection in countless spaghetti Westerns, horror pix and thrillers, but his best work came from his love-hate relationship with half-mad director Herzog. This tale of a maniacal conquistador's doomed trip along the Amazon has some stunning scenes: an exploding cannon pitching over a cliff, Kinski adrift amidst a horde of chattering monkeys … all backed by the hypnotic music of Popol Vuh, Herzog's perennial soundtrack collaborators. Imaginative epic entertainment.

THE AMERICAN FRIEND

DENNIS HOPPER, BRUNO GANZ, NICHOLAS RAY, SAM FULLER

WIM WENDERS

WEST GERMANY (CONNOISSEUR) 1977

127m (PG)

Based on Patricia Highsmith's novel *Ripley's Game*. Ganz is a hapless artisan, willing to be hired for murder by Hopper because he believes he's dying and wants to have cash to leave to his family. Oddly distant yet compelling, with cameos from expatriate USA directors Ray and Fuller. Very much a cult picture these days and I personally find it a better bet than many of Wenders' more acclaimed ramblings. Hopper is wonderful as ever, of course.

AND GOD CREATED WOMAN

BRIGITTE BARDOT, CURT JURGENS, JEAN LOUIS TRINTIGNANT

ROGER VADIM

FRANCE (ARROW) 1956

90m (18)

'B' gets her kit off for the delectation of several dirty old men. The film 'made' Bardot as well as St Tropez. Vadim, who used the same title for another story in 1987, was very adept at turning his paramours into sex symbols (see *Barbarella* on page 242). Widescreen.

BELLE DE JOUR

CATHERINE DENEUVE, MICHEL PICCOLI, JEAN SOREL, GENEVIEVE PAGE

LOUIS BUNUEL

FRANCE/ITALY (ELECTRIC) 1967

100m (18)

A massive hit when revived in the early 90s, this seductive story of an upper-class wife who has a secret life as a hooker retains its power 30 years after it was made. Bunuel chips away, as always, at the complacent veneer of polite society.

CINEMA PARADISO

PHILIPPE NOIRET, SALVATORE CASCIO, ANDREA MORRICONE

GIUSEPPE TORNATORE

ITALY/FRANCE (TARTAN) 1989

122m (PG)

A delightful film about the power of cinema to transform lives. A small boy forms a friendship with a grumpy old projectionist who runs the local film shows in their village. There's a great scene where all the clips cut by the censorious local priest are shown in tandem, to the delight of the now grown-up boy. Won an Oscar for best foreign film. Widescreen. Available in several different sets including one boxed with the script and one in an extended 155m version. Whichever you choose you'll be smiling at the end!

THE CITY OF LOST CHILDREN

RON PERLMAN, JEAN-CLAUDE DREYFUS, GENEVIEVE BRUNET

JEAN-PIERRE JEUNET, MARC CARO

FRANCE (ENTERTAINMENT) 1995

108m (15)

From the makers of cult arthouse film *Delicatessen*, this is a bizzare adult fairy tale: in a dark, decaying seaside dive, a circus strongman helps an orphan regain a pal from the clutches of a mad scientist who steals people's dreams. The baddy hangs out on a rotting oil rig surrounded by freaks and eye-dazzling retro machinery. Daft, but it's a treat for the senses. With killer fleas and a brain floating in an aquarium, the pic led to Jeunet directing the latest 'Aliens' episode, *Alien Resurrection* (see page 241).

CYRANO DE BERGERAC [4]

GERARD DEPARDIEU, ANNE BROCHET, VINCENT PEREZ

JEAN-PAUL RAPPENEAU

FRANCE (ARTIFICIAL EYE) 1990

138m (U)

Depardieu excels in this colour-packed version of Edmond Rostand's play about the long-nosed romancer, and rightly won the best actor award at Cannes. Nimble subtitling by Anthony Burgess makes this the most authentic of all the versions of this classic story to be lensed. Widescreen and boxed set available.

THE DIARY OF A CHAMBERMAID [3]

JEANNE MOREAU, MICHEL PICCOLI, FRANCOISE LUGAGNE

LUIS BUNUEL

FRANCE/ITALY (ELECTRIC) 1964

79m (15)

Bunuel's typically subversive version of Octave Mirbeau's story, updated to the 30s and taking a stab at right wing/bourgeois mores. Previously filmed in the USA by Jean Renoir in 1946. Widescreen.

ELVIRA MADIGAN [3]

PIA DEGERMARK, THOMMY BERGGREN, LENNART MALMER

BO WIDERBERG

SWEDEN (TARTAN) 1967

95m (PG)

Lush slow-motion romance which was a big hit worldwide and bagged Degermark the actress of the year award at Cannes. Widescreen.

JEAN DE FLORETTE [5]

GERARD DEPARDIEU, YVES MONTAND, DANIEL AUTEUIL, ELISABETH DEPARDIEU

CLAUDE BERRI

FRANCE (ELECTRIC) 1986

121m (PG)

Shot back to back with *Manon Des Sources* (see page 317), this tells author Marcel Pagnol's epic tale of love and greed in his beloved Provence. Depardieu is a city fellow thwarted by wily countrymen led by scheming patriarch Montand. Deservedly a smash. The first subtitled movie I ever managed to get my mother to sit through until the end and, like audiences the world over, she loved it. You will too! Widescreen.

LA DOLCE VITA ▣3

★ MARCELLO MASTROIANNI, ANITA EKBERG, ANOUK AIMEE, NICO

🎬 FREDERICO FELLINI

ITALY (ELECTRIC) 1960 B&W

⏱ 173m (15)

Fellini's view of the depraved, sleazy underbelly of 60s café society, seen via the lives of journalists, strippers and starlets who come (!) together in a final licentious orgy. Best film winner at Cannes. Widescreen available.

LES DIABOLIQUES ▣4

★ SIMONE SIGNORET, VERA CLOUZOT, PAUL MEURISSE, CHARLES VANEL

🎬 HENRI GEORGES CLOUZOT

FRANCE (ARROW) 1954 B&W

⏱ 114m (18)

This classy thriller comes from the Boileau/Narcejac team which later wrote *Vertigo* for Hitchcock (see page 276). A dingy school is the setting for a plot by two women to murder the man in their lives; but is he really dead? Grisly stuff, remade twice to no great purpose. This remains the top version.

M ▣5

★ PETER LORRE, OTTO WERNICKE, GUSTAV GRUNDGENS

🎬 FRITZ LANG

GERMANY (REDEMPTION) 1931 B&W

⏱ 118m (PG)

Lorre's debut, in which he stars as a childkiller pursued through pre-war Germany by a temporary alliance of cops and crooks. Lang and Lorre manage the unlikely feat of making a serial murderer a sympathetic character, even as he admits his guilt. Also released in a newly restored version, available from the BFI.

MAN BITES DOG ▣4

★ BENOIT POELVOORDE, NELLY PAPPAERT, MALOU MADOU

🎬 REMY BELVAUX, ANDRE BONZEL, BENOIT POELVOORDE

BELGIUM (TARTAN) 1992 B&W

⏱ 96m (18)

Outrageous fake documentary in which a film crew follow a serial killer around as he talks them through his acts of rape and butchery, gradually seducing them with his charmingly savage persona. Made by triumvirate of film students, it won three prizes at Cannes. Widescreen and boxed set available.

WORLD GREATS

MANON DES SOURCES [5]

YVES MONTAND, DANIEL AUTEUIL, EMMANUELLE BEART, ELISABETH DEPARDIEU

CLAUDE BERRI

FRANCE (ELECTRIC) 1986

114m (PG)

Sequel to *Jean De Florette* (see page 315) in which the daughter of crafty Yves Montand's victim grows up to take her revenge on the village for causing her dad's death. Wonderful entertainment, shot in beautiful golden colours. Widescreen. (Both films are based on *L'Eau Des Collines* by Maurice Pagnol).

MEPHISTO [5]

KLAUS MARIA BRANDAUER, ILDIKO BANSAGI, KRYSTYNA JANDA

ISTVAN SZABO

HUNGARY (ARTHOUSE) 1981

144m (15)

The film that shot Brandauer to stardom. Based on a novel by Klaus Mann about his real-life actor uncle Gustav Grundgens (who appears in *M*, see page 316). The film sees him find acclaim from the Nazis for his stage portrayal of the Devil, as he sells his soul for fame and rejects his black girlfriend at the behest of the fascists. Brandauer is magnetic in the starring role. Oscar for best foreign film.

MISHIMA: A LIFE IN FOUR CHAPTERS [4]

KEN OGATA, KANJI SAWADA, YASOSUKE BANDO

PAUL SCHRADER

USA (WARNER) 1985 COL/B&W

120m (15)

Schrader (who wrote such hits as *Taxi Driver*, see page 276) intersperses the life of gay Japanese writer Mishima with excerpts from his work. Oddly, he wanted a return to strict militarism after World War Two and tried to stage a coup. When it failed he committed hara-kiri. Great score by Philip Glass. For those who snipe at the commercial *oeuvres* of Francis Ford Coppola and George Lucas, it should be noted that they both helped finance this wondrous (but doggedly uncommercial) movie.

NIKITA [4]

ANNE PARILLAUD, JEAN RENO, JEANNE MOREAU

LUC BESSON

FRANCE/ITALY (ARTIFICIAL EYE) 1990

117m (18)

Improbably wild but entertaining story of a junkie girl reprieved from a death sentence (after a shoot-out at a chemist's shop) and subsequently groomed as a hit woman for the state. Remade in the USA in 1993 as *Assassin* with Bridget Fonda in the lead. Besson has become a major director with films like *Leon* (see page 270) and *The Fifth Element* (see page 246). Widescreen.

317

ONIBABA

NOBUKO OTOWA, YITSUKO YOSHIMURA, KEI SATO

KANETO SHINDO

JAPAN (TARTAN) 1964 B&W

104m (15)

Scary Japanese horror about two women who ambush stray samurai – but lust intervenes. Atmospheric and very disturbing film that makes the most of the small cast and smaller budget. Highly recommended for fans of the bizarre. Widescreen.

THE RETURN OF MARTIN GUERRE

GERARD DEPARDIEU, NATHALIE BAYE, MAURICE BARRIER

DANIEL VIGNE

FRANCE (ARROW) 1982

123m (15)

Medieval story of a man who returns to his wife and home a changed fellow: but is it really him? Intriguing fable, later remade in the USA as *Sommersby* (see page 233).

A SHORT FILM ABOUT KILLING

MIROSLAW BAKA, KRZYSZTOF GLOVISZ, JAN TESARZ

KRZYSZTOF KIESLOWSKI

POLAND (TARTAN) 1988

84m (18)

The fifth of the director's 'Ten Commandments' series is a sad little story about a youth who murders a taxi driver for no apparent reason, only to suffer the death penalty. Shows how sordid both the crime and the punishment inevitably are. A Cannes winner which is credited with causing a temporary hold on capital punishment in Poland. Widescreen.

UN HOMME ET UNE FEMME

ANOUK AIMEE, JEAN LOUIS TRINTIGNANT, VALERIE LAGRANGE

CLAUDE LELOUCH

FRANCE (WARNER) 1966

102m (PG)

Sloppy hit-romance/no-brainer with slushy Francis Lai music. Yuk. The director made a worse sequel 20 years later – but the magic (if you can call it that) didn't gel second time around. Not for me.

Further Reading

Magazines

There are numerous video consumer titles in newsagents such as *Video World*, and fans of populist cinema might try *Empire*. For serious film fans, there are the BFI magazine *Sight and Sound*, or USA imports *Film Comment* and *American Cinematographer*. Also from the USA is the more sociopolitically-minded *Cineaste*.

Horror fans should enjoy *The Dark Side*; or the mind-boggling *Flesh & Blood* (sex/horror/exploitation), *Eyeball* (ditto but with arthouse leanings) and *Diabolik* (Italian horror/trash). Write for information on those three titles to PO BOX 178, Guildford, Surrey, GU3 2YU.

If you're keen on knowing about cuts/variant versions, the best mag is *Video Watchdog*, PO BOX 5283, Cincinnati, OH 45205-0283, USA.

Serious special effects fans must buy *Cinefex*, a USA import.

Lastly, for fans of trashy cinema I hear that *Ungawa!*, a legendary title, is soon to resume after a long hiatus.

Books

The Aurum Film Encyclopaedia is in three separate volumes, *The Western*, *Horror* and *Science Fiction*, all indispensable. Edited by Phil Hardy. (Aurum Press).

Epic Films by Gary A Smith (McFarland).

Immoral Tales (Sex and Horror Cinema in Europe 1956–84) by Cathal Tohill and Pete Tombs (Titan).

Radio Times Film & Video Guide by Derek Winnert (Hodder & Stoughton).

Red Hot and Blue: A Smithsonian Salute to the American Musical by Amy Henderson and Dwight Blocker Bowers (Smithsonian).

Sex and Zen and a Bullet in the Head: the Essential Guide to Hong Kong's Mind-bending Films by Stefan Hammond & Mike Wilkins (Titan).

Spaghetti Westerns by Thomas Weisser (McFarland).

The X Factory by Anthony Petkovich (Critical Vision) is a background guide to the USA sex film industry.

This is just a selection of the numerous books/magazines available on all genres. If you can't find what you need locally, write, call or visit the following:

Zwemmers, 80 Charing Cross Road, London, WC2H 0BB (0171 240 4157).

Cinema Bookshop, 14 Great Russell Street, London, WC1B 3NH (0171 637 0206)

Cinema Store, 4b/c Orion House, Upper St. Martin's Lane, London, WC2H 9EJ (0171 379 7838).

Forbidden Planet, 71 New Oxford Street, London, WC1A 1DG (0171 836 4179)

Psychotronic Video, Unit 30C, 1st Floor, Camden Lock Buildings, Chalk Farm Road, Camden Town, London, NW1 8AF (0181 699 5375)

Cinema Store, Forbidden Planet and Psychotronic also sell videos; Cinema Store specialises in laserdisc/imports and Psychotronic in rare material. Tell 'em I sent you!

Index of Titles

10 62
10 Commandments, The 123
10 Rillington Place 258
101 Dalmatians 54
12 Monkeys 238
13 Ghosts 139
1941 62
2001 – A Space Odyssey 123, 237, 238
2010 – The Year We Make Contact 239
48 Hours 15
55 Days At Peking 123
633 Squadron 277
7 Brides For Seven Brothers 205
7 Years In Tibet 87
7th Voyage Of Sinbad, The 54
9½ Weeks 40
About Last Night 221
Absence Of Malice 87
Absolute Beginners 205
Abyss, The 239
Accidental Tourist, The 221
Accused, The 88
Ace Ventura: Pet Detective 62
Addams Family, The 62
Addams Family Values 63
Addiction, The 175
Adventures Of Pinocchio, The 139
Adventures Of Robin Hood, The 15
Affair To Remember, The 221
African Queen, The 16
Age Of Consent 222
Age Of Innocence, The 222
Aguirre, The Wrath Of God 313
Ai No Borei 40
Air Force One 16
Airplane 63
Al Capone 150

Aladdin 55
Alamo, The 293
Alcove, The 40
Alien 240
Alien3 240
Alien Resurrection 241
Aliens 240
All Quiet On The Western Front 277
All That Jazz 206
All The President's Men 88
Alphaville 241
Altered States 244
American Buffalo 88
American Friend, The 313
American Gigolo 89
American Graffiti 63
American In Paris, An 206
American President, The 222
American Tail, An 55
American Werewolf In London, An 175
And God Created Woman 314
And Now For Something Completely Different 63
Angel Enforcers 168
Angel Heart 176
Angel Of Vengeance 258
Angels 168
Animal Crackers 64
Animal House 64
Anne Of The Thousand Days 222
Annie Hall 11, 64
Apocalypse Now 278
Apollo 13 89
Arachnophobia 176
Arsenic And Old Lace 64
Art Of Love, The 40
Arthur 65

Asphalt, Jungle, The 150
Austin Powers – International Man
   of Mystery 65
Awakenings 89
Awful Doctor Orlof, The 176

Babe 140
Baby Face 39
Back To The Future 16
Back To The Future Part 2 16
Back To The Future Part 3 17
Backdraft 89
Bad And The Beautiful, The 90
Bad Day At Black Rock 90
Bad Lieutenant, The 150
Bad Taste 65
Ballad Of Cable Hogue, The 293
Barabbas 124
Barbarella 242
Barbarian, The 124
Barton Pink 90
Basic Instinct 257, 258
Basil, The Great Mouse Detective 55
Basquiat 90
Batman 17
Batman and Robin 18
Batman Forever 17
Batman Returns 17
Battle Of Britain, The 278
Battle Of Midway, The 278
Battle Of The Bulge 279
Beaches 91
Beauty And The Beast 55
Becket 124
Bedazzled 65
Bedford Incident, The 91
Beethoven 66
Beetlejuice 66
Belle De Jour 314
Belt, The 41
Ben Hur 124
Better Tomorrow 2, A 168
Better Tomorrow, A 168

Beverly Hills Cop 66
Beyond The Valley Of The Dolls 41
Bible, The 125
Big 140
Big Blue, The 91
Big Country, The 294
Big Red One, The 277, 279
Big Sleep, The 259
Big Wednesday 91
Bill And Ted's Bogus Journey 67
Bill And Ted's Excellent Adventure 67
Billionaire Boys Club 92
Billy Bathgate 151
Billy Liar 67
Birdman Of Alcatraz, The 92
Birds, The 259
Black Candles 41
Black Rain 151
Black Widow 259
Blackboard Jungle, The 92
Blade Runner 242
Blanche 42
Blazing Saddles 68
Blood And Sand 222
Blood For Dracula 177
Blood Simple 259
Blow Out 260
Blue Hawaii 206
Blue Lagoon, The 223
Blue Max, The 279
Blue Steel 260
Blue Thunder 18
Blue Velvet 260
Blues Brothers, The 68
Boat, The 280
Bob Roberts 68
Body Double 261
Body Heat 92
Bodyguard, The 223
Boiling Point 18
Bonnie And Clyde 151
Born Free 140
Born On The Fourth Of July 277, 280

INDEX OF TITLES

Bounty, The 93
Boyfriend, The 206
Boys Club, The 140
Boys From Brazil, The 261
Boyz 'N' The Hood 93
Bram Stoker's Count Dracula 177
Bram Stoker's Dracula 178
Braveheart 125
Brazil 243
Breakfast Club, The 69
Breaking Glass 207
Breaking The Waves 93
Breathless 223
Bridge On The River Kwai, The 280
Bridges Of Madison County, The 223
Brigadoon 207
Bring Me The Head Of Alfredo Garcia 151
Britannia Hospital 69
Broadcast News 69
Broken Arrow 18
Bronx Warriors 152
Brood, The 178
Brubaker 261
Buddy Holly Story, The 207
Bugs Bunny 53
Bugsy 152
Bullet For The General, A 294
Bullitt 262
Burbs, The 69

Cabaret 208
Cable Guy, The 70
Caine Mutiny, The 93
Calamity Jane 208
Caligula 125
Camelot 208
Can-Can 208
Cape Fear (1991) 262
Cape Fear (1961) 262
Capone 152
Captain Blood 19
Carlito's Way 153

Carry On ... 61, 70
Casanova's Big Night 70
Casino 153
Castaway 224
Casualties Of War 281
Cat On A Hot Tin Roof 94
Cemetery Man 179
Chamber, The 94
Charge Of The Light Brigade, The 126
Chariots Of Fire 94
Children Of A Lesser God 224
Chinatown 94
Chisum 294
Chitty Chitty Bang Bang 141
Church, The 179
Cincinnati Kid, The 95
Cinema Paradiso 314
Citizen Kane 95
City Of Lost Children, The 314
City Slickers 71
Clear And Present Danger 19
Cleopatra 126
Cliffhanger 19
Close Encounters Of The Third Kind 243
Cocoon 243
Colditz Story, The 281
Color Of Money, The 95
Color Purple, The 96
Colors 153
Coma 263
Comin Home 224
Commitments, The 205, 209
Common-Law Cabin 42
Companeros 294
Con Air 19
Conan The Barbarian 20
Conan The Destroyer 20
Confessions Of A Police Captain 149
Contact 243
Cool Hand Luke 96
Copland 263

323

Copycat 263
Courage Under Fire 96
Crash 42
Crimes And Misdemeanors 71
Crimes Of Passion 42
Criminal, The 154
Crocodile Dundee 71
Cromwell 126
Cronos 179
Cross Of Iron 281
Crow, The 180
Cruel Sea, The 281
Cruising 263
Cry Freedom 97
Cry In The Dark, A 96
Cry-Baby 209
Crying Game, The 97
Cujo 264
Curse Of The Daemon 181
Cyrano De Bergerac 315

D-Day The 6th Of June 282
Daddy Long Legs 209
Daleks – Invasion Earth 2150 AD 141
Dam Busters, The 282
Dances With Wolves 295
Dangerous Game 97
Dangerous Liaisons 97
Danny The Champion Of The World 141
Dante's Peak 20
Danton 126
Dark Habits 43
Dark Side Of Love, The 43
Daughters Of Darkness 181
Day At The Races, A 71
Day Of The Jackal, The 264
Day The Earth Stood Still, The 244
Daylight 20
Dead Man 295
Dead Man Walking 98
Dead Men Don't Wear Plaid 72
Dead Poets' Society 98

Dead Zone, The 264
Death Becomes Her 72
Death Rides A Horse 295
Deer Hunter, The 282
Defiant Ones, The 98
Deliverance 21
Dementia 13 182
Demetrius And The Gladiators 127
Demolition Man 21
Demon Seed 244
Demons 182
Desert Fox, The 283
Detour 99
Devil's Advocate 99
Devils, The 99
Dial M For Murder 264
Diary Of A Chambermaid, The 315
Dick Tracy 21
Die Hard 22
Dirty Dozen, The 283
Dirty Harry 22
Dirty Rotten Scoundrels 72
Dirty Weekend 43
Disclosure 100
Django 296
Django Strikes Again 296
Django The Bastard 296
Do The Right Thing 100
DOA (1949) 265
DOA (1988) 265
Doctor Doolittle 209
Doctor No 22
Doctor Zhivago 127
Dog Day Afternoon 100
Dogs Of War, The 23
Don't Look Now 182
Donnie Brasco 154
Doors, The 101
Dr Strangelove, Or ... 73, 237
Dracula (1931) 183
Dracula (1958) 183
Dracula – Prince Of Darkness 184
Dragonheart 141

INDEX OF TITLES

Dripping Red Wax 184
Driving Miss Daisy 61, 73
Drop Zone 23
Drugstore Cowboy 101
Dumb And Dumber 73
Dune 245

East Of Eden 101
Eastern Condors 169
Easy Rider 102
Ed Wood 102
Educating Rita 73
Education Anglaise 43
Edward Scissorhands 142
Egon Schiele Excesses 44
Eiger Sanction, The 23
El Cid 127
El Dorado 296
Elephant Man, The 102
Elmer Gantry 103
Elvira Madigan 315
Emilienne 44
Emperor Of The North 23
Empire Of The Sun 103
Empire Strikes Back, The 245
Encounters Of The Spooky Kind 169
Enemy Mine 245
English Patient, The 103
Enter The Dragon 169
Entertaining Mr Sloane 74
Erotic Dreams Of Cleopatra, The 44
Erotika 44
Escape From Alcatraz 265
Escape From Brothel 45
Escape From LA 24
Escape From New York 24
Eskimo Nell 45
ET – The Extra-Terrestrial 245
Evil Dead, The 184
Evil Senses 45
Excalibur 127
Exorcist, The 175
Exorcist, The 175

Expresso Bongo 210
Eyes Without A Face 185

Face/Off 24
Face To Face 297
Fail Safe 103
Fall Of The Roman Empire, The 128
Falling Down 104
Falling In Love 224
Fame 210
Fantasia 56
Fantastic Voyage 246
Far and Away 225
Farewell To Arms 225
Fargo 104
Faster Pussycat, Kill ... Kill 46
Fatal Attraction 104
Fearless Vampire Killers, The 185
Fellini Satyricon 128
Female Vampire 186
Few Good Men, A 105
Fiddler On The Roof 210
Field Of Dreams 105
Field, The 105
Fifth Element, The 246
Firefox 24
First Blood 25
First Men In The Moon 246
First Wives Club 74
Fish Called Wanda, A 74
Fistful Of Dollars, A 297
Fistful Of Dynamite, A 128
Fists Of Fury 170
Five Venoms 170
Flash Gordon 246
Flashdance 210
Flatliners 265
Flavia The Heretic 129
Flesh and Blood 25
Flesh Gordon 46
Fly Away Home 142
Fly, The 247
Fog, The 186

325

For A Few Dollars More 297
For The Boys 225
Forbidden Planet 247
Force Of Evil 154
Foreign Correspondent 266
Forever Young 225
Forrest Gump 226
Fort Apache 298
Four Weddings And A Funeral 226
Frankenstein 187
Frankenstein Must Be Destroyed 187
Freaks 188
Free Willy 139, 142
French Lieutenant's Woman, The 226
Frenzy 266
Fried Green Tomatoes At The Whistle Stop Café 106
From Dusk Till Dawn 188
From Here To Eternity 106
Fugitive, The 266
Full Metal Jacket 283
Full Monty, The 74
Funny Girl 211
Fury, The 188

Gallipolli 284
Gandhi 129
Genghis Khan 129
George Of The Jungle 75
Geronimo 298
Get Carter 267
Get Shorty 154
Getaway, The 155
Ghost 227
Ghost And The Darkness, The 53
Ghostbusters 75
GI Jane 106
Gigi 211
Glory 284
Godfather Part II, The 155
Godfather Part III, The 156
Godfather, The 149, 155

Goldeneye 25
Goldfinger 26
Gone With The Wind 129
Good Morning, Vietnam 75
Good, The Bad And The Ugly, The 298
Goodfellas 156
Goonies, The 143
Gorillas In The Mist 106
Gothic 189
Gotti 156
Grapes Of Wrath, The 107
Grease 211
Great Escape, The 284
Great Gatsby, The 227
Great Rock'n'Roll Swindle 212
Green Berets, The 284
Gremlins 75
Greystoke 130
Grifters, The 156
Groundhog Day 76
Guarding Tess 61
Gunfighter, The 298
Guns Of Navarone, The 285
Gypsy 212

Hair 213
Halloween 189
Hamburger Hill 285
Hamlet 130
Hand Of Death 170
Hand That Rocks The Cradle, The 267
Hang 'Em High 299
Hannah And Her Sisters 76
Hard Day's Night, A 213
Harrison Bergeron 238
Harvey 76
Haunting, The 190
Hear My Song 76
Heat 157
Heathers 77
Heaven's Gate 299
Hello, Dolly! 214

INDEX OF TITLES

Hellraiser 190
Help! 214
Henry – Portrait Of A Serial
    Killer 107
Henry V 130
Henry VIII And His Six Wives 130
Hercules 54
Hercules Conquers Atlantis 131
Heroes Shed No Tears 170
High Plains Drifter 299
High Society 205, 214
Highlander 26
Hindenburg, The 131
Hitcher, The 190
Home Alone 139, 143
Home Alone 2 143
Home Alone 3 143
Homicide 267
Homme Et Une Femme, Un 318
Honey, I Blew Up The Kid 144
Honey, I Shrunk The Kids 144
Horse Soldiers, The 300
Hot Shots 77
Hot, The Cool And The Vicious,
    The 171
House Of Games 267
How Green Was My Valley 107
How The West Was Won 123, 300
Howling, The 191
Hudsucker Proxy, The 77
Hunchback Of Notre Dame, The
    (1939) 227
Hunchback Of Notre Dame, The
    (Disney) 54
Hunger, The 191
Hunt For Red October, The 26

I Wake Up Screaming 268
I Was Monty's Double 285
Ice Cold In Alex 285
Ice Station Zebra 27
Illustrated Man, The 247
Immoral Tales 46

Importance Of Being Earnest, The 77
In Harm's Way 286
In Search Of The Castaways 144
In The Heat Of The Night 268
In The Line Of Fire 268
In The Name Of The Father 107
Indecent Proposal 228
Independence Day 237, 247
Inferno 191
Innerspace 144
Internal Affairs 269
Interview With The Vampire 192
Invasion Of The Body Snatchers 248
Island Of Lost Souls 192
Island On Fire 171
It's A Mad, Mad, Mad, Mad World 78
Italian Job, The 27
Ivan The Terrible 131

Jackal, The 27
Jagged Edge 257, 269
James And The Giant Peach 56
Jason And The Argonauts 56
Jaws 27
Jean De Florette 315
Jennifer Eight 269
Jeremiah Johnson 300
Jerry Maguire 78
Jesse James 300
Jewel Of The Nile, The 27
JFK 108
Journey To The Centre Of The
    Earth 28
Judgment At Nuremberg 131
Jumanji 145
Jurassic Park 28, 53

Kalifornia 269
Karate Kid, The 145
Kelly's Heroes 286
Keoma ... The Violent Breed 301
Key Largo 157
Khartoum 132

Killer Elite, The 28
Killer, The 171
Killing Fields, The 108
Killing Of A Chinese Bookie, The 157
Kind Hearts And Coronets 78
King Creole 214
King David 132
King Kong 57
King Of Comedy 78
King Of New York 158
Kiss Of The Spider Woman 108
Klute 270
Krays, The 158

LA Confidential 109
La Dolce Vita 316
LA Takedown 158
Lady And The Tramp 57
Last Emperor, The 132
Last Exit To Brooklyn 109
Last Man Standing 159
Last Of The Mohicans, The 132
Last Temptation Of Christ, The 133
Last Train From Gun Hill, The 301
Lavender Hill Mob, The 79
Lawrence Of Arabia 133
Left-Handed Gun, The 301
Legend 29
Legends Of The Fall 109
Lenny 109
Leon 270
Lepke 159
Les Diaboliques 316
Lethal Weapon 29
Lethal Weapon 2 29
Lethal Weapon 3 29
Life And Times Of Judge Roy Bean, The 301
Lion King, The 57
Little Big Man 302
Little Caesar 159
Logan's Run 248
Lone Star 110

Long And The Short And The Tall, The 286
Long Good Friday, The 270
Long Kiss Goodnight, The 30
Long Riders, The 302
Longest Day, The 286
Looking For Richard 110
Lord Jim 133
Lost Boys, The 193
Lost In America 79
Lost World, The: Jurassic Park 30
Love At First Bite 79
Love Field 228
Love Is A Many Splendored Thing 228

M 316
Macbeth 134
Mad Max 30
Mad Max 2: The Road Warrior 30
Mad Max: Beyond The Thunderdome 31
Madness Of King George, The 110
Magnificent Seven, The 302
Man Bites Dog 316
Man For All Seasons, A 134
Man Who Shot Liberty Valance, The 303
Man With The Golden Arm, The 110
Manchurian Candidate, The 270
Manhunter 271
Maniac Cop 193
Manon Des Sources 317
Marathon Man 271
Mark Of The Devil, The 193
Mark Of Zorro, The 31
Marnie 271
Mars Attacks! 237, 248
Mary Poppins 145
Mary Shelley's Frankenstein 194
Mask Of Satan 194
Matilda 145
Matter Of Life And Death, A 229

INDEX OF TITLES

Mayerling 229
McVicar 160
Mean Streets 160
Meaning Of Life, The 79
Memphis Belle 287
Men In Black 249
Men Of Respect 160
Mephisto 317
Mermaid, The Little 58
Mesa Of Lost Women, The 249
Miami Blues 160
Michael Collins 111
Midnight Cowboy 111
Midnight Express 111
Miler's Crossing 161
Miranda 46
Misery 272
Mishima: A Life In Four Chapters 317
Mission: Impossible 31
Mississippi Burning 272
Missouri Breaks, The 303
Mobsters 161
Mona Lisa 272
Mondo Topless 47
Monty Python And The Holy Grail 80
Monty Python's Life Of Brian 80
Moonstruck 229
Mr Sardonicus 195
Mrs Brown 112
Mutiny On The Bounty 134
My Beautiful Launderette 112
My Cousin Vinny 80
My Darling Clementine 303
My Left Foot 112
Mysterious Island 58
Mystery Of The Wax Museum 195

Naked And The Dead, The 287
Naked – As Nature Intended 47
Naked Gun 80
Naked Killer 172
Naked Lunch 113

Name Of The Rose, 113
National Lampoon's Vacation 81
Near Dark 195
Nell 113
Never Say Never Again 31
Neverending Story, The 146
New Jack City 161
New York, New York 215
Night Moves 272
Night Of The Generals, 287
Night Of The Living Dead 196
Nightmare Before Christmas, The 59
Nightwatch 273
Nikita 317
No Way Out 273
North By Northwest 273
Nosferatu The Vampire 196
Nutty Professor, The 81

Odd Couple, The 81
Of Mice And Men 113
Officer And A Gentleman, An 230
Oliver! 215
Omega Man, The 249
On Golden Pond 114
On The Beach 237
On The Waterfront 114
Once Upon A Time In America 161
Once Upon A Time In The West 304
One Flew Over The Cuckoo's Nest 114
One Million Years BC 58
One-Armed Boxer 172
One-Eyed Jacks 304
Onibaba 318
Orgy Of The Dead 47
Original Gangstas 162
Out Of Africa 230
Outbreak 32
Outland 250
Outlaw Josey Wales, The 304

Pacific Heights 115

Paint Your Wagon 215
Pal Joey 215
Pale Rider 305
Passage To India, A 115
Pat Garrett And Billy The Kid 305
Patriot Games 32
Patton 287
Peacemaker, The 32
Peeping Tom 197
Pennies From Heaven 216
People vs Larry Flynt, The 115
Performance 116
Peyton Place 230
Philadelphia 116
Piano, The 221, 230
Pink Floyd – The Wall 216
Pinocchio 58
Plan 9 From Outer Space 250
Planet Of The Apes 250
Platoon 277, 288
Pocahontas 59
Point Blank 273
Point Break 162
Poltergeist 197
Poseidon Adventure, The 32
Postcards From The Edge 116
Predator 33
Presumed Innocent 116
Pretty Baby 231
Pretty In Pink 231
Pretty Woman 231
Prick Up Your Ears 117
Primal Fear 274
Prince Of Tides, The 231
Princess Bride, 146
Prisoner Of Zenda, The 33
Private Benjamin 81
Private Parts 82
Producers, The 82
Project A 172
Psycho 198
PT 109 288
Public Enemey 162

Pulp Fiction 149, 163
Purple Rain 216

Quadrophenia 217
Quiz Show 87, 117
Quo Vadis 134

Rabid 198
Raging Bull 117
Raiders Of The Lost Ark 33
Railway Children, The 146
Rain Man 117
Raising Cain 274
Rambo: First Blood Part 2 33
Rambo 3 34
Ransom 274
Rasputin The Mad Monk 198
Red Dawn 288
Red River 306
Remains Of The Day 118
Repulsion 274
Reservoir Dogs 149, 163
Return Of Martin Guerre, The 318
Return Of The Jedi 251
Reversal Of Fortune 118
Richie Rich 146
Ride The High Country 306
Right Stuff, The 135
Ring Of Bright Water 147
Rio Bravo 306
Rio Grande 306
Rio Lobo 307
Road Runner 53
Rob Roy 34
Robe, The 135
Robocop 251
Rock, The 34
Rocky 118
Rocky Horror Picture Show, The 217
Rollerball 251
Roman Holiday 232
Romancing The Stone 34
Romantic Englishwoman, The 232

INDEX OF TITLES

Romeo And Juliet 221, 232
Rosemary's Baby 199
Run Silent, Run Deep 288
Running Man, The 35

Salvador 277, 289
Samourai, Le 159
Samson And Delilah 135
Sands Of Iwo Jima 289
Satan's Return 172
Scandalous Gilda 47
Scarface (1932) 163
Scarface (1983) 164
Scent Of A Woman 232
Schindler's List 118
School For Sex 48
Scream 199
Se7en 87, 119
Sea Hawk, The 35
Sea Of Love 275
Searchers, The 307
Sect, The 199
Sergeant York 289
Sexual Life Of The Belgians, The 48
Shane 307
Sharky's Machine 164
Shatter Dead 48
Shawshank Redemption 119
Shine 119
Shining, The 200
Shooting, The 308
Shootist, The 308
Short Film About Killing, A 318
Shot In The Dark, A 82
Showboat 205, 217
Showgirls 48
Sid And Nancy 120
Silence Of The Lambs, The 275
Silk Stockings 217
Singin' In The Rain 218
Single White Female 275
Sink The Bismarck 289
Sir Henry At Rawlinson's End 82

Sleepers 275
Sleeping Beauty 59
Sleepless In Seattle 221, 233
Sleuth 276
Smoke 120
Snake In The Eagle's Shadow 173
Solaris 251
Soldier Blue 308
Solomon And Sheba 135
Something Wicked This Way
  Comes 53
Somewhere In Time 233
Sommersby 233
Soylent Green 237, 252
Spanking The Monkey 49
Spartacus 136
Speed 35
Speed 2 – Cruise Control 35
Spirits Of The Dead 200
Stagecoach 309
Stalag 17 290
Stalker 252
Stanley And Iris 233
Star Is Born, A 205, 218
Star Trek – The Motion Picture 252
Star Trek II – The Wrath Of Khan 252
Star Trek III – The Search For
  Spock 253
Star Trek IV – The Voyage Home 253
Star Trek NG – First Contact 253
Star Trek V – The Final Frontier
Star Wars 254
Starman 254
Starship Troopers 254
State Of Grace 164
Strange Days 49
Stranglers Of Bombay, The 200
Study In Terror, A 200
Summer Of '42 234
Superman – The Movie 36
Supervixens 49
Suspiria 201
Sweet Charity 218

Sweet Smell Of Success, The 120
Swiss Family Robinson 147
Sword In The Stone, The 59

Tandem 49
Taps 290
Taxi Driver 276
Teenage Mutant Ninja Turtles 147
Tender Mercies 234
Terminal Velocity 36
Terminator, The 36
Terminator 2: Judgement Day 36
Terms Of Endearment 234
Terror Of Doctor Hitchcock, The 201
That'll Be The Day 218
That's Entertainment 219
Theatre Of Blood 201
They Were Expendable 290
Thing, The 201
This Is Spinal Tap 83
Those Magnificent Men In Their
    Flying Machines 147
Three Coins In The Fountain 234
Throne Of Blood 136
Thunderball 37
THX 1138 254
Tigers, The 173
Tim Burton's The Nightmare Before
    Christmas 59
Time Machine, The 237, 255
Time To Kill, A 120
Timemaster 148
Tin Cup 83
To Die For 83
Tobruk 290
Tom And Jerry 53
Tombs Of The Blind Dead 202
Tombstone 309
Tommy 219
Tomorrow Never Dies 37
Tootsie 83
Top Gun 37
Tora! Tora! Tora! 291

Torn Between Two Lovers 235
Total Recall 255
Towering Inferno, The 121
Toy Story 53, 60
Trading Places 84
Train, The 291
Trainspotting 121
Trees Lounge 121
Trip To Mars, A 237
True Grit 309
True Lies 38
True Romance 165
Twins 84
Twister 38

Unforgiven 310
Uncle Buck 84
Unsinkable Molly Brown, The 219
Untouchables, The 165
Up! 50
Usual Suspects, The 121

Valentino 235
Vampire Bat, The 202
Vampire Circus, The 202
Vampire Nue, La 192
Vampyros Lesbos 50
Venus In Furs 50
Vertigo 276
Videodrome 202
Vikings, The 136
Villain 165
Vixen 50
Von Ryan's Express 291

Wall Street 122
Wallace And Gromit 53
War And Peace (1956) 137
War And Peace (1967) 137
War Of The Roses, The 84
War Of The Worlds 255
Warlords Of Atlantis 255
Waterloo 137

INDEX OF TITLES

Way Ahead, The 291
Way We Were, The 235
Wayne's World 61, 85
West Side Story 219
Westworld 256
What's New Pussycat? 85
When Harry Met Sally 235
Where Eagles Dare 292
White Christmas 220
White Men Can't Junp 85
White Palace 236
White Zombie 203
Who Framed Roger Rabbit? 60
Who's Afraid of Virginia Wolfe? 122
Whore 51
Wicker Man, The 203
Wild At Heart 236
Wild Bill 310
Wild Bunch, The 311
Wilde 122
Wind In The Willows, The 148
Witches of Eastwick, The 85
Witchfinder General 203
Withnail And I 86

Witness 122
Wizard Of Oz, The 220
Wolf 204
Wolfen 204
Women In Love 236
Working Girl 86
WR Mysteries Of The Organism 51
Wuthering Heights 221, 236
Wyatt Earp 311

Xtro 256

Yankee Doodle Dandy 220
Year Of The Dragon 165
You Only Live Twice 256
Young Frankenstein 86
Young Guns 312
Young Guns II 312
Young Lions, The 292

Zardoz 256
Zeta One 51
Zombie Flesh Eaters 204
Zulu 137

Index of Stars

Abraham, F. Murray 113, 161
Ackland, Joss 67
Adams, Brooke 248, 264
Adams, Maud 251
Addams, Dawn 51
Addy, Mark 74
Adjani, Isabelle 196
Adrian, Max 99, 206
Agar, John 289
Agutter, Jenny 146, 175, 248
Aherne, Michael 209
Aiello, Danny 100, 270
Aimee, Anouk 316, 318
Alba, Rose 48
Albert, Eddie 232
Alda, Alan 71
Alderton, John 256
Alexander, Jane 261
Allen, Debbie 210
Allen, Joan 24
Allen, Karen 33, 254, 263
Allen, Nancy 62, 251, 260
Allen, Tim 60
Allen, Woody 61, 64, 71, 76, 85
Alonso, Maria Conchita 35, 153
Ameche, Don 84, 243
Anders, Luana 182
Anderson, Melody 246
Andres, Dana 181
Andress, Ursula 22, 85, 279
Andrews, Harry 74, 126, 285
Andrews, Julie 62, 145
Ann-Margret 95, 219
Annis, Francesca 134
Antolinos, Jean 43
Anwar, Gabrielle 232
Arana, Tomas 179, 199
Archer, Anne 19, 32, 104
Argento, Asia 179

Argento, Fiore 182
Ariane 165
Arkins, Robert 209
Arlen, Richard 192
Armstrong, Louis 214
Armstrong, Robert 57
Armstrong, Todd 56
Arno, Alice 186
Arnold, Tracy 107
Arquette, David 199, 310
Arquette, Patricia 165
Arquette, Rosanna 42
Arthur, Jean 307
Ash, Leslie 217
Ashcroft, Peggy 115
Assante, Armand 81, 156
Astaire, Fred 209, 217, 219
Astin, Sean 84, 143
Atherton, William 22
Atkins, Christopher 223
Atkins, Tom 29, 193
Atkinson, Jayne 142
Attenborough, Richard 28, 30, 209, 258, 284
Atwilll, Lionel 19, 195, 202
Auger, Claudine 37
Auteuil, Daniel 315, 317
Axton, Hoyt 75
Aykroyd, Dan 62, 68, 73, 75, 54
Aylward, Derek 48
Ayres, Lew 277

Bacall, Lauren 157, 259, 272, 308
Bacon, Kevin 89, 265, 275
Badel, Alan 264
Baio, Yuen 169, 172
Baka, Miroslaw 318
Baker, Betsy 184
Baker, Carroll 294

Baker, Diane 28, 271
Baker, Joe Don 25, 37
Baker, Stanley 137, 154, 281, 285
Balaban, Bob 87, 239, 242
Baldwin, Adam 283
Baldwin, Alec 66, 86, 110, 160
Baldwin, Stephen 109, 121, 280
Baldwin, William 89, 265, 269
Bale, Christian 103
Balkan, Florinda 129
Ball, Angeline 209
Balsam, Martin 88, 91, 149, 150, 198, 262, 291, 302
Bancroft, Anne 102, 106, 131
Banderas, Antonio 116, 192
Bando, Yasosuke 317
Banerjee, Victor 115
Banionis, Donatas 251
Bansagi, Ildiko 317
Barbeau, Adrienne 186
Barber, Frances 22
Barber, Paul 74
Barberini, Urbano 182
Barclanova, Olga 188
Bardot, Babette 42, 47
Bardot, Brigitte 200, 314
Barkin, Ellen 275, 310
Barr, Jean-Marc 91, 93
Barrier, Maurice 218
Barrile, Anthony 285
Barringer, Pat 47
Barry, Gene 255
Barrymore, Drew 199, 245
Barrymore, Lionel 157
Bassett, Angela 93
Basinger, Kim 17, 40, 109
Bass, Alfie 79
Bassett, Angela 49
Bates, Alan 130, 236
Bates, Kathy 106, 236, 272
Bauer, Belinda 210
Bauer, Steven 164, 274
Baxter, Anne 123

Baye, Nathalie 218
Beals, Jennifer 210
Bean, Sean 25, 32, 105
Beart, Emmanuelle 31, 317
Beatles, The 213, 214
Beatty, Ned 21, 76
Beatty, Warren 21, 151, 152
Bedelia, Bonnie 22
Beery, Noah, Jnr 289
Begley, Ed 219, 299
Bel Geddes, Barbara 276
Bellamy, Madge 203
Bellamy, Ralph 84, 231
Belle, Annie 40
Belton, Martha 41
Belushi, James 221, 289
Belushi, John 62, 64, 68
Bening, Annette 152, 156, 222, 248
Benjamin, Richard 79, 256
Bennent, David 29
Bennett, Jill 69
Bennett, Joan 201
Benny, Jack 78
Benson, Jodi 58
Benson, Robby 55
Berenger, Tom 23, 105, 280, 288
Berenson, Marisa 208
Bergen, Candice 129, 308
Berger, Helmut 232
Berger, William 297, 301
Bergin, Patrick 32
Bergman, Sandahl 20
Bergren, Thommy 315
Berkely, Elizabeth 48
Berkoff, Steven 33, 66, 158, 160
Berle, Milton 159
Bernard, Susan 46
Bernhard, Sarah 78
Beswick, Martine 58, 294
Beymer, Richard 219
Bickford, Charles 218
Biehn, Michael 34, 36, 239, 240
Biggins, Christopher 45

Biggs, Ronnie 212
Bikel, Theodore 98
Binoche, Juliette 103
Barkin, Ellen 234
Birkin, Jane 44
Birman, Serafina 131
Bisley, Steve 30
Bissell, Whit 255
Bisset, Jacqueline 262
Black, Isobel 258
Blackman, Honor 26, 56
Blackman, Joan 206
Blackmer, Sidney 159, 199
Blake, Robert 288
Blakely, Colin 23
Blessed, Brian 246
Blondell, Joan 162
Bloom, Claire 20, 71, 190, 247
Bloom, Verna 299
Blossom, Roberts 265
Blum, Mark 71
Boatman, Michael Patrick 285
Bodalo, Jose 296
Bodnia, Kim 273
Boehm, Carl 197
Bogart, Humphrey 16, 149, 157, 259
Bolger, Ray 220
Bologna, Joseph 235
Bond, Ward 290, 298, 307
Bondarchuk, Natalya 251
Bondarchuk, Sergei 137
Bonet, Lisa 176
Bonham Carter, Helena 194
Boone, Pat 28
Boone, Richard 283, 293
Boothe, Powers 288
Borgnine, Ernest 23, 24, 27, 32, 136, 311
Bosco, Philip 224
Bostwick, Barry 217
Bowie, David 90, 133, 191, 205
Boyd, Stephen 124, 128, 129, 246
Boyle, Peter 86, 160, 250, 276

Bracco, Lorraine 156
Bradford, Richard 232
Braga, Julia 108
Brambell, Wilfrid 213
Branagh, Kenneth 130, 194
Brand, Neville 92, 265
Brandauer, Klaus Maria 31, 230, 317
Brando, Marlon 36, 114, 134, 155, 278, 292, 303, 304
Branice, Ligia 42
Brasseur, Pierre 185
Brega, Maria 295
Bremner, Ewan 121
Brennan, Eileen 81, 236
Brennan, Walter 289, 303, 306
Breton, Michele 116
Bridges, Jeff 254, 269, 310
Bridges, Lloyd 63, 77, 144
Brigliadori, Eleonora 41
Brimley, Wilford 87, 201, 234, 243
Britton, Pamela 265
Brochet, Anne 315
Broderick, Matthew 70, 284
Brodie, Don 58
Brolin, James 256
Brolin, Josh 143
Bron, Eleanor 65, 214
Bronson, Charles 279, 283, 284, 304
Brook, Claudio 180
Brooks, Albert 69, 79, 276
Brooks, Elisabeth 191
Brooks, Mel 61
Brooks, Randy 153
Brooks, Ray 141
Brosnan, Pierce 20, 25, 37, 248
Brown, Blair 242
Brown, Bryan 106
Brown, Clancy 26, 260
Brown, Jim 27, 35, 162
Brown, Joe E. 217
Browne, Coral 201
Brunet, Genevieve 314
Brynner, Yul 135, 256, 302

Bucholz, Horst 302
Bujold, Genevieve 139, 222, 263
Bull, Peter 16
Bullock, Sandra 21, 35, 120
Burke, Kathleen 192
Burner, Cesar 202
Burns, Tim 30
Burroughs, William S. 101
Burton, Kevar 253
Burton, Richard 122, 124, 126, 135, 165, 222, 292
Buscemi, Steve 19, 24, 90, 104, 121, 158, 163
Busey, Gary 23, 29, 162, 207
Busey, Jake 254
Bush, Bill Green 190
Butler, Yancy 23
Byrne, Gabriel 121, 161, 189, 295

Caan, James 28, 155, 225, 251, 272, 296
Cabot, Bruce 57
Caesar, Sid 211
Cage, Nicholas 19, 24, 34, 229, 236
Cagney, James 149, 162, 220
Caine, Michael 27, 72, 73, 76, 137, 159, 232, 267, 272, 276
Callan, Michael 278
Callow, Simon 56
Calloway, Cab 68
Cameron-Glickenhaus, Jesse 148
Campbell, Bruce 184, 193
Campbell, Glen 309
Campbell, Neve 199
Campbell, William 182
Canada, Ron 110
Candy, John 81, 84, 143
Cantazaro, Veronique 43
Capaldi, Peter 97
Capri, Alaina 42
Capshaw, Kate 151
Capucine 128
Cara, Irene 210

Carati, Lilli 40
Cardinale, Claudia 304
Carey, Philip 208
Carey, Tim 157
Carlin, George 67
Carlson, Veronica 187
Carlyle, Robert 74, 121
Caron, Leslie 206, 209, 211, 235
Carradine, David 302
Carradine, John 107, 191, 309
Carradine, Keith 23, 231, 302, 310
Carradine, Robert 224, 279
Carrere, Tia 38, 85
Carrey, Jim 17, 61, 62, 70, 73
Carriere, Mathieu 44
Carroll, Leo G. 273
Carson, Jack 94, 218
Carter, Tk 201
Cartier, Caroline 192
Cartwright, Veronica 248
Caruso, David 25
Carvey, Dana 85
Casares, Maria 129
Cascio, Salvatore 314
Casey, Bernie 67
Cash, Rosalind 249
Cassavetes, John 152, 188, 199, 283
Cassel, Seymour 157
Cassidy, Jack 23
Cassidy, Joanna 60
Cassinelli, Claudio 129
Castel, Lou 294
Cates, Phoebe 75
Cazale, John 100
Cecchi, Andrea 194
Cei, Pina 47
Celi, Adolfo 37
Cepeda, Laura 43
Chakiris, George 219, 277
Chamberlain, Wilt 20
Chambers, Marilyn 198
Chan, Jackie 167, 170, 171, 172, 173
Chan-A-Hung, Meredith 50

Chandler, Helen 183
Chaney, Lon, Jnr 98
Channing, Stockard 120, 211
Chapman, Graham 63, 79, 80
Charelson, Ian 94
Charisse, Cyd 207, 217, 218, 255
Charles, Josh 98
Chase, Chevy 81
Chen, Joan 132
Chen, Pauline 45
Cher 85, 229
Chereau, Patrice 126
Cherkassov, Nikolai 131
Cheung, Leslie 168
Chevalier, Maurice 144, 208, 211
Chi, Ma 172
Chiaki, Minoru 136
Chiles, Lois 235
Chong, Rae Dawn 96
Christie, Julie 67, 127, 182, 244
Cilento, Diane 203
Cing, Jack 299
Cioffi, Charles 270
Clark, Candy 18
Clark, Fred 209
Clarke, Mae 162, 187
Clarke, Warren 24
Cleese, John 63, 74, 75, 79, 80, 148, 194
Clift, Montgomery 106, 131, 292, 306
Clifton-James, M.E. 285
Clive, Colin 187
Cliver, Al 40, 203
Clooney, George 18, 32, 188
Clooney, Rosemary 220
Close, Glenn 97, 104, 118, 130, 248, 269
Clouzot, Vera 316
Cobb, Lee J. 114
Coburn, James 81, 128, 278, 281, 284, 302, 305
Cole, George 126

Coleman, Dabney 114
Colouris, George 95
Coltrane, Robbie 141, 272
Comer, Anjanette 159
Comingore, Dorothy 95
Compere, Jean-Henri 48
Connery, Sean 22, 26, 31, 34, 37, 113, 141, 165, 250, 256
Connery, Sean 271
Connick, Harry, Jnr 263
Connolly, Billy 59
Connolly, Christopher 152, 296
Connor, Kenneth 70
Constantine, Eddie 241, 270
Coogan, Jackie 249
Coogan, Steve 148
Cook, Elisha, Jnr 23, 259
Cook, Peter 65
Cooper, Gary 289
Coote, Robert 33
Coppola, Andrea 44
Coppola, Sofia 156
Cornthwaite, Robert 255
Corri, Adrienne 202
Cortes, Juan 202
Costa, Mary 59
Costner, Kevin 83, 105, 108, 165, 223, 273, 295, 311
Cotten, Joseph 95, 291
Coulson, Bernie 88
Courtenay, Tom 67, 287
Coward, Noel 27
Cox, Brian 34, 271
Cox, Courteney 62, 199
Cox, Ronny 21, 66
Coyote, Peter 245, 269
Craig, Michael 58
Crane, Norma 210
Crawford, Michael 214
Cregar, Laird 222, 268
Crenna, Richard 25, 33, 34, 92
Crisp, Donald 35, 107, 236
Cristal, Perla 176

Criswell 47
Cromwell, James 140
Cronenberg, David 83, 247
Cronyn, Hume 243
Crosby, Bing 214, 220
Cross, Ben 94
Crothers, Scatman 200
Crouse, Lindsay 267
Crowden, Graham 69
Crowe, Russel 109
Cruickshank, Andrew 200
Cruise, Tom 29, 31, 37, 78, 95, 105, 117, 192, 225, 280, 290
Crystal, Billy 71, 146, 235
Culkin, Macaulay 84, 143, 146
Cummings, Robert 264
Cummins, Peggy 181
Cupisti, Barbara 179
Curreri, Lee 210
Curry, Tim 29, 217
Curtis, Jackie 51
Curtis, Jamie Lee 38, 74, 84, 186, 189, 225, 260
Curtis, Kelly Leigh 199
Curtis, Tony 98, 120, 136, 159
Curzon, Jill 141
Cusack, Cyril 141
Cusack, Joan 63
Cusack, John 19, 156
Cushing, Peter 141, 183, 187, 254
Cuthbertson, Allan 200
Cuthbertson, Iain 106, 146
Czerny, Henry 31

D'Angelo, Beverly 81, 213
D'Onofrio, Vincent 283
Dafoe, Willem 19, 35, 103, 133, 236, 272, 280, 288
Dahl, Arlene 28
Dallesandro, Joe 177
Dalton, Audrey 195
Dalton, Timothy 246
Daltrey, Roger 160, 219

Dan, Yuen King 173
Dance, Charles 240
Daniels, Jeff 73, 142, 176
Daniels, Phil 207, 217
Danner, Blythe 231
Danson, Ted 92
Danvers, Lise 46
Darby, Kim 309
Darnell, Linda 31, 222
Darwell, Jane 107
Davenport, Nigel 165
Davi, Robert 48, 143
David, Angel 180
Davidovich, Lolita 18, 274
Davidson, Bruce 42
Davidson, Jaye 97
Davies, Jeremy 49
Davies, Ray 205
Davies, Rupert 203
Davis, Brad 111
Davis, Geena 30, 66, 83, 221, 247
Davis, Judy 90, 113, 115
Davis, Ossie 100
Davis, Sammi 272
Dawson, Anthony 264, 295
Day, Doris 208
Day, Laraine 266
Day, Morris 216
Day-Lewis, Daniel 93, 107, 112, 132, 222
De Havilland, Olivia 15, 19, 129
De Jonge, Marc 34
De La Croix, Raven 50
De Luise, Dom 55, 68
De Mornay, Rebecca 267
De Niro, Robert 78, 89, 117, 153, 155, 156, 157, 160, 161, 165 176, 194, 215, 224, 233, 243, 262, 263, 275 276, 282
De Sica, Vittorio 225
De Vito, Danny 17, 27, 34, 84, 109, 114, 154, 234, 248
De Young, Cliff 191

Dean, James 101
Dean, Loren 151
Degermark, Pia 315
Dehner, John 301
Del Rey, Marina 48
Delaney, Dana 142
Delon, Alain 159, 200
Delon, Nathalie 159
Dempsey, Patrick 161
Dench, Judi 112, 200
Deneuve, Catherine 191, 229, 274, 314
Dennehy, Brian 25, 116
Denning, Richard 221
Dennis, Sandy 122
Dennison, Michael 77
Depardieu, Elisabeth 315, 317
Depardieu, Gerard 126, 218, 315
Depp, Johnny 102, 142, 154, 209, 295
Derek, Bo 62
Dern, Bruce 69, 159, 224, 227, 271, 310
Dern, Laura 28, 236, 260
Devereux, Marie 200
Dexter, Brad 288, 291
Di Cicco, Bobby 279
Dickinson, Angie 273
Diffring, Anton 235
Digard, Uschi 49
Dillmann, Bradford 235
Dillon, Kevin 101, 288
Dillon, Matt 83, 101
Dillon, Melinda 243
Doherty, Shannon 77
Donlan, Yolande 210
Donohoe, Amanda 110, 224
Donovan, Tate 287
Doohan, James 252, 253
Douglas, Kirk 90, 136, 188, 286, 301
Douglas, Melvyn 202
Douglas, Michael 263
Douglas, Michael 27, 34, 84, 100,
104, 122, 151, 222, 258
Dourif, Brad 114, 272
Dow, Peggy 76
Drake, Claudia 99
Dravic, Milena 51
Dreyfus, Jean-Claude 314
Dreyfuss, Michael 27
Dreyfuss, Richard 56, 63, 116, 243
Drivas, Robert 247
Dru, Joanne 306
Drury, James 306
Duchovny, David 269
Duff, Howard 273
Dukakis, Olympia 229
Duke, Bill 33
Dullea, Keir 238
Dumont, Margaret 64
Dunaway, Faye 94, 121, 151, 302
Dunbar, Adrian 76
Dunne, Griffin 175
Dunst, Kirsten 145
Durning, Charles 77, 83, 100
Duvall, Robert 28, 104, 153, 155, 234, 254, 262, 278, 298, 309
Duvall, Shelley 200
Dvorak, Ann 163
Dwyer, Hilary 203
Dylan, Bob 305
Dysart, Richard 201
Dzunda, George 258

Earles, Harry 188
Eastwood, Clint 22, 23, 24, 215, 223, 265, 268, 286, 292, 297, 298, 299, 304, 305, 310
Eaton, Shirley 26
Ebersole, Christine 146
Edwards, Cliff 58
Eggar, Samantha 178, 209
Ehle, Jennifer 122
Ekberg, Anita 316
Ekland, Britt 203, 267
Elam, Jack 307

Eleman, Herb 81
Elfman, Danny 59
Elizondo, Hector 89
Elliott, Chris 76
Elliott, Denham 281
Elphick, Michael 86
Elwes, Cary 38, 77, 146, 284
Englund, Robert 91
Ermey, Lee 283
Esposito, Giancarlo 68
Essex, David 218
Estevez, Emilio 69, 312
Eubank, Shari 49
Evans, Edith 77
Evans, Maurice 199
Everett, Rupert 110, 179
Eyer, Richard 54

Fahey, Jeff 311
Fairbanks, Douglas, Jnr 159
Faith, Adam 160
Fajardo, Eduardo 296
Falchi, Anna 179
Falk, Peter 146
Fargas, Antonion 51
Farina, Dennis 160, 271
Farmer, Gary 295
Farmer, Mimsy 45
Farrell, Glenda 159, 195
Farrow, Mia 71, 76, 199, 227
Farrow, Tisa 203
Fat, Chow Yun 168, 171
Fat, Chung 169
Fauna, Flora 48
Fei, Lung 172
Feldman, Corey 69, 143
Feldman, Marty 86
Feng, Lu 170
Fenn, Sherilyn 113
Ferrer, Mel 137
Fiedler, Jon 81
Field, Sally 87, 197, 226
Field, Shirley Ann 76, 112

Fields, Suzanne 46
Fiennes, Ralph 49, 103, 117, 118
Finch, Jon 134, 207, 266
Finney, Albert 161, 203
Fiorentino, Linda 249
Fishburne, Larry 93, 158
Fisher, Carrie 68, 69, 76, 235, 245, 251, 254
Flemyng, Robert 201
Fletcher, Louise 114, 260
Flynn, Errol 15, 19, 35
Focas, Spiro 27
Foch, Nina 206
Foley, Ellen 83, 104, 213
Fonda, Bridget 275
Fonda, Henry 103, 107, 114, 137, 278, 279, 286, 298, 300
Fonda, Henry 303, 304
Fonda, Jane 114, 200, 224, 233, 242, 270
Fonda, Peter 24, 102, 200
Fong, Alen 45
Fontaine, Joan 70
Forbes, Brian 281
Forbes, Michelle 269
Ford, Glenn 92, 278
Ford, Harrison 16, 19, 32, 33, 63, 86, 116, 122, 242, 245, 251
Ford, Harrison 253, 266
Ford, Wallace 188
Forrest, Frederic 104, 278
Forsythe, William 156
Foster, Barry 266
Foster, Jodie 88, 113, 233, 244, 275, 276
Fowler, Harry 82
Fox, Edward 31, 93, 264
Fox, James 116, 118, 205
Fox, Michael J. 16, 17, 222, 281
Foy, Eddie, Jnr 220
Francis, Anne 90, 92, 211, 247
Francq, Noe 48
Franz, Dennis 88, 260, 261

INDEX OF STARS

Fraser, John 127, 200, 282
Fraser, Liz 212
Fraser, Ronald 286
Frazer, Robert 203
Frederick, Lynne 202
Freeman, Morgan 32, 73, 119, 284, 310
Freeman, Paul 33
Freberg, Stan 57
French, Dawn 139
Frewer, Matt 144
Fricka, Brenda 105, 112
Friedland, Alice 157
Frizell, Lou 234
Frobe, Gert 26
Fry, Stephen 122, 148
Frye, Dwight 183, 187, 202
Fu, Alex 168
Fuchs, Gaby 193
Fuji, Tatsuya 40
Fuller, Sam 313
Furlong, Edward 36
Furneaux, Yvonne 274
Fury, Billy 218

Gable, Christopher 206
Gable, Clark 129, 288
Gallagher, Bronagh 209
Galligan, Zach 75
Gallo, Carla 49
Gambon, Michael 161
Ganolfini, James 36
Ganz, Bruno, 196, 313
Garcia, Andy 151, 156, 165, 269
Gardenia, Vincent 229
Gardner, Ava 123, 125, 217, 229, 301
Garfield, John 154
Garland, Judy 131, 218, 220
Garner, James 284
Garr, Teri 83, 86, 243
Garrani, Ivo 194
Gassman, Vittorio 164
Gazzara, Ben 152, 157

Geer, Will 300
Geeson, Judy 258
Geldof, Bob 216
Gemser, Laura 40
Genn, Leo 134
George, Chief Dan 302, 304
Geraghty, Marita 76
Gere, Richard 27, 89, 132, 223, 230, 231, 233, 269, 274
Gershon, Gina 24, 48
Gerson, Betty Lou 54
Gertz, Jami 38
Getz, John 247, 259, 280
Gibson, Hoot 300
Gibson, Mel 29, 30, 31, 59, 93, 125, 130, 225, 274, 284
Gibson, Thomas 225
Gielgud, John 65, 94, 102, 199, 125, 126, 129
Gilliam, Terry 79
Gilmore, Peter 255
Gingold, Hermione 211
Girotti, Massimo 40
Glaser, Michael 210
Glenn, Scott 96, 135, 275
Glover, Brian 240
Glover, Danny 29, 96, 122, 265
Glovisz, Krzystof 318
Godenzi, Joyce 169
Goldberg, Whoopi 96, 227
Goldblum, Jeff 28, 30, 247
Golden, Annie 213, 238
Goldstein, Steve 267
Golino, Valeria 117
Gomez, Thomas 154
Goncalves, Milton 18
Goodall, Caroline 118
Gooding, Cuba, Jnr 78, 93
Goodman, John 90, 176, 275
Gordon, Ruth 199
Goring, Marius 229
Gorman, Cliff 206
Gorman, Lynne 202

343

Gorshin, Frank 238
Gossett, Louis, Jnr 230, 245
Gothard, Michael 99
Gough, Michael 17, 183
Gozuno, Paolo 296
Graaboel, Sofie 273
Grable, Betty 268
Graham, Gerrit 244
Grahame, Gloria 90
Grandi, Serena 46
Granger, Stewart 33
Grant, Cary 64, 221, 273
Grant, Hugh 226
Grant, Kathryn 54
Grant, Richard E. 86, 178
Grapewin, Charley 107
Graves, Peter 290
Gray, Charles 217
Gray, Spalding 91
Grayson, Kathryn 217
Green, Michael 79
Green, Nigel 56, 58, 137, 290
Green, Pamela 47
Greene, Graham 295
Greenwood, Joan 58, 77, 78
Gregory, James 288
Gregory, Mark 152
Greist, Kim 243
Grey, Joel 208
Griem, Helmut 208
Grier, Pam 162
Griest, Kim 271
Griffith, Melanie 86, 115, 261, 272
Griffiths, Hugh 124
Griffiths, Richard 86
Grimes, Gary 234
Grodin, Charles 66
Gronemeyer, Herbert 280
Grundgens, Gustav 316
Guardino, Harry 22, 152
Guerin, Nathalie 44
Guerra, Ruy 313
Guerritore, Monica 43, 45, 47

Guest, Christopher 83, 302
Guest, Nicholas 302
Guinness, Alec 78, 79, 115, 126,127, 128, 133, 254, 280
Gulpilil, Paul 71
Gunn, Moses 146
Gwynne, Fred 80

Haas, Lukas 122
Hackett, Buddy 58
Hackman, Gene 310, 311
Hackman, Gene 32, 36, 86, 94, 116, 151, 154, 272, 273, 298
Hadji-Lazaro, Francois 179
Hagerty, Julie 63, 79
Hagman, Larry 103
Haid, Charles 242
Haim, Corey 193
Haji 46, 49
Hale, Georgina 99, 160, 224
Haley, Jack 220
Hallahan, Charles 20
Hamill, Mark 245, 251, 254, 279
Hamilton, George 79
Hamilton, Linda 20, 36
Hamilton, Margaret 139, 220
Hamilton, Murray 27
Handl, Irene 212
Hanks, Tom 60, 69, 89, 116, 140, 226, 233
Hannah, Daryl 122, 188, 242
Hardin, Ty 288
Hardman, Karl 196
Hardwicke, Cedric 283
Hardwicke, Maureen 2327
Hargreaves, Christine 216
Harlow, Jean 162
Harper, Jessica 201, 216
Harper, Tess 234
Harrelson, Woody 85, 115, 228
Harris, Barbara 72
Harris, Ed 34, 89, 135, 164, 239, 265

Harris, Julie 101, 106, 190
Harris, Neil Patrick 254
Harris, Richard 105, 125, 126, 134, 208, 286, 310
Harrison, Rex 126, 209
Harrison, Susan 120
Harry, Debbie 202
Hartley, Mariette 306
Hartnell, William 291
Harvey, Don 281
Harvey, Laurence 210, 270, 286, 293
Hatcher, Teri 37
Hatfield, Hurd 127, 301
Hathaway, Noah 146
Hauer, Rutger 25, 190, 242
Havers, Nigel 94, 103, 115
Hawke, Ethan 98
Hawkins, Jack 124, 133, 137, 201, 280, 281
Hawn, Goldie 72, 74, 81
Hawthorne, Nigel 21, 24, 110
Hawtrey, Charles 70
Hayakawa, Sessue 280
Hayden, Sterling 73, 150
Hayes, Isaac 24
Hayes, Patricia 146
Hayman, David 120
Hays, Robert 63
Haysbert, Dennis 228
Hayward, Susan 127
Hayworth, Rita 215, 222
Headly, Glenne 72
Healey, Jeffrey 41
Heard, John 89, 140, 143
Heche, Anne 154
Hedaya, Dan 20, 62, 241, 259
Hedren, Tippi 259, 271
Heflin, Van 307
Helmore, Tom 276
Hemmings, David 126, 208, 242
Hendry, Ian 267, 274
Henriksen, Lance 36, 100, 195, 240, 269

Hepburn, Audrey 137, 232
Hepburn, Katherine 16, 114
Herbert, Charles 139
Herrmann, Edward 146
Hershey, Barbara 76, 91, 104
Heston, Charlton 123, 124, 127, 132, 249, 250, 252, 278, 294
Heston, Charlton 309
Hicks, Leonard 253
Higgins, Claire 190
Hill, Benny 27, 141
Hiller, Wendy 134
Hindle, Art 178
Hines, Gregory 203
Hingle, Pat 156
Hoag, Judith 147
Hoffman, Dustin 21, 32, 83, 88, 109, 111, 117, 151, 271, 275 302
Hogan, Paul 71
Holbrook, Hal 88, 186
Holden, William 121, 228, 290, 300, 311
Holliman, East 301
Holloway, Stanley 79, 291
Holly, Lauren 73
Holm, Celeste 214
Holm, Ian 94, 110, 113, 130, 194, 240, 243, 246
Homolka, Oscar 195, 225
Hope, Bob 61, 70
Hopkins, Anthony 93, 102, 109, 118, 178, 275
Hopkins, Bo 28, 111
Hopper, Dennis 18, 35, 90, 96, 102, 165, 259, 260, 278, 309, 313
Hordern, Michael 141, 285
Horne, Victoria 76
Hoskins, Bob 60, 216, 270, 272
Hotaru, Hazuki 49
Houseman, John 251
Houser, Jerry 234
Houston, Donald 200
Houston, Whitney 223

Hovey, Natasha 182
Howard, Arliss 30
Howard, Leslie 129
Howard, Ron 63, 308
Howard, Trevor 82, 126, 134, 291
Howell, Thomas C. 190
Howes, Sally Ann 141
Hoyt, John 46
Hudson, Ernie 180
Hudson, Rock 27, 225, 290
Hulce, Tom 64, 194
Hull, Henry 300
Hull, Josephine 76
Hung, Lee Che 168
Hung, Sammo 169, 170, 171, 172
Hunt, Bonnie 66
Hunt, Helen 38
Hunt, Linda 59
Hunt, Martita 124, 219
Hunter, Bill 284
Hunter, Holly 42, 69, 230
Hunter, Jeffrey 307
Hunter, Kim 229, 250
Huppert, Isabelle 299
Hurley, Elizabeth 65
Hurt, John 34, 102, 105, 111, 240, 244, 258, 299, 310
Hurt, William 69, 92, 108, 120, 221, 224, 242
Hussey, Olivia 232
Huston, Anjelica 62, 63, 156
Huston, John 94
Huston, Walter 220
Hutchins, Will 308
Hutton, Jim 284
Hutton, Lauren 89
Hutton, Tim 290
Hyde, Jonathan 145
Hyde-White, Alex 231
Hyer, Martin 246

Ice Cube 93
Ice-T 161

Idle, Eric 63, 79, 148
Ingham, Barrie 55
Irons, Jeremy 57, 141, 226
Irons, Samuel 141
Ironside, Michael 254
Irving, Amy 188
Ives, Burl 94
Ivey, Diane 72

Jackson, Glenda 232, 236
Jackson, Peter 65
Jackson, Samuel L. 30, 120, 163
Jacobi, Derek 130
Jaeckel, Richard 254, 287
Jaffe, Sam 150, 244
Jaffrey, Saeed 112
Jagger, Dean 103, 214, 220
Jagger, Mick 116
James, Brion 245
James, Sid 70, 79
Jameson, Jemma 82
Janda, Krystna 317
Janssen, David 284
Jarvet, Yuri 251
Jeffrey, Peter 147
Jeffries, Lionel 141, 246, 281
Jeter, Michael 23
Johns, Glynis 145
Johnson, Ben 155, 288, 294, 299, 304, 306, 311
Johnson, Richard 132, 190, 203
Johnson, Tor 250
Johnson, Van 93, 207
Jones, Angela 47
Jones, Carolyn 214, 301
Jones, Dean 66
Jones, Dickie 58
Jones, Duane 196
Jones, Freddie 24, 102, 187
Jones, Gemma 99
Jones, Grace 20
Jones, James Earl 19, 20, 57, 105, 233
Jones, Jennifer 225, 228

Jones, Sam 246
Jones, Shirley 103
Jones, Terry 63, 80, 148
Jones, Tommy Lee 17, 249, 266
Jourdan, Louis 211, 234
Jovovich, Milla 246
Judd, Edward 246
Julia, Raul 62, 63, 108, 116
Jurado, Katy 304
Jurgens, Curt 133, 314
Justice, James Robertson 51

Kahn, Madeline 68, 86
Kaidanovsky, Alesandr 252
Kanante, Lu 296
Kane, Carol 64
Kaprisky, Valerie 223
Karina, Anna 241
Karlatos, Olga 216
Karlen, John 181
Karloff, Boris 163, 187
Katt, William 91
Kaufman, Christine 44
Kaye, Danny 220
Kaye, Stubby 60
Keach, James 302
Keach, Stacy 24, 301, 302
Keaton, Diane 64, 74, 155
Keaton, Michael 17, 66, 115
Keel, Howard 205, 208, 217
Keen, Geoffrey 140
Keir, Andrew 141, 184
Keitel, Harvey 263, 276
Keitel, Harvey 97, 120, 133, 150, 152, 160, 163, 188, 224, 230
Keith, Brian 164
Keith, David 230
Keller, Hiram 128
Keller, Marthe 271
Kelly, David Patrick 180
Kelly, Gene 206, 207, 218, 219
Kelly, Grace 214, 264
Kelly, Jack 247

Kelly, Jim 169, 170
Kemp, Gary 158, 223
Kemp, Jeremy 279
Kemp, Martin 158
Kennedy, Arthur 124, 133, 230, 246
Kennedy, George 23, 80, 96
Kensit, Patsy 29, 205
Kerr, Bill 284
Kerr, Deborah 33, 106, 134, 221
Kerwin, Brian 228
Kidder, Margot 36
Kidman, Nicole 17, 32, 83, 151, 225
Kier, Udo 93, 139, 177, 193, 201
Kilmer, Val 17, 37, 101, 157, 165, 309
King, Dave 270
Kingsley, Ben 118, 129, 152
Kinnear, Roy 45
Kinski, Klaus 177, 196, 294, 313
Kinski, Natassja 36
Kirby, Bruno 71
Kirk, Tommy 147
Kitchen, Michael 230
Kline, Kevin 74, 97
Ko, Eddy 170
Koch, Marianne 297
Koteas, Elias 42, 147
Kotero, Appollonia 216
Kotto, Yaphet 35, 261
Kove, Martin 145
Kozak, Harley Jane 176
Kozlowski, Linda 71
Krabbe, Jeroen 266
Krige, Alice 132, 253
Kristofferson, Kris 110, 151, 299, 305
Kurtz, Swoozie 233

La Paglia, Anthony 121
Lacey, Ronald 25
Ladd, Alan 307
Ladd, Diane 236
Lagrange, Valerie 318
Lahr, Bert 220
Lake, Ricki 209

Lamarr, Hedy 135
Lambert, Christopher 26, 129
Lancaster, Burt 92, 103, 105, 106, 120, 131, 288, 291
Lancaster, Stuart 46
Landau, Martin 71, 102, 139, 273
Landis, Carole 268
Lane, Diane 310
Lane, Priscilla 64
Lang, Stephen 109
Lange, Hope 230, 292
Lange, Jessica 34, 83, 206, 262
Lanovoi, Vasily 137
Lansbury, Angela 55, 135, 206, 270
Larroquette, John 146
Lau, Andy 171, 173
Laughton, Charles 136, 192, 227
Laurence, Ashley 190
Laurence, Caroline 43
Laurenson, James 216
Laurie, Piper 224
Lavia, Gabrielle 45, 47
Law, John Phillip 242, 295
Law, Jude 122
Lazar, John 41
Le Gros, James 101
Le, Thuy Thu 281
Lee, Anna 107
Lee, Bernard 22
Lee, Brandon 180
Lee, Bruce 169, 179
Lee, Christopher 62, 177, 183, 184, 198, 203
Lee, Danny 171
Lee, Hwang Jang 173
Lee, Mark 284
Lee, Moon 168
Lee, Peggy 57
Lee, Spike 100
Lee, Tommy 171
Leeves, Jane 56
Lehne, Frederick 92
Leigh, Janet 136, 186, 198, 270

Leigh, Jennifer Jason 25, 77, 109, 160, 190, 275
Leigh, Vivien 129
Lemaitre, Maurice 192
Lemmon, Jack 81, 108
Lena, Lorenzo 43
Leon, Valerie 51
Leonard, Bridget 47
Leonard, Robert Sean 98
Leslie, Joan 220, 289
Lester, Mark 215
Leung, Tony 171, 173
Levant, Oscar 206
Levine, Ted 275
Lewis, Fiona 165, 188
Lewis, Jerry 78
Lewis, Juliette 49, 188, 262, 269
Lewis, Ronald 195
Leyton, John 291
Linden, Jennie 236
Lindo, Delroy 18, 274
Linney, Laura 274
Linz, Alex D. 143
Liotta, Ray 105, 156, 263
Lipman, Maureen 73
Lister, Moira 281
Lithgow, John 19, 206, 239, 260, 274
Little, Cleavon 68
Livesy, Roger 229
Lloyd, Christopher 16, 17, 60, 62, 63, 114
Lloyd, Danny 200
Lloyd, Kathleen 303
Loc, Tone 62
Locaine, Amy 209
Locke, Sondra 304
Lockwood, Gary 238
Loggia, Robert 140, 269
Lollobrigida, Gina 135
Lom, Herbert 58, 82, 127, 136, 137, 177, 193, 199, 264
Lone, John 132, 165
Longo, Malisa 46

INDEX OF STARS

Lords, Traci 209
Loren, Sophia 127, 128
Lorre, Peter 64, 217, 316
Love, Courtney 115
Lowe, Rob 85, 221
Luchini, Fabrice 46
Luddy, Barbara 57, 59
Lugagne, Francoise 315
Lugosi, Bela 183, 192, 203, 250
Lukoye, Peter 140
Lund, Zoe 150
Lung, Chan 169
Lunghi, Cherie 127
Lupone, Patti 73
Luppi, Federico 180
Lynch, Kelly 101
Lynn, Porsche 44

MacArthur James 91, 147
Macchio, Ralph 80, 145
MacDonald, Edmund 99
MacGinnis, Niall 56, 181
MacGowran, Jack 185, 222
Mackay, Fulton 69
MacLachlan, Kyle 48, 101, 245, 260
MacLaine, Shirley 116, 208, 218, 234
MacMurray, Fred 93
Macnee, Patrick 191
Macy, Wiliiam H. 267
Madigan, Amy 84, 105
Madonna 21
Madou, Malou 316
Madsen, Michael 101, 142, 154, 163
Magee, Patrick 82, 154, 182
Mahito, Kino 49
Mako 20, 87, 115
Malden, Karl 92, 95, 114, 212, 287, 298, 304
Malik, Art 38
Malkovich, John 19, 97, 103, 108, 113, 268, 269
Malleson, Miles 78
Malmer, Lennart 315

Man, Daisy 168
Managno, Silvano 124
Manchester, Melissa 55
Mann, Leslie 75
Manners, David 183
Manni, Ettore 131
Manning, Katy 45
Mantegna, Joe 152, 267`
Margolyes, Miriam 56
Margulies, David 40
Mars, Betty 44
Mars, Kenneth 58, 82
Marshall, Gary 79
Marshall, Herbert 266
Martin, Dean 292, 306
Martin, Oliver 192
Martin, Steve 216
Martin, Strother 96, 293
Marvin, Lee 23, 72, 90, 93, 215, 273, 279, 283, 303
Marx Brothers, The 61, 64, 71
Mason, Hilary 182
Mason, James 28, 33, 128, 133, 218, 222, 229, 261, 273, 279
Mason, James 281, 283
Massey, Anna 197, 266
Massey, Raymond 64, 101, 287
Masterson, Mary Stuart 106
Mastrantonio, Mary Elizabeth 95, 164, 239
Mastroianni, Marcello 316
Matania, Celia 182
Matheson, Tim 62, 64
Mathis, Samantha 18
Matlin, Marlee 224
Matthau, Walter 81, 103, 108, 214
Matthews, Francis 184, 198
Matthews, Kerwin 54
Mature, Victor 127, 135, 268, 303
Maura, Carmen 43
Mayne, Fred 185
McAnally, Ray 112
McArthur, Alex 158

McCallum, David 43, 76, 284
McCarthy, Andrew 231
McCarthy, Kevin 144
McClosky, Leigh 191
McClure, Doug 255
McConaughey, Matthew 110, 120, 244
McCormack, Mary 82
McCowen, Alec 97, 266
McCoy, Matt 267
McCrea, Joel 266, 306
McCulloch, Ian 203
McDermott, Dylan 268
McDonald, Christopher 36
McDonnell, Mary 295
McDormand, Frances 102, 104, 161, 259, 272, 274
McDowall, Roddy 32, 107, 250
McDowell, Andie 76, 130, 226
McDowell, Malcolm 18, 125
McEnery, Peter 74
McGann, Paul 86
McGavin, Darren 110
McGee, Vonetta 23
McGillis, Kelly 37, 88, 122
McGoohan, Patrick 27, 125, 265
McGovern, Elizabeth 161
McGraw, Ali 155
McGregor, Ewan 121
McGuire, Dorothy 147, 234
McKean, Michael 83
McKenna, Virginia 140, 147
McKern, Leo 134, 214, 223, 226
McLaglen, Victor 306
McLaren, Malcom 212
McLerie, Allyn Ann 208
McMartin, John 218
McMillan, Roddy 147
McQueen, Steve 95, 121, 155, 262, 284, 302
McShane, Ian 165
Meaney, Colm 19
Melvin, Murray 99

Meredith, Burgess 118, 131, 164
Mervyn, William 146
Metcalf, Laurie 84
Metrano, Art 223
Meurisse, Paul 316
Michell, Keith 130
Midler, Bette 74, 91, 225
Mifune, Toshiro 136, 278
Miles, Sarah 147
Miles, Sylvia 111
Miles, Vera 198, 307
Milian, Tomas 294, 297
Milland, Ray 264
Miller, Dennis 100
Miller, Dick 215
Miller, Johnny Lee 121
Miller, Penelope Ann 89, 153
Mills, Hayley 144
Mills, John 129, 147, 281, 285
Milner, Martin 120, 139, 289
Mimieux, Yvette 255
Miner, Jan 109
Minett, Mike 65
Minnelli, Liza 65, 208, 215
Minty, Emil 30
Miranda, Soledad 50, 177
Mirren, Helen 110, 125, 127, 222, 239, 270
Mitchell, Millard 298
Mitchell, Thomas 227, 309
Mitchum, Robert 262, 278, 286, 295, 296
Modine, Matthew 115, 283, 287
Mohner, Carl 289
Molina, Alfred 117
Monroe, Marilyn 150
Montalban, Ricardo 218, 252
Montand, Yves 315, 317
Montgomery, Robert 290
Moody, Ron 215
Moon, Keith 218
Moore, Demi 100, 105, 106, 221, 227, 228

INDEX OF STARS

Moore, Dudley 62, 65
Moore, Frank 198
Moore, Julianne 30, 267
Moore, Karen 41
Moorhead, Agnes 95
Moranis, Rick 75, 144
More, Kenneth 289
Moreau, Jeanne 291, 315, 317
Moreno, Rita 218, 219
Moriarty, Cathy 117
Moriarty, Michael 305
Morita, Noriyuki 'Pat' 145, 148
Morley, Robert 16, 126, 147
Morricone, Andrea 314
Morris, Haviland 143
Morrow, Jo 139
Morrow, Vic 92, 152, 214
Mortensen, Viggo 18, 20, 106, 153
Morton, Gary 109
Mostel, Zero 82
Mueller-Stahl, Armin 32, 119
Muni, Paul 163
Murakami, Rena 45
Murdock, Jack 117
Murphy, Eddie 15, 66, 81, 84
Murphy, Michael 289
Murray, Bill 75, 76, 83, 102
Muti, Ornella 246
Myers, Cynthia 41
Myers, Mike 65, 85
Naismith, Laurence 289
Nalder, Reggie 193
Napier, Alan 59
Napier, Charles 33, 49, 160
Natividad, Kitten 50
Naughton, David 175
Neal, Patricia 244, 286
Neal, Tom 99
Neeson, Liam 34, 93, 111, 113, 118
Neill, Sam 28, 96, 230
Nelligan, Kate 231, 232
Nelson, Craig T. 99, 197
Nelson, Judd 92, 69, 161

Nelson, Ricky 306
Nelson, Sean 88
Nero, Franco 208, 294, 296, 301
Nesbitt, Cathleen 221
Nevill, John 200
Newley, Anthony 209
Newman, Paul 77, 87, 94, 95, 96, 121, 301
Newmeyer, Jane 205
Newton-John, Olivia 211
Ng, Carrie 172
Ngor, Hain S 108
Nicholson, Jack 17, 69, 85, 94, 102, 105, 114, 200, 203, 219 234, 248, 303, 308
Nico 316
Nicolodi, Daria 191
Nielsen, Leslie 80, 247
Nimoy, Leonard 248, 252, 253
Niven, David 123, 229, 236, 285, 291
Nixon, Allan 249
Nogulich, Natalja 267
Noiret, Philippe 314
Nolte, Nick 15, 231, 262
Noonan, Tom 271
Norman, Zack 34
North, Sheree 193
Norton, Edward 274
Nouri, Michael 210
Novak, Gilla 43
Novak, Kim 110, 215, 276
Nureyev, Rudolph 235

O'Brien, Donald 301
O'Brien, Edmond 227, 265, 282, 311
O'Brien, Richard 217
O'Connell, Eddie 205
O'Connor, Carrol 273, 286
O'Connor, Donald 218
O'Connor, Hazel 207
O'Dea, Judith 196
O'Donnell, Chris 18, 94, 232
O'Donnell, Rosie 233

O'Hara, Catherine 143
O'Hara, Maureen 107, 227, 306
O'Hara, Paige 55
O'Herlihy, Dan 103, 251
O'Herne, Peter 65
O'Malley, J. Pat 54
O'Neal, Patrick 225
O'Neal, Ron 162
O'Neill, Amy 144
O'Neill, Jennifer 234, 307
O'Shea, Milo 232, 242
O'Sullivan, Maureen 71
O'Toole, Annette 15
O'Toole, Peter 85, 124, 125, 132, 133, 287
Oates, Warren 18, 151, 268, 308, 311
Oberon, Merle 236
Occhipinti, Andrea 46
Ogata, Ken 317
Ogilvy, Ian 203
Oiumet, Daniele 181
Oldman, Gary 16, 108, 117, 164, 165, 178, 246, 270
Oliver, Barrett 146
Olivier, Laurence 93, 132, 136, 236, 261, 271, 276, 278
Olmos, Edward James 203
Ormond, Julia 109
Osborne, John 267
Otowa, Nobuko 318
Oudry, Pierre 44

Pacino, Al 21, 99, 100, 110, 153, 154, 155, 157, 164, 232, 263 275
Page, Genevieve 314
Pai, Wei 170
Paige, Janis 217
Palance, Jack 17, 71, 124, 294, 307, 312
Palin, Michael 63, 74, 79, 80
Pallenberg, Anita 116, 242
Palmer, Geoffrey 112
Palmer, Lilli 261
Palminteri, Chaz 121
Paltrow, Gwynneth 119
Paluzzi, Luciana 37
Papas, Irene 222
Pappaert, Nelly 316
Paquin, Anna 142, 230
Parillaud, Anne 317
Park, Reg 131
Parker, Cecil 285
Parker, Eleanor 110
Parker, Mary Louise 106
Parker, Sarah Jessica 102
Parson, Beatrice 154
Parsons, Estelle 151
Pascal, Francoise 48
Pasco, Richard 198
Pascual, Cristina S. 43
Pasdar, Adrian 195
Pastell, George 200
Patinkin, Mandy 146
Patric, Jason 35, 193, 275, 298
Patrick, Robert 36
Patton, Bart 182
Paxton, Bill 38, 89, 195, 240, 309
Payne, Laurence 202
Pearlman, Ron 180
Peck, Gregory 232, 261, 262, 285, 294, 298
Penn, Christopher 140, 163, 305
Penn, Sean 98, 153, 164, 281, 290
Peppard, George 235, 279, 290
Perez, Rosie 85
Perez, Vincent 315
Perier, Francois 159
Perkins, Anthony 42, 198, 301
Perkins, Elizabeth 140, 221
Perkins, Milie 308
Perlman, Ron 113, 241, 314
Perrine, Valerie 109
Perschy, Maria 277
Persky, Lisa Jane 235
Persoff, Nehemiah 55, 150

INDEX OF STARS

Pesci, Joe 29, 80, 108, 117, 143, 153, 156
Peters, Bernadette 216
Peters, Jean 234
Petersen, William 271, 312
Petrelli, Marcella 44
Pettet, Joanna 287
Petty, Lori 142, 162
Pfeiffer, Michelle 17, 85, 97, 164, 203, 222, 228
Phillips, Lou Diamond 96, 312
Phillips, Michelle 235
Phoenix, Joaquin 83
Picasso, Paloma 46
Piccolli, Michel 314, 315
Pickens, Slim 73, 155, 237, 305
Pickles, Wilfred 67
Picon, Molly 210
Pidgeon, Walter 90, 107, 211, 24l7
Pierce, Bradley 145
Pierro, Marina 40
Pilgaard, Ulf 273
Pinkott, Jada 81
Pintauro, Danny 264
Pistill, Luigi 295
Pitt, Brad 87, 109, 119, 165, 192, 238, 269, 275
Pitt, Ingrid 203
Placido, Michelle 40
Plank, Scott 158
Pleasance, Donald 24, 130, 158, 189, 246, 254, 256, 284, 296
Pleasance, Donald 308
Pleshette, Suzanne 259
Plummer, Christopher 55, 137, 203, 233
Poelvoorde, Benoit 316
Poitier, Sydney, 27, 91, 92, 98, 268
Polanski, Roman 177, 185
Pollard, Michael J. 151
Pop, Iggy 209
Porter, Eric 264
Portman, Eric 281

Portman, Natalie 270
Postlethwaite, Peter 30, 107, 121
Potter, Martin 128
Potter, Terry 65
Potts, Annie 42
Pouget, Ely 158
Powell, Dick 90
Powell, Jane 205
Power, Tyrone 31, 222, 300
Powers, Alexandra 159
Preminger, Otto 290
Presley, Elvis 205, 206, 214
Presley, Priscilla 80
Presnell, Harve 104, 215, 219
Preston, Kelly 78, 84
Price, Dennis 50, 78
Price, Vincent 55, 70, 142, 201, 203
Prince 205, 216
Prochnow, Jurgen 280
Prosky, Robert 225
Prosky, Scott 98
Proval, David 160
Prowse, Juliet 208
Pryce, Jonathan 37, 207, 243
Pullman, Bill 221, 233, 247
Pyriev, Eric 131

Quaid, Dennis 116, 135, 141, 144, 245, 265, 302, 311
Quaid, Randy 81, 111, 237, 247, 302, 303
Quarshie, Hugh 26, 179
Quayle, Anna 45
Quayle, Anthony 133, 200, 222, 285
Quill, Tim 285
Quilley, Denis 132
Quinn, Adrian 109, 124, 156, 161, 194
Quinn, Anthony 285, 301
Quivers, Robin 82

Raft, George 163

Rain, Douglas 238
Rains, Claude 15, 35, 133
Rampling, Charlotte 130, 176, 256, 265
Randall, Tony 78
Rathbone, Basil 15, 19, 31, 70
Rave, Stark 48
Ray, Aldo 284, 287
Ray, Gene Anthony 210
Ray, Nicholas 313
Rea, Stephen 11, 97
Read, Dolly 41
Redford, Robert 88, 227, 228, 230, 235, 261, 300
Redgrave, Lynn 119
Redgrave, Michael 77, 282
Redgrave, Vanessa 99, 117, 122, 208
Reed, Donna 106, 290
Reed, Oliver 99, 178, 215, 219, 224, 236
Reeve, Christopher 36, 118, 233
Reeves, Keanu 35, 67, 97, 99, 162, 178
Regehr, Duncan 148
Reicher, Frank 57
Reid, Beryl 74
Rein, Adele 42
Reiner, Bob 83
Reiner, Carl 72
Reinhold, Judge 66, 75
Remar, James 15, 101
Remick, Lee 235
Rennie, Michael 127, 135, 244
Reno, Jean 91, 270, 317
Rey, Fernando 294
Reynolds, Burt 21, 164
Reynolds, Debbie 218, 219
Rhames, Ving 19, 267
Rhys-Davies, John 33
Richard, Cliff 210
Richardson, Ian 43
Richardson, John 58, 194
Richardson, Miranda 97, 103

Richardson, Natasha 113, 189
Richardson, Ralph 130, 132, 251
Richter, Jason James 142
Richwine, Maria 207
Rickman, Alan 22, 68, 111
Ridgely, John 259
Rigg, Diana 201
Rimmer, Shane 255
Ringwald, Molly 69, 231
Ritter, Thelma 92, 209
Rivera, Cecilia 313
Rivera, Chita 218
Robards, Jason 88, 116, 291, 293, 304
Robbins, Tim 68, 77, 119
Roberts, Julia 111, 231, 265
Roberts, Tony 64
Robertson, Cliff 277, 287, 288
Robinson, Amy 160
Robinson, Andrew 190
Robinson, Andy 22
Robinson, Ann 255
Robinson, Edgar G. 95, 123, 157, 159
Robson, Flora 35, 123, 236
Rodolfo, Ugo 184
Röeves, Maurice 132
Rogers, Mimi 65, 101
Rojo, Helena 313
Roland, Gilbert 90
Rolfe, Guy 195, 200
Roman, Susan 198
Romay, Lina 186
Rooker, Michael 19, 107, 108, 275
Rooney, Mickey 219
Rosier, Cathy 159
Ross, Ted 65
Rosselini, Isabella 72, 260
Rossi, Leo 88
Rossington, Norman 213
Rossiter, Leonard 69, 238
Rossitto, Angelo 31
Roth, Lillian 64
Roth, Tim 34, 163

INDEX OF STARS

Roundtree, Richard 75, 162, 193
Rourke, Mickey 40, 92, 165, 176
Rubinstein, Zelda 197
Ruddo, James 97
Ruggiero, Anthony 150
Rush, Geoffrey 119
Russell, Kurt 24, 89, 201, 309
Russell, Rosalind 212
Russell, Theresa 51, 259
Russo, Rene 29, 32, 83, 154, 268, 274
Russon, James 41
Ryan, Meg 96, 101, 144, 233, 265
Ryan, Mitchell 299
Ryan, Robert 90, 279, 283, 286, 311
Ryder, Winona 66, 77, 110, 142, 178, 222, 241

Saad, Margit 154
Saijo, Hideo 168
Saint, Eva Marie 114, 273
Saito, James 147
Sakata, Harold 26
Saldana, Theresa 117
Sallow S 227
Samples, Candy 50
Sampson, Will 114
Samuel, Joanne 30
San Martin, Conrado 176
Sanjay 51
Sanders, George 82, 135, 144, 266
Sands, Julian 108, 113, 176, 189
Sandweiss, Ellen 184
Sang, Lau Chau 170
Satana, Tura 46
Santoni, Reni 22, 72
Sara, Mia 29
Sarandon, Chris 59
Sarandon, Susan 56, 85, 98, 191, 217, 231, 236
Sato, Kei 318
Savage, Ann 99
Savage, John 213, 282, 289
Savalas, Telly 283

Savelyeva, Ludmila 137
Savoy, Teresa Ann 125
Sawada, Kanji 317
Saxon, John 169
Sayer, Philip 256
Scacchi, Greta 116
Scheider, Roy 18, 27, 113, 206, 239, 270, 271
Schell, Maximilian 281
Schneider, Sophie 48
Schwarzenegger, Arnold 18, 20, 33, 35, 36, 38, 84, 221, 255
Sciorra, Annabella 118, 175, 267
Scob, Edith 185
Scofield, Paul 117, 130, 134, 291
Scorsese, Martin 276
Scorupco, Isabella 25
Scott, George C. 73, 125, 131, 287, 290
Scott, Randolph 300, 306
Seberg, Jean 215
Segal, George 122, 225
Selleck, Tom 263
Sellers, Peter 61, 73, 82, 85
Seth, Joshan 112
Sevigny, Chloe 121
Sewell, Rufus 43
Sex Pistols, The 212
Seyler, Athene 181
Seymour, Jane 233
Seyrig, Delphine 181
Sharif, Omar 127, 129, 133, 211, 229, 287
Shatner, William 252, 253
Shaw, Fiona 112
Shaw, Martin 134
Shaw, Robert 27, 134, 278, 279
Shawn, Dick 79, 82
Shawn, Wallace 117
Shearer, Harry 83
Shearer, Moira 197
Sheedy, Ally 69
Sheen, Charlie 36, 77, 122, 288, 312

Sheen, Martin 129, 222, 264, 278
Shelley, Barbara 184, 198
Shelton, Deborah 261
Shenar, Paul 91
Sheng, Chiang 170
Shepard, Sam 135
Shepherd, Cybill 276
Sher, Anthony 112
Sheridan, Dinah 146
Sherwood, Bobby 215
Shields, Brooke 223, 231
Shire, Talia 118
Shirley, Bill 59
Shue, Elisabeth 145
Siemaszko, Casey 113
Signoret, Simone 316
Silva, Maria 202
Silva, Rita 44
Silver, Fawn 47
Silver, Joe 198
Silver, Ron 92, 118, 260
Silvers, Phil 78
Silverstone, Alicia 18
Simmons, Jean 103, 135, 136, 294
Simon, Michel 42
Simon, Paul 64
Simpson, OJ 80
Sims, Sylvia 285
Sinatra, Frank 106, 110, 208, 214, 215, 219, 270, 291
Sinden, Donald 264
Singer, Steve 258
Sinise, Gary 89, 113, 226, 274
Sinn, Nikki 44
Skala, Lilia 210, 267
Skerritt, Tom 37, 240, 244
Slater, Christian 18, 77, 113, 161, 165, 192, 312
Slater, Helen 71
Sloane, Everett 95
Smith, Charles Martin 63, 207, 254
Smith, Will 247, 249
Snipes, Wesley 18, 21, 23, 85, 158, 161

Snodgress, Carrie 188, 305
Soles, PJ 189
Sommer, Elke 82
Sondergaard, Gale 31
Sorel, Jean 314
Sorenson, Ricky 59
Sorvino, Paul 21, 156, 263
Spacek, Sissy 108
Spacey, Kevin 109, 110, 119, 120, 121
Spader, James 42, 203, 236
Spain, Fay 131, 150
Spall, Timothy 189
Spector, Phil 102
Spence, Bruce 30
Spinell, Joe 263, 276
Spiner, Brent 253
St James, Susan 79
Stack, Robert 63
Stallone, Sylvester 19, 20, 21, 25, 33, 34, 118, 152, 263
Stamp, Terence 122, 200, 312
Stander, Lionel, 215
Stanshall, Vivian 82
Stanton, Harry Dean 133, 231
Starr, Ringo 218
Steele, Barbara 194, 201, 231
Steenburgen, Mary 17, 116
Steffen, Anthony 296
Stegers, Bernice 256
Steiger, Rod 114, 127, 128, 137, 150, 160, 247, 268, 286
Stellar, Virginia 184
Stensgaard, Yutte 51
Stephens, Robert 232
Stern, Daniel 143
Stern, Howard 82
Sternhagen, Frances 250, 272, 274
Stevens, Inger 299
Stevens, Stella 293
Stewart, Elaine 207
Stewart, James 76, 276, 300, 303, 308
Stewart, Patrick 253
Sting 217, 245

INDEX OF STARS

Stock, Nigel 282
Stockwell, Dean 16, 245, 260
Stockwell, Guy 290
Stokowski, Leopold 56
Stoltz, Eric 287
Stone, Christopher 264
Stone, Sharon 153, 255, 258
Stone, Stuart 140
Stormare, Peter 104
Stowe, Madeleine 132, 238
Strassman, Marcia 144
Strauss, Peter 308
Streep, Meryl 72, 96, 116, 223, 224, 226, 230, 282
Streisand, Barbra 211, 214, 231, 235
Stribling, Melissa 183
Stride, John 134
Strode, Woody 301, 303
Stroemburg, Ewa 50
Strong, Michael 287
Strong, Samantha 44
Stroud, Don 207
Studi, Wes 132, 298
Sullivan, Barry 90
Sutherland, Donald 32, 89, 100, 108, 182, 248, 270, 283, 286
Sutherland, Kiefer 105, 193, 265, 312
Sutton, Dudley 99
Swayze, Patrick 162, 227, 288
Syms, Sylvia 43, 210

Takakura, Ken 151
Tamblyn, Russ 190, 205, 219, 230
Tamerlis, Zoe 258
Tamiroff, Akim 241
Tamura, Takahiro 40, 291
Tandy, Jessica 73, 106, 243, 259, 283
Tao, Wong 171
Tarantino, Quentin 163, 188
Tarita 134
Tate, Sharon 185
Taylor, Deems 56
Taylor, Don 290

Taylor, Elizabeth 94, 122, 126
Taylor, Ginny 59
Taylor, Holland 75
Taylor, Jack 186
Taylor, Lili 175
Taylor, Robert 134, 282
Taylor, Rod 54, 255, 259
Taylor-Young, Leigh 252
Termo, Leonard 165
Terry, Nigel 127
Terry-Thomas 78, 147
Tesarz, Jan 318
Thatcher, Torin 54, 228
Thaw, John 97
Therion, Charlize 99
Thewlis, David 56, 87, 141
Thibeau, Jack 258
Thiry, Raymond 50
Thomas, Henry 245
Thomas, Jonathan Taylor 139
Thomas, Kristin Scott 103, 226
Thompson, Emma 107, 118, 130
Thompson, Jack 25
Thompson, Lea 16, 17
Thring, Frank 31, 150, 222
Thurman, Uma 18, 97, 163, 269
Ticotin, Rachel 19, 255
Tien, James 170
Tien, Yuen Siu 173
Tierney, Laurence 163
Todd, Richard 282, 286
Tognazzi, Gian Maria 184
Tomei, Marisa 80
Tomelty, Frances 105
Tomlinson, David 145
Topol 210, 246
Topor, Roland 196
Torn, Rip 95, 249
Towers, Constance 300
Towles, Tom 107
Tracy, Spencer 78, 90, 131, 300
Tran, Tung Tuanh 75
Travers, Bill 140, 147

357

Travis, Nancy 269
Travis, Richard 249
Travolta, John 18, 24, 154, 163, 211, 260
Trevor, Claire 157, 309
Trintignant, Jean Louis 314, 318
Tripplehorn, Jeanne 258
Truffaut, Francois 243
Tucci, Stanley 66, 160
Tucker, Chris 246
Tucker, Forrest 289, 294
Tudor-Pole, Edward 120
Tune, Tommy 206
Turner, Kathleen 27, 34, 42, 84, 92, 221
Turner, Lana 90, 230
Turner, Tina 31, 219
Turney, Michael 147
Turturro, John 90, 95, 100, 117, 160, 161
Tutin, Dorothy 126
Twiggy 206
Tyson, Cathy 272

Unger, Deborah 42
Ure, Mary 292
Ustinov, Peter 134, 136, 248

Vaccaro, Brenda 111
Valentine, Anthony 116
Valli, Alida 185, 191, 201
Valli, Romolo
Vallone, Raf 27
Vampira 250
Van Cleef, Lee 24, 295, 297, 298
Van Der Ven, Anne 50
Van Diem, Casper 254
Van Dyke, Dick 141, 145
Van Fleet, Jo 101
Van Lee, Ron 168
Van Pallandt, Nina 89
Van Peebles, Mario 161
Van Sloan, Edward 183, 187

Vanel, Charles 316
Vaughn, Robert 262, 302
Vega, Isela 151
Venora, Diane 27, 203
Ventura, Jesse 33
Vernon, Howard 176, 241
Vernon, John 22, 64, 304
Vidal, Gore 68
Vidovic, Ivica 51
Vincent, Jan-Michael 91
Vitale, Milly 124
Viva 111
Voight, Jon 21, 31, 111, 157, 224
Volonte, Cian-Maria 294, 297
Von Sydow, Max 20, 31, 76, 245, 246

Wagner, Lori 125
Wai, Miu Ki 173
Wakabayashi, Akiko 256
Walcott, Gregory 250
Waldall, Nikolaj 273
Walken, Christopher 17, 23, 90, 158, 159, 163, 165, 175, 216
Walken, Christopher 264, 282, 299
Walker, Kim 77
Wallace, Dee 191, 245, 264
Wallace, Paul 212
Wallach, Eli 129, 133, 156. 298, 302
Wallis, Shani 215
Walsh, M. Emmet 259, 261
Walters, Julie 73, 117
Walters, Nancy 206
Walters, Thorley 202
Wanamaker, Sam 154
Wang, George 171
Ward, Fred 160
Ward, Rachel 72, 164
Ward, Sela 266
Ward, Simon 187
Warden, Jack 88, 288
Warner, David 226, 253, 281, 293
Warren, Jennifer 272
Washington, Denzel 96, 97, 116, 284

INDEX OF STARS

Wasson, Craig 261
Waterston, Sam 108, 227
Watson, Alberta 49
Watson, Emily 93
Wayne, John 284, 286, 289, 290, 293, 294, 296, 298, 300 303, 306, 307, 308, 309
Weathers, Carl 33
Weaver, Fritz 244
Weaver, Sigourney 75, 86, 106, 240, 241, 263
Webb, Alan 74
Webb, Chloe 84, 120
Webb, Clifton 234
Webber, Robert 62, 81
Weber, Steven 275
Webster, Betty 41
Welch, Raquel 58, 65, 246
Weld, Tuesday 95
Weller, Peter 113, 251
Welles, Orson 95, 137
Wells, Vernon 30
Wennemann, Klaus 280
Wernicke, Otto 316
Whaley, Frank 101
Whitaker, Forest 75, 97, 120
White, Harriet 201
White, Wilfred Hyde 144
Whitelaw, Billie 158
Whiting, Leonard 232
Whitman, Stuart 147
Whitmore, James 119, 150
Whitton, Margaret 40
Widmark, Richard 91, 263, 293
Wiest, Dianne 76, 142, 193, 224
Wild, Jack 215
Wilder, Gene 68, 82, 86
Wilkinson, Tom 74
Williams, Edys 41
Williams, Jason 46
Williams, Jo Beth 23, 197
Williams, Kenneth 70
Williams, Lia 43

Williams, Lori 46
Williams, Michael 73
Williams, Robin 55, 61, 75, 89, 98, 145
Williams, Treat 213
Williamson, Fred 152, 162
Williamson, Nicol 127, 259
Willis, Bruce 22, 27, 72, 151, 159, 163, 238, 246
Wilson, Georges 42
Wilson, Scott 98, 227, 268
Wilton, Penelope 97
Wills, Chill 293
Winger, Debra 230, 234, 259
Wingett, Mark 217
Winter, Alex 67
Winters, Shelley 32
Wiseman, Joseph 22
Washbourne, Mona 67
Wolfit, Donald 124, 133
Wolheim, Louis 277
Wong, Victor 132
Woo, John 170
Wood, Elijah 225
Wood, Natalie 212, 219, 307
Woods, James 153, 161, 202, 244, 272, 289
Woodward, Edward 132, 203
Wray, Fay 57, 195, 202
Wray, John 277
Wright, Jeffrey 90
Wright, Jenny 195
Wright, Robin 226
Wright, Teresa 233
Wuhl, Robert 75
Wyler, Richard 124
Wymark, Patrick 203, 274, 292
Wyngarde, Peter 246
Wynn, Keenan 273
Wynter, Dana 282, 289

Yam, Simon 172
Yamada, Isuzu 136

359

Yau, Chingamy 172
Yeh, Sally 171
Yellen, Peter 258
Yen, Donnie 172
Yeoh, Michelle 37
Yi, Maria 170
Ying, Lam Ching 170
York, Michael 208, 248
York, Susannah 278
Yoshimura, Yitsuko 318
Yoshiyuki, Kazuko 40
Young, Alan 255
Young, Burt 28, 94, 109, 118, 161
Young, Diane 47
Young, Gig 28, 151

Young, Sean 62, 122, 242, 273
Young, Sharon 168
Young, Stephen 287
Yu, Jimmy Wang 171
Yu, Wang 172
Yuri, Ishiwara 49

Zamprogna, Dominic 140
Zane, Billy 287
Zawa, Devon 140
Zellweger, Renee 78
Zerbe, Anthony 249
Zimbalist, Efrem, Jnr 77
Zucco, George 227

Index of Directors

Abrahams, Jim 63, 77
Aldrich, Robert 23, 283
Allen, Irwin 121
Allen, Woody 64, 71, 76
Allers, Roger 57
Almodovar, Pedro 43
Amiel, Jon 233, 263
Anderson, Lindsay 69
Anderson, Michael 248, 282
Annakin, Ken 147, 279, 286
Annaud, Jean-Jacques 87, 113, 143
Apostoloff, Stephen C. 47
Apted, Michael 106, 113
Archer, Ted 296
Argento, Dario 191, 201
Armitage, George 160
Armstrong, Michael 193
Ashby, Hal 224
Asquith, Anthony 77
Attenborough, Richard 97, 129
Avildsen, John G. 118, 145
Avnet, Jon 106

Babenco, Hector 108
Badham, John 18, 23
Ballard, Carroll 142
Barker, Clive 190
Barron, Steve 139, 147
Bava, Lamberto 182
Bava, Mario 194
Bay, Michael 34
Beatty, Warren 21
Becker, Harold 275, 290
Belvaux, Remy 316
Benton, Robert 151
Benveniste, Michael 46
Beresford, Bruce 73, 132, 234
Berri, Claude 315, 317
Bertolucci, Bernardo 132

Besson, Luc 91, 246, 270, 317
Bigelow, Kathryn 49, 161, 195, 260
Bluth, Don 55
Bondarchuk, Sergei 137
Bonzel, Andre 316
Boorman, John 21, 127, 256, 273
Bornedal, Ole 273
Borowczyk, Walerian 40, 42, 46
Boyle, Danny 121
Brambilla, Marco 21
Branagh, Kenneth 130, 194
Brando, Marlon 304
Brass, Tinto 46, 125
Brest, Martin 66, 232
Brooks, Albert 79
Brooks, James L. 69, 234
Brooks, Mel 68, 82, 86
Brooks, Richard 92, 94, 103, 133
Browning, Tod 183, 188
Bucquoy, Jean 48
Bunuel, Louis 314, 315
Burton, Tim 17, 66, 102, 142, 237, 248
Buscemi, Steve 121
Butler, David 208

Cain, Christopher 312
Cameron, James 36, 38, 239, 240
Cammell, Donald 116, 244
Campbell, Martin 25, 45
Campion, Jane 230
Capra, Frank 64
Caro, Marc 314
Carpenter, John 24, 186, 189, 201, 254
Carver, Steve 152
Casaril, Guy 44
Cassavetes, John 157
Castellari, Enzio G. 152, 301
Castle, William 139, 195

361

Caton-Jones, Michael 27, 34, 287
Cattaneo, Peter 74
Chaffey, Don 56, 58
Chan, Jackie 172
Cheh, Chan 170
Chelsom, Peter 76
Chomsky, Marvin J. 92
Cimino, Michael 165, 282, 299
Clayton, Jack 227
Clegg, Tom 160
Clemente, Ron 55, 58
Clouse, Robert 169
Clouzot, Henri Georges 316
Coen, Joel 77, 90, 104, 161, 259
Cohen, Larry 161
Cohen, Rob 20, 141
Collinson, Peter 27
Columbus, Chris 143
Connor, Kevin 255
Cooper, Meridian C. 57
Coppola, Francis Ford 149, 155, 156, 178, 182, 278
Corbucci, Sergio 294, 296
Corrente, Michael 88
Cort, Michael 51
Cosmatos, George P. 33, 309
Costner, Kevin 295
Cottafavi, Vittorio 131
Couffer, Jack 147
Cox, Alex 120
Craven, Wes 199
Crichton, Charles 74, 79
Crichton, Michael 256, 263
Cronenberg, David 42, 113, 178, 198, 202, 247, 264
Crowe, Cameron 78
Cukor, George 218
Curtiz, Michael 15, 19, 35, 195, 214, 220

D'Amato, Joe 40
Damiani, Damiano 149, 294
Dante, Joe 69, 75, 144, 191

Darabont, Frank 119
Davenport, Harry Bromley 256
Daves, Delmer 127
Davis, Andrew 266
De Bont, Jan 35, 38
De Mille, Cecil 123, 135
De Ossorio, Armando 202
De Palma, Brian 31, 153, 164, 165, 188, 260, 261, 274, 281
De Renzy, Alex 39
De Vito, Danny 84, 145
Dearden, Basil 132
Del Toro, Guillermo 180
Demme, Jonathan 116, 275
Deutch, Howard 231
Dieterle, William 227
Disney 53-4
Dmytryk, Edward 93, 292
Donaldson, Roger 20, 93, 273
Donen, Stanley 65, 205, 218
Donner, Clive 85
Donner, Richard 29, 36, 143
Dragoti, Stan 79
Dwan, Allan 289

Eastwood, Clint 23, 24, 223, 299, 304, 305, 310
Edel, Uli 109
Edwards, Blake 62, 82
Eisenstein, Sergi 131
Emmerich, Roland 247
Endfield, Cy 58, 137
Ephron, Nora 233

Faiman, Peter 71
Farrelly, Peter 73
Fawcett, John 140
Fellini, Federico 128, 200, 316
Ferrara, Abel 97, 150, 158, 175, 258
Figgis, Mike 269
Fincher, David 119, 240
Fisher, Terence 183, 184, 187, 200
Fleischer, Richard 20, 124, 136,

INDEX OF DIRECTORS

209, 246, 252, 258, 291
Fleming, Gordon 141
Fleming, Victor 129, 220
Foely, James 94
Ford, Clarence 172
Ford, John 107, 290, 298, 300, 303, 306, 307, 309
Forman, Milos 114, 115, 213
Fosse, Bob 109, 206, 208, 218
Frakes, Jonathan 253
Franco, Jess 50, 176, 177, 186
Franju, Georges 185
Frankenheimer, John 92, 270, 291
Frears, Stephen 97, 112, 117, 156
Freda, Riccardo 201
Frend, Charles 281
Friedkin, William 263
Fulci, Lucio 204
Fuller, Sam 277, 279

Gabriel, Mike 59
Gamba, Guiliana 41
Garrone, Sergio 296
Geronimi, Clyde 54, 57, 59
Gibson, Brian 207
Gibson, Mel 125
Gilbert, Brian 122
Gilbert, Lewis 73, 256, 289
Gilliam, Terry 80, 238, 243
Glaser, Paul Michael 35
Glenville, Peter, 124
Glickenhaus, James 148
Godard, Jean-Luc 241
Golan, Menahem 159
Goldberg, Eric 59
Gordon, Steve 65
Grauman, Walter 277
Grossbard, Ulu 224
Guccione, Bob 125
Guest, Val 210
Guillermin, John 121, 279, 285

Hackford, Taylor 99, 230

Haines, Randa 224
Haley, Jack, Jnr 219
Halperin, Victor 203
Hamer, Robert 78
Hamilton, Guy 26, 278, 281
Hanson, Curtis 109, 267
Hardy, Robin 203
Harlin, Renny 19, 30
Harmon, Robert 156, 190
Harris, James B. 18, 91
Haskin, Byron 255
Hathaway, Henry 283, 300, 309
Hawks, Howard 163, 259, 289, 296, 306, 307
Heerman, Victor 64
Hellman, Monte 308
Herek, Stephen 67
Herzog, Werner 196, 313
Hewitt, Peter 67
Hickox, Douglas 74, 201
Hicks, Scott 119
Hill, James 140, 200
Hill, Walter 15, 159, 298, 302, 310
Hiller, Arthur 290
Hitchcock, Alfred 198, 257, 259, 264, 266, 271, 273, 276
Ho, Godfrey 168
Hoblit, Gregory 274
Hodges, Mike 246, 2647
Hooper, Tobe 197
Hopper, Dennis 102, 153
Howard, Ron 89, 225, 243, 274
Hudson, Hugh 94, 130
Hughes, John 69, 84
Hughes, Ken 126, 141
Humberstone, Bruce 268
Hung, Sammo 169
Hussein, Waris 130
Huston, John 16, 125, 150, 157, 301
Hutton, Brian G. 286, 292
Hyams, Peter 239, 250
Hytner, Nicholas 110
Irvin, John 23, 285

Ivory, James 118

Jackson, Mick 223
Jackson, Peter 65
Jackson, Wilfred 57
Jankel, Annabel 265
Jarmusch, Jim 295
Jarrott, Charles 222
Jeffries, Lionel 146
Jeunet, Jean-Pierre 241, 314
Jewison, Norman 95, 210, 225, 251, 268
Joanoli, Phil 164
Joffe, Roland 108
Johnston, Joe 144, 145
Jones, Chuck 53
Jones, Terry 79, 80, 148
Jordan, Neil 97, 111, 192, 272
Juran, Nathan 54, 246

Kaplan, Jonathan 88, 228
Karbelnikoff, Michael 161
Kasdan, Lawrence 92, 221, 311
Kaufman, Philip 135, 248
Kazan, Elia 101, 114
Keighley, William 15
Kellogg, Ray 284
Kelly, Gene 214, 218
Kenton, Erle C. 192
Kershner, Irvin 31, 245
Kieslowski, Krzystof 318
King, Henry 228, 298, 300
Kleiser, Randal 144, 211, 223
Koster, Henry 76, 135, 282
Kotcheff, Ted 25
Kramer, Stanley 78, 97, 131
Kubrick, Stanley 73, 136, 200, 238, 283
Kumel, Harry 181
Kurosawa, Akiro 136

Landis, John 64, 68, 84, 175
Lang, Fritz 316

Lang, Walter 208
Larraz, Jose 41
Lasseter, John 60
Lavia, Gabrielle 45, 47
Le Roy, Mervyn 134, 159, 212
Lean, David 115, 127, 133, 280
Leder, Mimi 32
Lee, Spike 100
Lehmann, Michael 77
Lelouch, Claude 318
Leone, Sergio 128, 161, 297, 298, 304
Lester, Richard 213, 214
Levant, Brian 66
Levin, Henry 28, 129
Levinson, Barry 75, 100, 117, 152, 275
Litvak, Anatole 287
Logan, Joshua 208, 215
Losey, Joseph 154, 232
Lucas, George 63, 254
Lumet, Sidney 100, 103
Lun, Ah 172
Luske, Hamilton S. 54, 57, 58
Lustig, William 193
Lynch, David 102, 236, 245, 260
Lyne, Adrian 40, 104, 210, 228
Lynn, Jonathan 80

MacKendrick, Alexander 120
MacKenzie, John 269
Madden, John 112
Magnoli, Albert 216
Makavejev, Dusan 51
Malle, Louis 200, 231
Mamet, David 267
Mamoulian, Rouben 31, 217, 222
Mandoki, Louis 236
Mangold, James 263
Mankiewicz, Joseph L. 126, 276
Mann, Anthony 127, 128
Mann, Delbert 235
Mann, Michael 132, 157, 158, 271
Marks, George Harrison 47

INDEX OF DIRECTORS

Marquand, Richard 251, 269
Marshall, Frank 176
Marshall, Garry 91, 231
Marshall, George 300
Marshall, Penny 89, 140
Martin, Andrew 286
Martinson, Leslie H. 288
Mate, Rudolph 124, 265
Mattison, Burny 55
McBride, Jim 223
McCallum, Robert 44
McCarey, Leo 221
McCrae, Scooter 48
McDonald, Peter 34
McLaglen, Andrew 294
McLeod, Norman Z. 70
McNaughton, Ian 63
McNaughton, John 107
McTiernan, John 22, 26, 33
Medak, Peter 158
Melville, Jean-Pierre 159
Meyer, Nicholas 252
Meyer, Russ 41, 42, 46, 47, 49, 50
Michener, Dave 55
Milestone, Lewis 134, 277
Milius, John 20, 91, 288
Millar Gavin 141
Miller, George 30, 31, 85
Miner, Steve 225
Minghella, Anthony 103
Mingozzi, Gianfranco 129
Minkoff, Rob 57
Minnelli, Vincente 90, 206, 207, 211
Morrissey, Paul 177
Morton, Rocky 265
Mulcahy, Russell 26
Mulligan, Robert 234
Murphy, Geoff 312
Musker, John 55, 58

Nam, Lee Tso 171
Neame, Ronald 32
Negulesco, Jean 209, 234

Nelson, Ralph 308
Newell, Mike 154, 226
Nichols, Mike 86, 116, 122, 204
Nieuwenhuijs, Victor E. 50
Nimoy, Leonard 253
Ninn, Michael 39
Noonan, Chris 140
Norman, Leslie 286
Noyce, Philip 19, 32

Ogilvie, George 31
Oshima, Nagisa 40
Oz, Frank 72

Pacino, Al 110
Pakula, Alan J. 88, 116, 270
Pal, George 255
Parker, Alan 111, 176, 209, 210, 216, 272
Parks, Nick 53
Peckinpah Sam 28, 151, 155, 281, 293, 305, 306, 311
Penn, Arthur 151, 272, 301, 302, 303
Petersen, Wolfgang 16, 32, 146, 245, 268, 280
Petrie, Donald 146
Petroni, Giulio 295
Ping, Chu Yen 171
Poelvoorde, Benoit 316
Polanski, Roman 94, 134, 185, 199, 274
Pollack, Sydney 83, 87, 230, 235, 300
Polonsky, Abraham 154
Post, Ted 299
Powell, Michael 197, 222, 229
Preminger, Otto 110, 286
Pressburger, Emeric 229
Proyas, Alex 180

Rafelson, Bob 259
Raimi, Sam 184
Ramis, Harold 76, 81

Rappeneau, Jean-Paul 315
Rash, Steve 207
Ray, Nicholas 123
Redford, Robert 117
Reed, Carol 215, 291
Reeves, Michael 203
Reilly, William 160
Reiner, Carl 72
Reiner, Rob 83, 105, 146, 222, 235, 272
Reisz, Karel 226
Reitherman, Wolfgang 54, 59
Reitman, Ivan 75, 84
Reynolds, Burt 164
Richardson, Tony 126
Ritt, Martin 233
Roach, Jay 65
Robbins, Jerome 219
Robbins, Tim 68, 97
Roberts, Steve 82
Robinson, Bruce 86, 269
Robinson, Phil Alden 105
Robson, Mark 230, 291
Roddam, Franc 217
Rodriguez, Robert 188
Roeg, Nicholas 116, 182, 224
Rollin, Jean 192
Romero, George A. 196
Rosenberg, Stuart 96
Ross, Herbert 216
Rossati, Nello 296
Rosso, Sergio 184
Roy, Jean-Claude 43
Russell, David O. 49
Russell, Ken 51, 42, 99, 189, 206, 219, 235, 242
Rydell, Mark 114, 225

Sagal, Boris 249
Saks, Gene 81
Samperi, Salvatore 43
Sarafian, Deran 36
Sato, Toshiki 49
Sayles, John 110

Schaffner, Franklin J. 250, 261, 287
Schepisi, Fred 96
Schlesinger, John 67, 111, 115, 271
Schnabel, Julian 90
Schoedsack, Ernest 57
Schrader, Paul 89, 317
Schroeder, Barbet 118, 275
Schumacher, Joel 17, 18, 104, 120, 193, 265
Scorsese, Martin 78, 95, 117, 133, 153, 156, 160, 215, 222
Scorsese, Martin, 262, 276
Scott, Ridley 29, 106, 151, 240, 242
Scott, Tony 37, 165, 191
Selick, Henry 56, 59
Sena, Dominic 269
Seyferth, Maartje 50
Shadvac, Tom 62, 81
Sharman, Jim 217
Sharp, Don 198
Sharpsteen, Ben 56, 58
Shatner, William 253
Shelton, Ron 83, 85
Sheridan, Jim 105, 107, 112
Shindo, Kaneto 318
Sidney, George 215, 217
Siegel, Don 22, 265, 308
Singer, Bryan 121
Singleton, John 93
Sinise, Gary 113
Smight, Jack 247, 278
Soavi, Michele 179, 199
Sollima, Sergio 297
Sonnenfeld, Barry 62, 63, 154, 249
Spheeris, Penelope 85
Spielberg, Steven 27, 28, 30, 33, 62, 96, 103, 118, 243, 245
Spottiswoode, Roger 37
Stevens, George 307
Stevenson, Robert 144, 145
Stiller, Ben 70
Stone, Oliver 101, 108, 122, 277, 280, 288, 289

INDEX OF DIRECTORS

Strayer, Frank 202
Streisand, Barbra 231
Sturges, John 27, 90, 284, 301, 302
Szabo, Istvan 317
Szwarc, Jeannot 233

Tarantino, Quentin 149, 163
Tarkovsky, Andrei 251, 252
Taurog, Norman 206
Teague, Lewis 27, 264
Temple, Julien 205, 212
Tevos, Herbert 249
Thomas, Betty 82
Thompson, J. Lee 262, 285
Thorpe, Richard 33
Tien, Yuen Siu 173
Todd, Cesar 44
Tornatore, Giuseppe 314
Tourneur, Jacques 181
Trousdale, Gary 55
Tsang, Eric 173
Tuchner, Michael 165

Ulmer, Edgar G. 99
Underwood, Ron 71

Vadim, Roger 200, 242, 314
Van Peebles, Mario 161
Van Sant, Gus 83, 101
Verhoeven, Paul 25, 48, 251, 254, 255, 258
Vesely, Herbert 44
Vidor, King 135, 137, 225
Vigne, Daniel 318
Von Trier, Lars 93

Wadja, Andrzej 126
Wadleigh, Michael 204
Walker, Pete 48
Walsh, Raoul 287
Walters, Charles 214, 219
Wang, Wayne 120
Waters, John 209

Wayne, John 284, 293
Wei, Lo 170
Wei, Wong Lung 45
Weir, Peter 97, 122, 284
Welles, Orson 95
Wellman, William 162
Wenders, Wim 313
Wesman, Sam 75
West, Simon 19
Whale, James 187
Whatham, Claude 218
Wicki, Bernard
Widerberg, Bo 315
Wilcox, Fred M. 247
Wilder, Billy 290
Wilson, Hugh 74
Wilson, Richard 150
Wince, Simon 142
Winner, Michael 43
Wise, Kirk 55
Wise, Robert 131, 190, 219, 244, 252, 288
Woo, John 18, 24, 167, 168, 170, 171
Woo, Teresa 168
Wood, Edward D. 250
Wood, Sam 71
Wyler, William 124, 211, 232, 236
Wyler, Willliam 294

Yates, Peter 262
Young, Robert 202
Young, Terence 22, 37, 229
Yu, Wang 172

Zefirelli, Franco 130, 232
Zemeckis, Robert 16, 34, 60, 72, 226, 244
Zieff, Howard 81
Ziehm, Howard 46
Zinnemann, Fred 106, 134, 264
Zucker, David 63, 80
Zucker, Jerry 63, 227
Zwick, Edward 96, 109, 221, 284